Steffen Zschaler

Non-functional Specifications of Components and Systems

Steffen Zschaler

Non-functional Specifications of Components and Systems

A Generic Semantic Framework and its Applications

VDM Verlag Dr. Müller

Imprint

Bibliographic information by the German National Library: The German National Library lists this publication at the German National Bibliography; detailed bibliographic information is available on the Internet at http://dnb.d-nb.de.

Cover image: www.purestockx.com

Publisher:
VDM Verlag Dr. Müller Aktiengesellschaft & Co. KG , Dudweiler Landstr. 125 a, 66123 Saarbrücken, Germany,
Phone +49 681 9100-698, Fax +49 681 9100-988,
Email: info@vdm-verlag.de

Zugl.: Dresden, Technische Universität, Dissertation, 2007

Produced in USA and UK by:
Lightning Source Inc., La Vergne, Tennessee, USA
Lightning Source UK Ltd., Milton Keynes, UK
BookSurge LLC, 5341 Dorchester Road, Suite 16, North Charleston, SC 29418, USA

ISBN: 978-3-639-05402-6

Abstract

Component-based software development is considered a way of dealing with the increasing complexity of modern software systems. Applications can be built from software components pre-fabricated by third parties. To this end, it is important that all relevant properties of the components are specified as precisely and formally as possible, so that properties of the resulting application can be derived from properties of the component without the need to inspect component implementations. Much research has been done regarding specification of the functionality of software. However, the area of non-functional properties, while just as important, has not been researched at equal depth. Intuitively, non-functional properties are all properties that do not refer to *what* the software does, but to *how well* it does it.

In this thesis we propose a formal technique for specifying non-functional properties of components and component-based systems. We use temporal logic as our formalism. We begin by discussing the core concepts, then extend them to component networks and to the specification of multiple non-functional properties. We apply our approach to formally define the semantics of a current non-functional specification language and to derive analysis models for performance analysis. Finally, we show how our approach integrates into the component-oriented software development process.

Contents

I Overview   **1**

1 Introduction   **3**
  1.1 Background and Motivation   3
  1.2 Problem   4
  1.3 Envisioned Solution   5
  1.4 Contributions of the Thesis   6
       1.4.1 Major Contributions   6
       1.4.2 Secondary Contributions   6
  1.5 Research Methods   7
  1.6 Extended Temporal Logic of Actions (TLA$^+$)   7
  1.7 Organisation of the Thesis   9

2 Overview of the Approach   **11**
  2.1 Services   12
  2.2 Components   12
  2.3 Resources   12
  2.4 Container   13
  2.5 Measurements   13
  2.6 Non-functional Properties   14
  2.7 Feasible Systems   15
  2.8 Example   16
  2.9 Summary   18

II The Semantic Framework   **19**

3 Core Framework   **21**
  3.1 The System Model   21
  3.2 Measurements   23
       3.2.1 Context Models and Application Models   24
       3.2.2 Formal Representation of Measurements   26
       3.2.3 Mapping Measurements onto Actual Applications   27
       3.2.4 A Remark on the Different Types of Models   34
  3.3 Non-functional Properties   35
       3.3.1 Intrinsic vs Extrinsic Specifications   36
       3.3.2 Resource Specification   38
       3.3.3 Container Specification   38
       3.3.4 System Specification   39
  3.4 Feasible System   40
  3.5 Examples   40
       3.5.1 A Simple Performance Example Based on Request–Response
              Communication   41

3.5.2 A Data Quality Example 48
3.5.3 A Performance Example Based on Stream-Based Communication
and an Active Component 49
3.6 Summary 50

4 Extension to Component Networks   **51**
4.1 Container Strategies for Component Networks 52
4.1.1 Global Container Strategies 52
4.1.2 Local Container Strategies 54
4.1.3 Comparison and Summary 56
4.2 Component Interconnection 57
4.3 Component Specification 58
4.3.1 Extending Intrinsic Specifications 58
4.3.2 Extending Container Strategy Specifications 58
4.3.3 Comparison and Summary 59
4.4 Example 59
4.5 Summary 63

5 Describing Multiple Non-functional Properties of the Same Service   **65**
5.1 Relations between Measurements 66
5.2 Extending the Container Specification to Combine Multiple Properties . . . 66
5.3 Examples 69
5.3.1 Jitter-Constrained Components 69
5.3.2 Reliable Components 71
5.4 Summary 77

III Application to Specification Languages   **79**

6 A Semantic Mapping for μCQML   **81**
6.1 Introduction to CQML$^+$ 81
6.2 μCQML 83
6.3 The Semantic Mapping 85
6.3.1 Computational Model 86
6.3.2 Semantic Mapping Function 86
6.4 Evaluation 95
6.5 Summary 98

IV Concepts for System Analysis and Development   **101**

7 Performance Analysis of System Specifications   **103**
7.1 Software Performance Engineering and Performance Analysis Using
SPE·ED 103
7.2 SPE Analysis of Component-Based Specifications 106
7.2.1 An SPE Model for Use-Case–Based Analysis 107
7.2.2 An SPE Model for the Analysis of a Single Operation 109
7.3 Formal Support for Analysis Experts 112
7.4 Summary 115

8 Connection to a Development Process — 117
8.1 A Development Process for Component-Based Software with Special Consideration of Non-functional Properties — 117
8.2 Specification of Non-functional Properties in the Context of the Development Process — 118
8.3 Example — 119
8.4 Summary — 122

V Summary — 123

9 Related Work — 125
9.1 Application Structuring Techniques — 125
9.2 Non-functional Properties — 128
9.2.1 Non-functional Requirements — 129
9.2.2 Basic Contract Concepts — 130
9.2.3 Characteristic-Specific Approaches — 131
9.2.4 Measurement-Based Approaches — 134
9.3 Related Projects — 137
9.4 Summary — 138

10 Conclusions — 139
10.1 General Conclusions — 139
10.2 Contributions of the Thesis and Problems Solved — 140

11 Outlook — 145

VI Appendices — 149

A Acronyms — 151

B Complete Example Specifications — 155
B.1 A Simple Performance Example Based on Request–Response Communication — 155
B.2 A Data Quality Example — 177
B.3 A Performance Example Based on Stream-Based Communication and an Active Component — 181
B.4 An Example for Component Network Specification — 188
B.5 Component Specification with Two Non-functional Properties — 220
B.6 Jitter-Constrained Components — 221
B.7 Reliable Components — 230

C Detailed Proofs — 233
C.1 Proofs on the specification schemes — 233
C.1.1 The Measurement Specification Scheme Produces Measurements — 233
C.1.2 The Measurement Specification Scheme is a Simple Extension of the Context Model — 234
C.2 Proving Conditions $\Phi 1$ thru $\Phi 3$ for ϕ_{App}^{Ctx} — 235
C.3 Proofs for the Example Specifications — 237
C.3.1 Proving That Response Time Is a Measurement — 237
C.3.2 Proving That (3.12) Is a Model Mapping — 237
C.3.3 Proving Feasibility — 238

List of Figures — 245

List of Examples   247

List of Definitions, Propositions, and Theorems   249

Bibliography   251

Index   263

Acknowledgements

A piece of work like this can, of course, never be successfully created without the support of others.

First and foremost, I wish to thank my supervisor Prof. Heinrich Hußmann for valuable discussions and his supervision of this work. It is also because of his insistence on concreteness that this has not become a work of philosophical abstractness. Thomas Santen, Sten Löcher, and Simone Röttger provided opportunities for discussions of my work as well as valuable insights and hints on where to refine and progress. Furthermore, they were ever ready to read and criticise draft versions of papers or chapters.

I also wish to express my gratefulness to Deutsche Forschungsgemeinschaft (DFG) for paying for part of my employment at the university as part of the COMQUAD project. Everybody else working in that project must also be mentioned here: Steffen Göbel, Christoph Pohl, Marcus Meyerhöfer, Elke Franz, Ronald Aigner, Martin Pohlack, Frank Wehner.

A special thank you must go out to Raffaela Mirandola. From the time we just missed each other at the Doctoral Symposium of ICSE'04, which I attended probably way too early in my studies, she has been around to give advise, point out interesting literature, and read and comment early drafts of my thesis. Jan Øyvind Aagedal I also thank for reading and commenting the final draft of my thesis.

Part I

Overview

In this part we give an overview of both the context of this work and the approach taken in this thesis.

We begin in Chapt. 1 by motivating the need for our work, discussing problems with current specification approaches, listing the contributions this thesis is going to provide, and introducing the formalism we are going to use. Chapter 2 gives a bird's-eye overview of the main concepts of our approach.

Chapter 1

Introduction

In this chapter we introduce the background of this thesis, present the problem the thesis sets out to solve, and enumerate the contributions this thesis will make to the research area. Additionally, we give a short introduction to Extended Temporal Logic of Actions (TLA$^+$) [78], the formalism used in the remainder of the thesis.

1.1 Background and Motivation

Modern software systems are becoming increasingly more complex. At the same time, competition enforces decreasing time-to-market—that is, the time between the inception of a software solution and the actual deployment in a software market. If we want to create high-quality software even under these circumstances, we need an approach to software development that can produce highly complex software efficiently. Component-Based Software Engineering (CBSE) is considered such an approach by many researchers and practitioners. Here, software systems are assembled from pre-fabricated, reusable pieces of software—so-called *software components*. In particular, there is the vision of a *component market* (e.g., [140]): An industry where companies develop and market software components that are then bought and reused by other companies to develop larger pieces of software or even complete applications. This is seen as a means of reducing complexity and raising efficiency (and, thus, reducing time-to-market) in software development.

In order for components to be reusable by third-parties in an efficient manner, their relevant properties need to be described precisely, concisely, and in a form that is understood by all parties involved in the CBSE process. These descriptions must allow the component user to obtain sufficient information for correctly reusing the component in his[1] context. The component user should not need to inspect the component implementation in order to use the component correctly. This has led many researchers to ask questions similar to the following:

> "How to specify a component so that its specification can be properly understood in the context of system requirements and how to predict/derive the system properties from the measurable and specified components?" [45]

Additionally, the component description needs to abstract from the details of the component's behaviour, because we can only increase efficiency and decrease complexity if the amount of information a single developer needs to cope with at any moment can be reduced.

While the description of functional properties has been researched for quite some time, the description of non-functional properties has been focused on only comparatively recently. It is, however, clear, that these properties are becoming increasingly more impor-

---

[1] Of course, when using the masculine or feminine in this thesis we always mean to include both sexes.

tant. Therefore, they, too, must be considered at the specification level for component-based software.

Non-functional properties need to be treated differently from functional properties, because they have some fundamentally different characteristics (the following is not an exhaustive listing):

- The functionality of a component typically does not change with its usage context. Its non-functional properties, on the other hand, will. For example, the response time of a component operation depends on the availability of required resources (in particular, Central Processing Unit (CPU)), but also on the time required by other components used to complete the job. All of these cannot be predicted by the original component developer, in particular not in the context of a component market.

- Functional properties are always boolean properties. Therefore, a system either satisfies a functional property (provides a certain functionality) or it does not do so. *Tertium non datur.* In contrast, systems can have non-functional properties *to degrees.* For example, the non-functional property "operation op has a maximum response time of 50ms" can be satisfied by an implementation with exactly 50ms response time, but also with one that is faster than 50ms. We will typically assume the latter implementation to have a *better* response time than the former. Thus, with non-functional properties, there is a notion of one system satisfying a property *better than* some other system.

1.2 Problem

There exist various approaches for the formal specification of certain non-functional properties [13, 46, 61, 81]. However, although these approaches are quite good in terms of formality, they are all restricted to one property, or a very limited set of properties. This is problematic in the context of component markets, because every new formalism forces all players in the market to learn new techniques and concepts. Therefore, in a component-market world, we need a generic means of description for non-functional properties. This is also supported by the following quotation:

> "When systems are designed and built from components, many system properties can be derived from the component properties. Hence, a generic support for the definition and measurement of the properties, which is built into the component models and technologies, would be greatly welcomed." [44]

Some generic approaches towards non-functional specifications have been developed [1, 56, 57, 69, 80, 84, 101, 117, 120, 128]. However, these approaches are lacking in formality, and thus allow for ambiguities. Also, some of the conceptualisations are not adequate for component-based software. To understand what we mean by this, we discuss a few examples from Extended Component Quality Modelling Language (CQML$^+$) [117] the most advanced such language known to us:

Example 1.1 (Insufficiencies in CQML$^+$)

1. CQML$^+$ provides the concept of a `quality_characteristic` to represent a non-functional dimension of a system. A `quality_characteristic` can be seen as a function that can be applied to a running system to obtain a value characterising some non-functional property of the system. It is also possible to define `quality_characteristics` that cumulate such values and, for example, determine their mean value. However, the definition of CQML$^+$ makes no statement

about *when* quality_characteristic values are determined. Without this information, the value of cumulative quality_characteristics is underspecified. For example, it is important to know whether response-time values are determined once for every operation call or once every 10ms (even though operations may be invoked more or less often). This can neither be specified explicitly nor does CQML$^+$ define a standard interpretation. This is a case of missing formalisation.

2. CQML$^+$ does not distinguish properties of components from properties induced by the usage context of a component. As discussed in Sect. 1.1, non-functional properties are strongly affected by the context in which a component is used. Because CQML$^+$ does not support this distinction, it can only be used when the usage context is known. This is incompatible with the notion of a component market, where component developers have only very limited knowledge about potential uses of the components they develop, but still need to describe non-functional properties of these components. This is a case of inadequate conceptualisation.

3. CQML$^+$ provides the so-called resources-clause for the specification of a component's resource demand. There are at least two problems with this:

   (a) The resource demand of a component depends heavily on how the component is used. Thus, the component developer alone cannot make statements about a component's resource requirements. At the same time, resource demand also depends on the component's implementation. Thus, component users cannot make statements about resource demand on their own. Only component developer and user together can make statements about a component's resource demand. Because in a component market they must be able to work independently, both need to be able to specify their part of knowledge about a component so that it can later be combined to obtain a complete picture of the component's properties. This cannot be done in CQML$^+$. This is a case of inadequate conceptualisation.

   (b) The formalisation chosen for resource demand is highly specific to the underlying real-time operating system Dresden Real-Time Operating System (DROpS) [65]. It cannot be translated easily for other resource management systems and is not usable for any kind of reasoning. This is a case of inadequate formalisation.

It is, therefore, necessary to define a formal and generic approach to the specification of non-functional properties of component-based applications. Such an approach should, in particular, support the specific distribution of knowledge in a component market.

1.3 Envisioned Solution

In this thesis, we define a formal and generic approach for the specification of non-functional properties of component-based applications. The approach is based on temporal-logic specifications using TLA$^+$ by Abadi and Lamport. Temporal logic is used to model both application functionality, and non-functional dimensions and properties. The basis of the non-functional part is formed by the formal definition of measurements (also called quality characteristics or non-functional dimensions) as values of flexible variables in TLA$^+$ expressions. A formal mapping of states connects the definition of a measurement and the model of a software system and, thus, leads to an application of the measurement to the software system.

To support the specific distribution of knowledge in component markets, we split a system specification into several partial specifications, one for each stakeholder (party) in the market. These specifications contain place holders defining how such partial specifications can be combined to obtain a system specification. We make use of Abadi and Lamport's composition theorem [5] to enable reasoning about system properties.

1.4 Contributions of the Thesis

In this section we point out the contributions of this thesis to the research on non-functional specifications of component-based systems. We have divided the set of contributions into major contributions and secondary contributions, often resulting as by-products of evaluation.

1.4.1 Major Contributions

The thesis makes the following major contributions to the research on non-functional specifications of component-based systems:

1. The thesis provides an approach for the formal specification of non-functional properties of component-based systems that takes into account the limited knowledge of the various parties involved in a component market. At the same time this approach allows formal reasoning about system specifications. To the best of our knowledge, this is the first such approach available.

2. The thesis shows that and how non-functional properties can be understood formally as constraints over history-determined variables based on an abstract context-model state machine. The general possibility of representing non-functional dimensions as history-determined variables has been speculated on by Abadi and Lamport in [4]. However, they only specifically discussed it for certain timing properties. This thesis is the first work to substantiate Abadi/Lamport's speculations.

3. The thesis improves understanding of the concepts underlying non-functional specifications in particular in the context of CBSE. Based on this, formal semantics and deficiencies of current non-functional specification languages are discussed.

1.4.2 Secondary Contributions

Apart from the major contributions discussed above, the thesis makes a number of secondary contributions to the research area:

1. The thesis provides a formal semantics for a sub-language of CQML$^+$, one of the most advanced specification languages for non-functional properties of software components. The basic structure of this semantics is similar to the approach used in denotational semantics: The thesis provides a semantic mapping function from CQML$^+$ to TLA$^+$-based specifications following our approach.

2. The thesis demonstrates how the approach can be used for the formal description of analysis techniques for certain non-functional properties and how this can be used to extract analysis parameters from system specifications. This is particularly relevant in the context of emerging Model-Driven Architecture (MDA) [75, 104] component (MDAC) [21] technology.

3. The thesis discusses the embedding of formal specifications of non-functional properties into a component-oriented development process.

4. The thesis provides a comprehensive overview and classification of the literature on non-functional specification and semantics.

5. The thesis proposes an architecture for component runtime environments where a container selects from a set of container strategies one strategy that can handle the non-functional properties relevant for a specific application.

6. A negative outcome of the thesis is that formal specifications techniques for non-functional properties can never be completely generic: As a minimum they require an agreed-upon underlying computational model.

1.5 Research Methods

The basic research approach in this thesis is to study various examples and derive a model of the semantic domain of non-functional specifications. Various sources form the basis for such a model: literature on measurement theory [54], on specific approaches to non-functional specifications [1, 4, 81, 137], existing research on real-time and QoS-aware systems, but also literature on component-based software [140] and composability [2, 148]. An important tool in developing the semantic model is—as stated above—generalisation from examples. Consequently, a number of examples will be discussed in the thesis to show how the abstract concepts of the semantic model apply to actual non-functional specifications. To ensure generality of the approach, we have chosen examples covering different non-functional properties.

Another important method used is evaluation in various areas of application. In this thesis we use three types of evaluation:

1. A semantic model is only really useful if it can be used to define the semantics of some programming or modelling language. Consequently, we use our approach to provide a semantics for a sublanguage of CQML$^+$.

2. Although in this thesis we are not looking for new analysis technologies for non-functional properties, we equally must not reduce the opportunities for analysis. Consequently, we need to show how existing analysis techniques can be combined with our approach. We do so for the example of Software Performance Engineering (SPE) [130, 133] performance analysis.

3. The introduction of individual partial specifications is only sensible if each of these partial specifications can be completely created and maintained by one party in the software development process. We, therefore, show how our approach integrates with a development process.

1.6 Extended Temporal Logic of Actions (TLA$^+$)

In this thesis, we use temporal logic as the formalism to describe our semantic framework. In particular, we use Extended Temporal Logic of Actions (TLA$^+$) [78], a temporal logic introduced by Abadi and Lamport. It is important to note that this design decision slightly limits the expressiveness of our approach, because although temporal logic is capable of expressing a very broad range of properties, it cannot be easily used to express stochastic properties. However, the advantages of temporal logic—comparative ease of use, support of proof rules and model checking analysis techniques, compatibility to formal notions commonly used in specifying functional properties of components (e.g., state machines), and relatively large range of specifiable systems—in our opinion outweigh this limitation. In the following, we give a quick introduction to TLA$^+$ to ease understanding of the thesis. For further details as well as the formal definition of the concepts used, please refer to the literature.

In TLA$^+$, systems are characterized by the set of behaviours they can perform. A behaviour is an infinite sequence of states. For a given set of states Σ, the set of all behaviours over Σ is denoted by Σ^∞. A sequence of states is also called a trace. The set of all finite traces over Σ is denoted by Σ^*. We typically use σ and τ to refer to traces (or behaviours) and σ_i to refer to the ith state in σ. $\sigma|_n$ refers to a sub-trace of σ that only contains the first n states. In the other direction, we can use $\sigma \circ \tau$ to produce a new trace by concatenating traces σ and τ. A pair of consecutive states in a trace is called a step.

A state is defined by the values of so-called flexible variables. Two states where all variables have the same values are considered equal. Σ is, thus, the cross-product of the domains of all flexible variables. A step where both states are equal in variables v is called a stuttering step in v. Two traces are called stuttering equivalent in v ($\simeq_v$) iff they are equal once all stuttering steps in v have been removed. In the proofs we will occasionally use $\pi_{App}(s)$ to refer to only a part of the variables of state s—namely to those variables belonging to the application model.

Systems are described by TLA$^+$ formulas, which express constraints over flexible variables. The notation $\sigma \models F$ indicates that formula F holds for behaviour σ. There are two basic types of formulas:

State functions A state function maps a state to a value. Of particular interest are predicates, which are boolean-valued state functions.

Transition functions A transition function maps a pair of states to a value. Of particular interest are actions, which are boolean-valued transition functions.

For a predicate P, $\sigma \models P$ holds iff[2] $P(\sigma_1) = $ TRUE; that is, iff P holds for the first state in σ. For an action A, $\sigma \models A$ iff $A(\sigma_1, \sigma_2) = $ TRUE; that is, iff A holds for the first pair of states in σ. In any transition function, we use v' to refer to the value of variable v in the second state.

Based on these basic types of formulas, we can construct temporal-logic specifications of systems. In particular, we will use the following constructions in this thesis:

- Conjunction and disjunction as known from standard predicate logic. TLA$^+$ uses a special notation to save parentheses: Alignment of junctors can be used to group subexpressions. Thus:

$$(A \vee B) \wedge C \equiv \begin{array}{l} \wedge \vee A \\ \vee B \\ \wedge C \end{array}$$

- UNCHANGED v is the same as saying $v' = v$; that is, it is the action asserting that v does not change.

- $\Box[A]_v$ where A is an action and v is a variable or a sequence of variables. This is the same as saying $\Box(A \vee$ UNCHANGED $v)$. In other words, it asserts that each step in a behaviour where v changes is an A step. Note that in TLA$^+$ the operator $\Box$ can only be used within this construction. This is required to allow specifications to be composed simply by conjoining them. The TLA$^+$ motto is "Composition is Conjunction" [2].

- $A \overset{+}{\Rightarrow} B$ asserts that B holds *at least as long as* A. In fact, the formal definition of $\overset{+}{\Rightarrow}$ requires that B holds for at least one step longer than A, if A ever stops to hold. This is useful for modelling open systems, that provide a service B as long as the environment behaves in a certain way, described by A. Using $\Rightarrow$ would allow the system to cease providing the service *before* the environment stops behaving correctly. It would, thus, allow for systems that predict the future, which is not realistic. $\overset{+}{\Rightarrow}$ explicitly excludes such systems. This is helpful when discussing compositions of open systems and is the basis of the composition theorem from [2, 5].

---

[2] if and only if

- $\exists\, v \,:\, F$ is a means of hiding variable v in F. It asserts that we can find a sequence of values for v so that F holds.

- **if** A **then** B **else** C evaluates to B if A evaluates to TRUE and to C, otherwise. The formal definition is actually a little more subtle, but for our purposes it is sufficient to interpret it in this way.

- Functions are expressed as follows:

    - $[S \rightarrow T]$ denotes the set of all functions from S to T.
    - $[x \in S \mapsto e]$ is the function f with domain S so that $f[x] = e$; that is, the value of f for argument x is the value of expression e (which may refer to x).
    - This can also be used to define records by saying, for example, $[a \mapsto 1, b \mapsto 17]$.
    - To update a function at one argument without changing the function value for any other argument, we can use the EXCEPT construction: $f' = [f \text{ EXCEPT } ![c] = e]$ which replaces the value of f at argument c by the value of expression e. e may contain the special character @ which means $f[c]$.

- We use $\wp\,(X)$ to denote the power set of a set X—that is, the set of all subsets of X.

Finally, we use $\triangleq$ to give names to formulas.

A system is described in TLA$^+$ by a specification, which typically represents a state machine. A state machine is a triple $S = (\Sigma, F, N)$ with Σ the set of states, $F \subseteq \Sigma$ a set of initial states, and $N \subseteq \Sigma \times \Sigma$ the next-state relation representing legal state transitions. A state machine can be represented by a TLA$^+$ formula of the form

$$S \;\triangleq\; \wedge\, INIT$$
$$\wedge\, \Box[NEXT]_{vars}$$

where $INIT$ is a predicate describing the initial states F, $NEXT$ is an action describing N, and $vars$ is a sequence of all variables, effectively describing Σ. A state machine specification S describes a property Π, such that $\forall\, \sigma \,:\, \sigma \models S \Leftrightarrow \sigma \in \Pi$. A property is a set of behaviours closed under stuttering equivalence. In other words: $\forall\, \sigma, \tau \,:\, (\sigma \simeq \tau \wedge \sigma \in \Pi) \Rightarrow \tau \in \Pi$.

TLA$^+$ specifications are organised into modules. A module can instantiate another module by using $MVar \;\triangleq\;$ **instance** $ModuleName$ **with** $VarReplacements$. This creates the name $MVar$ which is a reference to module $ModuleName$ with all variables replaced by variables of the using module in accordance with the replacement rules given in $VarReplacements$. We can then refer to formula F in module $ModuleName$ through $MVar!F$.

TLA$^+$ comes with a certain amount of tooling. All specifications in this thesis have been checked for static consistency and syntactic and semantic correctness using TLASAny the syntactic and static semantics analyser of TLA$^+$.

1.7   Organisation of the Thesis

The thesis is structured into five parts:

Part I contains this introduction as well as a high-level overview of the specification approach presented in this thesis (Chapt. 2).

Part II—the central part of the thesis—contains three chapters that incrementally present our specification approach. The first of these chapters—Chapt. 3—presents the basic concepts for systems consisting of exactly one component and restricted to exactly one non-functional dimension per system. The following two chapters extend this to component networks (Chapt. 4) and to the specification of multiple non-functional properties (Chapt. 5).

The following two parts evaluate the proposed approach in various contexts: Part III and Chapt. 6 show how the approach can be used to define the semantics of a non-functional specification language. Part IV discusses using the approach to specify non-functional analysis techniques and extract analysis parameters from system specifications (Chapt. 7) and the integration of the approach into a development process (Chapt. 8).

Finally, Part V provides a summary and conclusion of the thesis. It contains a discussion of related work in Chapt. 9, conclusions in Chapt. 10, and a discussion of potential further research in Chapt. 11.

Some of the work presented in this thesis has also been reported on in workshop and conference publications by the author of this thesis [151, 152].

Chapter 2

Overview of the Approach

This chapter gives a high-level overview of the approach presented in this thesis. We give intuitive descriptions of the core concepts and their relationships, but omit any formal discussions; these can be found in Part II of this thesis.

There are two sides to developing component-based systems with defined non-functional properties:

1. Component developers must *implement* components in such a way that they have determinable non-functional properties.

2. Application designers and the runtime system must *use* these components so that the non-functional properties required from the application can be guaranteed.

Example 2.1 (Implementation vs Usage) We will never be able to make any guarantees about the memory consumption (or time for data retrieval) for a FIFO queue component which was implemented using a linked list without any limits on its maximum size. But even if the queue was implemented with a fixed-size array of length 64 kB, the runtime system can still use this implementation in such a way that it consumes 256 kB of memory: by creating four instances. ◇

We call properties that depend only on the implementation of a component *intrinsic properties*. Properties depending on how components are used—by application assemblers and the runtime environment—to provide a certain service are called *extrinsic properties*.

In this thesis, we are not primarily interested in how components must be implemented so that their non-functional properties become determinable; these questions are only contingently related to CBSE. Instead, we assume components with determinable non-functional properties to be available. Based on this, we provide a semantic framework, which allows

- component developers to describe the non-functional properties of the components they have developed, and

- application designers to describe how these components are used to provide guaranteed non-functional properties of an application.

Figure 2.1 presents an overview of the various specifications defined by our approach. Each of these specifications is created by a different player in the component market and each of them represents a different important concept. All of them share the common terminology provided by a repository of formal measurement definitions. In the following sections we give a short overview of these core concepts in our approach.

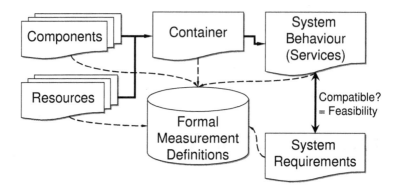

Figure 2.1: Overview of the semantic framework. The document symbols indicate specifications, the cylinder represents a repository of measurement definitions. Dashed arrows
denote usage, solid arrows denote information flow, and the double-headed arrow denotes
a required consistency proof

2.1 Services

Users view a system in terms of the services it provides. They do not care about how
these services are implemented, whether from monolithic or from component-structured
software. A *service* is a causally closed part of the complete functionality provided by a
system. As various authors [76, 121] have pointed out, we can model services as partial
specifications of a system. Multiple services can then be combined into a total specification of the system's functionality. Users associate non-functional properties with individual
services—for example, they will talk about the frame rate provided by a video player service independently of the response time of a cast query for that same film. So, from the
user's perspective, the non-functional properties of individual services should be described
independently. Note that this does not imply that the non-functional properties of two
services cannot interact—for example, because their respective implementations run on the
same system and share the same resources. However, although users may be able to specify
preferences on services, indicating which service should prevail in case of resource contention, they need to be able to describe their non-functional requirements independently
for each service.

2.2 Components

Components provide implementations for services. As has been pointed out in the literature
[76, 121] a component can provide implementations for multiple services. In addition,
services can be implemented by networks of multiple cooperating components. In this case,
the service's functionality is composed from the functionality of the individual components.

2.3 Resources

The term *resource* is used in the literature essentially to refer to everything in the system
which is required by an application in order to provide its services (e.g., [60, 141]). More
specifically, Goscinski defines a resource as:

"[...] each reusable, relatively stable hardware or software component of a
computer system that is useful to system users or their processes, and because
of this [...] is requested, used and released by processes during their activity."
[60, Page 440*f.*]

The most important properties of a resource are that it can be allocated to, and used by,
applications, and that each resource has a maximum capacity. We do not consider resources
with unlimited availability, because they do not have any effect on the non-functional properties of an application. We distinguish between the actual resource (e.g., CPU, memory)
and the aspect it enables (e.g., execution of program code/computation, availability of space
to store data).

2.4   Container

The components implementing a service require a runtime environment which executes
them. We call this runtime environment the *container*, inspired by the terminology used,
for example, in the Java Enterprise computing framework. The container instantiates components, connects these instances to other instances according to the functional specification, and provides various middleware services to the components, including access to the
underlying platform. In short, the container manages and uses the components such that it
can provide the services clients require. Extending this notion to non-functional properties,
we see that the container needs to use components and resources in such a way that it can
guarantee the required non-functional properties of the services it provides.

Additionally, the system's environment also plays an important role. In particular, the
container may need to make assumptions about the environment in order to provide its
services. In this case, the container will only be able to provide a certain level of non-
functional properties as long as its assumptions about the environment are still valid. Environment assumptions may include information on the interarrival times of requests (for
time-based properties), assumptions about the abilities of system attackers (for security
properties), usage profiles (for dependability properties), and so on.

2.5   Measurements

We use the concept of a *measurement* to represent non-functional dimensions of systems.
Non-functional specifications can then be expressed as constraints over measurements. A
concept equivalent to our measurement is usually called *characteristic* in the literature
(most notably [1, 69]). We prefer the term measurement, because the concept is indeed
based on the same concept from measurement theory (e.g., [55]) where a measurement is a
mapping from physical or empirical objects to formal objects. The "physical or empirical
objects" in our case are the systems under discussion—represented by state-based models
of these systems—thus measurements can be represented as state functions. We use *context
models* (state-based specifications of the parts of a system which are relevant for the definition of a measurement) to specify measurements independently of the concrete applications
on which they are to be used.

We distinguish two kinds of measurements:

1. *Extrinsic measurements* describe non-functional dimensions which are applicable
   to a service and are relevant from a user perspective. They view the system as a
   whole and do not make distinctions to allow for other services, other components, or
   resource contention. In effect, extrinsic measurements can be used to describe users'
   non-functional requirements on a service. An example for an extrinsic measurement
   is response time of a service.

2. *Intrinsic measurements* describe non-functional dimensions of component implementations. The value of an intrinsic measurement for a specific implementation
   depends principally on the way the implementation is realised. If two implementations differ in their values for an intrinsic measurement, they use different algorithms
   or implementation techniques to provide their functions. Definitions of intrinsic measurements account for the presence of other components, and for resource contention;
   that is, for the environment in which the component will be executed. In effect, intrinsic measurements can be used to describe the properties of an actually existing
   implementation independently of how this implementation is used. An example for
   an intrinsic measurement is execution time of an operation.

2.6   Non-functional Properties

Non-functional properties are constraints over measurements. Examples are properties like
"The response time of service `login` is always less than 50 ms", or "The execution time of
operation `login` is always less than 30 ms." As usual, any non-functional property can be
interpreted as a non-functional specification, stating that the property holds for the element
being specified.

We distinguish four kinds of non-functional specifications:

Intrinsic specifications Component implementation properties are described using constraints over intrinsic measurements. These constraints describe relations between
the various intrinsic measurements relevant for the component implementation. The
most simple example is a statement like: "The execution time of operation `login` is
less than 30 ms". More complex properties constrain the relation between multiple
measurements. For example, for a component computing a numerical value the execution time might depend on the number of exact decimals the component computes.
Intrinsic specifications describe the effect of the algorithms and implementation techniques used to create a component implementation.

Note, that component implementation specifications make no explicit mention of the
resources required to provide the component's services. It is not useful to express resource demand of a component as an intrinsic property, because it depends largely on
how the component is used. For example, CPU demand depends on both the intrinsic
property execution time, and the number of requests per second the component has to
serve. For this reason, component implementation specifications constrain intrinsic
properties only, but some of these intrinsic properties (e.g., execution time) corre-
spond to an aspect enabled by a certain resource (e.g., CPU). The relation between
resource specifications and component implementation specifications is established
by the container specification.

Extrinsic specifications Service specifications essentially constrain extrinsic measurements for a single service. These constraints express how users expect the system
to behave or how a system as a whole behaves. The property "The response time of
service `login` is always less than 50 ms" from above is an example for an extrinsic
specification.

Resource specifications As we explained in Sect. 2.3, resources enable some non-
functional aspect, provided their capacity is sufficient to serve the specified load.
This leads directly to resource specifications that consist of two parts: a) an antecedent describing the capacity limits, and b) a consequence describing the non-
functional aspect enabled by the resource. For example, for a CPU with a scheduler
based on Rate-Monotonic Scheduling (RMS) [83] the capacity limit can be expressed

by the following formula:

$$\sum_{i=1}^{n} \frac{t_i}{p_i} \leq n \cdot \left(\sqrt[n]{2} - 1 \right) \qquad (2.1)$$

where n is the number of tasks, and t_i and p_i refer to the worst case execution time
and period of the ith task, resp. The non-functional aspect enabled by this resource
is that the n tasks described by these parameters can be scheduled to execute jobs
with a period p_i which are allowed to execute for at least t_i units of time between
the begin and end of their respective period. This is in essence a constraint over
execution time.

As shown in the example above, resource specifications are the 'hook' at which the
well understood theories from operating-systems research can be plugged into the
semantic framework.

Container specifications The container uses resources and components to provide a service with certain non-functional properties. In order to reason about the extrinsic
properties of a system based on the intrinsic properties of its components and the
available resources we need to specify precisely how the container uses the components and resources. A container specification is written in rely–guarantee style [72]
with the antecedent asserting that:

1. the available component implementations have the provided intrinsic properties. This pre-condition essentially enumerates the intrinsic properties the container takes into account.

2. the system's environment guarantees certain properties. Depending on the algorithms implemented by the container, the container will make different assumptions about the system environment. A typical example of the kind of guarantees given by the system environment is the distribution of request-interarrival
   times. This can be used together with queuing-theory–based techniques to determine the optimal number of components and buffer size to achieve a required
   response time using components with a known execution time [10, 64].

3. the available resources will enable the required non-functional aspects. What
   non-functional aspects are required depends on the intrinsic properties of the
   available components, the extrinsic property to be provided, the guarantees
   given by the system environment, and the algorithms implemented by the container. This antecedent is the central part of the container specification which
   describes the mapping from extrinsic and intrinsic non-functional properties of
   services and components to the lower-level concepts of resource specifications.

Provided these conditions hold, the container guarantees that it will deliver a certain
service with specified extrinsic properties. The container specification thus forms a
second 'hook' at which results from performance analysis, security analysis, etc. can
be plugged into the framework.

2.7   Feasible Systems

In the last subsections we have described four types of specifications. All these specifications are only useful if we can compose them to obtain a global view of the system
which we can use for analysis. One useful analysis is to test whether the available resources are sufficient to provide the required extrinsic properties given the available components and the container specification. This is equivalent to proving that the composition
of resource specifications, container specification, intrinsic specifications, and system environment guarantees implies the extrinsic specification. We define a *feasible system* to

be a system made up from components, resources, and a container for which together this condition can be proved.

In the core chapters, this thesis provides a formal definition of the term 'feasibility'. Based on work by Abadi and Lamport in [2, 5], we provide proof obligations for feasibility proofs. We also prove feasibility for example specifications. These proofs have been manually constructed. Currently, there exists only limited tool support for proofs of TLA$^+$ specifications [93]. However, manual proofs are possible and more advanced proof-support systems will be developed as the need arises.

2.8 Example

To make the abstract concepts discussed above a little more concrete, we introduce a small and simple example. We will use a simple pseudo-code notation inspired by modern programming languages. Note that this language does not exist. We have simply set it up to illustrate our concepts. This language will be used again in Chapt. 8 for illustrative purposes.

Assume, we want to reason about the response time of the increment() operation of a simple Counter application. Obviously, the first thing we need to do is to define the vocabulary for our specifications. We do so by defining the measurements execution_time and response_time as follows:

```
declare real response_time   (ServiceOperation    op);
declare real execution_time  (ComponentOperation op);
```

This simply declares that response_time can be applied to operations of services and delivers a real value, and that execution_time can be applied to operations of components and delivers a real value, too. To ensure that different developers—for example, component developers and application designers—understand and use these concepts in the same way, we need to provide formal definitions of the semantics of response and execution time. Section 3.2.2 is about how we can use temporal-logic formulas to do so. The specification of what response or execution time are can be done completely independently of specific components or applications.

Next, we need to specify the component we have implemented. It looks like this:

```
declare component Counter {
  public void inc();
  public integer getValue();

  always execution_time (inc) <= 7;
}
```

This is meant to convey that the Counter component offers two operations—inc() and getValue()—and that the execution time of the inc() operation is known to be always less than 7 (units of time—for example, milliseconds). Section 3.2.3 is about how we can formally represent the application of the execution time measurement to operation inc() by defining an appropriate model mapping between the application model and the context model. The specification of a component's non-functional properties must be done independently of usage context, because we want to enable third-party development and provision of components.

Similarly,

```
declare service CounterS {
  public void inc();
  public integer getValue();
```

```
    always response_time (inc) <= 15;
}
```

specifies the service we expect from our system. This information is typically provided by
the customers who initiated the production of the application system. Note that, because
this is a very simple example with only one component, the functional interface of the service is the same as that of the component. In a more realistic example, in particular, when
a network of collaborating components provide the service, this need not be the case. In
most applications, however, there will be one component that realises the interactions with
the user and uses the other components in the network to provide the application's functionality. The functional interface of the service will then match the functional interface of
that component.

In order to have a complete system specification, we need to provide a specification
of the available resources. This is done by describing the relevant properties of these resources; in our case the only relevant resource is the CPU:

```
declare abstract resource CPU {
  capacitylimit boolean canSchedule (TaskSet ts);
}

declare resource RMS_CPU : CPU {
  capacitylimit boolean canSchedule (TaskSet ts);
}
```

Each resource has an associated capacity limit. For a CPU this is represented by the maximum number of tasks it can safely schedule. To represent sets of tasks, the specification
introduces the TaskSet type, which is specified separately. We do not show its specification here; it essentially represents tasks as tupels of worst-case execution time and period
(which is assumed to also represent the relative deadline). In our specific case, we use an
RMS-scheduled CPU. Section 3.3.2 discusses formal specification of resources.

The central element in every component-based application is the container. It provides
a runtime environment for the components and manages their non-functional properties so
that it can guarantee certain non-functional properties to clients of the system as a whole.
We need a container that can translate execution time into response time. In order to do so,
it must reserve a certain amount of CPU time, which it can use to execute the components
code (execTime and responseTime are two real valued parameters representing the
intrinsic execution time constraint and the extrinsic response time constraint, resp.):

```
declare container Cont (execTime, responseTime) {
  requires
    component C {
      operation op;
      always execution_time(op) <= execTime
    },
    resource CPU {
      canSchedule (TaskSet {execTime,
                            responseTime});
    };

  provides
    service CS implemented by C {
      always response_time (op) <= responseTime;
    }
}
```

The `TaskSet` constructor used creates a task set containing one task with a worst-case execution time of `execTime` and a period (and relative deadline) of `responseTime`. Section 3.3.3 talks about formal specification of containers.

Now we can instantiate the specifications of the individual parts of our system and assemble the system specification from these parts:

```
system CompleteSystem {
  instance Counter c;
  instance RMS_CPU cpu;
  instance Cont container;

  container uses c, cpu;
  container provides CounterS cs;
}

prove: CompleteSystem is feasible!
```

Section 3.3.4 explores formal system specifications in more detail. The last line above should be read as "Prove that this system is feasible as defined in Sect. 3.4!"

2.9 Summary

In this chapter we have given an overview of the core concepts to be presented in this thesis. They are graphically represented in Fig. 2.1. Container specifications define how components and resources (both described by individual specifications) of a system are used to provide certain services, which consequently form the system behaviour. System behaviour must then be checked against the system requirements specification. For this purpose we introduce the notion of a feasible system. So that all these specifications can be defined independently, we use formally defined measurement specifications to serve as an interface between individual specifications.

The overview given in this chapter was very high-level, its main purpose was to provide an overall understanding of the approach. The next part of this thesis will elaborate each of the concepts in depth. We will give formal definitions, discussions and examples, and will also discuss how this approach extends to services provided by multiple components, and to systems where more than one extrinsic property are of interest. The remainder of the thesis will then apply the approach to a current specification language for non-functional properties of component-based systems (namely, CQML[+]), to an analysis technique (namely, performance analysis using *SPE·ED*), and show how it fits together with a component-oriented development process.

Part II

The Semantic Framework

In this part, we present the core concepts of this thesis. We begin in Chapt. 3 with the fundamental concepts and then extend them in two directions: Chapter 4 discusses services delivered by networks of interacting components. Chapter 5 is about systems where more than one interacting non-functional properties need to be considered.

Chapter 3

Core Framework

In this chapter we will formally develop the core framework concepts. We begin by explaining our system model, introducing the core concepts of components, resources, containers, and services. Next, we define how we use measurements to specify non-functional characteristics. We then show how we derive non-functional property specifications of components and services from these measurements. Finally, we discuss three example specifications to illustrate the concepts introduced in this chapter.

3.1 The System Model

Figure 3.1 shows a Unified Modelling Language (UML) [105] class diagram presenting the core concepts of the system model underlying the semantic framework. Only applications structured in a way compliant to this system model can be described using a specification technique based on our framework. The system model, thus, shows the assumptions we make about the systems to be described. We will explain each element of the system model in more detail in this section.

The business logic of an application is coded into *components*. We base our understanding of a component on the definition given by Szyperski:

> "A software component is a unit of composition with contractually specified interfaces and explicit context dependencies only. A software component can

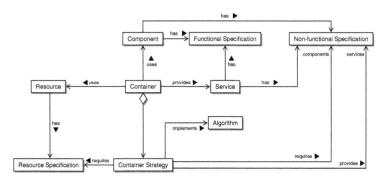

Figure 3.1: System model

be deployed independently and is subject to composition by third parties."
[140]

Components come with a specification of their *functional* as well as their *non-functional properties*. In this thesis we are going to concentrate mainly on the non-functional properties. These are, however, always expressed in relation to some specific functionality. For example, we may talk about the "response time of an Internet query", or the "reliability of the ignition sequence implementation of an Ariadne rocket", but it is rather meaningless to talk about a general response time or reliability. We will, therefore, need to consider what parts of the functionality to represent, and how best to represent these parts.

Components work together to provide an application's functionality. Users view application functionality in terms of *services*. For each service, they have *functional* as well as *non-functional requirements,* which must be fulfilled by corresponding properties of the service.

Allowing components to interact directly to provide the desired functionality defeats the idea of independent component realisation and deployment. If the developer of component A has not anticipated its interaction with a component B, it would be impossible for the two components to interact, even if their functional specifications give a perfect match [59]. We, therefore, assume that a runtime environment—also known as the *container*—manages all interactions between components. In addition, to shield component developers from platform details and other aspects (such as transaction and other middleware services), the container implements life-cycle management as well as a set of standardised services usable inside components.[1] All information about the components that the container requires to perform this task are to be provided in the form of declarative specifications. In summary, it is the container's responsibility to use available components and *resources* intelligently in order to provide a certain service with certain properties.

There exists a quite diverse set of non-functional properties that could be of interest for an application. *Container strategies* encapsulate *algorithms* which consider a specific set of non-functional properties and resources, and describe what needs to be done to support them. A container knows a set of such strategies that it applies when setting up an application. Each container strategy maps a set of non-functional properties of components and a set of constraints over resources (resource specifications in Fig. 3.1) to a set of non-functional properties of the corresponding service. Container strategies are considered to be *functionality preserving;* that is, the functionality of the service is derived only from the functionality of the components.

Example 3.1 (Container Strategy for Responsibility) Users of business-critical applications may want to file charges against the producers of these systems if the system fails to provide the services contractually agreed on. We will say that systems allowing this provide the property of *responsibility* [50, 146, 147]. In order to provide responsibility in a component-based setting, two criteria must be met:

1. When a failure occurs, it must be possible to identify the component which caused it.

2. For each component, it must be possible to identify who produced it. In addition, the producer of the component must be ready to take up responsibility for his or her work.

To be able to blame failures to specific components, we need to intercept and log all information crossing any of the interfaces of the component. By comparing these logs to the specification of the component, we can identify components which behave incorrectly. This may not be enough, because the failure may actually have been caused by the platform

---

[1]This has not been shown in Fig. 3.1.

on which the component runs [41], but we will ignore this further complication for the sake of this example.

A component developer is only ready to take responsibility for his or her product's failures, if it can be shown that the product was used unaltered and according to its specification. The component code, therefore, needs to be signed with a digital signature to guard its integrity, and, at the same time, assert the identity of the producer. For the sake of simplicity in this example, we will assume that by providing such a signature the component developer consents to taking responsibility for failures of his or her code.

Looking at this situation through the looking glass of our system model, we can rephrase it as follows: Component code can be signed. The presence of a signature is a non-functional property of a component (*is_signed*). In order to provide a service with the non-functional property *responsibility* from components with the non-functional property *is_signed*, the container needs to perform the following two steps:

1. Check all signatures of all components cooperating to provide the service.

2. Log all events at all interfaces of the component instances while the service is being provided.

This algorithm can be captured in a container strategy for responsibility, which supports the transformation from *is_signed* to *responsibility* by checking signatures and logging interactions.   ◇

Example 3.2 (Response time) [64] presents another container strategy: Given a component with one operation with a worst-case execution time, and information about the stream of incoming requests for this operation in the form of a jitter-constrained stream [63] this strategy computes the required number of component instances, the amount of memory required to buffer incoming requests for the operation's service, the task set to be scheduled by the underlying CPU, and the worst-case response time for each operation invocation. ◇

In the following sections we will discuss the formal specifications of the core parts of this system model—components, services, container strategies, and resources—in detail.

3.2   Measurements

All specifications of non-functional properties of components or services are essentially constraints over non-functional dimensions of these systems. Such dimensions are often also called *characteristics* [69]. A formal definition of such a characteristic must explain how its value can be measured in a running system. Therefore, it must be represented as a mapping from the system state to the value of the characteristic. This description is very close to the definition of a *measurement* in *measurement theory* (e.g., [55]) where a measurement is a mapping from physical or empirical objects to formal objects. We, therefore, use the term *measurement* to talk about the formal specification of a non-functional dimension or characteristic.

As we already explained in the previous section, a measurement can only be defined relative to some functional characterisation of the system to be constrained. This characterisation does not need to be complete, but it must contain the elements, structures, and behaviours on which the measurement relies. Because such a model gives the context of a measurement, we call it a *context model*.[2] A context model explicitly expresses the assumptions a measurement makes about the functional environment to which it will be

---

[2]The term *context* should not be confused with the same term used in the area of *context-aware computation*. There, context refers to the environment in which an application is executing, and in particular to those aspects of the environment that influence the behaviour of the application. Here, context denotes the aspects of an application that are relevant for the definition of a measurement.

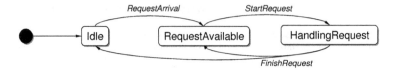

Figure 3.2: An example of a context model defining the relevant steps in an operation call

applied. Using context models, we can specify measurements independently of their usage in concrete applications.

When specifying non-functional properties of an application, we need to map the concepts from the measurement's context model to the structures and behaviours present in the application model. In other words, we need to explain that, and how, the application model can be seen as an instance of the measurement's context model. This serves two purposes: (i) to check whether the measurement can indeed be applied in this specific case, and (ii) to bind parameters; that is to express specifically, to which part of our system the measurement should be applied.

We will discuss formal definitions for these concepts in the following subsections. We begin by defining context models and discussing their relation to application models in Sect. 3.2.1. Section 3.2.2 then presents the formal definition of a measurement. These concepts are combined by the definition of a model mapping in Sect. 3.2.3. The discussion closes with a comparison of the different types of models involved (Sect. 3.2.4).

3.2.1   Context Models and Application Models

We use temporal logic as our base formalism, and, thus, we use temporal logic also to describe context and application models.

Definition 3.1 (Context Model and Application Model) A context model S_{Ctx} is given by a state machine (*cf.* Sect. 1.6) $S_{Ctx} = (\Sigma_{Ctx}, F_{Ctx}, N_{Ctx})$, an application model S_{App} is analogously given by $S_{App} = (\Sigma_{App}, F_{App}, N_{App})$.

Context models are distinguished from application models by the fact that they have been constructed for the definition of a specific measurement m and model only those structures which are relevant to m.   ■

Context models are more generic than application models. They do not define specific components, operations, or attributes, but the *concept* of a component, an operation, or an attribute. The relationship between context models and application models can be likened to the relationship between a meta-model [40, p. 19*f.*] and an actual model. The context model is a measurement-specific abstraction of the application model. There is, however, no formal distinction between context models and application models: they are both normal TLA$^+$ specifications.

Example 3.3 (Context Model and Application Model) Figure 3.2 shows an example of a context model defining the relevant steps in an operation call. The notation is based on UML state diagrams. Hence, the black circle indicates an initial state, named boxes indicate states, and arrows indicate transitions between states. The transition labels either refer to action names (as in the figure) or they indicate assignments occurring when the transition fires (as will be seen in later figures).

The component is in state 'Idle' as long as no request for the execution of an operation has arrived. As soon as such a request arrives, the component changes to state 'RequestAvailable'. At some point, the component begins handling the request. As long as it is in the process of handling the request, the component is in state 'HandlingRequest'. When

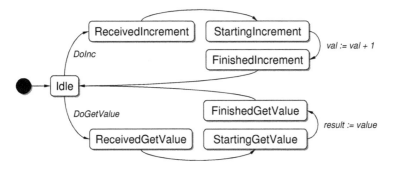

Figure 3.3: An example of an application model describing a simple Counter component

the request has been handled completely, the component returns to state 'Idle' or 'RequestAvailable', depending on whether a new request has arrived in the meantime. Note that this way of modelling a service operation is just one possible way of doing it. Depending on the domain, other aspects of an operation call may be important and need to be modelled in a different manner.

Figure 3.3 shows an application model for a simple Counter component. The component offers two operations: inc, represented by the upper branch, which increments an internal value variable, and getValue, represented by the lower branch, which returns the current value. ◇

When specifying context models, we typically follow a simple specification scheme. Although we could use any legal TLA$^+$ specification, these restrictions make it much easier to define measurements based on these context models.

Definition 3.2 (Specification Scheme for Context Models) A context model S_{Ctx} should be specified using the following specification scheme:

1. The complete specification consists of the conjunction of an initial-states predicate $INIT$ and the next-state clause $NEXT$:

$$S_{Ctx} \triangleq \land INIT$$
$$\land \Box[NEXT]_{vars_{Ctx}}$$

where $vars_{Ctx}$ are the state variables referenced in $INIT$ or $NEXT$.

2. $NEXT$ is a disjunction of different actions A_i, which are pairwise disjoint and none of which does not modify any state variable:

$$NEXT \triangleq \bigvee_i A_i$$
$$\forall i, j : (i \neq j) \implies (A_i \implies \neg A_j)$$
$$\forall i : (A_i \implies \neg\text{UNCHANGED } vars_{Ctx})$$ ∎

In practice, these constraints do not cause much suffering. The first condition has already been laid down by Lamport when presenting TLA$^+$. He states that this style of specification helps reasoning about specifications in general. The second condition is natural to most specifications anyway. Technically it usually only means that one needs to add UNCHANGED v clauses for each v not directly referenced by the action to each action specification.

3.2.2 Formal Representation of Measurements

The formal specifications used to define measurements must not influence the behaviour of the systems to which they are applied. Abadi/Lamport [3] formally define the concept of a *history variable* to represent state components that can be added to a specification without changing the externally observable behaviour of this specification. In [4] they apply history variables to define timers which can be used to express timing constraints in TLA$^+$ specifications. We use history variables as the basis of our definition of a measurement:[3]

Definition 3.3 (Measurement) A measurement m is given by state functions f, g, and v, such that

$$Hist(m, f, g, v) \triangleq (m = f) \land \Box[m' = g \land v' \neq v]_{\langle m, v \rangle}$$

m does not occur free in either f or v, and m' does not occur free in g.

Measurements are defined relative to a context model S_{Ctx}^m with externally visible property Π_{Ctx}^m. For every measurement

$$\forall \sigma \in \Sigma^\infty : \sigma \in \Pi_{Ctx}^m \Rightarrow \sigma \models \exists m : S_{Ctx}^m \land Hist(m, f, g, v)$$

must hold. The complete measurement specification is then given by $S_{Ctx}^m \land Hist(m, f, g, v)$ ∎

Intuitively, f specifies the initial value for the measurement, g defines the actual process of measuring—that is, how the measurement reacts to actions in the context model S_{Ctx}^m. v is a sequence of context-model variables that the measurement watches. Measurement updates can occur if and only if any one of the variables in v changes. Abadi/Lamport showed in [4] that conjoining $Hist(m, f, g, v)$ to S_{Ctx}^m does not affect the behaviour represented by S_{Ctx}^m.

Again, when specifying measurements, we usually follow a specification scheme:

Definition 3.4 (Specification Scheme for Measurements) Measurements should be specified using the following specification scheme:

1. The complete specification is the conjunction of the context-model specification and the measurement specification:

$$S_m \triangleq \land S_{Ctx}^m$$
$$\land MeasureSpec_m$$

2. The measurement specification $MeasureSpec_m$ is the conjunction of an initial-states predicate and the next-state clause $NEXT_m$:

$$MeasureSpec_m \triangleq \land m = INIT_m$$
$$\land \Box[NEXT_m \land vars'_{Ctx} \neq vars_{Ctx}]_{vars}$$

where $vars = \langle m, var_{Ctx} \rangle$, and m does not occur free in $INIT_m$.

3. $NEXT_m$ is the conjunction of reactions $R_i \triangleq A_i \Rightarrow m' = B_i$ one for each action A_i in the context model. B_i is a function computing the new value of the measurement. m' does not occur free in any B_i.

$$NEXT_m \triangleq \land \bigwedge_i A_i \Rightarrow m' = B_i$$
$$\land (\forall i : \neg A_i) \Rightarrow \text{UNCHANGED } m$$
∎

---

[3]The specific formalisation of a measurement is closely modelled along the definition of a history-determined variable given in [4].

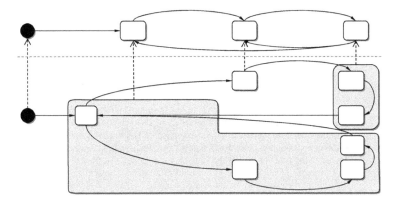

Figure 3.4: An example model mapping. The upper part represents the context model from Fig. 3.2, the lower part is the application model from Fig. 3.3. The dashed arrows and shaded areas indicate which application-model states are mapped onto which context-model states

Using this specification scheme automatically renders measurements according to Def. 3.3 (see proof in Appendix C.1.1). The most interesting part of this specification scheme is the definition of $NEXT_m$. Intuitively, we write it as a list, where for each action the context model can perform (A_i), we define how the measurement changes as a reaction $(m' = B_i)$. It can be seen easily, through a few standard TLA$^+$ transformations, that defining a measurement in this way essentially conjoins $m' = B_i$ to the corresponding A_i of the context model (see Appendix C.1.2 for the proof).

3.2.3   Mapping Measurements onto Actual Applications

Once we have specified non-functional dimensions using measurements, we need to apply these definitions to concrete applications. This requires a formal relation to be established between the measurement's context model and the application model. We want to combine context and application model such that we can reason about the combination as an instance of the context model without having to reason about—or know of—the specific application's functionality. We can do so by having the context model *observe* the behaviour of the application model; that is the two models "run" in parallel and the context model's behaviour is additionally constrained by the application model and a mapping between state variables. To put this a little more formally, we will represent the mapping as a relation $\phi_{App}^{Ctx} \subseteq \Sigma_{App} \times \Sigma_{Ctx}$, so that we can represent the application by

$$\Pi_{Ctx}^{App} \triangleq \Pi_{App} \wedge \Pi_{Ctx} \wedge \Box\left(\langle v_{App}, v_{Ctx}\rangle \in \phi_{App}^{Ctx}\right) \tag{3.1}$$

where v_{App} refers to all flexible variables of the application state and, correspondingly, v_{Ctx} refers to the flexible variables of the context model. Because $\models \Pi_{Ctx}^{App} \Rightarrow \Pi_{Ctx}$, we can, thus, reason about our application as though it was an instance of our context model.

Example 3.4 (Model Mapping) Figure 3.4 shows an example of a simple model mapping. It maps the context model from Fig. 3.2 onto the `inc` operation call defined in the application model from Fig. 3.3. We have introduced a few hierarchical states to group application-model states that are mapped to the same context-model state.

Two things should be noted about this example:

1. All application-model states that represent the invocation of the `getValue` operation have been mapped to the 'Idle' state in the context model. This means, that at the context-model level, we only observe calls to `inc`, because these cause state changes in the context model; all calls to `getValue` are ignored by this mapping. We will use this approach further down to associate measurements with individual operations, streams, or other parts of an application's behaviour.

2. In order for such a mapping to be possible, the application model's state machine must be fine-grained enough to allow the states required by the context model to be discerned. The context model then serves as an abstraction of the states of the application model. In particular, in our example, we had to model the mechanics of operation invocation in more detail than what would have been necessary purely for expressing the functionality of the Counter component. It is, however, conceivable that Computer-Aided Software Engineering (CASE) tools providing a higher-level language for the expression of application models (e.g., a combination of UML and CQML$^+$ such as reported in [?]) may use the context-model information to introduce the additional states necessary at the application-model level in a way that is transparent to the modeller.   ◇

Of course, not all mappings ϕ_{App}^{Ctx} are equally well suited. They represent how a certain measurement is being applied to a certain concrete application, and thus must maintain the semantics of the measurement and of the application. So, what are the conditions, ϕ_{App}^{Ctx} must fulfil? Most importantly, we want to retain the observational property of a measurement. Recall from Sect. 3.2.2 that we used history-determined variables to define measurements so that adding a measurement to a specification will not change the set of behaviours described by this specification. To maintain this property also when mapping to concrete applications, we require that

$$\models \Pi_{App} \equiv \mathbf{\exists}\, v_{Ctx} \,:\, \Pi_{Ctx}^{App} \qquad\qquad (3.2)$$

where v_{Ctx} means all flexible variables introduced by the context model. That is, for every behaviour satisfying the application model, we can find a sequence of values for the context model's variables so that both the model mapping and the context model are satisfied by the combined behaviour.

Two remarks about this requirement may be in order:

1. Determining the non-functional properties of a running application is a difficult problem. In particular, it can be very hard to design a measuring set-up such that the functional or non-functional properties of the application under measurement are not changed by the process of measuring some of its properties. However, in this thesis, we are concerned purely with the *specification* of applications and their non-functional properties. It is reasonable to require that the addition of measurement specifications to a functional specification does not affect the behaviour defined by this functional specification.

2. Of course, at some point, we want our non-functional specifications to restrict the set of possible behaviours of the system specified. We will discuss in Sect. 3.3 how constraining the possible *values* of measurements can constrain the set of possible behaviours of a system.

Condition (3.2) can be a little cumbersome to check. Therefore, we provide sufficient requirements on ϕ_{App}^{Ctx} directly:

Φ1) Every initial state of the application model is mapped to at least one initial state of the context model:

$$\forall s_{App}^f \in F_{App} \,:\, \exists s_{Ctx}^f \in F_{Ctx} \,:\, \langle s_{App}^f, s_{Ctx}^f \rangle \in \phi_{App}^{Ctx}$$

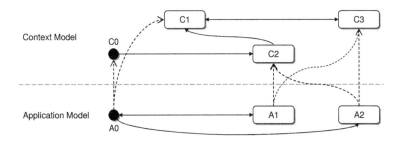

Figure 3.5: Typical mappings for initial application states

Figure 3.5 shows a mapping respecting this condition. Initially, the application model starts out in A0 and the context model starts in C0, both of which are initial states so that this is possible for both state machines. The application may eventually return to state A0, in which case the context model will go to state C1. This is not an initial state, but because the application has been running for some time already, this is not a problem. If A0 had not been mapped to any initial state of the context model, conjoining the context model to the application model would effectively remove A0 from the set of valid initial application states and so change the application's behaviour.

Φ2) Any legal state transition in the application model is mapped to at least one legal state transition or to a stuttering step in the context model:

$$\forall s_{App}^1, s_{App}^2 \in \Sigma_{App} \; : \; \langle s_{App}^1, s_{App}^2 \rangle \in N_{App}$$
$$\Rightarrow \forall s_{Ctx}^1 \in \Sigma_{Ctx} \; :$$
$$\langle s_{App}^1, s_{Ctx}^1 \rangle \in \phi_{App}^{Ctx}$$
$$\Rightarrow \exists s_{Ctx}^2 \in \Sigma_{Ctx} \; :$$
$$\wedge \langle s_{App}^2, s_{Ctx}^2 \rangle \in \phi_{App}^{Ctx}$$
$$\wedge \vee \langle s_{Ctx}^1, s_{Ctx}^2 \rangle \in N_{Ctx}$$
$$\vee s_{Ctx}^1 = s_{Ctx}^2$$

Figure 3.6a shows a situation where this condition is violated. It can be seen that the set of behaviours allowed by the application model is restricted by the context model and the model mapping. The behaviour shown in the lower compartment, which had been allowed by the application model, is ruled out by the combination of application model and context model.

The rule above is overly strict, however. It also excludes the model mapping shown in Fig. 3.6b, although the application model is at no time blocked by the context model. In many situations, it may be completely reasonable for the context model to perform multiple steps for one step of the application model. It is, therefore, reasonable to weaken the above condition as follows:

Any legal state transition in the application model is mapped to a sequence of legal

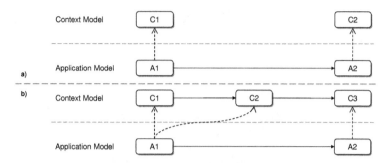

Figure 3.6: Two examples for mappings constrained by $\Phi2$: a) is an example of a violation of the strict rule; b) shows a mapping where the context model is allowed to observe an application model step in a sequence of steps

state transitions or to stuttering steps in the context model:

$$
\begin{aligned}
\forall\, s_{App}^1, s_{App}^2 &\in \Sigma_{App} \;:\; \langle s_{App}^1, s_{App}^2 \rangle \in N_{App} \\
\Rightarrow \forall\, s_{Ctx}^1 &\in \Sigma_{Ctx} \;:\; \langle s_{App}^1, s_{Ctx}^1 \rangle \in \phi_{App}^{Ctx} \\
\Rightarrow \exists\, s_{Ctx}^2 &\in \Sigma_{Ctx} \;: \\
&\wedge \langle s_{App}^2, s_{Ctx}^2 \rangle \in \phi_{App}^{Ctx} \\
&\wedge \vee \langle s_{Ctx}^1, s_{Ctx}^2 \rangle \in N_{Ctx} \\
&\quad \vee \exists\, n \in \mathbb{N}, \widehat{s}_{Ctx}^0, \dots, \widehat{s}_{Ctx}^n \in \Sigma_{Ctx} \;: \\
&\qquad \wedge \langle s_{Ctx}^1, \widehat{s}_{Ctx}^0 \rangle \in N_{Ctx} \\
&\qquad \wedge \langle \widehat{s}_{Ctx}^n, s_{Ctx}^2 \rangle \in N_{Ctx} \\
&\qquad \wedge \forall\, i = 0, \dots, n-1 \;:\; \langle \widehat{s}_{Ctx}^i, \widehat{s}_{Ctx}^{i+1} \rangle \in N_{Ctx} \\
&\qquad \wedge \forall\, i = 0, \dots, n \;:\; \langle s_{App}^1, \widehat{s}_{Ctx}^i \rangle \in \phi_{App}^{Ctx} \\
&\quad \vee s_{Ctx}^1 = s_{Ctx}^2
\end{aligned}
$$

Note that we require that all states in the sequence of context-model states have been mapped to the first application-model state. This is exactly as we did in our example in Fig. 3.6b, where A1 is the first application-model state, and A2 is the second one. If this condition is respected, the application model can always perform a series of stuttering steps while the context model moves along, preparing the application-model transition. Moreover, all situations where the context models needs to perform more steps than the application model can be represented in this way.

$\Phi3$) The mapping is complete; that is every state of the application model is mapped to at least one state in the context model:[4]

$$
\forall\, s_{App} \in \Sigma_{App} \;:\; \exists\, s_{Ctx} \in \Sigma_{Ctx} \;:\; \langle s_{App}, s_{Ctx} \rangle \in \phi_{App}^{Ctx}
$$

Figure 3.7 shows an example where this condition has been violated. It can be seen that the application model is blocked by this model mapping, because it is completely unclear what context-model state should be chosen to go with A2 .

Theorem 3.1 (Conditions for Model-Mappings) Conditions $\Phi1$ thru $\Phi3$ are sufficient conditions to produce a ϕ_{App}^{Ctx} fulfilling Cond. (3.2). $\square$

---

[4]This condition is a little over-exacting. It would be sufficient to demand that all *reachable* application states are mapped to some context-model state. However, the requirement that all states must be mapped can be fulfilled easily by providing a dummy mapping for unreachable states, and phrasing the condition so makes the proofs a lot simpler.

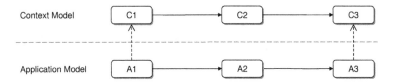

Figure 3.7: An example mapping that violates rule $\Phi3$

The proof of this theorem can be found in Sect. C.2 in the appendix.

Conditions $\Phi1$ thru $\Phi3$ look very similar to the conditions defined for refinement mappings in [3]. The major difference is that there is no externally visible state component which needs to remain identical. For very similar reasons, ϕ_{App}^{Ctx} only reminds one of the concept of observable simulation relation as defined, for example, in [139, p. 68]. A relation B between states is an *observable simulation relation* iff for each $(s_1, s_2) \in B$ and for each action A, $s_1 \overset{A}{\Rightarrow} s_3$ there exists a state s_4 so that $s_2 \overset{A}{\Rightarrow} s_4$ and $(s_3, s_4) \in B$.[5] Our conditions stipulate, rather, that there must exist some action C (which may also be the empty action ϵ) so that $s_2 \overset{C}{\Rightarrow} s_4$ and $(s_3, s_4) \in B$. This is a much weaker set of conditions.

The formalism most closely related to our notion of model mapping is the notion of a correct refinement for Abstract State Machines (ASMs) [25] as defined by Börger in [24]. Börger requires an equivalence relation $\equiv$ to be defined between states—this can be our relation ϕ_{App}^{Ctx}. An ASM M is then a *correct refinement* of another ASM M^* iff for every run R of M there exists a run R^* of M^* so that some subsequence of the states from R can be mapped to some subsequence of the states from R^* using $\equiv$. Thus, Börger allows both state machines to perform arbitrary steps between equivalent states. In contrast, we require every step of the application model to be matched by a step of the context model. Either step may be a stuttering step, but still, ϕ_{App}^{Ctx} must relate all states involved. Börger's approach works well for defining a notion of equivalence or refinement between specifications. However, we require a definition that allows usage of ϕ_{App}^{Ctx} as part of a specification, following Equation (3.1).

The lack of externally visible state or identically named actions, however, is also the biggest problem with conditions $\Phi1$ thru $\Phi3$, because the effects of the mapping are, thus, difficult to capture formally. This is similar to the situation with interface refinements as discussed in [78]. There, the point is made that such mappings actually add information to the specification. This is the reason why it is not possible to provide a complete definition of what a correct mapping looks like. All we can do, is to provide conditions that enable us to identify *incorrect* mappings. Conditions $\Phi1$ thru $\Phi3$ are a good start on this way.

Example 3.5 (Bad Model Mapping) Consider the following mapping relation ξ_{App}^{Ctx}:

$$\exists f_{Ctx} \in F_{Ctx} : \wedge \forall s_{App} \in \Sigma_{App} : \langle s_{App}, f_{Ctx} \rangle \in \xi_{App}^{Ctx} \qquad (3.3)$$
$$\wedge \forall s_{Ctx} \in \Sigma_{Ctx} : \vee f_{Ctx} = s_{Ctx}$$
$$\vee \forall s_{App} \in \Sigma_{App} : \langle s_{App}, s_{Ctx} \rangle \notin \xi_{App}^{Ctx}$$

mapping every state of the application onto the same initial state of the context model. This is fully consistent with the conditions above, as well as with Cond. (3.2). However, the context model does not *observe* the application model at all, and any measurements defined based on this context model become meaningless. ξ_{App}^{Ctx} fulfils Cond. (3.2), which means that this condition is not sufficiently strict. $\diamond$

The issue is located not at the formal level, but rather it is an issue about the relation between the formalism and reality, or about the *intended semantics* of a measurement

---

[5]$E \overset{A}{\Rightarrow} E'$ stipulates that state E can be evolved to E' through a number of hidden actions and the action A.

definition. By this we mean, the structure or function in reality that the original specifier intended to denote by the formal specification. Because any conditions we place on ϕ_{App}^{Ctx} can only express constraints on the formal level, they are not appropriate to capture intended semantics. Because in a component market, different people will develop different parts of the final and complete application specification, we need a common formal basis among these people, which allows them to communicate correctly. Note that this does not solve the initial problem of the intended semantics, but it makes it accessible to negotiation between the stakeholders outside the formal system. Once all parties agree on a common formal basis, everything else can be treated at the formal level. We call this common conceptual basis a *computational model:*

Definition 3.5 (Computational Model) A computational model S_{CM} is given by a state machine $S_{CM} = (\Sigma_{CM}, F_{CM}, N_{CM})$.

A computational model is similar to a context model (*cf.* Def. 3.1) in that it is defined at the meta-level, but it is not constructed with view to a specific measurement definition. In contrast, a computational model captures the terms, structures and behaviours commonly agreed between different stakeholders in a *domain*. It captures the concepts relevant to this domain and thus limits and grounds the set of possible measurement definitions of this domain. ∎

Once we have defined a computational model, all context models in a domain can be formally mapped onto this computational model. Thus, the computational model provides a commonly agreed basis for communication between different players in a domain.

It seems important to point out, that agreeing on a computational model is a consequential step in defining a domain, and that it *limits* the set of measurements that can be expressed in this domain. Because every measurement definition references variables already present in the context model, and because the context model will eventually be mapped onto the computational model, every variable to be referenced by a measurement specification must be representable in the computational model. A computational model which only considers operation calls will not allow measurements related to stream-based communication to be defined. This statement is in contrast to the—often implicit—notion in other works on measurement-based specification (most notably [1, 57]) that these approaches can be used to specify any arbitrary measurement. While it remains true that they have the potential to do so, an important step toward making them useful is to agree on a computational model, and as soon as a computational model has been fixed, the expressiveness has been restricted. This shows up implicitly in Aagedal's thesis [1] when he presents characteristics without a definition of their semantics (i.e., without a `values`-clause).

To summarise the discussion in this section, we define measurement mappings in the following way (this definition summarises conditions $\Phi 1$ thru $\Phi 3$ and applies them to both context models and computational models):

Definition 3.6 (Measurement Mapping) A relation $\phi_{M_1}^{M_2} \subseteq \Sigma_{M_1} \times \Sigma_{M_2}$ where

1. Every initial state of M_1 is mapped to at least one initial state of M_2:

$$\forall s_{M_1}^f \in F_{M_1} \ : \ \exists s_{M_2}^f \in F_{M_2} \ : \ \langle s_{M_1}^f, s_{M_2}^f \rangle \in \phi_{M_1}^{M_2}$$

2. Any legal state transition in M_1 is mapped to a sequence of legal state transitions or

to stuttering steps in M_2:

$$\forall s_{M_1}^1, s_{M_1}^2 \in \Sigma_{M_1} :$$
$$\langle s_{M_1}^1, s_{M_1}^2 \rangle \in N_{M_1}$$
$$\Rightarrow \forall s_{M_2}^1, s_{M_2}^2 \in \Sigma_{M_2} : \wedge \langle s_{M_1}^1, s_{M_2}^1 \rangle \in \phi_{M_1}^{M_2}$$
$$\wedge \langle s_{M_1}^2, s_{M_2}^2 \rangle \in \phi_{M_1}^{M_2}$$
$$\Rightarrow \vee \langle s_{M_2}^1, s_{M_2}^2 \rangle \in N_{M_2}$$
$$\vee \exists n \in \mathbb{N}, \widehat{s}_{M_2}^0, \ldots, \widehat{s}_{M_2}^n \in \Sigma_{M_2} :$$
$$\wedge \langle s_{M_2}^1, \widehat{s}_{M_2}^0 \rangle \in N_{M_2}$$
$$\wedge \langle \widehat{s}_{M_2}^n, s_{M_2}^2 \rangle \in N_{M_2}$$
$$\wedge \forall i = 0, \ldots, n-1 : \langle \widehat{s}_{M_2}^i, \widehat{s}_{M_2}^{i+1} \rangle \in N_{M_2}$$
$$\wedge \forall i = 0, \ldots, n : \langle s_{M_1}^1, \widehat{s}_{M_2}^i \rangle \in \phi_{M_1}^{M_2}$$
$$\vee s_{M_2}^1 = s_{M_2}^2$$

3. The mapping is complete; that is every state of M_1 is mapped to at least one state in M_2:

$$\forall s_{M_1} \in \Sigma_{M_1} : \exists s_{M_2} \in \Sigma_{M_2} : \langle s_{M_1}, s_{M_2} \rangle \in \phi_{M_1}^{M_2} \qquad \blacksquare$$

is called a *measurement mapping*.

There are two types of measurement mappings:

1. *Mapping context models to the computational model:* Here, M_1 is the computational model, and M_2 is a context model.

2. *Mapping the computational model to an application:* Here, M_1 is an application model, and M_2 is the computational model.

Because context models and computational models are both defined at the meta-level, and because context models will eventually need to be mapped onto the computational model anyway, it can be argued that there is no need for context models at all. We have discussed in other publications [118, 119] how multiple context models can be used to support the application designer's refinement decisions in incremental design. For the purposes of this thesis we will not consider this aspect and we will no further discuss the distinction between computational model and context models. For the remainder of this thesis we will use these terms interchangeably.

Context models, and sometimes even application models, are rather abstract. It is, therefore, often undesirable to spell out the complete state information and all state changes explicitly, as this may break encapsulation of implementation details. To avoid such problems, TLA$^+$ allows specifiers to use unspecified actions in their specifications. The example in Sect. 3.5.2 uses such actions. However, because the state information is not made explicit, measurement mappings cannot be defined as a direct relation between state components. Hence, we extend (3.1) as follows:

$$\Pi_{Ctx}^{App} \triangleq \Pi_{Ctx} \wedge \Pi_{App} \wedge \Box ModelMappingRule \qquad (3.4)$$

where

$$ModelMappingRule \triangleq \wedge \left(\langle v_{App}, v_{Ctx} \rangle \in \phi_{App}^{Ctx} \right) \qquad (3.5)$$
$$\wedge \forall A \in Action_{App} : A \Rightarrow B_A$$

where $Action_{App}$ is the set of actions from the application model to be mapped to context-model actions, and B_A is the context-model action to which application-model action A is to be mapped.

Of course, we need to impose some additional condition on the mapping to make it a valid mapping. For each rule of the form $A \Rightarrow B_A$ we require the following to hold:

$$
\begin{aligned}
\forall s_{App}^1, s_{App}^2 \in \Sigma_{App} : \forall s_{Ctx}^1, s_{Ctx}^2 \in \Sigma_{Ctx} : \; & \wedge \langle s_{App}^1, s_{App}^2 \rangle \models A \qquad\qquad (3.6) \\
& \wedge \langle s_{App}^1, s_{App}^2 \rangle \in N_{App} \\
& \wedge \langle s_{App}^1, s_{Ctx}^1 \rangle \in \phi_{App}^{Ctx} \\
& \wedge \langle s_{App}^2, s_{Ctx}^2 \rangle \in \phi_{App}^{Ctx} \\
\Rightarrow \; & \wedge \langle s_{Ctx}^1, s_{Ctx}^2 \rangle \models B_A \\
& \wedge \langle s_{Ctx}^1, s_{Ctx}^2 \rangle \in N_{Ctx}
\end{aligned}
$$

That is, ϕ_{App}^{Ctx} must not drive the system into a situation, where the application would like to perform an A step, but the context model cannot perform the corresponding B_A step.

3.2.4   A Remark on the Different Types of Models

After we have introduced definitions of different types of models—context models, application models, and computational models—in the preceding sections, it is perhaps prudent to summarise their interrelations and discuss their relationships to other (component-oriented) models, such as component models, interface models, and meta-models. Although these various models are referred to quite often in the literature, it is astonishingly difficult to find precise, let alone commonly accepted, definitions. For the sake of our discussion in this thesis, we, therefore, introduce the following definitions:

Definition 3.7 (Component Model) A *component model* defines rules to be obeyed by components following this model. The purpose of these rules is to achieve technical interoperability between components implemented by third-party component developers. They include concepts such as special interfaces to be implemented by components in order to be accessible by the component runtime environment, certain types of interfaces a component may provide (these are normally related to the underlying interface model or models), additional specification requirements (such as component descriptor formats), binary format definitions, and so on. ∎

Definition 3.8 (Interface Model) [6] An *interface model* defines the concepts and constraints governing the interactions between components. Interface models are more general than component models, but each component model is based on one or more interface models—together with a definition of how they are realised within this specific component model. The three most common interface models are:

1. *request–response-based communication,* also sometimes called the Remote Procedure Call (RPC) interface model

2. *asynchronous communication,* or event notification

3. *stream-based communication* ∎

Definition 3.9 (Meta-model (derived from [40])) A *meta-model* is a model of a modelling language. Meta-models capture the essential features and properties of a modelling language—that is, the concrete syntax, the abstract syntax, and semantics. ∎

Application models are models in the sense of meta-modelling. They conform to a specific component model and one or more interface model(s). They describe concrete applications. In contrast, both the computational model and the context model are meta-models of possible application models. Many, but not all, of the concepts defined in a context or a computational model can be found in interface models. For example, the

---

[6]This definition has been inspired particularly by [22].

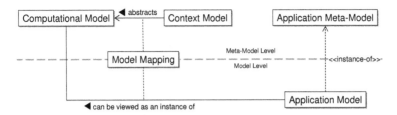

Figure 3.8: Relations between the major model types in our approach

concept of interfaces with operations comes from the RPC interface model. Context and computational models need to be mapped (typically by container designers) onto concrete component models by explaining how their concepts are realised in the specific component model. As we have explained in Sect. 3.2.3, context models and computational models are very closely related.

Figure 3.8 gives an overview of the most important relations between models in our approach. Application models are written as instances of an application meta-model—for example, the UML meta-model. When applying a measurement to an application model, we need to show that the application model "can be seen as" an instance of the computational model that is the basis of definition of the measurement. We can do so by providing an appropriate model mapping. A similar relationship exists between context models and computational models, where the former are essentially an abstraction of the latter—again demonstrated by a model mapping. Application meta-models, computational models, and context models are similar in that they all reside on the meta-modelling level.

After we have discussed the basic building blocks—measurements—in the last sections, the next section looks at how we use these building blocks to construct complete specifications of components, services, and systems.

3.3 Non-functional Properties

It is common in temporal logics to define *properties* as sets of traces or behaviours—that is, infinite sequences of states. A property, thus, characterises a subset of the set of all behaviours. Recall that above we defined a measurement by using history-determined variables so that the set of valid behaviours was not affected by the addition of a measurement to the specification. Therefore, a measurement alone is *not* a non-functional property. A *non-functional property* is derived from a measurement, or a set of measurements, by specifying constraints over the measurement values.

Definition 3.10 (Non-functional Property) Given a set $M = \{m_1, m_2, \ldots\}$ of measurements, a non-functional property over this set $\Pi_{Nf}(M)$ is given by any formula constraining the values of the measurements in M. ∎

In this chapter, we focus on cases where M only contains one measurement m and discuss the fundamental definitions of our approach. Some of the definitions in the following will be general enough to include other cases—to be discussed in Chapt. 5. In particular, we will not discuss the relations between different context models of different measurements, or interactions between measurements in this chapter.

It should be noted that the above definition, together with the definition of a measurement, means that our approach cannot be used for properties that are not "measurable" as functions of the state of the product. Any product property that can be so measured, however, is also covered by our approach.

As we have already mentioned in Sect. 2.6, we distinguish four kinds of non-functional specifications:

Intrinsic specifications specify component implementation properties.

Extrinsic specifications specify properties of a service.

Resource specifications specify the aspect enabled by a resource.

Container specifications specify container behaviour with respect to non-functional properties.

We will discuss these four types of specifications in the following, beginning with a discussion of the most fundamental distinction: that between intrinsic and extrinsic properties. Note that we will use the terms non-functional property and *non-functional specification* interchangeably in the following. We understand a specification to be a statement that a certain property must hold for a system satisfying the specification.

3.3.1 Intrinsic vs Extrinsic Specifications

As components are essentially subsystems, we would expect non-functional component specifications to be very similar to non-functional system specifications. However, there is one important difference between the two, which is related to the contextual knowledge of their producers and specifiers. While application designers will usually know about the specific system they use, in particular about the available resources and container strategies, component developers may not have such knowledge. Even worse, CBSE stipulates for components to be "[...] subject to composition by third parties" [140]. This implies that it is undesirable for component developers to make assumptions about the context of use of their components. Therefore, non-functional component specifications can only talk about properties intrinsic to the component (and thus independent of the component's context of use). Independence of the context of use can be achieved by modelling explicitly in the measurement definition the parts of the context which can affect the measurement value.

Definition 3.11 (Intrinsic vs Extrinsic Specifications) We distinguish two kinds of specifications, and—correspondingly—two kinds of non-functional measurements:

1. *Intrinsic specifications* and *intrinsic measurements:* Intrinsic properties apply to components and can be specified by component developers without further knowledge of the context of use of the components being specified. They are specified in the form of constraints over the relative values of intrinsic measurements, only. Intrinsic measurements are measurements the value of which can be determined exclusively from the implementation of a component without consideration of context of use. The definition of an intrinsic measurement will typically include hooks describing explicitly the assumptions made about the context of use. We use S_{Cmp} to denote an intrinsic specification of non-functional properties of a component.

2. *Extrinsic specifications* and *extrinsic measurements:* Extrinsic properties apply to services and systems and can be derived by application designers using knowledge of the context of use. They can also be specified by system users to express their requirements on a system or service. Extrinsic specifications are based on extrinsic measurements, which assume the context of use to be known and, therefore, provide no hooks to explicitly describe assumptions about the context of use.   ∎

We will see in one of the examples (Sect. 3.5.2) that for some non-functional dimensions, such as data quality, the difference between intrinsic and extrinsic measurements is somewhat hazy. Still, even for those the runtime environment may influence the resulting properties, so that the difference between intrinsic and extrinsic property exists.[7]

It is important to be a bit more specific about what we mean by 'context of use' in the above discussion and definition. We need to distinguish two types of context of use:

1. *The specific hardware on which the component will be executed:* This includes processor architecture, memory protocol, floating point unit precision, and similar issues.

2. *The platform which will execute the component and the usage profile:* This includes the container strategies and resource availability, but also the frequency of requests, risk level of the machine (is it inside a firewall, not connected to the Internet, freely accessible from anywhere on the Internet, and so on).

When talking about 'context of use' in relation to the distinction between intrinsic and extrinsic measurements and properties, we always refer to type 2. We assume that component developers know the machine for which they have developed their components and can, therefore, include machine-specific information in the intrinsic specification. This is not necessarily true, however. For example, the Intel family of personal computer processors share a common instruction set—which means that most components developed for execution on an Intel processor can be executed on any specific processor type—but have fundamentally different architectures, leading to fundamentally different performance. Where such effects become important, we need to introduce another distinction, which we call *machine-independent* vs *machine-dependent* specification. There has been some discussion of this topic in the literature (see Chapt. 9 for references), but machine dependency is not the subject of this thesis.

Another important distinction concerns the data to be processed by a component or a system. Some non-functional properties (again, most notably performance) are heavily dependent on the data to be processed. We, therefore, need to distinguish between *data-independent* specifications, which, similarly to intrinsic specifications, can be given by component developers and provide the information only depending on the component itself, with some hooks where information about the data to be processed should be placed, and *data specifications* which describe relevant properties of the data to be processed and can be combined with the data-independent specification to give a complete system specification. Again, we do not discuss this issue any further in this thesis, but leave it for future work.

Intrinsic and extrinsic specifications can also be classified according to their structure (and correspondingly according to their complexity). We distinguish the following three classes:

1. *Simple constraints* constrain exactly one measurement. Typically they are of the form $\Box(m \leq Value)$ or $\Box(m \geq Value)$ where *Value* is an arbitrary constant value.

2. *Relational constraints* describe relations between two (or more) measurements. Their generic form is $\Box\left(m_1 \lessgtr F\left(m_2\right)\right)$ where F is some arbitrary function from the domain of m_2 into the domain of m_1.

3. *Arbitrary constraints* on multiple measurements.

In the following discussions in this chapter we will focus on the first case. The latter two cases will be discussed in Chapt. 5.

The next two sections discuss two types of specifications that describe the context of use, effectively formalising the transformation of intrinsic properties into extrinsic properties.

---

[7]For example, the runtime system may employ multiple instances of the same component and attempt to compute an improved results from the individual results.

3.3.2   Resource Specification

Many applications require system resources, such as CPU, memory, hard disks, databases, and so on, to provide their functionality. The availability of these resources is an important factor determining the extrinsic non-functional properties of the system. Therefore, in order to determine the extrinsic properties of a system, we need to understand—and model—the resources available to it.

A resource specification consists of three layers, very similarly to intrinsic or extrinsic specifications:

1. The *resource-service layer:* This layer models the service provided by the resource. For example, a CPU provides execution slots to various tasks. This layer is very similar to the context models used with intrinsic or extrinsic properties in that it defines the terminology to be used in the other layers.

2. The *resource-measurement layer:* This layer uses history variables to describe the non-functional aspects of the resource. For our CPU example this would be the periods, worst-case execution times, and actual execution times per period for each task. This layer is very similar to the definition of measurements for intrinsic or extrinsic specifications.

3. The *resource-property layer:* This layer defines constraints over the history variables defined in the resource-measurement layer. For example, for an RMS-scheduled CPU, such a constraint would express that all tasks will meet their deadlines provided the schedulability criterion (Cond. (2.1)) is satisfied.

Definition 3.12 (Resource Specification) A *resource specification* is a formula of the form

$$CapacityBoundsSpecification \stackrel{+}{\mapsto} ResourceServiceSpecification$$

where

$CapacityBoundsSpecification$ is a predicate that is true if the current resource demand for the resource is below the capacity limit for the resource, and

$ResourceServiceSpecification$ specifies the service delivered by the resource.   ∎

Such a specification resides at the resource-property layer. The other two layers provide the terminology to be used in the final resource specification. In effect, they define the abstract resource, while the resource-property layer defines a concrete resource. So, both $CapacityBoundsSpecification$ and $ResourceServiceSpecification$ make use of concepts defined at the resource-measurement and the resource-service layer. To continue with the CPU-example from above, $CapacityBoundsSpecification$ would use the measurements defined at the resource-measurement layer to express the RMS schedulability criterion, and $ResourceServiceSpecification$ would use those measurements to express the fact that all tasks scheduled will meet their respective deadlines.

3.3.3   Container Specification

Container strategies need to bind together the available resources and the intrinsic properties of the available components. In order to reason about the extrinsic properties of a component-based system we need formal models of these container strategies. We, therefore, introduce another type of specification: *container-strategy specifications.* Each container-strategy specification describes which intrinsic properties and which services provided by resources the modelled container strategy transforms into which extrinsic properties of the resulting system.

There are at least two possible approaches to represent this transformation formally:

1. Using rewrite rules [74], expressing the transformation as a deduction system.

2. Using a TLA$^+$ rely–guarantee-style [72] specification.

While the first approach appears to be more expressive, in particular, because it can model algorithmically container strategies whose decision procedures cannot be expressed in closed-form terms, such models are also more complicated to analyse. We therefore use the second alternative in the context of this thesis:

Definition 3.13 (Container Specification) A container is given by the specification of its container strategy. Each container strategy is specified by a *container-strategy specification* S_{CS}. Container strategy specifications are formulas of the form

$$\begin{aligned}
&\wedge\ IntrinsicProperties \\
&\wedge\ ResourceRequirements \\
&\wedge\ EnvironmentConditions \\
&\wedge\ ComponentFunctionalityHook \\
&\stackrel{+}{\triangleright}\ ExtrinsicSpecification \wedge ServiceFunctionalityHook
\end{aligned}$$

where

$IntrinsicProperties$ is a conjunction of constraints over intrinsic measurements expressing the requirements of the container strategy on the available components.

$ResourceRequirements$ is a conjunction of constraints over resource measurements expressing the requirements of the container strategy regarding the available resources.

$EnvironmentConditions$ represent the assumptions the resulting system makes about environment behaviour. For example, this may include assumptions about the frequency of incoming requests, or the accuracy of data entered.

$ExtrinsicSpecification$ is a conjunction of constraints over extrinsic measurements, expressing the behaviour of the resulting system.

$ComponentFunctionalityHook$ and $ServiceFunctionalityHook$ represent the fact that each container strategy preserves the functionality provided by the components. $ComponentFunctionalityHook \triangleq CompFun \wedge CompMap \wedge (CompFun \Rightarrow ServFun)$ where $CompFun$ is a predicate parameter for the functionality provided by the component, $CompMap$ is a predicate parameter for the mapping between functional model and context model, and $CompFun \Rightarrow ServFun$ is the actual statement of functionality preservation. $ServiceFunctionalityHook \triangleq ServFun \wedge ServMap$ with analogous meanings of the conjuncts.   ∎

This definition is limited to containers with only one container strategy. We will discuss containers with more than one strategy in Sect. 5.2.

3.3.4   System Specification

As a summary of the preceding sections we define the *system specification*:

Definition 3.14 (System Specification) A *system specification* is given by the conjunction of intrinsic specifications of the available components, resource specifications of available resources, and a container strategy applied to the components and resources in the system:

$$\begin{aligned}
S_{System}\ \triangleq\ &\wedge \bigwedge{}_i S_{Cmp}{}^i \\
&\wedge \bigwedge{}_i S_R{}^i \\
&\wedge S_{CS}(S_{Cmp}{}^i, S_R{}^i)
\end{aligned}$$

where $S_{CS}(S_{Cmp}{}^i, S_R{}^i)$ expresses the application of a container strategy to the components and resources in the system. This can be done by substituting the strategy's parameters with variables from the component or resource definitions.   ∎

3.4 Feasible System

In the previous section we have seen the different types of specifications that comprise a complete system specification: Container specifications describe how intrinsic specifications of components and resource specifications of available resources are transformed into extrinsic specifications of the services offered by the system. Users' non-functional requirements on the system can also be expressed using extrinsic specifications. It becomes important then to analyse whether "supply meets demand"; that is, whether the extrinsic properties provided by the system satisfy the requirements of the users.

Definition 3.15 (Feasible System) Given a system specification S_{System}, and a requirements specification $S_{Rqmts} \triangleq Environment \xrightarrow{+} ExtrinsicProperty$ we call the system specified by S_{System} *feasible* with respect to S_{Rqmts}, denoted by $IsFeasible (S_{System}, S_{Rqmts})$, iff the system specification is an implementation of the requirements specification:

$$IsFeasible (S_{System}, S_{Rqmts}) \triangleq S_{System} \Rightarrow S_{Rqmts} \qquad \blacksquare$$

Of course, we would like to be able to prove feasibility of a system specification with respect to certain requirements. Fortunately, Abadi/Lamport [5] have shown the *Composition Principle* which allows us to perform implementation proofs based on conjunctions of individual specifications, provided some conditions hold. In this thesis, we can limit ourselves to safety properties. This is because we are mainly interested in checking that a system's non-functional properties will hold *whenever it does something useful*, not necessarily in checking *that* it does something useful at all. Checking that the system does something useful at all is mostly concerned with the system's functional properties, and we will consider this a separate task to be performed prior to checking any non-functional properties. Because we can thus limit ourselves to safety properties, we can use Abadi/Lamport's Composition Principle in a simplified form, ignoring liveness.[8] It should be noted, however, that the composition principle developed by Abadi/Lamport does support liveness under certain conditions, but at the cost of additional complexity of proofs.

Theorem 3.2 (Composition Principle (simplified from Theorem 3 from [5]))
If, for $i = 1, \ldots, n$,

1. E, M, E_i, M_i are safety properties,

2. $\models E \wedge \bigwedge_{j=1}^{n} M_j \Rightarrow E_i$

3. (a) $\models E_{+v} \wedge \bigwedge_{j=1}^{n} M_j \Rightarrow M$ where v a tuple of variables including all the free variables of M

   (b) $\models E \wedge \bigwedge_{j=1}^{n} M_j \Rightarrow M$

then $\models \bigwedge_{j=1}^{n} (E_j \xrightarrow{+} M_j) \Rightarrow (E \xrightarrow{+} M)$. $\qquad \square$

Using this composition principle we can prove that the composition of component, resource and container strategy specifications (all of which are of the form $E_j \xrightarrow{+} M_j$) implement the system requirements specification (which again is of the form $E \xrightarrow{+} M$). That is, the theorem provides the proof obligations for feasibility proofs.

3.5 Examples

In this section we look at different example specifications to clarify the concepts discussed so far. We start by looking at the execution-time–response-time example in detail. We then look at some other measurements to show that the approach presented so far is not limited to execution-time or response-time specification.

---

[8]Intuitively, safety properties specify that 'nothing bad happens', while liveness properties state that 'something good eventually happens'. A more formal definition can, for example, be found in [97].

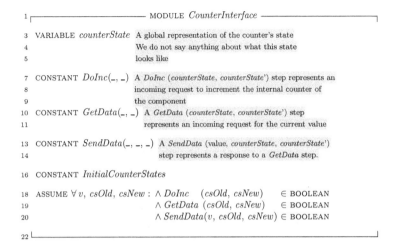

Figure 3.9: Interface specification for the counting application

3.5.1 A Simple Performance Example Based on Request–Response Communication

Assume we are to develop a small application realising a counting service. There are to be two operations, namely an increment() operation that increments an internal counter and a getValue() operation that returns the current value of the internal counter. Figure 3.9 shows a TLA$^+$ specification of the interface provided by such a service. The $DoInc(\_,\_)$ predicate represents a call to the increment() operation; $GetData(\_,\_)$ represents an invocation of getValue(), and $SendData(\_,\_,\_)$ represents the corresponding response. A simple implementation can be seen on Page 155 in Appendix B.

Apart from the functionality of this example, we are interested in its non-functional properties. In particular, our users care about the response time of calls to getValue(). Response time is an extrinsic property of operational services. Therefore, we first need to define a context model for such services.[9] Figure 3.10 shows a state-machine representation of the context model: A service starts out idle until it receives a request, which it then proceeds to handle in some manner. After this, the service returns to the idle state. Because requests may have arrived in the meantime, it may be ready to start handling a second request right after returning from handling the first one. Figure 3.11 shows the corresponding TLA$^+$ specification. Note that we have split information about the service's control state (idle or handling a request) from information about the availability of new requests. We have done so merely because this makes it more convenient to write the TLA$^+$ specifications. We have abstracted from this separation in the state-machine diagrams, and will continue to do so in further examples.

Next, we need to define the response time measurement based on this context model. Figures 3.12 and 3.13 show the TLA$^+$ specification of response time. The variable $LastResponseTime$ is introduced and defined so that it always contains the response time of the last invocation of the service. Response time is measured as the time spent in state

---

[9]Note that we will use individual context models in these examples. If all of the properties are required within a domain, these context models must of course be merged into a common computational model. We will not do so in this thesis, but we have taken care to structure the context models sufficiently similarly to simplify the merging.

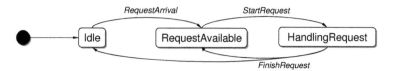

Figure 3.10: State-machine representation of the service context model. Note that this is the same as in Fig. 3.2

HandlingRequest. Figure 3.14 shows how the state machine from Fig. 3.10 is extended by the specification of response time. We use a helper variable *Start* to remember the time when the service entered into state *HandlingRequest*. From this we derive the actual response time when the services returns; that is on action *FinishRequest*. The TLA$^+$ specification works as follows: We define a new component (Line 58 of Fig. 3.12) *RespSpec*, which reacts to some actions in the service context model by setting the variables *Start* and *LastResponseTime*. This reaction is achieved through the implications on Lines 43 and 47 of Fig. 3.12. The complete specification is an instance of the specification scheme defined in Def. 3.4.

Note that we have not specified response time as the time from the arrival of a request to the sending of the response. This definition may or may not be exactly what we want in an actual project. The important message this example should convey, however, is that, because we have formally specified exactly what we mean when we say 'response time', we are now able to reason unambiguously about this definition and to judge whether it is right for our purposes. All other non-functional specification techniques known to us, leave this to informal and potentially ambiguous explanations.

It can easily be verified that this measurement specification follows the specification scheme laid down in Def. 3.4. It must, therefore, define a valid measurement as defined in Def. 3.3. Some simple TLA$^+$ transformations show that it indeed defines the following measurement:[10]

$$Hist(m_{RT}, f_{RT}, g_{RT}, v_{RT}) \;\triangleq\; \wedge\, m_{RT} = f_{RT} \tag{3.7}$$
$$\wedge\, \square[m_{RT}' = g_{RT} \wedge v_{RT}' \neq v_{RT}]_{\langle m_{RT}, v_{RT}\rangle}$$

$$m_{RT} \;\triangleq\; \langle Start, LastResponseTime \rangle \tag{3.8}$$

$$f_{RT} \;\triangleq\; \langle 0, 0 \rangle \tag{3.9}$$

$$g_{RT} \;\triangleq\; \textbf{if } (Serv!StartRequest) \tag{3.10}$$
$$\textbf{then } \langle now, LastResponseTime \rangle$$
$$\textbf{else if } (Serv!FinishRequest)$$
$$\textbf{then } \langle Start, now - Start \rangle$$
$$\textbf{else } \langle Start, LastResponseTime \rangle$$

$$v_{RT} \;\triangleq\; \langle inState, unhandledRequest \rangle \tag{3.11}$$

This is a measurement for the service context model, because it does not constrain any variables of the service context model.

The specification we have shown here does in fact a bit more than just define the response time measurement. The expression

$$\square(LastResponseTime \leq ResponseTime)$$

---

[10]We use the notation *Serv!X* to refer to symbol *X* as defined in the service context model. This notation is based on the notation for the instantiation of a specification in TLA$^+$: The TLA$^+$ module defining the response time measurement instantiates the service context model and makes it available under the name *Serv*.

```
 1 ┌──────────────────── MODULE Service ────────────────────┐
    Service Context Model

    Variables:

    inState        – the current state of the service execution machinery.
    unhandledRequest – TRUE indicates a fresh request has been placed in the system.
13  VARIABLES inState, unhandledRequest

15  vars ≜ ⟨inState, unhandledRequest⟩

17 ├────────────────────────────────────────────────────────┤
18   The environment model

20   InitEnv ≜ unhandledRequest = FALSE  Initially there are no requests.

22   The environment sets the unhandledRequest flag at some arbitrary moment to
23   indicate a new request.
24   RequestArrival ≜ ∧ unhandledRequest = FALSE
25                    ∧ unhandledRequest' = TRUE
26                    ∧ UNCHANGED inState

28   EnvSpec ≜ ∧ InitEnv
29             ∧ □[RequestArrival]_vars

31 ├────────────────────────────────────────────────────────┤
32   The actual service.

34   InitServ ≜ inState = "Idle"  Initially we start out in the Idle state

36   The transition from idle to handling request is triggered by an incoming
37   request
38   StartRequest ≜ ∧ inState = "Idle" ∧ unhandledRequest = TRUE
39                  ∧ inState' = "HandlingRequest" ∧ unhandledRequest' = FALSE

41   Request handling can finish any time
42   FinishRequest ≜ ∧ inState = "HandlingRequest"
43                   ∧ inState' = "Idle"
44                   ∧ UNCHANGED unhandledRequest

46   NextServ ≜ StartRequest ∨ FinishRequest

48   ServiceSpec ≜ ∧ InitServ
49                 ∧ □[NextServ]_vars

51 ├────────────────────────────────────────────────────────┤
53   Service ≜ EnvSpec ⁺▷ ServiceSpec

55 └────────────────────────────────────────────────────────┘
```

Figure 3.11: TLA$^+$ representation of the service context model

```
 1 ┌─────────────── MODULE ResponseTimeConstrainedService ───────────────┐
 2 │ EXTENDS RealTime
   │
   │ Parameter:
   │ ResponseTime − Maximum response time a request should exhibit.
 9 │ CONSTANT ResponseTime
10 │ ASSUME (ResponseTime ∈ Real) ∧ (ResponseTime > 0)
   │
   │ Variables:
   │ LastResponseTime − the response time of the last request serviced.
   │ inState      − the current state of the service machinery.
   │ unhandledRequest − TRUE indicates the arrival of a new request.
19 │ VARIABLES LastResponseTime, inState, unhandledRequest
   │
21 ├────────────────────────────────────────────────────────────────────┤
   │
23 │   ┌─────────────────── MODULE Inner ───────────────────┐
   │   │ The actual specification.
   │   │
   │   │ Variables:
   │   │ Start − the start of the last request.
33 │   │ VARIABLE Start
   │   │
35 │   │ Serv ≜ INSTANCE Service   Based on the Service context model
   │   │
37 │   ├────────────────────────────────────────────────────┤
   │   │
39 │   │   Init ≜ ∧ Start = 0
40 │   │          ∧ LastResponseTime = 0
   │   │
42 │   │   StartNext reacts to a StartRequest step
43 │   │   StartNext ≜ Serv!StartRequest ⇒ ∧ Start' = now
44 │   │                                   ∧ UNCHANGED LastResponseTime
   │   │
46 │   │   RespNext reacts to a FinishRequest step
47 │   │   RespNext ≜ Serv!FinishRequest ⇒ ∧ LastResponseTime' = now − Start
48 │   │                                   ∧ UNCHANGED Start
   │   │
50 │   │   ExcludeOtherChange ≜ ¬(Serv!StartRequest ∨ Serv!FinishRequest)
51 │   │                        ⇒ UNCHANGED ⟨Start, LastResponseTime⟩
   │   │
53 │   │   Next ≜ StartNext ∧ RespNext ∧ ExcludeOtherChange
   │   │
55 │   │   ctxvars ≜ ⟨inState, unhandledRequest⟩
56 │   │   vars ≜ ⟨Start, LastResponseTime, inState, unhandledRequest⟩
   │   │
58 │   │   RespSpec ≜ ∧ Init
59 │   │             ∧ □[Next ∧ ctxvars' ≠ ctxvars]_vars
   │   │
61 │   │   Service ≜ ∧ Serv!Service
62 │   │            ∧ RTnow(vars)   This incorporates the realtime definitions
63 │   │            ∧ RespSpec
64 │   │            ∧ □(LastResponseTime ≤ ResponseTime)
   │   │
66 │   └────────────────────────────────────────────────────┘
```

Figure 3.12: TLA$^+$ representation of the response time measurement

```
68 ├──────────────────────────────────────────────────────────────────┤

70   _Service(Start) ≜ INSTANCE Inner
71   Service ≜ ∃ s : _Service(s)!Service

73 └──────────────────────────────────────────────────────────────────┘
```

Figure 3.13: TLA⁺ representation of the response time measurement (end)

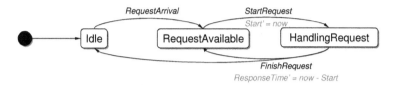

Figure 3.14: State-machine representation of the response time measurement

on Line 64 of Fig. 3.12 actually defines a simple non-functional property, constraining response time by an upper bound given through the *ResponseTime* parameter.

This specification uses the module *RealTime*, which defines the variable *now* as an abstraction of real time. This module has been introduced by Abadi/Lamport in [4] and can be found on Page 156 in Appendix B. *RealTime* only contains the constraints absolutely necessary to characterise *now*, namely that time never runs backward. We thus model response time constraints as a safety property only, with the meaning that if the service returns at all, it will do so within the time specified by the constraint. We could add a so-called *NonZeno* condition—which states that time eventually exceeds all bounds—to incorporate liveness, but Abadi/Lamport showed that this condition can be considered implicit for all specifications which represent realisable systems. Adding liveness, on the other hand, makes proofs and derivations much more complicated. We, therefore, do not explicitly consider the *NonZeno* condition and limit ourselves to a safety version of response time.

The developer of our `Counter` component cannot know the response time of its operations as this depends heavily on how the component is being used. Two major factors determining response time are a) whether buffers have been inserted to queue incoming requests, and b) the amount of resources allocated for the `Counter` component—in particular, the deadline chosen for the underlying CPU task. Another important aspect is the rate at which incoming requests are received. Hence, the component developer can only safely talk about the execution time of her component, which is an intrinsic property of the component. Figure 3.15 shows a state machine which incorporates both the context model of a component and the definitions for the execution time measurement (represented by the *LastExecutionTime* variable). The corresponding TLA⁺ specifications can be found in Appendix B.1.

The most important difference to the state machine for a service is the new state 'Blocked', which indicates that the component would be handling a request, but cannot do so, because it is lacking the required resources or is waiting for another component to complete its part of the job. This state represents one of the assumptions of the component about its environment. In effect, it is saying that component developers expect the response time of their components to be influenced by the time spent in state 'HandlingRequest' and the additional time spent blocking, because of scheduling decisions made by the environment. It is interesting to note that we did not provide a similar hook for the buffering of incoming requests. This is something happening outside the component; that is in the way the component's operation is mapped onto the service's operation by the runtime system.

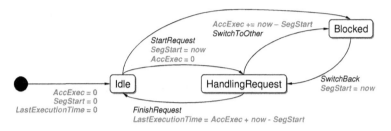

Figure 3.15: State-machine representation of the component context model with attached specifications for the execution time measurement

It is therefore not necessary to model this in the component context model.

Now we still need to map these abstract models onto our Counter application. This means, we need to say which operation in our counter should be measured by providing mappings from the Counter specification to the component and the service context models. For the execution time part, the mapping looks as follows:

$$
\begin{aligned}
ModelMapping \triangleq\ &\wedge\ doHandle = 0 \Rightarrow\ \wedge\ inState = \text{``Idle''} \\
&\qquad\qquad\qquad\qquad \wedge\ unhandledRequest = \text{FALSE} \\
&\wedge\ doHandle = 1 \Rightarrow\ \wedge\ inState = \text{``Idle''} \\
&\qquad\qquad\qquad\qquad \wedge\ unhandledRequest = \text{TRUE} \\
&\wedge\ doHandle = 2 \Rightarrow\ \wedge\ inState \in \{\text{``HandlingRequest''},\\
&\qquad\qquad\qquad\qquad\qquad\qquad \text{``Blocking''}\} \\
&\qquad\qquad\qquad\qquad \wedge\ unhandledRequest = \text{FALSE} \\
&\wedge\ (doHandle \notin \{0,1,2\}) \Rightarrow\ \wedge\ inState = \text{``Idle''} \\
&\qquad\qquad\qquad\qquad \wedge\ unhandledRequest = \text{FALSE}
\end{aligned}
$$

$$(3.12)$$

which maps the `getValue()` operation, but not the `increment()` operation as an operation of the component context model (*cf.* Fig. 3.4 for an illustration). The complete specification, also of the mapping to the service context model can be found in Appendix B.1. We also prove, in Sect. C.3.2, that this is indeed a measurement mapping as defined in Def. 3.6.

The most important resource in this context is certainly the CPU. The key characteristic of this resource in this context is that it is allocated to a certain task for a certain amount of time in each period. We can model this behaviour with a first specification of a resource, allocation of which is shifted between a number of tasks in a task set. In a next step, we add some history-determined variables to measure the amount of time each task 'possessed' the resource in each period. Finally, we extend this abstract model of a CPU by defining a concrete CPU—for example, one that is scheduled using RMS. The corresponding TLA$^+$ specifications can again be found in the appendix; we are not going to discuss them in detail. We concentrate only on the final specification of the RMS-scheduled CPU:

$$
\begin{aligned}
&\wedge\ TimedCPUSched\,!\,TimedCPUScheduler \\
&\wedge\ \Box Schedulable \overset{+}{\leadsto} \Box TimedCPUSched\,!\,ExecutionTimesOk
\end{aligned}
$$

The first conjunct expresses that an RMS CPU is a CPU. The second conjunct expresses the capacity limits of the RMS CPU: As long as the tasks to be scheduled meet a certain schedulability criterion, all tasks will meet their deadlines. The schedulability criterion is the RMS criterion (2.1). This specification, thus, has the general form given in Def. 3.12.

As the last part of our system, we need to say something about the container's behaviour. For this purpose, we write a container strategy specification (*cf.* Pages 168–170).

In our example, this is a very simple strategy which merely tries to allocate one instance of the component, and does not place any buffers before or after the component. The specification begins by including various definitions of the measurements to be used. In our example, these are exactly the definitions of response time and execution time as well as the resource specifications we have seen so far, but this does not need to be the case. Container designers may use their own definitions of these measurements. In this case, the container strategy will be applicable, if the measurements provided by, for example, a component can be shown to be an implementation of the measurements required by the container specification. For the sake of simplicity we leave this additional complexity out of our example. The container expects a component with an execution time (given by the parameter $ExecutionTime$) of less than the expected response time (given by the parameter $ResponseTime$) to be available:

$$\land\ ExecutionTime \leq ResponseTime$$
$$\land\ ComponentMaxExecTime(ExecutionTime)$$

Furthermore, it expects the CPU to be able to schedule exactly one task with a period (and deadline) equal to the required response time, and a worst-case execution time (WCET) equal to the execution time given as a parameter:

$$CPUCanSchedule(1,$$
$$[n \in \{1\} \mapsto ResponseTime],$$
$$[n \in \{1\} \mapsto ExecutionTime])$$

Finally, it expects the environment to send requests with at least $ResponseTime$ time units between requests:

$$MinInterrequestTime(ResponseTime)$$

These expectations are combined by conjunction into formula $ContainerPreCond$. If all these pre-conditions hold, the container can use exactly one instance of the component to provide the service. This is expressed in the conclusion of the specification:

$$ContainerPostCond \ \triangleq\ \land\ ServiceResponseTime(ResponseTime)$$
$$\land\ \Box\land\ TaskCount = 1$$
$$\land\ Periods = [n \in \{1\} \mapsto ResponseTime]$$
$$\land\ Wcets = [n \in \{1\} \mapsto ExecutionTime]$$
$$\land\ \Box(CmpUnhandledRequest =$$
$$EnvUnhandledRequest)$$

The complete container specification is then

$$ContainerPreCond \xrightarrow{+} ContainerPostCond$$

It is important to note that this container strategy specification has not made any reference to *existing* resources or components. It has only stated that if such components and resources are made available, the container will behave in a certain way. It is, therefore, a complete specification of the container's behaviour, which can be written without knowledge of the concrete components and the concrete CPU to be used. Note also that this container strategy specification does not say anything about *how* the container will do the things it does, it only makes statements about the effect of the container's behaviour.

The container specification contains one more set of clauses, which concern the functionality of the component and the service provided by the system. These are necessary mainly for technical reasons, their primary purpose is to express that the container strategy preserves the functionality of the application. For this purpose, the specification defines additional parameters $CompFunc$, $CompMap$, $ServFunc$, and $ServMap$, which represent a specification of the component's functionality, the model mapping for the component, the service functionality specification, and the model mapping for the service, resp. These must be provided when instantiating the container specification. We use parameters for these parts of the specification, because the specific functionality is not important here. All we need to say is that the container expects the component to provide the functionality and will in turn provide the service functionality. For this, it is necessary, that the component specification be an implementation of the service specification. $ContainerPreCond$ is extended by adding $CompFunc \wedge CompMap \wedge CompFunc \Rightarrow ServFunc$. $ContainerPostCond$ is extended by $ServFunc \wedge ServMap$.

We can now pull all our specifications together into a sample system specification (*cf.* Pages 173–176). This system contains exactly one component with an execution time of 20 milliseconds, a CPU scheduled with RMS, and a container supporting the simple container strategy from above. We will look at the most salient parts of the specification only. The actual system specification is obtained by conjoining the individual specifications of the different parts and providing some wiring, thus:

$$
\begin{aligned}
System \ \triangleq \ & \wedge \ MyComponent \\
& \wedge \ MyCPU(CPUTaskCount, CPUPeriods, CPUWcets) \\
& \wedge \ MyContainer(20, ResponseTime, SCTaskCount, \\
& \qquad\qquad SCPeriods, SCWcets) \\
& \wedge \ \Box \wedge \ ServLastResponseTime = SCServLastResponseTime \\
& \qquad \wedge \ ServInState = SCServInState \\
& \qquad \wedge \ ServUnhandledRequest = SCServUnhandledRequest \\
& \wedge \ \Box \wedge \ MYCPU\_MinExecTime = SCCPUMinExecTime \\
& \qquad \wedge \ MYCPU\_AssignedTo = SCCPUAssignedTo \\
& \qquad \wedge \ CPUTaskCount = SCTaskCount \\
& \qquad \wedge \ CPUPeriods = SCPeriods \\
& \qquad \wedge \ CPUWcets = SCWcets \\
& \wedge \ \Box \wedge \ SCCmpLastExecutionTime = MyCompLastExec \\
& \qquad \wedge \ SCCmpInState = MyCompInState \\
& \qquad \wedge \ SCCmpUnhandledRequest = MyCompUnhandledRequest \\
& \wedge \ \Box \wedge \ SCEnvLastDeltaTime = EnvLastDeltaTime \\
& \qquad \wedge \ SCEnvInState = EnvInState \\
& \qquad \wedge \ SCEnvUnhandledRequest = EnvUnhandledRequest
\end{aligned}
$$

The specification contains another interesting formula,

$$
IsFeasible \ \triangleq \ System \Rightarrow \big(Environment(RequestPeriod) \overset{+}{\Rightarrow} Service\big) \qquad (3.13)
$$

which is a predicate expressing feasibility of the system (*cf.* Sect. 3.4). This formula can be proved using the composition principle (Theorem 3.2) to hold for the system specification. The complete proof can be found in Appendix C.3.3.

3.5.2   A Data Quality Example

The concept of 'data quality' is rather complex and somewhat fuzzy [145]. However, there seems to be some agreement in the literature that 'data quality' can be quantified by the loss of information happening when real-world data (of potentially infinite precision or resolution) is modelled or represented in a system with finite resources. In this example, we only consider the aspect of accuracy, which we take to mean—in the spirit of [136, 145]— the difference between the correct result and the result actually delivered from an operation call. We restrict ourselves even further, by only considering operations returning real-valued results. One operation which meets these criteria is the getValue() operation from our Counter example above.

As it has been proposed by Staehli et al. [136], we base our formalisation on an actual result and an ideal result. Both are represented by flexible variables in our context model

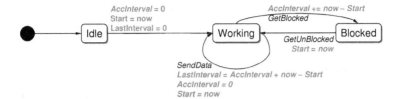

Figure 3.16: State-machine representation of data rate for an active component

(*cf.* Page 177 in Appendix B.2). The variable *idealResult* is especially interesting here, because this variable is constrained neither by the context model nor by the measurement definitions. The sequence of values for this variable is only determined in the model mapping when the measurement is actually applied to an application. This is a result of the close link between the data-quality properties of an application and its functionality. For, what determines the ideal result depends only on the intended functionality of the application.

In the measurement specification for accuracy (*cf.* Page 178), the measurement—represented by variable *LastAccuracy*—is defined as the absolute value of the difference between the actual and the ideal result. The example specification further shows how this measurement can be applied to an application.

3.5.3 A Performance Example Based on Stream-Based Communication and an Active Component

Multimedia systems are an important group of applications where non-functional properties play a major role. Many of these systems consume and produce continuous streams of data instead of working on a request–response basis. One very important criterion in this context is the minimum data rate the application can provide through a certain stream—for example, the frame rate of a video player application. We, therefore, walk through an example using stream-based communication. We discuss the core specifications of the context models for components and services, the corresponding measurement definitions, and a simple container strategy specification. The actual specifications can be found in Appendix B.3.

Figure 3.16 shows the state machine for the component context model annotated with the expressions determining the data rate. The corresponding specification for the service context model is very similar: Only the 'Blocked' state and the 'AccInterval' variable are not used. The specification does not directly define data rate, but rather the interval between two successive data emissions, *LastInterval*. From this it is very simple to derive the data rate: $\Box(LastInterval = 0 \lor DataRate = 1/LastInterval)$. Note, that we could have chosen to derive *DataRate* in a different manner—for example, by averaging over all intervals since the start of the system. The formalism forces us to make the derivation explicit. This solves an issue frequently found with languages such as Component Quality Modelling Language (CQML) [1], or Quality Modelling Language (QML) [57], which is that they only implicitly define when and how often measurement values are determined, and how statistical derivations are derived.

The biggest difference to the request–response based example in Sect. 3.5.1 is certainly, that no requests come into the system. Instead, the component performs work in its own thread of control and periodically sends out data. We call such a component an *active component*. Similarly, the service behaves as though it had a thread of control of its own and periodically sends out data. Therefore, we call such a service an *active service*. Because no requests ever arrive, the environment condition on request interarrival times is not needed in the container strategy specifications. The container derives execution times, periods, and deadlines of tasks to be scheduled by the CPU directly from the *LastInterval*, and the requirements of the service (see the container strategy specification on Pages 185–187).

3.6   Summary

In this chapter we have discussed the fundamental concepts of our semantic framework. We began by defining the underlying system model, which consists of component-based applications that are executed by a container using various container strategies to map intrinsic component properties to extrinsic properties of services provided by the system. Next, we formally defined the concept of a measurement, the fundamental building block of any non-functional specification. Measurements are always defined relative to context models, which represent the structural and behavioural hooks required to define the measurement. Applying a measurement to a specific component or system requires to map the measurement's context model to the component's or system's model. We showed that in order for independently working component developers and application designers to do this consistently, all stakeholders need to reach agreement on a computational model defining all concepts required for the measurements relevant in a particular domain. It is important to keep in mind that this also implies a restriction of the expressiveness of this specification approach, because only measurements supported by the computational model can be defined.

Based on the definition of measurements, we went on to discuss non-functional properties or specifications, which are constraints over measurements. We distinguished different kinds of specifications based on who creates them concerning what part of the overall system. In particular, we distinguished intrinsic, extrinsic, resource and container strategy specifications. Finally, we introduced the notion of a feasible system, defined as a system that has sufficient resources and appropriate components to provide a certain service with certain non-functional properties.

The discussion in this chapter needs to be extended in two directions: First, we need to discuss systems constructed from networks of interoperating components, and second, we need to discuss specifications which constrain more than one property in the same specification.

Chapter 4

Extension to Component Networks

In the previous chapter we have presented the central concepts of the semantic framework. We have confined ourselves to systems consisting of *one* component, managed by *one* container and providing *one* service. Of course, the whole point of CBSE is to build applications where *networks* of components cooperate to realise the various services provided by the system. In this chapter we, therefore, extend our approach to situations where more than one components cooperate.

A component network provides its functionality through interactions between the constituting components. The structure of such a component network, also called its architecture, is typically modelled using an Architecture Description Language (ADL) [90, 91, 92] (or an ADL-like language, such as some parts of the UML). ADLs provide three basic concepts to model system architecture:

1. *Components* for modelling the actual loci of computation,

2. *Connectors* for modelling the interactions between components, and

3. *Configurations* for modelling component networks.

In a specification of non-functional properties of a component-based system, we need to provide information about non-functional properties for each of these. Therefore, there are three major sections in this chapter:

1. *Component Specification (Sect. 4.3):* The non-functional properties exhibited by a component C_0 depend on non-functional properties exhibited by other components C_i used by C_0. An important question is how these dependencies should be specified.

2. *Component Interconnection (Sect. 4.2):* We need to specify the non-functional properties of connectors, as they can have a major effect on non-functional properties of a component-based system. For example, data security provisions differ massively between systems where all components are co-located on the same machine (or even in the same process), and systems where all information exchange happens through a (possibly open and insecure) network.

3. *Configuration Specification (Sect. 4.1):* Container strategies must be extended to cope with cooperating components. Here, we need to balance expressive power in the container strategy specification against simplicity of the approach. An important sub-issue is the question of combining the resource demands for the individual components to describe the overall resource demand of the system.

Finally, Sect. 4.4 presents an example specification of a simple component network using the specification scheme resulting from these discussions.

4.1   Container Strategies for Component Networks

There are essentially two ways in which we can extend the concept of a container strategy
discussed in the previous chapter to support interoperating networks of components:

1. *Global Strategies:* A global strategy describes the way the container manages the
   complete network of components making up a service. In addition to the intrinsic and
   extrinsic properties for which it is applicable, a global container strategy also specifies certain architectural constraints describing the kinds of component networks for
   which it can be used.

2. *Local Strategies:* A local strategy describes the way the container manages a single
   component. The complete container behaviour is then composed from individual
   container strategies, which have been selected for each component in the component
   network.

These two approaches represent the spectrum of available approaches. It is, of course, possible to mix them by having some of the components be managed as a group by one strategy
and having other components be managed by other strategies. Figure 4.1 summarizes these
three options, which we inspect in more detail in the following.

4.1.1   Global Container Strategies

Global container strategies extend the container strategies from the previous chapter so that
they can handle *many* components and transform their interaction into one service. Hence,
they allow the specification of global optimisations.

Example 4.1 (Global Container Strategies) In a radar tracking system the container may
balance the amount of time spent in the actual sensor component against the amount of time
spent in the ensuing analysis component, thus trading overall response time against precision of results; however, it can only do so, if it knows of the interaction of these two components and their relative contribution to the extrinsic properties of the system. As another
example, knowing all components cooperating to provide the service, the container can
decide where to place buffers and how to dimension these buffers, thus balancing response
time against jitter.   ◇

     The specific strategies typically depend on the architecture of the component network.
For example, the contribution the execution time of an individual component makes towards the response time of the complete system depends on how the components are in-
terconnected, and how often they invoke each other. Because we want to specify container
strategies independently of the concrete components they are going to manage, we need to
make assumptions about the system's architecture and make them explicit in the specification of the container strategy. Thus, a *global container strategy* is the result of conjoining a
container specification and a set of architectural constraints specifying the assumptions the
container strategy makes about the system's architecture.
     The specification of architectural constraints must fulfil at least the following require-
ments:

1. It needs to express the essential properties the architecture must possess to be managed by the container strategy.

2. It should be generic, meaning that it should not fit only one specific architecture, but
   as many concrete architectures as possible.

3. It must allow a clear identification of individual components, so that the components
   can be referenced in the actual container strategy specification.

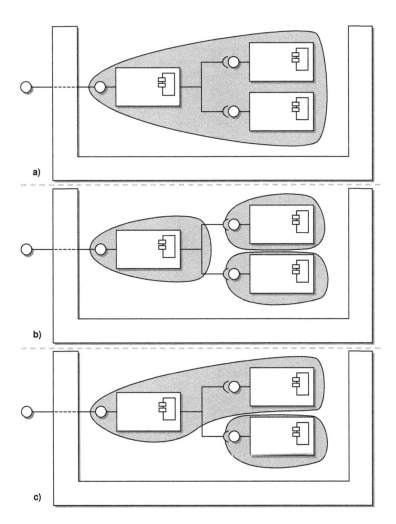

Figure 4.1: Three approaches to specifying container strategies for component networks: a) one global strategy for all components, b) one local strategy for each component, and c) mixed approach. The container is shown as a trough, each shaded area indicates the components managed by a separate strategy

Of course, the first two constraints must be balanced against each other depending on the specific container strategies. Some container strategies (e.g., the radar tracking example above) perform very application-specific optimisations; for these the architectural constraints need to pin the application rather specifically. Other strategies (e.g., the strategy trading response time for jitter) are only concerned with a certain set of non-functional properties; here the architectural constraints should be as generic as possible.

ADLs serve to describe the architecture of one specific application at a relatively high level of abstraction. As a generalisation of this idea, several researchers developed the concept of an *architectural style* [6, 7, 11, 58], a specification that collects constraints to be fulfilled by instantiating architectures. An architectural style can thus be considered a template for an architecture description. In particular, the discussion in [6, 7] gives a formalisation of architectural styles using Z, showing that architectural styles can be used to specify architectural constraints fulfilling the above constraints.

4.1.2   Local Container Strategies

The container strategies we defined in Sect. 3.3.3 took intrinsic properties of the component and available resources, and transformed them into a service complete with its extrinsic properties. The container strategy essentially worked as a wrapper around the component and the resources used by it, and also as an adapter producing a service from a component. This situation changes when we consider component networks: The extrinsic non-functional properties provided through a component A may now depend upon extrinsic properties of other components (namely the components used by A). However, assuming the container strategy has only knowledge of component A (the component it is local to), it cannot produce a complete service specification. Additionally, the system's resources may be shared between components in the same system. Again, the container strategy has no knowledge of the other components with which it needs to share resources. Thus, the application of a local container strategy to a component can only result in a conditional service specification, which still depends on the properties of other components and on global system resource sharing and availability. We call such a component wrapped by a local container strategy an *encapsulated component:*

Definition 4.1 (Encapsulated Component) An *encapsulated component* is the result of composing (i.e., conjoining the specifications of) a component and a local container strategy. Its external view can be represented by a formula following the following schema:

$$ECS \quad \stackrel{\triangle}{=} \quad \wedge \; ResourceRequirements$$
$$\wedge \; RequiredQualitySpecification$$
$$\wedge \; EnvironmentAssumption$$
$$\stackrel{+}{\Rightarrow} \; ExtrinsicProperties$$

where

ResourceRequirements specifies the resource demand of the encapsulated component.

RequiredQualitySpecification specifies what non-functional properties the encapsulated component requires from the components it uses. These normally specify constraints over extrinsic properties, because encapsulated components are intended to be composed with other encapsulated components.

EnvironmentAssumption specifies assumptions the encapsulated component makes about its usage context.

ExtrinsicProperties specifies the extrinsic properties the encapsulated component provides.   ∎

RequiredQualitySpecification and *EnvironmentAssumption* are very similar in their intention. The difference is that *RequiredQualitySpecification* specifies what the encapsulated component requires from components it uses, whereas *EnvironmentAssumption* refers to how the encapsulated component itself is being used. For example, in the case of response time, *RequiredQualitySpecification* would specify constraints on the response times of used components, whereas *EnvironmentAssumption* could specify a constraint on the maximum invocation frequency.

We can use feasibility proofs quite similar to those introduced in Sect. 3.4 to show that a system composed from a component C and a local container strategy LCS indeed implements the more abstract encapsulated component specification ECS from Def. 4.1. In a complete system specification, we can thus replace every component C_i by its corresponding encapsulated component ECS_i, conjoining them to a specification of the available system resources and component interconnections. We can then attempt to prove feasibility for the complete system.

Resource sharing requires some more preparations in our specifications. The container strategies as discussed in Chapt. 3 assume that they are the only thing in the system requiring resources. Therefore, they use a precondition which essentially states "I need a resource which can handle *exactly* this demand." In contrast, in a component network, the local container strategy may need to share resources with other encapsulated components, but there is no way to know, when writing the container strategy specification, which components these are. Indeed this may be different from system to system in which the container strategy is to be employed. Therefore, we need a precondition which states intuitively: "There needs to be a resource that handles my demand and that can still handle its complete load." Then, in the system specification, we can specify how the various resource requirements are combined and handed to the various available resources.

For different resources, combining resource demands means different things. For a simple resource such as main memory, resource demands are combined by adding their values (i.e., the kilobytes of memory required). For more complex resources, no single figure can appropriately express the combination of multiple resource demands. For example, in the case of a CPU, a set of tasks can often be boiled down to a single figure called *utilisation*(expressing the average percentage of time the CPU is occupied), but this figure is not always useful for determining schedulability of this set of tasks. Instead, sometimes we require more detailed knowledge of the tasks involved. In our specifications, we want to keep all knowledge of how resource demands are combined confined to resource specifications. Outside of resource specifications we only need to know how to express an individual resource demand.

Definition 4.2 (Shared Resource) A *shared resource* R is a resource (*cf.* Def. 3.12) that defines a set D_R of potential resource demands, and accepts elements from $\wp(D_R)$ as descriptions of the total load.   ∎

Example 4.2 (Shared Resources) Here are some resource demand models for a few typical shared resources:

CPU Individual resource demands are called tasks. Different scheduling models define different task models, for example:

  • most standard scheduling models characterise a task by its ID, a worst-case execution time, and a period

  • approaches based on imprecise scheduling [35] characterise a task by its ID, a distribution function for the execution time of a mandatory part, distribution functions for the execution times of one or more optional parts, a period and a quality figure indicating what percentage of the optional parts must be executed before the period end.

Memory Memory has the most simple resource demand model: Resource demand is simply expressed by a number of kilobytes required.

Network For network connections the simplest way to express resource demand is by giving a required bandwidth (be it constant or average rate) together with a source and a target address. More elaborate network management schemes require more information about resource demand—for example, a characterisation of the traffic to be transported.   ◇

With such a shared resource, combining resource demands becomes the union over sets. Testing whether a certain resource demand is contained in a certain set becomes testing for set inclusion. All knowledge of how resource demands are actually combined is hidden behind this interface. This approach is similar to that described in [98], where a central Quality of Service (QoS) Manager provides a resource-independent interface for specifying application resource demands based on Extended Markup Language (XML) [26]. However, while that approach is an implementation solution for a real-time operating system, we provide an approach that allows for independent *specification* of resource demands and available resources.

For each encapsulated component we can now define two resource demand parameters per resource used:

1. the *global resource load* d_{global}—an input parameter of the specification, set in the system specification—and

2. the *local resource demand* of the encapsulated component d_{local}—an output parameter of the specification.

We use d_{local} to describe the resource demand of the encapsulated component, but use d_{global} to check resource availability. To make the underlying assumption explicit, we conjoin $d_{local} \subseteq d_{global}$ to the pre-condition of the encapsulated component. In the system specification we collect all the d_{local}^i and combine them using $d_{global} = \bigcup_i d_{local}^i$. Note that in order to avoid circular specifications, we cannot put the constraints defining d_{local} into the post-condition of the encapsulated component. Instead, we must make this a separate statement conjoined to the standard specification of the encapsulated component as defined in Def. 4.1.

4.1.3 Comparison and Summary

We have discussed two polar approaches to extending container strategies to support interacting networks of components. *Global* container strategies manage *all* components forming an application. On the other hand, *local* container strategies manage *exactly one* component and, by wrapping it, transform it into an encapsulated component that provides a certain service under the condition that it receives certain resources and that other components it uses also provide certain extrinsic properties.

Both approaches have their advantages and disadvantages: For local container strategies the required extension is comparatively simple: all that is needed is to export the environment expectations (including resource demand and requirements on other components) and a mechanism specifying how resource demands are distributed on the actually available system resources. However, every container strategy can only influence the environment for one component in the network, and it can do so based essentially only on the properties of this component, and the components this component uses *directly*. On the other hand, global container strategies can query the properties of all components in the system, and, therefore, allow for global optimisations of the extrinsic properties of the complete system. Unfortunately, global container strategies are much more complex, because they require a separate specification of architectural constraints describing the types of architectures the strategy supports, and they must balance the demands and properties of more than one component.

It is, therefore, sensible to combine the two approaches when constructing a system. To this end, we extend the definition of an encapsulated component as follows:

Definition 4.3 (Composite Encapsulated Component) A *composite encapsulated component* is an encapsulated component, which is internally composed of more than one component (encapsulated or simple). Its external view can be represented as for any other encapsulated component. Resource demand and requirements on other components may be derived from any of the internal components.   ∎

In Fig. 4.1 c), the upper shaded area represents a composite encapsulated component consisting of two subcomponents. The lower shaded area represents an atomic encapsulated component. Note that this definition encloses both polar approaches: Global container strategies turn the complete system into a single composite encapsulated component, while local container strategies use only atomic encapsulated components.

The concept of composite encapsulated components is very similar to the notion of hierarchical or nested components as used by many ADLs. However, for an encapsulated component, the behaviour of the complete component is always determined from the behaviours of the internal component *by a container strategy*. This introduces an additional layer not considered for hierarchical components in ADLs.

4.2   Component Interconnection

Component connection can have a profound effect on the non-functional properties of a component-based system. For example, a connection over a network incurs a much greater performance penalty than a direct connection inside the same address space (for which the performance penalty may even be zero in the ideal case). As another example, consider a measurement determining the security of some data in terms of who may become aware of the contents of this data.[1] Here, the measurement value is primarily influenced by the connection between the components: is it via an open network, via Interprocess Communication (IPC), or directly inside the same address space on the same machine? We, therefore, need to attach specifications of the non-functional properties of the components' environment to the connectors that are part of the functional specification of a component-based application.

Formally, connectors are not much different from components. We can define context models and measurements for connectors as for components and services, and use model mappings to constrain the behaviour of specific connectors. However, connectors are not managed by the container, and, therefore, do not distinguish between intrinsic and extrinsic properties.

From a separation-of-concerns perspective we would like to specify connectors in the functional specification without regard for any non-functional properties, and then add in non-functional specifications on top of the functional one. Unfortunately, this is not possible: At least when we are using local container strategies, the connectors need to connect encapsulated components, so that at the semantic level, we cannot hide the non-functional specifications when writing connector specifications. However, because the functionality of a component and its corresponding encapsulated component are equal, it is possible to hide this distinction in dedicated languages built on top of the semantic level and provide application designers with a view of the application where they do not have to worry about the non-functional properties of connectors or components. Therefore, this is a technical issue, which does not effect the usability of the approach proposed.

---

[1] see [85] for a discussion of how to model such properties in TLA$^+$

4.3   Component Specification

In component networks, the properties exhibited by an individual (encapsulated) component typically depend on properties of the components used by this component. As with container strategies, the specification of these component dependencies can follow one of two polar approaches:

1. We can extend intrinsic specifications (*cf.* Sect. 3.3.1) to include a description of how the intrinsic properties of a component depend on properties exhibited by the components used by this component.

2. We can extend container strategies with a specification that uses the intrinsic specification, the functional specification of the component network (e.g., provided by an ADL specification), and the properties of other components when determining extrinsic properties of an encapsulated component.

The following two subsections discuss these options in more detail.

4.3.1   Extending Intrinsic Specifications

Intrinsic specifications, as we discussed them in Sect. 3.3.1, describe the relations between the different intrinsic properties of a component. However, nothing stops us from including properties of used components in such a specification.

Example 4.3 (Extending intrinsic specifications) We could, for example, write a specification that intuitively asserts that the execution time of a `getData` operation in an object-relational–mapper (OR mapper) component is at most 100 ms plus the amount of time it takes the used database component to process a certain type of SQL query. It is important to realise that the amount of time used by the database is expressed as a constraint over database response time—that is, an *extrinsic* property. This is so because the OR mapper always communicates with the database component through the container (even if both components are managed by the same global container strategy). Therefore, it views the database component as an encapsulated component. We do not care, in the specification of the OR mapper, how much of the database time is due to database execution time, and how much is due to some management work of the container.   ◇

Extending intrinsic specifications in this manner has the advantage of simplicity. We do not need new concepts or specification constructs. However, there is also a disadvantage: As we have seen in the example, such an extension causes intrinsic specifications to become a mixture of constraints over intrinsic and extrinsic measurements. This does not agree with the separation of concerns we aim at with our approach.

4.3.2   Extending Container Strategy Specifications

In many cases, the relation between properties of the components used and properties of the using component are quite independent of the computation performed by the component itself. In the execution time example in the previous subsection, the formula for the total time spent in the operation is always

$$ExecutionTime + \Sigma_{co \in CalledOps} ResponseTime(co)$$

irrespective of whether the component under consideration is an OR-mapper or a hotel-management component. In this example, the formula is specific to the set of measurements; the actual properties are only parameters to the formula. It is, therefore, sensible to move the specification of this relation from the intrinsic specification of the component into the container strategy specification dealing with this combination of properties.

When we do this, the functional specification (e.g., the architectural specification using an ADL) must provide explicit information on relevant properties of component interaction—namely the number of invocations of other operations in our example. Parametrised contracts—discussed by Reussner in his dissertation [111]—are an interesting approach for this, but sometimes we may be able to derive the required information directly from the functional specification.

4.3.3 Comparison and Summary

Two aspects underlie the distinction between the two approaches we have discussed:

1. *Separation of intrinsic and extrinsic properties:* The first approach of extending the intrinsic specification of a component forced us to mix constraints over intrinsic and extrinsic measurements in the component specification. Ideally, we should separate these concerns as much as possible, for two reasons: First, it mixes two levels of specification, making the specifications harder to understand. Secondly, mingling concerns keeps architectural information, such as the number of invocations made to a used component implicit.

2. *Generality of the dependency:* For some properties—for example, for execution time, as discussed above—the effect of component-interaction on the property is completely independent of the specific components. For other properties, however, the dependency of a component's property on the properties of used components is specific to this component. An example for such a property is accuracy (as discussed in Sect. 3.5.2): The error of the result of some computation obviously depends on the error of the input values, but the precise dependency hinges on the specific computation being performed. For such properties we cannot move the specification of the component dependency into the container strategy, but have to keep it in the intrinsic component specification.

It can be seen that of the two approaches we discussed each favours one of these aspects over the other: The extension of intrinsic specifications is useful for properties whose dependencies are very component-specific, but mixes intrinsic and extrinsic properties and keeps architectural information implicit. On the other hand, the extension for container strategies is good at separating intrinsic and extrinsic specifications and at making architectural information explicit, but fails to support properties with component-specific dependencies. Therefore, in general we should strive to keep property dependencies in the container strategy specifications, but for properties which have component-specific dependencies, we need to resort to using extended intrinsic specifications.

4.4 Example

In this section we walk through an example application consisting of three components. As usual, we present only the most salient parts of the specification here, the full specification can be found in Appendix B.4. Figure 4.2 shows the architecture of the example application—a simple calculator, offering a `getResult` operation, which performs a certain computation and returns the result. Specifically, the `Calculator` uses two `DataDeliverer` instances called `summands` and `factors`, which provide a fresh item of data for each invocation of their respective `getData` operation. The `Calculator` invokes `getData` twice on `summands` and adds the two values thus obtained. It then invokes `getData` on `factors` and multiplies the result with the sum obtained in the previous step. The resulting value is returned as the result value of `getResult`.

We want to talk about execution time and response time of the components and the service in this example. As we discussed in Sect. 4.3.3, the dependencies of such timing

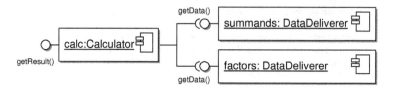

Figure 4.2: Architecture of the example application

properties are typically independent of the specific component and can, therefore, be specified with the container strategy. Also, there is not a lot of global optimization we could perform, so that we decide to use local container strategies. Finally, we use a very simple, idealised connector, which transports requests and results in zero time.

First, we specify the `DataDeliverer` component, and provide a simpler form of the specification using the external view of the encapsulated component. The actual nonfunctional specification (see Appendix B.4) is not very different from those shown in Sect. 3.5, so we do not need to discuss too many details here. The only major difference is that we do not provide a specification of a concrete resource. Instead, the resource remains a precondition of the encapsulated component (*cf.* Lines 132–141 of module `DataDelivererService` on Page 196):

$$
\begin{aligned}
ExternalService \;\triangleq\; &\wedge \Box \wedge\; TaskCount = 1 \\
&\wedge\; Periods = [n \in \{1\} \mapsto ResponseTimeConstraint] \\
&\wedge\; Wcets = [n \in \{1\} \mapsto 7] \\
&\wedge \wedge\; CPUCanSchedule(1 \\
&\qquad\qquad\qquad [n \in \{1\} \mapsto ResponseTimeConstraint] \\
&\qquad\qquad\qquad [n \in \{1\} \mapsto 7]) \\
&\wedge\; EnvCalls \\
&\overset{+}{\Rightarrow}\; Service
\end{aligned}
$$

Recall that *TaskCount*, *Periods*, and *Wcets* are our means of expressing CPU demand. Here, we state that we need to be able to schedule one task with a period (and relative deadline) of *ResponseTimeConstraint* and a WCET of 7 (units of time—for example, milliseconds).

We can still use the principle of the feasibility proof we used in Sect. C.3.3 to show that the component together with the container form the encapsulated component specified in module `DataDelivererService`, except for the treatment of resource demand of the container, which is now provided for by the environment assumption of the encapsulated component instead of by an explicit resource specification. We can, therefore, use this simpler external view of the encapsulated component in the remaining specifications, allowing us to deal with components one at a time.

The response time of the `Calculator` component depends on the execution time of the component itself, on the response time of the components `factors` and `summands`, and on the number of times these components are invoked. We can generalise the second part by adding up all times when a component has invoked operations on another component while processing an operation call of its own. The corresponding measurement we name the *call time* of the component. Figure 4.3 shows the state machine for this measurement and the corresponding context model. It is a slightly extended version of the state machine for execution time, in that the 'Blocked' state has been split into an 'OperationCall' state representing calls to operations of other components, and a 'Blocked' state representing all other kinds of interruptions. Combining all operation calls into one global state allows us to treat uniformly any number of calls to any number of different operations

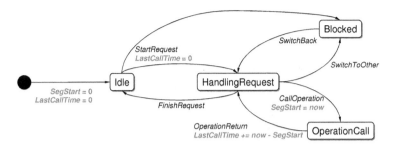

Figure 4.3: State machine with context model and measurement definition for call time

from different components. The model mapping for a component then defines what are the external operations it calls. This model is sufficient for our example because the container only needs to know the maximum amount of time spent in all operation calls triggered by one call to one component. More complicated models would be required if we needed to know the specific time spent in each individual call.

Based on this additional measurement, we can now define an extended version of the container strategy from Sect. 3.5.1: *ContainerRespectingCalledOperations* (*cf.* Pages 208–211). This container strategy uses the maximum call time and the execution time of the component to determine the response time of the corresponding encapsulated component. This is expressed on Lines 179–201, where *ContainerPreCond*(*MaxCallTime*) is defined as:

$$
\begin{aligned}
ContainerPreConde(MaxCallTime) \ &\triangleq \\
\wedge \ &\dots \\
\wedge \ &ComponentMaxExecTime(ExecutionTime) \\
\wedge \ &\dots \\
\wedge \ &ComponentMaxCallTime(MaxCalLTime) \\
\wedge \ &\dots
\end{aligned}
$$

This is later (Lines 213–218) used to define the actual container strategy:

$$
\begin{aligned}
Container \ \triangleq \ \exists MaxCallTime \ : \\
\wedge \ \Box\wedge \ TaskCount = 1 \\
\wedge \ Periods = [n \in \{1\} \mapsto ResponseTime - MaxCallTime] \\
\wedge \ Wcets - [n \in \{1\} \mapsto ExecutionTime] \\
\wedge \ ContainerPreCond(MaxCallTime) \xrightarrow{+} ContainerPostCond
\end{aligned}
$$

The first conjunct declares the resource allocation performed by this container strategy. This is d_{local} as defined in Sect. 4.1.2. As stated there, we must not put this into *ContainerPostCond* in order to avoid circular reasoning. It should also be noted how the specification uses existential quantification so that it does not constrain the call time, but only determines its value.

We have three interacting encapsulated components, which need to share the same resource—namely the CPU. We, therefore, need to model CPU as a shared resource according to Def. 4.2. This requires that we define the set of possible resource demands D_{CPU}. As explained above, CPU demand is modelled using task sets. In this example, we use the simplest definition of a task set, which only considers WCET and period of each task. For reasons of simplicity in the specification with TLA$^+$,[2] we represent a set of tasks by the

---

[2]In particular, we can so reuse the resource specifications from previous examples.

following three values:

$$
\begin{aligned}
TaskCount &\in Nat \\
Periods &\in [\{1..TaskCount\} \rightarrow Real] \\
Wcets &\in [\{1..TaskCount\} \rightarrow Real]
\end{aligned}
$$

Set inclusion is then expressed as follows for two task sets A and B:

$$
\begin{aligned}
A \subseteq B \quad \triangleq \quad &\wedge A.TaskCount \leq B.TaskCount \\
&\wedge \forall i \in \{1..A.TaskCount\} : \exists j \in \{1..B.TaskCount\} : \\
&\quad \wedge A.Periods[i] = B.Periods[j] \\
&\quad \wedge A.Wcets[i] = B.Wcets[j]
\end{aligned}
$$

Note that the above specification is not quite complete. It would allow situations in which A contained two tasks with identical properties, but B contained only one such task, but in which $A \subseteq {}_{CPU} B$ was still considered to hold. To avoid such situations, we would have to assign a unique ID to each task in a task set, and to make use of this ID in the comparison. However, the effort for this improvement would be very large[3] in comparison with the gain, so that we have not included this complication in our example specification.

Finally, task set union is simply done by creating a task set that contains all the constituent task sets one after the other:

$$
\begin{aligned}
\Box \wedge\ &CPUTaskCount = SCSumTaskCount+ \\
&\qquad\qquad\qquad SCFactTaskCount+ \\
&\qquad\qquad\qquad SCCalcTaskCount \\
\wedge\ &CPUPeriods = [n \in \{1..CPUTaskCount\} \mapsto \\
&\qquad \textbf{if }(n \leq SCSumTaskCount) \\
&\qquad \textbf{then } SCSumPeriods[n] \\
&\qquad\quad \textbf{else if }(n \leq SCSumTaskCount + SCFactTaskCount) \\
&\qquad\qquad \textbf{then } SCFactPeriods[n - SCSumTaskCount] \\
&\qquad\qquad \textbf{else } SCCalcPeriods[n - SCSumTaskCount \\
&\qquad\qquad\qquad\qquad\qquad\qquad -SCFactTaskCount] \\
&\ ] \\
\wedge\ &CPUWcets = [n \in \{1..CPUTaskCount\} \mapsto \\
&\qquad \textbf{if }(n \leq SCSumTaskCount) \\
&\qquad \textbf{then } SCSumWcets[n] \\
&\qquad\quad \textbf{else if }(n \leq SCSumTaskCount + SCFactTaskCount) \\
&\qquad\qquad \textbf{then } SCFactWcets[n - SCSumTaskCount] \\
&\qquad\qquad \textbf{else } SCCalcWcets[n - SCSumTaskCount \\
&\qquad\qquad\qquad\qquad\qquad\qquad -SCFactTaskCount] \\
&\ ]
\end{aligned}
$$

So far, we have discussed how the resource demands of the different encapsulated components are mapped onto the actual resources contained in the system, and how the container makes use of the properties of other components to determine properties of the component using them. There is one more effect that we need to consider: The specifications of the encapsulated `DataDeliverer` components state that the response time constraints holds only if (and as long as) calls to `getData` occur with a certain maximum frequency. In order to prove feasibility, our specifications must allow us to derive this from the external call frequency of the application as a whole. That is, we must be able to reason about how often calls to a used component occur, based on our knowledge of how often calls to the using component occur. In general, this kind of derivation can be supported by parametrised contracts, as described in [111]. Additionally, we need to take into

---

[3] Because we need additional specifications to make sure that task IDs don't clash between different components sharing the same resource

consideration the effect of the container encapsulating the using component: Parametrised contracts only describe how properties are propagated inside the component, the container strategy needs to specify how properties are propagated between the service interface and the component. For example, the container might buffer incoming requests, thereby regularising the time between calls and potentially lowering the maximum call frequency by removing bursts of calls. In the case of our example, life is much simpler, though: Because only one instance of `Calculator` will be created, and because this instance performs all work strictly sequentially, the minimum time between calls to `summands.getData` and `factors.getData`, respectively, is determined by the minimum of the response time of the `getData` operation and the execution time of `Calculator.getResult`. For simplicity, this has been reflected in the module `System` on Pages 214–219 on Lines 71 and 111 by directly mentioning the correct value

$$RequestPeriod \leftarrow 10,$$

Finally, a remark concerning the complexity of the specifications. Although some of the examples may look very complex for the amount of information actually expressed, this is only the case, because they are being expressed at the semantic level. What is required are more high-level languages that can express the same information more compactly.

4.5   Summary

In this chapter we have discussed an extension of our core framework toward the specification of services provided by interacting networks of components. In correspondence to the three basic concepts of software architecture—components, connectors, and configurations—we have identified three major areas in need of extension: 1) Component specifications, 2) specification of component interconnection, and 3) container strategy specifications. We have discussed the range of possible design decisions, with particular focus on the polar forms. This has led us to distinguish between global and local container strategies (and with them normal and encapsulated components), and between extension of implicit specifications and an extension of container strategies for component-internal dependencies between non-functional properties.

Furthermore, we have found that, for component networks, the clean separation between functional and non-functional specification, which was still possible in the case of only one component, can no longer be upheld at the semantic level. Functional specifications at least need to be aware of the existence of a non-functional specification, because connectors must connect encapsulated components instead of simple components in this case. This is, at first sight, an unfortunate result. However, because the mapping between components and encapsulated components is schematic the existence of encapsulated components can be hidden from the authors of functional specifications by appropriate modelling tools. Therefore, this issue only exists at the technical level and does not affect the usability of the specification approach developed in this thesis.

In this chapter, we have discussed only one important dimension of extension. We are now going to deal with the other dimension—supporting more than one non-functional property in a specification.

Chapter 5

Describing Multiple Non-functional Properties of the Same Service

In the previous chapters we have discussed the central notions of our semantic framework as well as an extension to networks of interacting components. However, these discussions have always focused on specifications of *one* intrinsic property to be transformed into *one* extrinsic property. In this chapter we are going to extend our discussions to specifications of multiple, possibly interacting, non-functional properties.

There are three aspects of this problem, which we need to discuss:

1. *Support for multiple intrinsic non-functional properties in component specifications:* We need a possibility to specify more than one non-functional property of the same component. In addition, we need to be able to describe interactions between these properties—such as the increase in response time caused by a certain increase in data quality.

2. *Support for multiple extrinsic non-functional properties in a service specification:* Similarly, we need a possibility to specify a combination of non-functional properties for a service provided by an application.

3. *Support for multiple non-functional properties in container specifications:* Ideally, we want to be able to combine individual container strategies for individual non-functional properties to form a container specification managing all of these properties.

We will see in Sect. 5.1 that the first two points are very similar, and can be solved straightforwardly using the specification techniques we have already developed in previous chapters. The main focus of this chapter (Sect. 5.2) will, therefore, be a discussion of problems and some solution ideas for combining individual container strategies to specify the behaviour of a container when faced with a set of intrinsic properties to be transformed into a set of extrinsic properties. The most prominent issue in this area is the problem of "feature interaction"—that is in our case the effect the application of one container strategy may have on the results of another one. This issue forms a research area of its own and leads us out of the scope of this thesis, so that we will only give some initial comments and possible research directions.

5.1   Relations between Measurements

When a component exhibits multiple non-functional properties, there often exists a relationship between them. For example, a component may offer different levels of accuracy of the result, but at the cost of increased execution time. Thus, the component must specify (in addition to specifying the individual properties themselves) how they are interrelated for this component. As another example, the execution time of an operation depends on whether parameters and result value must be de- and encrypted before and after the actual execution of the operation. Thus, if a component offers a non-functional property describing whether de-/encryption happens, and an execution time specification, it also needs to specify how the de-/encryption affects execution time. In a complete specification of the component, such relations must be formally expressed.

In the two examples above, we have not indicated one specific component. However, the precise (quantitative) relationship between intrinsic properties typically depends on the specific component. Of course, examples like the ones above are common place, and we always talk about them without mentioning specific components. All such discussions reflect the general trend only, however, and as soon as we want to be more concrete, it seems that we always need to talk about specific components. To the best of our knowledge, no intrinsic properties exist about whose relationships meaningful statements can be made without reference to concrete components. We leave the search for such properties open as a research topic.

Modelling multiple intrinsic properties of the same component is actually quite easy. Each property can be modelled as though it existed in isolation. That is, for each intrinsic measurement we provide a model mapping from the corresponding context model to the underlying application model of the concrete component, and we specify any constraints required for expressing the property we are interested in. In extension to the simple constraints discussed in Chapt. 3, we now allow more complex constraints including more than one measurement.

Example 5.1 (Accuracy and Execution Time) Figure 5.1 shows a sample specification expressing the relation between the accuracy of a Counter component and its execution time. This specification reuses the specifications of accuracy and execution time as well as the Counter component specifications from Chapt. 3.

Notice how the two different measurements are applied to the same component (Lines 11–25) and how these two specifications are then conjoined together with a constraint over both execution time and accuracy to form the complete specification of the component (Lines 27–30). A specification like this can be used wherever a component specification can be used. In particular, it can be used to model a system and can then be formally evaluated in a feasibility proof.   ◇

The extrinsic properties of a service are the result of a transformation of the intrinsic properties of components by the container. Therefore, the corresponding constraints are typically known individually for each extrinsic measurement rather than in the form of relations between measurements. In any case the specification technique is the same as for the specification of intrinsic properties of components, of course using service-related context models instead of component-oriented ones.

5.2   Extending the Container Specification to Combine Multiple Properties

The container strategies discussed in Chapt. 3 map one intrinsic property to one extrinsic property. Of course, there is nothing in Def. 3.13 that prevents us from mapping one or more intrinsic properties to one or more extrinsic properties. However, in this case,

```
 1 ┌──────────────── MODULE CompleteCounter ────────────────┐
     A counter components with constraints on accuracy and execution time.
 5 EXTENDS Reals, CounterInterface, RealTime

 7 ├────────────────────────────────────────────────────────┤
 8 VARIABLES MyCompExec, MyCompInState, MyLastAccuracy
 9 VARIABLES MyInternalCounter, MyDoHandle

11   Worst-case execution time measurement
12 _ExecTimeSpec ≜ INSTANCE CounterAppExecTime
13                 WITH ExecutionTime ← MyCompExec,
14                      inState ← MyCompInState,
15                      internalCounter ← MyInternalCounter,
16                      doHandle ← MyDoHandle,
17                          . . .

19   Accuracy measurement
20 _AccuracySpec ≜ INSTANCE AccuracyLimitedCounter
21                 WITH LastAccuracy ← MyLastAccuracy,
22                      inState ← MyCompInState,
23                      internalCounter ← MyInternalCounter,
24                      doHandle ← MyDoHandle,
25                          . . .

27   The actual (combined) component specification.
28 Counter ≜ ∧ _ExecTimeSpec! CounterComponent
29           ∧ _AccuracySpec! CompleteSpec
30           ∧ □(MyCompExec ≥ 4 + (2 − MyLastAccuracy))

32 └────────────────────────────────────────────────────────┘
```

Figure 5.1: Sample component specification showing a relation between accuracy and execution time. We have removed some variable renamings to focus on the relevant parts. The complete specification can be found in the appendix

container designers would have to predict and pre-specify every combination of intrinsic non-functional properties that could occur. This is undesirable for at least three reasons:

1. *Combinatorial explosion:* even for a comparatively small number of intrinsic properties, the number of potential combinations becomes huge,

2. *Redundancy through a lack in modularity of the container strategies:* dealing with one property is often done the same way irrespective of the other properties supported in parallel, but may have to be reimplemented for every combination, and

3. *Unpredictability:* the container designer cannot predict the combinations of non-functional properties for which the container will be used; therefore, he must provide all combinations.

All of these issues could be resolved, if we follow a more orthogonal approach, in which container strategies only deal with individual non-functional properties and are combined to deal with multiple properties for a specific application. Thus, each non-functional property with its corresponding container strategy is essentially treated as an aspect in the sense of Aspect-Oriented Programming (AOP) [51, 73]. There have been a few approaches towards building such containers in the research community; for examples see [9, 143, 144, 149].

Before we can discuss such a more orthogonal approach, we need to revisit our definition of a container specification from Sect. 3.3.3. There, we identified the specification of the container and the container strategy, in effect only considering containers with exactly one container strategy. We already indicated in Sect. 3.1, however, that a container may provide more than one container strategy. In fact, if we want to support more than one non-functional property in an orthogonal manner, containers *must* support more than one strategy. We, therefore, refine our definition of a container specification:

Definition 5.1 (Container Specification (Multiple Container Strategies)) A container specification S_C is a set of container strategy specifications:

$$S_C = \bigcup_{i=1}^{n} \left\{ S_{CS}{}^i \right\} \quad , \text{for some } n \in \mathbb{N} \qquad \blacksquare$$

In a specification supporting such a modularised container we need to solve the following issues:

1. *Selection of appropriate strategies:* We need to select the container strategies to be applied in the context of a specific system. This is comparatively easy in the case where S_C contains only one strategy for each intrinsic property relevant to the system. However, a container may support more than one container strategy dealing with the same intrinsic property, possibly in different ways. In each case, it must eventually be clear which strategies to apply.

   Example 5.2 (Container Strategy Selection) A container may have two strategies based on a component's execution time and determining CPU demand for this component: One strategy that guarantees maximum response time and one that minimizes jitter of the result stream based on parameters of the request stream. Depending on the requirements of a certain application one of these strategies—or both— must be selected. ◇

   We have two basic possibilities for realising container strategy selection:

   (a) We can specify the container strategies to be used explicitly in the system specification (*cf.* Sect. 3.3.4).

   (b) The system can select an optimal set of container strategies, based on the available strategies, components, and resources, and the requirements and preferences of the user (*cf.* e.g. [80, 108, 109]).

   The second possibility is still an open field for research. In this thesis, we will, therefore, restrict ourselves to the first possibility.

2. *Interactions between container strategies:* Different strategies (even for different properties) may have an influence on each other. For example, consider again the two strategies from above. The strategy dealing with jitter will likely make a decision about CPU allocation which differs from the decision made by the response-time strategy. A conflict arises when both strategies need to affect the same component.

   This issue can be split into two sub-problems:

   (a) *Description of possible interactions:* We need to specify where and how interactions between container strategies can occur.

   (b) *Resolution of conflicts created by strategy interactions:* We need to specify what to do when an interaction occurs.

   These sub-problems depend on the way container strategies are selected: When explicitly specifying the container strategies to be used, we only need to check for conflicts; this is much simplified by a formal specification of the container strategy as proposed in this thesis. When container strategies are selected by the system based on some optimisation criterion, these sub-problems become much more difficult.

5.3 Examples

In this section, we will discuss a few examples to allow for a more detailed discussion of some issues. These examples represent two different ways of combining container strategies:

1. *Simple conjunction of the container strategies in the system specification (Sect. 5.3.1):* This approach is suitable for container strategies that are completely orthogonal.

2. *Wrapping container strategies around other strategies (Sect. 5.3.2):* This is suitable if a container strategy can be thought of as producing an encapsulated component with a component-like external view.

5.3.1 Jitter-Constrained Components

In Sect. 3.5.1 we discussed a container strategy that guarantees a maximum response time for an operation call. Sometimes it is equally important to guarantee a certain *minimum* response time—in particular if the operation is invoked periodically and the jitter of the corresponding result stream must be minimized. One simple way of doing this is by buffering operation results until the minimum response time before actually sending them to the receiver. Figures 5.2 and 5.3 show a container strategy that does exactly this. It uses a specification of memory, which can be found in the appendix. The important bits in this container-strategy specification are the usage of module `JitterConstrainedService`, which defines the measurement jitter, on Lines 29–35, and the definition of the buffer (one block of 1024 kB memory) on Lines 50–58.

Most of the time, it is not useful to use the jitter-constraining container strategy alone, without also using a strategy that guarantees a certain maximum response time. Figures 5.4–5.6 show how the jitter-constraining specification can be combined with the response-time-guaranteeing strategy from Sect. 3.5.1. Because the two strategies do not have any conflicts in the way they handle components or allocate resources, their specifications can simply be conjoined to express that they may be used in any order modifying the behaviour of the same component. This is reflected in Fig. 5.6 where the two corresponding container strategies are simply conjoined on Lines 115–117:

$$\wedge\ SchedulingContainer(MyCompExec, ServResponseTime,$$
$$SCTaskCount, SCPeriods, SCWcets)$$
$$\wedge\ JitterContainer(ServResponseTime, MEMRequestCount, MEMRequests)$$

Another way to maintain a certain minimum response time would be to schedule execution of the operation so that the minimum response time can be guaranteed without having to resort to buffering. This strategy is interesting in our context because it creates a resource conflict with the maximum–response-time strategy. How to formally represent, let alone resolve, this conflict is as yet an unsolved problem and outside the scope of this thesis. We will, however, discuss the main issues that arise: The central problem is that we will have a system specification in which *multiple container strategies* define *different resource allocations* for *the same component.* With the current structure of our resource specifications (see Sect. 4.1.2), all of these specifications would be conjoined in the system specification. Therefore, we would obtain a specification stipulating that *all* resource allocations be met, instead of selecting *one,* or deriving a new one through a process of conflict resolution between the individual resource allocations. In order to be able to resolve this problem, we would require some means of expressing component identities in a specification that could then be used to connect resource allocations to the components on whose behalf they have been defined and thus to check that there are no conflicts in the resource allocations for one component. Appropriate representation of component identifiers and

```
 1 ┌──────────────────── MODULE FixedJitterContainer ─────────────────────┐
 2  EXTENDS RealTime

 4  CONSTANT ResponseTime
 5  ASSUME (ResponseTime ∈ Real) ∧ (ResponseTime > 0)

 7 ├──────────────────────────────────────────────────────────────────────┤

    Specification of required component behaviour.
12  _Component(ExecutionTimeConstraint)
13      ≜ INSTANCE ExecTimeConstrainedComponent
14          WITH ExecutionTime ← ExecutionTimeConstraint,
15              . . .

17  ComponentMaxExecTime(ExecutionTimeConstraint)
18      ≜ _Component(ExecutionTimeConstraint)!Component

20  CONSTANT CompFun
21  ASSUME CompFun ∈ BOOLEAN
22  CONSTANT CompModelMapping
23  ASSUME CompModelMapping ⊂ BOOLEAN

25 ├──────────────────────────────────────────────────────────────────────┤

    Specification of guaranteed service behaviour.
29  _ServiceJitter(ResponseTimeConstraint)
30      ≜ INSTANCE JitterConstrainedService
31          WITH ResponseTime ← ResponseTimeConstraint,
32              . . .

34  ServiceJitter(ResponseTimeConstraint)
35      ≜ _ServiceJitter(ResponseTimeConstraint)!Service

37  CONSTANT ServFun
38  ASSUME ServFun ∈ BOOLEAN
39  CONSTANT ServModelMapping
40  ASSUME ServModelMapping ∈ BOOLEAN

42 ├──────────────────────────────────────────────────────────────────────┤
    The resources required by this container, namely some memory.

    This has been simplified for the sake of the example. Actually, the buffer space requirement
    depends at least on request frequency and worst-case execution time of the component to be
    managed.
50  VARIABLES ContAllocationCount, ContAllocations

52  _Buffer(Requests, RequestCount) ≜ INSTANCE Memory WITH
53                                        AllocationCount ← ContAllocationCount,
54                                        Allocations ← ContAllocations
55  BufferAvailable ≜ ∧ _Buffer([n ∈ {1} ↦ [id ↦ 0, size ↦ 1024]], 1)
56                        !MemoryInvariants
57                    ∧ □(_Buffer([n ∈ {1} ↦ [id ↦ 0, size ↦ 1024]], 1)
58                        !AllRequestsSuccessful)
```

Figure 5.2: A container guaranteeing a minimum response time. Some variable renamings
have been removed for clarity. The full specification can be found in the appendix

```
60 ├─────────────────────────────────────────────────────────────────────────────────┤
61   ContainerPreCond  ≜  ∧   A component with some execution time is available.
62                             ∧ ∃ ExecutionTime :
63                                   ComponentMaxExecTime(ExecutionTime)
64                             ∧ CompFun
65                             ∧ CompModelMapping
66                         ∧   There is sufficient buffer space
67                             ∧ BufferAvailable
68                         ∧   The component functionality implements the service
69                             functionality.
70                             CompFun ⇒ ServFun

72   VARIABLES ContRequestCount, ContRequests

74   ContainerPostCond  ≜  ∧   The promised jitter can be guaranteed
75                              ∧ ServiceJitter(ResponseTime)
76                              ∧ ServFun
77                              ∧ ServModelMapping
78                          ∧   The container will allocate a buffer for the requests
79                              □ ∧ ContRequestCount = 1
80                                ∧ ContRequests = [n ∈ {1} ↦ [id ↦ 0,
81                                                             size ↦ 1024]]

83   Container  ≜  ContainerPreCond ⁺↦ ContainerPostCond

85 └─────────────────────────────────────────────────────────────────────────────────┘
```

Figure 5.3: A container guaranteeing a minimum response time (shortened, end)

their usage in specifications of resource demand and allocations will need to be understood in more detail before this issue can be resolved.

5.3.2 Reliable Components

Reliability of a software system [86] is an important non-functional property. Because any piece of software may contain faults and because it is hard to impossible to find, let alone remove, them all, it is important to construct fault-tolerant systems, which increase reliability by masking certain faults. In hardware fault tolerance, a good way of increasing reliability is to have a number of identical units of hardware work in parallel and use some sort of adjudicator to determine the (hopefully correct) result from the individual results of the individual units. This can increase the reliability of the overall system, because faults occur more or less randomly and correlated coincident failures are typically rare. This is different in the software world where "[...] faults are for the most part the result of software specification and design errors" [88]. Therefore, duplicated software components will tend to fail simultaneously, which means that there will be no gain of reliability in simple replication (refer to the Ariane 5 Flight 501 failure report [82] for a famous example).

A typical solution to this problem is to have different development teams realise independent implementations of the same component specification, so that—ideally—these different implementations will fail on different subsets of the input space [88]. Different variations of this principle occur in the literature: *N-version programming* or *recovery-block* systems are the two major groups. All of these systems consist of a number of implementations (or versions) of the component and a so-called *adjudicator* that decides about the correctness of results. In recovery-block systems, the adjudicator is an acceptance test; that is, it can determine the correctness of a result by performing certain tests on that result. In N-version programming the adjudicator is a voter which considers the result delivered

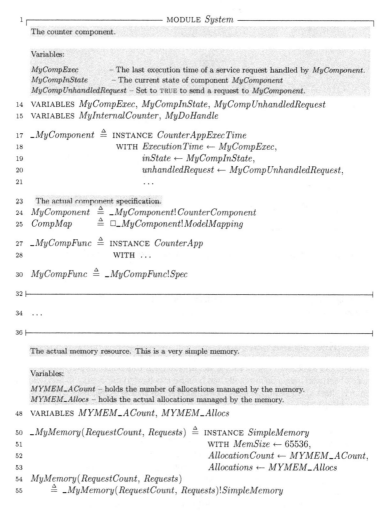

```
 1 ┌──────────────────── MODULE System ─────────────────────┐
    The counter component.

    Variables:

    MyCompExec          – The last execution time of a service request handled by MyComponent.
    MyCompInState       – The current state of component MyComponent
    MyCompUnhandledRequest – Set to TRUE to send a request to MyComponent.
14 VARIABLES MyCompExec, MyCompInState, MyCompUnhandledRequest
15 VARIABLES MyInternalCounter, MyDoHandle

17 _MyComponent ≜ INSTANCE CounterAppExecTime
18               WITH ExecutionTime ← MyCompExec,
19                    inState ← MyCompInState,
20                    unhandledRequest ← MyCompUnhandledRequest,
21                    ...

23   The actual component specification.
24 MyComponent ≜ _MyComponent!CounterComponent
25 CompMap     ≜ □_MyComponent!ModelMapping

27 _MyCompFunc ≜ INSTANCE CounterApp
28               WITH ...

30 MyCompFunc ≜ _MyCompFunc!Spec

32 ├──────────────────────────────────────────────────────┤

34 ...

36 ├──────────────────────────────────────────────────────┤

    The actual memory resource. This is a very simple memory.

    Variables:

    MYMEM_ACount – holds the number of allocations managed by the memory.
    MYMEM_Allocs – holds the actual allocations managed by the memory.
48 VARIABLES MYMEM_ACount, MYMEM_Allocs

50 _MyMemory(RequestCount, Requests) ≜ INSTANCE SimpleMemory
51                                      WITH MemSize ← 65536,
52                                           AllocationCount ← MYMEM_ACount,
53                                           Allocations ← MYMEM_Allocs
54 MyMemory(RequestCount, Requests)
55    ≜ _MyMemory(RequestCount, Requests)!SimpleMemory
```

Figure 5.4: Using jitter-constrained and response-time container together. Some variable renamings have been removed for clarity. The full specification can be found in the appendix

57

Container specification 1: The Response-time guaranteeing container.

62 VARIABLES $SCCmpInState$, $SCCmpUnhandledRequest$, $SCCmpLastExecutionTime$

64 $\_SchedulingContainer(ExecutionTimeConstr,\ ResponseTimeConstr,$
65 $\qquad\qquad\qquad TaskCount,\ Periods,\ Wcets)$
66 $\qquad \triangleq$ INSTANCE $SimpleContainer$
67 $\qquad\qquad$ WITH $ExecutionTime \leftarrow ExecutionTimeConstr,$
68 $\qquad\qquad\qquad ResponseTime \leftarrow ResponseTimeConstr,$
69 $\qquad\qquad\qquad CmpInState \leftarrow SCCmpInState,$
70 $\qquad\qquad\qquad CmpUnhandledRequest \leftarrow SCCmpUnhandledRequest,$
71 $\qquad\qquad\qquad CmpLastExecutionTime \leftarrow SCCmpLastExecutionTime,$
72 $\qquad\qquad\qquad CompFun \leftarrow MyCompFunc,$
73 $\qquad\qquad\qquad CompModelMapping \leftarrow CompMap,$
74 $\qquad\qquad\qquad \ldots$

76 $SchedulingContainer(ExecutionTimeConstr,\ ResponseTimeConstr,$
77 $\qquad\qquad\qquad TaskCount,\ Periods,\ Wcets)$
78 $\qquad \triangleq \_SchedulingContainer(ExecutionTimeConstr,\ ResponseTimeConstr,$
79 $\qquad\qquad\qquad TaskCount,\ Periods,\ Wcets)!Container$

81

Container specification 2: The Jitter-constraining container.

86 $\_JitterContainer(ResponseTimeConstr,\ MemReqCount,\ MemRequests)$
87 $\qquad \triangleq$ INSTANCE $FixedJitterContainer$
88 $\qquad\qquad$ WITH $ResponseTime \leftarrow ResponseTimeConstr,$
89 $\qquad\qquad\qquad CompFun \leftarrow MyCompFunc,$
90 $\qquad\qquad\qquad CompModelMapping \leftarrow CompMap,$
91 $\qquad\qquad\qquad CmpInState \leftarrow SCCmpInState,$
92 $\qquad\qquad\qquad CmpUnhandledRequest \leftarrow SCCmpUnhandledRequest,$
93 $\qquad\qquad\qquad CmpLastExecutionTime \leftarrow SCCmpLastExecutionTime,$
94 $\qquad\qquad\qquad ContRequestCount \leftarrow MemReqCount,$
95 $\qquad\qquad\qquad ContRequests \leftarrow MemRequests,$
96 $\qquad\qquad\qquad ContAllocationCount \leftarrow MYMEM\_ACount,$
97 $\qquad\qquad\qquad ContAllocations \leftarrow MYMEM\_Allocs,$
98 $\qquad\qquad\qquad \ldots$

100 $JitterContainer(ResponseTime,\ MemReqCount,\ MemRequests)$
101 $\qquad \triangleq \_JitterContainer(ResponseTime,\ MemReqCount,\ MemRequests)!Container$

Figure 5.5: Using jitter-constrained and response-time container together (shortened, ctd.)

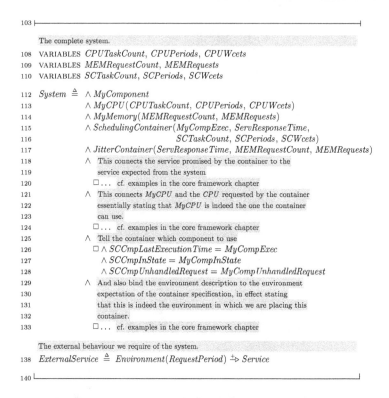

Figure 5.6: Using jitter-constrained and response-time container together (shortened, end)

by a majority of the implementations to be the correct result. Recovery-block systems run the first implementation, then the adjudicator checks the result. If this is correct the result is delivered, otherwise the system state is rolled back (or 'recovered') and the next component implementation is executed, etc. In N-version programming, all versions are executed in parallel, and the adjudicator determines the global result based on the majority of the individual results.

Figures 5.7 to 5.8 show a container strategy using recovery block with two versions. Assuming the adjudicator accepts a correct answer and rejects an incorrect answer with the probability B, we can determine (using a derivation similar to that in [88]) that the reliability produced by combining two versions (with their individual reliabilities r_1 and r_2) is

$$r_1 B + [(1 - r_1) B + r_1 (1 - B)] r_2 B$$

The specification assumes $B = 0.99$ (*cf.* Lines 90–98 in Fig. 5.8).

Reliability is modelled using a somewhat modified component context model with an additional state called 'Exception'. This state indicates that the component has run into a problem while handling a request and that it could not produce a correct answer. Reliability is then computed by counting the number of requests and the number of successfully completed requests and comparing them. Figure 5.9 shows a graphical representation of the context model together with the measurement definition, the TLA$^+$ specification can be

```
 1 ┌──────────────── MODULE TwoVersionContainer ──────────────────┐
   A container that takes two functionally identical but independently implemented components and
   produces an encapsulated component by adjudicating their results and thus hopefully improving
   reliability.
 7 EXTENDS RealTime, Reals

 9 CONSTANTS Reliability1, Reliability2
10 CONSTANTS ExecutionTime1, ExecutionTime2

12 ├──────────────────────────────────────────────────────────────┤

   The first component.
17 VARIABLES CMP1InState, CMP1UnhandledRequest, CMP1AllRequests
18 VARIABLES CMP1FailedRequests, CMP1LastExecutionTime

20 _Component1Rel ≜ INSTANCE ReliabilityConstrainedComponent
21                    WITH inState ← CMP1InState,
22                         unhandledRequest ← CMP1UnhandledRequest,
23                         AllRequests ← CMP1AllRequests,
24                         FailedRequests ← CMP1FailedRequests

26 _Component1Exe ≜ INSTANCE ExecTimeConstrainedComponent
27                    WITH inState ← CMP1InState,
28                         unhandledRequest ← CMP1UnhandledRequest,
29                         LastExecutionTime ← CMP1LastExecutionTime,
30                         ExecutionTime ← ExecutionTime1

32 Component1 ≜ ∧ ∧ _Component1Rel!Component
33                ∧ _Component1Rel!Reliability(Reliability1)
34                ∧ _Component1Exe!Component

36 CONSTANT Comp1Fun
37 ASSUME Comp1Fun ∈ BOOLEAN
38 CONSTANT Comp1ModelMapping
39 ASSUME Comp1ModelMapping ∈ BOOLEAN

41 ├──────────────────────────────────────────────────────────────┤

   The second component.
46 VARIABLES CMP2InState, CMP2UnhandledRequest, CMP2AllRequests
47 VARIABLE CMP2FailedRequests, CMP2LastExecutionTime

49 _Component2Rel ≜ INSTANCE ReliabilityConstrainedComponent
50                    WITH inState ← CMP2InState,
51                         unhandledRequest ← CMP2UnhandledRequest,
52                         AllRequests ← CMP2AllRequests,
53                         FailedRequests ← CMP2FailedRequests

55 _Component2Exe ≜ INSTANCE ExecTimeConstrainedComponent
56                    WITH inState ← CMP2InState,
57                         unhandledRequest ← CMP2UnhandledRequest,
58                         LastExecutionTime ← CMP2LastExecutionTime,
59                         ExecutionTime ← ExecutionTime2

61 Component2 ≜ ∧ ∧ _Component2Rel!Component
62                ∧ _Component2Rel!Reliability(Reliability2)
63                ∧ _Component2Exe!Component
```

Figure 5.7: Container strategy for recovery block software redundancy

65   CONSTANT $Comp2Fun$
66   ASSUME $Comp2Fun \in$ BOOLEAN
67   CONSTANT $Comp2ModelMapping$
68   ASSUME $Comp2ModelMapping \in$ BOOLEAN

70 ├──┤

The result component.

75   VARIABLES $CMPRInState, CMPRUnhandledRequest, CMPRAllRequests$
76   VARIABLE $CMPRFailedRequests, CMPRLastExecutionTime$

78   $\_ComponentRRel \triangleq$ INSTANCE $ReliabilityConstrainedComponent$
79   WITH $inState \leftarrow CMPRInState,$
80                       $unhandledRequest \leftarrow CMPRUnhandledRequest,$
81                       $AllRequests \leftarrow CMPRAllRequests,$
82                       $FailedRequests \leftarrow CMPRFailedRequests$

84   $\_ComponentRExe \triangleq$ INSTANCE $ExecTimeConstrainedComponent$
85   WITH $inState \leftarrow CMPRInState,$
86                       $unhandledRequest \leftarrow CMPRUnhandledRequest,$
87                       $LastExecutionTime \leftarrow CMPRLastExecutionTime,$
88                       $ExecutionTime \leftarrow ExecutionTime1 + ExecutionTime2$

90   $AdjudicatorReliability \triangleq 0.99$
91   $ComponentR \triangleq \wedge \wedge \_ComponentRRel!Component$
92                 $\wedge \_ComponentRRel!Reliability($
93                      $Reliability1 * AdjudicatorReliability +$
94                      $Reliability2 * AdjudicatorReliability *$
95                      $((1 - Reliability1) * AdjudicatorReliability +$
96                      $Reliability1 * (1 - AdjudicatorReliability))$
97                      $)$
98                 $\wedge \_ComponentRExe!Component$

100   CONSTANT $CompRFun$
101   ASSUME $CompRFun \in$ BOOLEAN
102   CONSTANT $CompRModelMapping$
103   ASSUME $CompRModelMapping \in$ BOOLEAN

105 ├──┤

107   $ContainerPreCond \triangleq \wedge Component1$
108                      $\wedge Component2$
109                      $\wedge \wedge Comp1Fun \Rightarrow Comp2Fun$
110                          $\wedge Comp2Fun \Rightarrow Comp1Fun$

112   $ContainerPostCond \triangleq \wedge ComponentR$
113                      $\wedge Comp1Fun \Rightarrow CompRFun$

115   $Container \triangleq ContainerPreCond \overset{+}{\Rightarrow} ContainerPostCond$

117 └──┘

Figure 5.8: Container strategy for recovery block software redundancy (end)

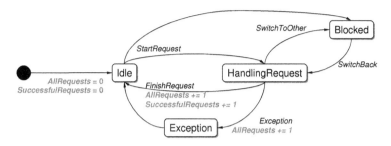

Figure 5.9: State-machine representation of the reliability measurement

found in the appendix. This model of reliability uses exceptions as an external acceptance test (*cf.* [88]) to identify failures.

Executing two components instead of one of course has an influence on the execution time. This is also accounted for by the container strategy in Figs. 5.7 to 5.8, which takes two components and produces a new component whose WCET is the sum of the WCETs of those two components. By making this strategy produce a component instead of a service, we have also clarified how to use this strategy together with the strategy from Sect. 3.5.1. In effect we have defined that these strategies are to be wrapped around the component in the manner of onion skins: First the reliability strategy produces a combined and more reliable component and then the response time strategy ensures a maximum response time for this component. For the specification of the response time strategy we can reuse the specification from Sect. 3.5.1, we do not need to consider the fact that the component to be executed has in fact been created on demand by another container strategy.

It is important to note that the difference in context models between the reliability definition and the execution time definition from Sect. 3.5.1 is not a problem in reality, because, as we have discussed in Sect. 3.2.3, in order for the two measurements to be used together at all, we need to base them on a common computational model, which would need to contain all states required by any of the measurements—that is, including the 'Exception' state.

5.4 Summary

In this section we have discussed specifications concerning more than one non-functional property of the same component or service. We have seen that multiple intrinsic properties of the same component and their relations are unproblematic and do not require additional means of specification. However, specifying individual container strategies for individual properties and merging them to specify support for a combination of properties is a far more difficult issue. This issue must be solved, however, because it is the only approach that allows to cope successfully with the combinatorial explosion of the number of possible property combinations containers should be able to deal with. We have discussed two examples, showing two different solution approaches for this problem: 1) conjunction of container strategies in the system specification, which is applicable for completely independent container strategies only, and 2) wrapping container strategies around components and encapsulated components, which is applicable for capturing simple dependencies between strategies. The problems underlying the specification of multiple non-functional properties in a modular manner would easily justify a whole dissertation in its own right. They are, thus, outside the scope of this thesis.

This chapter concludes the core part of this thesis in which we have presented and discussed our semantic framework. We have started from the very basics providing support for the specification of one non-functional property of one component and then have extended this first to networks of components and then to the specification of multiple non-functional properties. Of course, complete specifications will feature a combination of the solutions provided in these last three chapters, namely they will cover both component networks and multiple non-functional properties.

In the following chapters we will evaluate the usefulness of our approach in various contexts, namely:

- *Using it as a means of defining the semantics of CQML:* As we have seen, specifications at the semantic level are quite unwieldy even for simple examples. Therefore, we need to provide higher-level specification languages for non-functional properties of component-based systems. In Chapt. 6 we discuss how our approach can be used to formally define the semantics of one such specification language.

- *In the context of analysis methods, in particular for performance analysis:* Any specification is only useful if it can be analysed. Thus, our approach must not hinder analysis. Chapter 7 discusses connections between our approach and analysis techniques, using performance analysis as a specific example.

- *In relation to a component-based software development process:* A specification technique that does not match the development process, is of little use. Hence, Chapt. 8 looks at how our approach can be integrated with a component-based development process.

Part III

Application to Specification Languages

In this part, the concepts developed in the previous part are used to define the semantics of an existing specification language for non-functional properties of component-based applications.

Chapter 6

A Semantic Mapping for μCQML

In the previous chapters we have seen that specifications written entirely at the semantic level easily become quite unwieldy. Therefore, we need higher-level specification languages that can express the same information more compactly. Such languages are frequently called quality modelling languages. In this chapter we study how the specification concepts developed in the previous chapters can be used to define the semantics of a quality modelling language for component-based systems. Specifically, we study the Extended Component Quality Modelling Language (CQML$^+$) [117], a language co-developed by the author of this thesis and based on Jan Aagedal's Component Quality Modelling Language (CQML) [1]. We have chosen CQML$^+$, because it seems to be the most advanced among the existing languages for the specification of non-functional properties. QML—the predecessor of CQML—does not support component specification, the UML profile on schedulability, performance and time specification [101] is limited to time-based properties. Semantic Web Specification Language for Web Services (OWL-S) [30] also has some support for specifying resource demand, but it is very simple and allows only for the most basic specifications. To the best of our knowledge, there are no other generic languages for the description of non-functional properties of component-based systems.

Many elements in CQML$^+$ exist solely for readability or reusability of specifications and specification parts and are irrelevant semantically. Furthermore, CQML$^+$ also covers adaptivity—that is, the ability of an application to change its non-functional properties in a controlled manner depending on resource availability and other environmental factors. Adaptability is beyond the scope of our discussions. For the purposes of this thesis we, therefore, define a subset of CQML$^+$ where we reduce the original language to its salient features and remove support for adaptability. We use mathematical notation to present the abstract syntax of this CQML$^+$ subset, because it is more directly accessible to the formal definition of semantics. We call this language μCQML.

We will first give a quick overview of the essential concepts of CQML$^+$, after which we proceed to presenting μCQML. In Sect. 6.3, we define the semantics of μCQML using the specification techniques proposed in the previous chapters. Finally, we evaluate our findings and draw conclusions regarding our semantic framework.

6.1 Introduction to CQML$^+$

In his thesis [1], Aagedal defines the Component Quality Modelling Language (CQML), a specification language to describe QoS offers and requirements in component-based systems. Its terminology is based on the ISO QoS Framework [69]. CQML$^+$ [117] is an extension of Aagedal's language developed as part of the Components with Quantitative properties and Adaptation (COMQUAD) [8, ?] project. The main contributions of CQML$^+$ are simple support for the specification of resource demand of components and explicitly

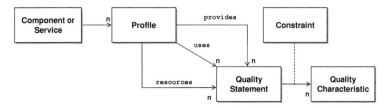

Figure 6.1: Core concepts of CQML$^+$

defined context models.

Figure 6.1 shows the fundamental concepts of CQML$^+$. The notation has been inspired by Meta-Object Facility (MOF) [102] meta-modelling conventions. The basic building block of a CQML$^+$ specification is the quality characteristic. It represents a quality dimension to be constrained by the specification and is, thus, very similar to our concept of a measurement. The most important part of the definition of a characteristic is the specification of how the current value of this characteristic could be determined in a running system. Examples for characteristics are delay, jitter, screen resolution, but also—in a different context—learnability. Quality statements are then used to specify constraints over quality characteristics. Because both quality characteristics and quality statements are parametrised and can be specialised, they allow for reuse of parts of the specification in different contexts.

The specification is completed by associating the quality statements to components of the application to be modelled. For this, CQML$^+$ offers the concept of quality profiles. Here, the formal parameters of the quality statements are replaced by actual elements (e.g., operations, streams) of the component for which the QoS constraint is meant to hold. There are three ways in which a quality statement can be associated to a component: as a QoS offer, a QoS requirement, or as a resource demand. CQML$^+$ offers the three corresponding keywords `provides`, `uses`, and `resources`, resp. Profiles can contain multiple sub-profiles which are used as a means to express adaptivity. Finally, CQML$^+$ specifications can be structured using quality categories (not shown in the figure), similarly to using name spaces in other languages.

Example 6.1 (A simple CQML$^+$ specification) The following CQML$^+$ listing shows a simple example specification. It models the same application as the example in Sect. 3.5.1: The response time of the `getValue()` service of a Counter application is constrained to 50 milliseconds.

```
1  quality_characteristic response_time (op: ServiceOperation) {
     domain: numeric milliseconds;

     values: op.invocations->last().endTime -
             op.invocations->last().startTime;
6  }

   quality good_response (op: ServiceOperation) {
     response_time (op) < 50;
   }
11
   profile good for Counter {
     provides good_response (getValue);
   }
```

The listing begins (Lines 1 thru 6) with the definition of a quality characteristic `response_time`, which is defined for individual service operations `op` as the difference between end and start time of the last invocation of that operation. The `domain` keyword is used to specify the type of the quality characteristic—that is, the set of possible values

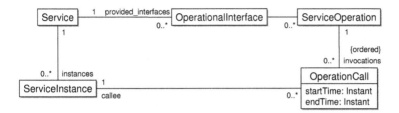

Figure 6.2: Static structure diagram of the CQML context model for the definition of response time

the characteristic may exhibit when applied to a running system. In our case we define that the values of the `response_time` characteristic are numeric values given in units of milliseconds. The `values` clause uses a syntax based on Object Constraint Language (OCL) [103] to specify the meaning of this characteristic. This is done by stating how the characteristic's values could be obtained in a running system.

The OCL-based specification of a characteristic's meaning relies on the existence of a context model that defines the concept of an operation, its sequence of invocations, and their start and end time. Figure 6.2 shows the static structure of the corresponding context model. Underlying this model is a dynamic model stipulating that a new instance of `OperationCall` is added whenever an operation is invoked, registering start and end of the call in the corresponding attributes.

The next lines of the listing above (Lines 8 to 10) use the response-time characteristic to define that an operation's response time is considered good when it is always less than 50 milliseconds. Finally, Lines 12 to 14 use the `profile` construct to state that this constraint holds for operation `getValue` of service `Counter`.   ◇

After this short overview of the core concepts of CQML⁺, we will now define a simplified version of this language that we will use in our further analysis.

6.2   μCQML

In this section, we inductively define the abstract syntax of μCQML, a version of CQML⁺ that has been reduced to the semantically relevant constructs. In particular, we have removed the concepts of quality category and inheritance between characteristics and quality statements, because their main purpose is to structure a specification and to make partial specifications reusable. We have also removed all concepts related to adaptation (namely sub-profiles and profile-transition specifications) as adaptation is outside the scope of this thesis. Finally, we have left out the unit from the domain description of CQML⁺, because it is without formal meaning [1, p. 48].

We begin by defining a few helper concepts:

Definition 6.1 (μCQML helper concepts) $NAMES$ is a set of names. Two names can be combined to form a new name using the operator

$$\text{conc} : NAMES \times NAMES \rightarrow NAMES$$

For some set $N \subseteq NAMES$ there exists with $EXPS(N)$ a set of expressions over these names. We do not make any statements about these expressions other than a) the names from N may appear as free variables in the expressions, and b) the mapping of the computational model to TLA⁺ also induces a mapping of expressions to TLA⁺.

$PARAMTYPES_{S_{CM}}$ is a set of type names indicating all types a formal parameter can have. This set is determined by the selection of a computational model S_{CM} (cf. Sect. 3.2.3). From the computational model there also exists an operator

$$\nu_{S_{CM}} : PARAMTYPES_{S_{CM}} \rightarrow \wp(NAMES)$$ ∎

that retrieves all names that a parameter type induces in the computational model and that can, thus, be used in an expression over a parameter of this type.

$FORMALPARAMS_{S_{CM}} = NAMES \times PARAMTYPES_{S_{CM}}$ is the set of all possible formal parameters.

$DOMAINS$ is the set of all types a characteristic can have: $DOMAINS = \{\mathbb{N}, \mathbb{R}\}$.

Example 6.2 (Parameter types and induced names) The computational model we are going to use knows about operations of services and components. We represent these by the μCQML parameter types $SERVOP$ and $COMPOP$, respectively. Thus, $PARAMTYPES_{S_{CM}} = \{SERVOP, COMPOP\}$.

For $\nu_{S_{CM}}(SERVOP)$ we have:

$$\{\text{invocations->last().startTime,}$$
$$\text{invocations->last().endTime}\} \subseteq \nu_{S_{CM}}(SERVOP)$$ ◇

Next, we make use of these basic definitions to define the actual language constructs of μCQML:

Definition 6.2 (μCQML language constructs) The set $CHARACTERISTICS_{S_{CM}}$ of all characteristic definitions over a given computational model S_{CM} is defined by:

$$CHARACTERISTICS_{S_{CM}} =$$
$$\{(n, fp, d, exp) \mid n \in NAMES \wedge$$
$$fp \in \wp(FORMALPARAMS_{S_{CM}}) \wedge$$
$$d \in DOMAINS \wedge$$
$$exp \in EXPS\left(\bigcup_{(n,t) \in fp} \left(\bigcup_{mn \in \nu(t)} \text{conc}(n, mn) \cup \{n\}\right)\right)\}$$

Thus, the expression exp associated to a characteristic may range over all formal parameter names, as well as all names resulting from concatenating a parameter name and any name induced by the computational model for the type of that parameter.

For some application model S_{App}, the set of constraints over characteristics is given by:

$$CHARCONSTRS_{S_{App}} =$$
$$\{(cn, n, paramMap, op, val) \mid cn \in NAMES \wedge$$
$$n \in NAMES \wedge$$
$$paramMap \subseteq \{(n, e) \mid n \in NAMES \wedge$$
$$e \in S_{App}\} \wedge$$
$$op \in \{<, >\} \wedge$$
$$\exists Q \in DOMAINS : val \in Q\}$$

The set of all possible profiles is given by:

$$PROFILES = \{(name, p, r) \mid name \in NAMES \wedge$$
$$p \in \wp(NAMES) \wedge$$
$$r \in \wp(NAMES)\}$$

Finally, a μCQML specification is given by a tuple

$$Spec_{(S_{App}, S_{CM})} = (chars, constrs, profs)$$

where $profs \in \wp(PROFILES)$, $constrs \in \wp(CHARCONSTRS_{S_{App}})$, and $chars \in \wp(CHARACTERISTICS_{S_{CM}})$; and the following consistency rules hold:

1. Characteristics, constraints, and profiles must be uniquely named:

$$\forall \ (cn_1, n_1, paramMap_1, op_1, val_1) \ , (cn_2, n_2, paramMap_2, op_2, val_2) :$$
$$cn_1 = cn_2 \Rightarrow n_1 = n_2 \ \wedge$$
$$\qquad paramMap_1 = paramMap_2 \ \wedge$$
$$\qquad op_1 = op_2 \ \wedge$$
$$\qquad val_1 = val = 2$$
$$\forall \ (n_1, fp_1, d_1, p_1) \ , (n_2, fp_2, d_2, p_2) \in chars :$$
$$n_1 = n_2 \Rightarrow fp_1 = fp_2 \ \wedge$$
$$\qquad d_1 = d_2 \ \wedge$$
$$\qquad p_1 = p_2$$
$$\forall \ (name_1, p_1, r_1) \ , (name_2, p_2, r_2) \in profs :$$
$$name_1 = name_2 \Rightarrow (p_1 = p_2 \wedge r_1 = r_2)$$

2. Every characteristic referenced from a constraint, and every constraint referenced by a profile, must exist:

$$\forall \ (cn, n, paramMap, op, val) \in constrs : \exists \ (n, fp, d, p) \in chars :$$
$$|paramMap| = |fp| \ \wedge$$
$$\forall \ (pn, pt) \in fp : \exists \ (pn, me) \in paramMap \ \wedge$$
$$val \in d$$
$$\forall \ (name, p, r) \in profs :$$
$$(\forall n \in p : \exists \ (n, cn, paramMap, op, val) \in constrs) \ \wedge$$
$$(\forall n \in r : \exists \ (n, cn, paramMap, op, val) \in constrs) \qquad\blacksquare$$

Example 6.3 (A simple μCQML specification) Translating the CQML$^+$ specification from Example 6.1 into a μCQML specification produces the following (We only show the three sets of characteristics, constraints, and profiles; of course, the complete specification is the tuple formed from these three sets.):

$$chars = \{(response\_time, \{(op, SERVOP)\}, \mathbb{R},$$
$$\qquad\quad \text{conc}(op, invocations\text{->}last().endTime) -$$
$$\qquad\quad \text{conc}(op, invocations\text{->}last().startTime))\}$$
$$constrs = \{(good\_response, respone\_time, \{(op, Counter.getValue)\}, <, 50)\}$$
$$profs = \{(good, \{good\_response\}, \emptyset)\} \qquad\qquad\qquad\qquad\qquad \diamond$$

6.3   The Semantic Mapping

Defining the semantics of μCQML consists of two steps:

1. *Definition of a computational model* on which to base our semantics definition. As we already stated in Sect. 3.2.3, specifications of non-functional properties can only be interpreted relative to a computational model.

2. *Definition of a semantic mapping function*

$$[\![.]\!] : (\wp\,(CHARACTERISTICS_{S_{CM}}) \times$$
$$\qquad\quad \wp\,(CHARCONSTRS_{S_{App}}) \times$$
$$\qquad\quad \wp\,(PROFILES)) \qquad\qquad \rightarrow TLA^+$$

that maps μCQML specifications into TLA$^+$ specifications.

It is, thus, similar to the way the denotational semantics [12] of a programming language can be defined. However, the similarities do not extend too far, for several reasons. First, we are dealing with a specification language, which has other requirements on semantics than a programming language. Secondly, we are not interested in the functionality of an application, as is the case with traditional denotational semantics. Therefore, two operations that would be quite different from the point of view of traditional denotational semantics may be considered equal in our semantics, if they have the same non-functional properties.

We will look at the two steps from above in the following two subsections.

6.3.1   Computational Model

It is important to realise that the principle of the semantic mapping is independent of the concrete computational model. It is sufficient if some computational model has been defined and mapping functions for this model exist so that it can be represented in TLA$^+$ and application models can be related to the TLA$^+$ representation of the computational model.

We can, therefore, without loss of generality define a very simple computational model to use in further discussions and to expose the principles underlying the semantics definition for μCQML. The sample computational model visible in Figs. 6.3 and 6.4 only knows about components and services with operations; for each invocation of an operation start and end time are recorded. This computational model is a TLA$^+$ representation of the computational model in Fig. 6.2, enhanced by the concept of components with their respective operations. The specifications in the figures are based on the context model specifications of component and service from Sect. 3.5.1. However, we needed to make some adjustments to the computational model. In particular, OCL—which is used as the expression language in CQML$^+$ and thus in μCQML—does not support temporal logic expressions. Therefore, any computation relying on temporal issues must be treated completely in the computational model. The OCL expressions can merely use the probes provided by the computational model and combine their respective values to obtain the value of a characteristic. This is why we have enhanced the context models from Sect. 3.5.1 with variables storing the start and end time of the last operation call. Note that temporal aspects are still implied by a μCQML specification.

Notice that we have essentially reused the context models from Sect. 3.5.1, so that mapping an application model onto this context model can be done very much like there. Of course this requires that every application model is represented similarly to how we modelled the `Counter` service in Sect. 3.5.1. We assume that application designers represent their models using some higher-level modelling language—for example UML. Therefore, before a model mapping between the application model and the computational model can be specified, the application model must be translated from the higher-level modelling language into TLA$^+$. This translation also ensures that the application model is represented using the mechanisms we used in Sect. 3.5.1.

6.3.2   Semantic Mapping Function

In this subsection, we discuss the actual semantic mapping function for μCQML specifications. The semantic mapping defines the meaning of any μCQML specification in terms of our specification approach and, thus, in TLA$^+$. Hence, it is a function

$$[\![.]\!] : (\wp(CHARACTERISTICS_{S_{CM}}) \times \\ \wp(CHARCONSTRS_{S_{App}}) \times \\ \wp(PROFILES)) \qquad \rightarrow TLA^+$$

mapping a μCQML specification—consisting of characteristics, constraints and profiles—into a TLA$^+$ specification. This semantic mapping is always parametrised by a computational model and an application model, just as the μCQML specification. We will point out the effects of this parametrisation as we define $[\![.]\!]$.

```
 1 ┌──────────────── MODULE muCQMLContext ────────────────┐

 3  EXTENDS RealTime

 5  VARIABLES ServUnhandledRequest, ServInState
 6  Service ≜ INSTANCE Service
 7            WITH unhandledRequest ← ServUnhandledRequest,
 8                 inState ← ServInState

10  VARIABLES ServOpStart, ServOpEnd, ServInCall

12  ServInit ≜ ∧ ServInCall = FALSE
13             ∧ ServOpStart = 0
14             ∧ ServOpEnd = 0

16  OnServStartRequest ≜ Service!StartRequest ⇒ ∧ ServInCall' = TRUE
17                                              ∧ ServOpStart' = now
18                                              ∧ UNCHANGED ServOpEnd

20  OnServFinishRequest ≜ Service!FinishRequest ⇒ ∧ ServInCall' = FALSE
21                                                ∧ ServOpEnd' = now
22                                                ∧ UNCHANGED ServOpStart

24  ServNext ≜ ∧ OnServStartRequest
25             ∧ OnServFinishRequest

27  ServVars ≜ ⟨ServOpStart, ServOpEnd, ServInCall⟩

29  ServSpec ≜ ∧ ServInit
30             ∧ □[ServNext]_ServVars

32 ├──────────────────────────────────────────────────────┤

34  VARIABLES CmpUnhandledRequest, CmpInState
35  Component ≜ INSTANCE Component
36              WITH unhandledRequest ← CmpUnhandledRequest,
37                   inState ← CmpInState

39  VARIABLES CmpOpStart, CmpOpEnd, CmpInCall

41  CmpInit ≜ ∧ CmpInCall = FALSE
42            ∧ CmpOpStart = 0
43            ∧ CmpOpEnd = 0

45  OnCmpStartRequest ≜ Component!StartRequest ⇒ ∧ CmpInCall' = TRUE
46                                               ∧ CmpOpStart' = now
47                                               ∧ UNCHANGED CmpOpEnd

49  OnCmpFinishRequest ≜ Component!FinishRequest ⇒ ∧ CmpInCall' = FALSE
50                                                 ∧ CmpOpEnd' = now
51                                                 ∧ UNCHANGED CmpOpStart

53  CmpNext ≜ ∧ OnCmpStartRequest
54            ∧ OnCmpFinishRequest

56  CmpVars ≜ ⟨CmpOpStart, CmpOpEnd, CmpInCall⟩

58  CmpSpec ≜ ∧ CmpInit
59            ∧ □[CmpNext]_CmpVars
```

Figure 6.3: Context model for use in defining the μCQML semantics

61 ├──┤

63   $ContextSpec \triangleq \wedge CmpSpec$
64                              $\wedge ServSpec$

66 └──┘

Figure 6.4: Context model for use in defining the μCQML semantics (end)

TLA$^+$ can be quite unwieldy at times. In order to make the following definitions easier to understand, we introduce a template-based mechanism for the creation of TLA$^+$ specifications from μCQML: We define a function $\iota\,(T, n, p)$ taking a TLA$^+$ template T, a name n, and a list of parameters p and producing a TLA$^+$ specification. Such a template is very similar to a specification: It starts with a comment indicating the formal parameters of the template—these will be mapped to the actual parameters in p by the call to $\iota\,(T, n, p)$. The rest of the template is essentially a normal TLA$^+$ module. The name of the module is replaced with n by $\iota\,(T, n, p)$. In the body of the module definition, $\iota\,(T, n, p)$ will replace any occurrence of a formal parameter with the corresponding (by order) actual parameter from p. Additionally, we use the construction $\hat{\forall}x \in y : t$ in the template to produce an instantiation of the TLA$^+$ text t for every x in y, where y typically is a formal parameter of the template.

The semantic mapping function $[\![.]\!]$ can be split up into four functions as follows:

$$[\![chars, constrs, profs]\!] = [\![chars]\!] \cup [\![constrs]\!]\,(chars)\,\cup$$
$$[\![profs]\!] \cup \{\mathbb{S}\,(chars, constrs, profs)\}$$

This means, the semantic mapping of a μCQML specification is the union of the semantic mappings of its constituents plus a system specification defined by $\mathbb{S}\,(chars, constrs, profs)$, which combines these elementary specifications. Note that the semantic mapping functions to the right of the above equation are different from the semantic mapping functions for the complete specification, even though we reuse the symbol. In the following, we will look at each of these functions in turn.

We begin with the mapping of characteristic definitions. In general, mapping a set of things results in a set of mapped elements:

$$[\![C \in \wp(CHARACTERISTICS_{S_{CM}})]\!] = \bigcup_{c \in C} [\![c]\!]$$

For each individual characteristic, we define a corresponding measurement, using the computational model as the context model. The type(s) of the formal parameters of our characteristic definition determine(s) which part of the computational model will be used as the context model for the measurement and when measurement values will be determined. Our computational model only considers operation invocation and we have decided to update any operation-related measurements always at the end of each operation invocation. Notice, that our choice for the latter has been arbitrary, because neither the specification of CQML$^+$ nor the definition of CQML$^+$ or μCQML make any statements about this. Also, for this example, we only consider characteristics with at most one parameter.

$$[\![(n, fp, d, p)]\!] = \mathbf{if}\ |fp| = 1 \wedge fp.t = SERVOP$$
$$\mathbf{then}\ \iota\,(ServOp, Char_n, n, fp, d, p)$$
$$\mathbf{else\ if}\ |fp| = 1 \wedge fp.t = COMPOP$$
$$\mathbf{then}\ \iota\,(CompOp, Char_n, n, fp, d, p)$$
$$\mathbf{else}\ \perp$$

The $\perp$ symbol indicates that no semantics can be given for the characteristic specification. We use $|x|$ to indicate the cardinality of set x. $fp.t$ refers to the type part of an arbitrary

```
    \ * (n, fp, d, p)

2  ┌──────────────────────── MODULE ServOp ────────────────────────┐

4  EXTENDS RealTime

6    Importing the context model

8  VARIABLES ServUnhandledRequest, ServInState
9  VARIABLES ServOpStart, ServOpEnd, ServInCall
10 VARIABLES CmpUnhandledRequest, CmpInState
11 VARIABLES CmpOpStart, CmpOpEnd, CmpInCall

13 fp.n ≜ INSTANCE muCQMLContext

15 ├────────────────────────────────────────────────────────────────┤

17 VARIABLE n  The actual measurement
18 VARIABLE hadOpCall  Helper

20 ├────────────────────────────────────────────────────────────────┤

22 Init ≜ ∧ n ∈ d
23        ∧ hadOpCall = FALSE

25 OnFinishRequest ≜ fp.n!Service!FinishRequest ⇒ ∧ n' = ⟦p⟧ₛ(fp)
26                                                 ∧ hadOpCall' = TRUE

28 Spec ≜ ∧ fp.n!ServSpec
29        ∧ Init
30        ∧ □[OnFinishRequest]⟨n, hadOpCall⟩
31 └────────────────────────────────────────────────────────────────┘
```

Figure 6.5: Measurement definition template for the semantic mapping of service operations. **Bold** font indicates place holders to be replaced with information from the characteristic specification

element of fp; because of $|fp| = 1$, this element is unambiguously defined. $ServOp$ and $CompOp$ refer to the TLA$^+$ templates shown in Figs. 6.5 and 6.6.

Particularly, note how the characteristic's value expression p is inserted into the template on Line 25: Again, a semantic mapping function is applied to it, but this time it maps OCL expressions to TLA$^+$. This mapping is a parameter to the semantic mapping of μCQML, completely dependent on the mapping of the computational model to TLA$^+$. This is the same mapping that has been mentioned in Def. 6.1. We will restrict ourselves to explaining intuitively its important properties: The mapping translates the value expression to TLA$^+$. In particular, expressions like conc(op, invocations->last().endTime) are translated into $CmpOpEnd$ or $ServOpEnd$ depending on whether op represents a component's or a service's operation. The decision whether to use the component or the service variant has been made by using two slightly different mapping functions: $\llbracket . \rrbracket_c$ is the mapping for the component version and $\llbracket . \rrbracket_s$ is the one for the service version.

We have only considered characteristics with one formal parameter above. In theory, a characteristic can have any number of parameters, although in practice our experience shows that this is very rare. In any case, the above schema can easily be extended to more than one parameter. In such a case one mapping template would have to be provided per relevant combination of parameter types.

Example 6.4 (Semantics of response_time) Figure 6.7 shows the TLA$^+$ specification

```
   \ * (n, fp, d, p)
 2 ┌─────────────────────────── MODULE CompOp ──────────────────────────┐

 4 EXTENDS RealTime

 6   Importing the context model

 8 VARIABLES ServUnhandledRequest, ServInState
 9 VARIABLES ServOpStart, ServOpEnd, ServInCall
10 VARIABLES CmpUnhandledRequest, CmpInState
11 VARIABLES CmpOpStart, CmpOpEnd, CmpInCall

13 fp.n ≜ INSTANCE muCQMLContext

15 ├─────────────────────────────────────────────────────────────────────┤

17 VARIABLE n  The actual measurement
18 VARIABLE hadOpCall  Helper

20 ├─────────────────────────────────────────────────────────────────────┤

22 Init ≜ ∧ n ∈ d
23          ∧ hadOpCall = FALSE

25 OnFinishRequest ≜ fp.n!Component!FinishRequest ⇒ ∧ n′ = [[p]]_c(fp)
26                                                   ∧ hadOpCall′ = TRUE

28 Spec ≜ ∧ fp.n!CmpSpec
29          ∧ Init
30          ∧ □[OnFinishRequest]_⟨n, hadOpCall⟩
31 └─────────────────────────────────────────────────────────────────────┘
```

Figure 6.6: Measurement definition template for the semantic mapping of component operations. **Bold** font indicates place holders to be replaced with information from the characteristic specification

corresponding to the μCQML definition of response_time. It has been created quite straight-forwardly by instantiating the $ServOp$ template in Fig. 6.5.

The most interesting part is probably the result of $[[p]]_s(fp)$, which can be seen on Lines 22–23. In the computational model, $ServOpStart$ and $ServOpEnd$ are used to represent conc(op, invocations->last().startTime) and conc(op, invocations->last().endTime) for a service operation op, respectively. Note that this mapping depends only on the way the computational model is represented in the CQML$^+$ world and how it is mapped to its TLA$^+$ representation.   ◇

Next, we define the semantic mapping of μCQML constraints, by defining a function

$$[[.]] : CHARCONSTRS_{S_{App}} \times \wp(CHARACTERISTICS_{S_{CM}}) \to TLA^+$$

As in the case of the semantic mapping for characteristics, we define the mapping of a set of constraints to be the set of mappings of the individual constraints. Therefore, we only present the mapping of an individual constraint:

$[[(cn, n, paramMap, op, val)]](c) =$
  if $|paramMap| = 1 \wedge \exists (n, fp, d, p) \in c : fp(paramMap.n) = SERVOP$
    then $\iota (ServOpConstr, Constr_{cn}, n, paramMap, op, val, (n, fp, d, p))$
    else if $|paramMap| = 1 \wedge \exists (n, fp, d, p) \in c : fp(paramMap.n) = COMPOP$
      then $\iota (CompOpConstr, Constr_{cn}, n, paramMap, op, val, (n, fp, d, p))$

```
 1 ┌──────────────── MODULE char_response_time ──────────────┐

 3   EXTENDS RealTime

 5   VARIABLES ServUnhandledRequest, ServInState
 6   VARIABLES ServOpStart, ServOpEnd, ServInCall
 7   VARIABLES CmpUnhandledRequest, CmpInState
 8   VARIABLES CmpOpStart, CmpOpEnd, CmpInCall

10   op ≜ INSTANCE muCQMLContext

12 ├──────────────────────────────────────────────────────────┤

14   VARIABLE response_time
15   VARIABLE hadOpCall

17 ├──────────────────────────────────────────────────────────┤

19   Init ≜  ∧ response_time ∈ Real
20           ∧ hadOpCall = FALSE

22   OnFinishRequest ≜ op!Service!FinishRequest ⇒ ∧ response_time′ = ServOpEnd −
23                                                                   ServOpStart
24                                                ∧ hadOpCall′ = TRUE

26   Spec ≜  ∧ op!ServSpec
27           ∧ Init
28           ∧ □[OnFinishRequest]⟨response_time, hadOpCall⟩

30 └──────────────────────────────────────────────────────────┘
```

Figure 6.7: The TLA$^+$ specification for response_time

Here, we use the notation $fp(paramMap.n)$ to interpret fp as a mapping from parameter names to parameter types and get the type corresponding to the parameter named $paramMap.n$. Figures 6.8 and 6.9 show the referenced specification templates $ServOpConstr$ and $CompOpConstr$. The mapping is quite straight-forward: A μCQML constraint is mapped onto a TLA$^+$ constraint over the measurement n. As with characteristics, the semantic mapping depends on the combination of parameters given, because the context models and model mappings depend on the parameter types. Again, we have only considered constraints over characteristics with exactly one parameter, and the same arguments apply for extending this to situations with more than one parameter.

Notice how we use $hadOpCall$ to state that the response-time constraint will only be evaluated when the operation has been invoked at least once. This is different from the semantics implied by the examples in [1] where such a constraint is apparently evaluated at all times, and the case that no operation invocation has happened yet must be handled explicitly in the definition of the characteristic.

Note how the model mapping specification is derived on Line 14 in Figs. 6.8 and 6.9. The model mapping represents the binding of formal parameters with elements from the application model in a μCQML specification. The definition of the mapping function translating $paramMap$ to TLA$^+$ depends on the application model and the computational model, and can, thus, not be given in all generality. It has, therefore, been encapsulated into a mapping function

$$[\![.]\!] : (NAMES \times S_{App}) \times CHARACTERISTICS_{S_{CM}} \rightarrow TLA^+$$

This mapping results in a TLA$^+$ expression relating variables of the computational model (as imported by the instantiation in the first part of the TLA$^+$ template) to variables of the application model (as imported through the **extends** clause). Typically, these expressions will be structured along the lines shown in the example in Sect. 3.5.1.

```
      \ * (n, paramMap, op, val, c)
 2  ┌──────────────────── MODULE ServOpConstr ─────────────────────┐
 4  EXTENDS $S_{App}$, RealTime

 6  VARIABLES ServUnhandledRequest, ServInState
 7  VARIABLES ServOpStart, ServOpEnd, ServInCall
 8  VARIABLES CmpUnhandledRequest, CmpInState
 9  VARIABLES CmpOpStart, CmpOpEnd, CmpInCall
10  VARIABLES n, hadOpCall

12  nSpec ≜ INSTANCE $Char_n$

14  ModelMapping ≜ □⟦paramMap⟧(c)

16  Spec ≜ ∧ ModelMapping
17         ∧ nSpec!Spec
18         ∧ □(hadOpCall ⇒ (n op val))

20  └────────────────────────────────────────────────────────────┘
```

Figure 6.8: Constraint template for the semantic mapping of service operations. **Bold** font indicates place holders to be replaced with information from the constraint specification

Example 6.5 (Semantics of `good_response`) Figure 6.10 shows the TLA$^+$ specification of the `good_response` quality statement from Example 6.1.

The most interesting part of this specification is certainly the model mapping defined on Lines 13–22. Before we can define a model mapping, we require an application model. Here, we can reuse the one from Sect. 3.5.1. We include it into our specification by naming $CounterApp$ in the **extends** -clause of the specification. The model mapping then declares that the `getValue` operation of this Counter application is the service operation to be constrained.[1]   ◇

We also need to define a mapping for the set of profiles. Again, we map a set of profiles to a set of mapped profiles, so that we only need to discuss the mapping of an individual profile:

$$⟦.⟧ : PROFILES → TLA^+$$

A profile intuitively states that a certain set of non-functional properties will be provided by a component (or service) provided that the environment provides a certain (different) set of properties:

$$⟦(name, p, r)⟧ = \iota\,(ProfileTemplate, name, p, r)$$

where $ProfileTemplate$ references the TLA$^+$ template shown in Fig. 6.11. The three dots on Lines 6 and 7 stand for a renaming of all variables of the instantiated specification (except those from the application model) to unique variable names.

Through this mapping, a profile guarantees all constraints in p as long as it can rely on the constraints in r. Note that this is only one possible interpretation of the definition of a CQML$^+$ profile as given in [1, p. 62 *ff.*].

Example 6.6 (Semantics of `good` profile) Figure 6.12 shows the mapping for the `good` profile from Example 6.1. Lines 5–24 are one instance of the pattern on Line 6 in Fig. 6.11. Note how the **with** -statement with the three dots has been expanded to a listing of all variables from the specification in Fig. 6.10. Because no required constraints have been specified, the precondition on Line 27 is TRUE.   ◇

---

[1]A technical remark: In this and the following example, the resulting specifications had to be named different from what the template stipulates, because *Spec* has already been defined in *CounterApp*. This is only a technical issue and has no influence on the information conveyed by the specification.

$\setminus *$ $(n,\ paramMap,\ op,\ val,\ c)$

2 ——————————— MODULE $CompOpConstr$ ————————————

4 EXTENDS S_{App}, $RealTime$

6 VARIABLES $ServUnhandledRequest$, $ServInState$
7 VARIABLES $ServOpStart$, $ServOpEnd$, $ServInCall$
8 VARIABLES $CmpUnhandledRequest$, $CmpInState$
9 VARIABLES $CmpOpStart$, $CmpOpEnd$, $CmpInCall$
10 VARIABLES **n**, $hadOpCall$

12 **nSpec** $\triangleq$ INSTANCE $Char_n$

14 $ModelMapping \triangleq \Box[\textbf{paramMap}](\textbf{c})$

16 $Spec \triangleq\ \wedge ModelMapping$
17 $\wedge \textbf{nSpec}!Spec$
18 $\wedge \Box(hadOpCall \Rightarrow (\textbf{n op val}))$

20

Figure 6.9: Constraint template for the semantic mapping of component operations. **Bold** font indicates place holders to be replaced with information from the constraint specification

Finally, we define how to create a system specification from a μCQML specification:

$$\mathbb{S} : (\wp\,(CHARACTERISTICS_{S_{CM}}) \times$$
$$\wp\,(CHARCONSTRS_{S_{App}}) \times$$
$$\wp\,(PROFILES)) \rightarrow TLA^+$$

A system specification is the conjunction of all profiles for all components in the system, the appropriate container strategies, and a specification of the available resources (*cf.* Sect. 3.3.4):

$\mathbb{S}\,(chars, constrs, profs) = \textbf{let}\ \ c\ \ \triangleq\ \ \{(name, p, r) \in profs\,|\,\forall\,n \in (p \cup r)\ :$
$$\exists\,co \in constrs\ :$$
$$\exists\,c \in chars\ :$$
$$\wedge\ co.cn = n$$
$$\wedge\ c.n = co.n$$
$$\wedge\ \forall fp \in c.fp\ :$$
$$fp.t - CompOp\},$$
$$s\ \ \triangleq\ \ \{(name, p, r) \in profs\,|\,\forall\,n \in (p \cup r)\ :$$
$$\exists\,co \in constrs\ :$$
$$\exists\,c \in chars\ :$$
$$\wedge\ co.cn = n$$
$$\wedge\ c.n = co.n$$
$$\wedge\ \forall fp \in c.fp\ :$$
$$fp.t = ServOp\}$$
$$\textbf{in}\ \ \iota\,(SysSpecTemplate, SystemSpecification, c, s)$$

c and s are helpers capturing the set of all profiles for components or services, respectively. $SysSpecTemplate$ refers to the TLA$^+$ template in Fig. 6.13. The template first imports all profiles describing non-functional properties of components (Lines 6–8 in Fig. 6.13). Next, it defines the system as the conjunction of the application model (denoted by $S_{App}!AppSpec$ in the template), container strategies, and a specification of available system resources (Lines 10–15 in Fig. 6.13). Next, the system specification presents

```
1  ┌─────────────────── MODULE constr_good_response ───────────────────┐

3  EXTENDS CounterApp, RealTime

5  VARIABLES ServUnhandledRequest, ServInState
6  VARIABLES ServOpStart, ServOpEnd, ServInCall
7  VARIABLES CmpUnhandledRequest, CmpInState
8  VARIABLES CmpOpStart, CmpOpEnd, CmpInCall
9  VARIABLES response_time, hadOpCall

11 response_timeSpec ≜ INSTANCE char_response_time

13 ModelMapping ≜ □ ∧ IF (doHandle = 0 ∨ doHandle = 1)
14                        THEN ServInState = "Idle"
15                        ELSE IF doHandle = 2
16                            THEN ServInState = "HandlingRequest"
17                            ELSE FALSE
18                   ∧ IF (doHandle = 0 ∨ doHandle = 2)
19                        THEN ServUnhandledRequest = FALSE
20                        ELSE IF doHandle = 1
21                                THEN ServUnhandledRequest = TRUE
22                                ELSE FALSE

24 constr_good_response_Spec ≜ ∧ ModelMapping
25                             ∧ response_timeSpec!Spec
26                             ∧ □(hadOpCall ⇒ (response_time < 50))

28 └──────────────────────────────────────────────────────────────────┘
```

Figure 6.10: The TLA$^+$ specification for good_response

```
   \* (p, r)
2  ┌─────────────────── MODULE Profile Template ───────────────────┐

4  EXTENDS $S_{App}$, RealTime

6  ∀̂n ∈ p : n_prov ≜ INSTANCE nConstr WITH ...
7  ∀̂n ∈ r : n_req  ≜ INSTANCE nConstr WITH ...

9  ├────────────────────────────────────────────────────────────────┤

11 Spec ≜ ∀̂n ∈ r : ∧ n_req!Spec
12          ⁺▷
13        ∀̂n ∈ p : ∧ n_prov!Spec

15 └──────────────────────────────────────────────────────────────────┘
```

Figure 6.11: Profile mapping template. **Bold** font indicates place holders to be replaced with information from the constraint specification

```
 1  ┌──────────────────────── MODULE good ────────────────────────┐
 3  EXTENDS CounterApp, RealTime

 5  VARIABLE   good_response_prov_ServUnhandledRequest
 6  VARIABLES good_response_prov_ServInState, good_response_prov_ServOpStart
 7  VARIABLES good_response_prov_ServOpEnd, good_response_prov_ServInCall
 8  VARIABLE   good_response_prov_CmpUnhandledRequest
 9  VARIABLES good_response_prov_CmpInState, good_response_prov_CmpOpStart
10  VARIABLES good_response_prov_CmpOpEnd, good_response_prov_CmpInCall
11  VARIABLES good_response_prov_response_time, good_response_prov_hadOpCall
12  good_response_prov ≜ INSTANCE constr_good_response
13       WITH ServUnhandledRequest ← good_response_prov_ServUnhandledRequest,
14            ServInState ← good_response_prov_ServInState,
15            ServOpStart ← good_response_prov_ServOpStart,
16            ServOpEnd ← good_response_prov_ServOpEnd,
17            ServInCall ← good_response_prov_ServInCall,
18            CmpUnhandledRequest ← good_response_prov_CmpUnhandledRequest,
19            CmpInState ← good_response_prov_CmpInState,
20            CmpOpStart ← good_response_prov_CmpOpStart,
21            CmpOpEnd ← good_response_prov_CmpOpEnd,
22            CmpInCall ← good_response_prov_CmpInCall,
23            response_time ← good_response_prov_response_time,
24            hadOpCall ← good_response_prov_hadOpCall
25  ├─────────────────────────────────────────────────────────────┤

27  good_Spec ≜ TRUE ⇸ good_response_prov!constr_good_response_Spec

29  └─────────────────────────────────────────────────────────────┘
```

Figure 6.12: The TLA$^+$ specification for `good`

a service view of the system by including only those profiles that define extrinsic properties (Lines 19–25 in Fig. 6.13). Finally, Line 31 states that a feasible system is a system
where the available components, resources, and container strategies combine to provide the
requested service.

Note that neither available resources nor container strategies to be used can be specified in CQML$^+$. This must either be done in an extended form of CQML$^+$ or through a
completely separate specification using a different language. At the same time, CQML$^+$
allows for the specification of resource demand directly in a component's profile. As we
have seen in Chapt. 3, this is the wrong approach as it prevents a clean separation between
intrinsic and extrinsic information about the component. Because information on resources
and container strategy is, thus, not present in the μCQML specification, we cannot give an
example for the mapping to TLA$^+$.

6.4   Evaluation

In the previous section, we have discussed a semantic mapping for μCQML—a mathemat-
ically represented subset of CQML$^+$.[2] We have seen that, for the most part, the mapping
was quite straight-forward. In this section, we are going to discuss some of the properties
of the semantic mapping we have proposed. In particular, we will point out where we were
able to fix short-comings in CQML$^+$, where problems occurred because our approach is
more expressive than CQML$^+$ and enhancing CQML$^+$ would require great design effort.
We will, also, discuss generality and efficiency of the semantic mapping approach we have
presented, and elaborate on why a language like CQML$^+$ with a semantic underpinning is
useful:

---

[2]In the following discussion we will make no distinction between the two languages.

```
   \ * (component_profs, service_profs)
 2 ┌──────────────────── MODULE SysSpecTemplate ────────────────────┐

 4   EXTENDS S_App

 6     collect profile INSTANCE s that deal with components not with services
 7     ∀p ∈ component_profs :
 8        {p.name}_comp ≜ INSTANCE p.name WITH ...

10     System Specification is conjunction of profiles and conjunction of
11     application model and container strategies and resource specifications
12     System  ≜  ∧ S_App!AppSpec
13                ∧ ContainerStrategy
14                ∧ ResourceSpecification
15                ∧ ∀p ∈ component_profs : ∧ {p.name}_comp!Spec

17 ├────────────────────────────────────────────────────────────────┤

19     The service to be provided is the conjunction of all profiles concerning
20     services, but not components
21     ∀p ∈ service_profs :
22        {p.name}_service ≜ INSTANCE p.name WITH ...

24     Service ≜ ∧ S_App!AppSpec
25                ∧ ∀p ∈ service_profs : ∧ {p.name}_service!Spec

27 ├────────────────────────────────────────────────────────────────┤

29     Feasible Systems are those where the service view follows from the system
30     view
31     IsFeasible ≜ System ⁺⇒ Service

33 └────────────────────────────────────────────────────────────────┘
```

Figure 6.13: System specification mapping template. **Bold** font indicates place holders to be replaced with information from the constraint specification

- *Fixing short-comings of CQML$^+$:*

  - Through the semantic mapping we can make precise and formal statements about the meaning of a CQML$^+$ specification. In particular, we can give a clear definition of many aspects that remain implicit in CQML$^+$. One example for such an implicit aspect is the question of when in the execution of an application a measurement's value should be determined. In our example mapping above, we have chosen to determine measurement values always at the end of an operation call, taking care to ignore the measurement's value as long as the corresponding operation has not yet been invoked.

    The time when a measurement's value is determined is particularly interesting in connection with CQML$^+$'s concept of *statistical aspects* (*cf.* [1, p. 49 *ff.*]). A statistical aspect allows to derive a new characteristic from an existing one by defining that only statistical derivations of the characteristic should be measured. For example, the following CQML$^+$ snippet defines the characteristic average_response_time as the average value of the response_time characteristic defined above:

```
 1  quality_characteristic average_response_time (op: SERVOP)
                         : response_time (op) {
      mean;
    }
```

The CQML specification defines that "[...]**mean** represents the arithmetic mean of the values of the characteristic" [1, p. 50]. But: when are these values measured? There are at least two possibilities:

1. the values are measured whenever an operation invocation returns, or
2. the values are measured continuously; if no operation invocation is just returning, the value of the last invocation is taken instead.

It is immediately clear, that the selection of one of these two alternatives has a profound influence on the value of the "arithmetic mean". Still, [1] does not state explicitly which alternative is meant. With the semantic mapping we have proposed in this chapter, we are now able to express this selection explicitly, formally, and precisely.

- *Issues due to greater expressiveness of our approach:*

  - We were not able to derive a complete system specification from a CQML$^+$ specification. In particular, we could not derive a specification of the available resources and of the container strategies to be used. These information are simply not given by a CQML$^+$ specification. We have seen in Chapt. 3 that they are very important when describing the non-functional properties of a complete component-based application. CQML$^+$ is, therefore, not able to describe a complete application. It can be used well, however, for specifying individual components and services. Beyond that, we need to provide extensions of CQML$^+$ based on our findings in this chapter.

  - Our specification approach is based on temporal logic. However, in the semantic mapping we could not use the full power of temporal logic, because this is not supported by OCL, which is the language used for defining characteristics in CQML$^+$. For our sample computational model we were able to circumvent this problem by providing probes $ServOpStart$, $ServOpEnd$, $CompOpStart$, and $CompOpEnd$ directly in the computational model. Further research will be required to understand whether this problem can always be treated in this manner or whether it represents a serious issue with the expressive power of CQML$^+$. If the latter is the case, it should also be studied how the various works on temporal-logics extensions for OCL ([42, 53, 150] to name a few) can be used here.

  - In our mapping of a characteristic definition, we have mainly used the characteristic's `values` clause. The CQML$^+$ specification also allows characteristic definitions without a `values` clause—for example, `learnability` as defined in [1, p. 118]. However, even with CQML$^+$ it is not clear what such a characteristic definition means, so our semantic mapping does not lose any relevant information.

- *Generality and efficiency of the semantic mapping approach:*

  - We have given the semantic mapping based on a concrete computational model and using an example with a concrete application model. Nonetheless, the principle of the semantic mapping is generic and does not depend on application model or computational model:

    * *Dependence on application model:* The semantic mapping is independent of concrete application models. It only depends on the way the application model is represented in TLA$^+$, in particular on the mapping of names used in the CQML$^+$ specification onto names and specification structures used in the TLA$^+$ specification. This dependency has been completely encapsulated in the semantic mapping function that creates a TLA$^+$ model mapping specification (used in the templates in Figs. 6.8 and 6.9).

* *Dependence on computational model:* The semantic mapping depends on the concrete computational model to be used. In particular, the mapping of characteristics and constraints must be defined through a separate specification template for each $p \in PARAMTYPES_{S_{CM}}$ (and possibly for relevant combinations of such types). Thus, the principle of the semantic mapping stays the same, even though there are different instances of the mapping depending on the parameter types as defined by the computational model. In Sect. 3.2.3 we have already discussed why every specification of non-functional properties of component-based software makes sense only relative to a specific computational model. The dependence of the semantic mapping on the computational model is only a natural consequence of this. Because the principle of the semantic mapping remains the same independently of the computational model, the usability of the approach is not restricted in any way.

– Because the TLA$^+$ specifications corresponding to CQML$^+$ expressions can be quite large at times, we have introduced a template-based mechanism for expressing the semantic mapping. Thus we can separate the constant parts of the TLA$^+$ specification more easily from the parts changing due to changes in the CQML$^+$ expression.

• *Usefulness of more abstract languages like CQML$^+$:*

– A TLA$^+$ specification can be quite big and unwieldy, even for expressing comparatively simple facts. In contrast, a CQML$^+$ specification expressing the same information is typically much more compact and much easier to understand. This can be seen very well from the example used throughout this chapter. Therefore, languages like CQML$^+$ are a good way for practically specifying non-functional properties in real-world settings. By providing a semantic mapping for μCQML, we have given these languages a more solid foundation, preparing for improved precision and tool support. Also, by showing the deficiencies of CQML$^+$ we have opened the way for extensions to be created so that a new language can be developed that fully supports non-functional specifications for component-based applications. The pseudo-language used in Sects. 2.8 and 8.3 can form the basis for such a new language.

6.5   Summary

In this chapter we have used our specification approach to define a semantics for μCQML, a derivation of Extended Component Quality Modelling Language (CQML$^+$). We have defined this semantics by providing a template-based semantic mapping function relating μCQML expressions to TLA$^+$ expressions. For the most part, the mapping has been quite straight-forward, but there have been some particularities:

1. Not all elements of our specification approach could be covered by μCQML. This is due to the fact that μCQML is a specification language for components, but not for complete component-based applications. To the best of our knowledge, currently no languages exist that support the specification of non-functional properties of complete component-based applications. Our approach is the first specification technique to support this.

2. The semantic mapping is specific to a concrete computational model and a concrete representation style for application models. However, the principle of the mapping is independent of these.

In this chapter we have shown that our specification approach is usable and useful for the specification of non-functional properties of component-based systems. The semantic mapping we defined allows us to understand precisely and unambiguously what is meant by a μCQML—and by extension a CQML$^+$—specification. Thus, it opens the way for advanced reasoning capabilities and tool support for languages like CQML$^+$.

In addition, we have seen where CQML$^+$ is missing concepts that are important for correct modelling of component-based applications and their non-functional properties and that have been defined in this thesis. This should form the basis for an extension of CQML$^+$ supporting these new concepts. The pseudo-language we used in Sect. 2.8 could form the basis of such an extension. It already provides notation for defining components, services, container strategies and systems. We leave the precise definition of such an extension (including the precise definition of semantics for the pseudo-language from Sect. 2.8) to future work.

Part IV

Concepts for System Analysis and Development

This part presents two directions of evaluation for the approach introduced in this thesis:

1. *Chapter 7:* A way to perform analysis based on specifications written using the approach. This chapter shows that the approach allows analysis of specifications and presents a general approach for this.

2. *Chapter 8:* A connection to a component-based software development process. This serves to demonstrate that we achieved our major goal of allowing different roles in the development of an application to provide their specifications independently.

Chapter 7

Performance Analysis of System Specifications

This chapter is about analysing the non-functional properties of component-based systems. We have already seen one type of analysis when we discussed the concept of a *feasible system* in Sect. 3.4, but of course there are many more we may wish to perform.

It is important to realise in this context that, while we can (as shown in the previous chapters) provide a generic framework for the *specification and description* of non-functional properties, such a generic framework does not exist for the *analysis* of non-functional properties. The algorithms and techniques required are very specific to the property under analysis, and to attempt to abstract them to some generic technique does not make sense. Therefore, for the purposes of this thesis, we focus on one property, namely on performance, which is one of the most important non-functional properties for non–real-time applications. In particular, we look at how to estimate an application's performance using techniques from Software Performance Engineering (SPE) [130, 133].

The main focus of our work is on providing means for specifying non-functional properties. In the area of analysis, we are, therefore, interested primarily in demonstrating that our approach does not prohibit the application of analysis techniques.

The chapter begins with an introduction to the key elements of SPE and an SPE analysis tool called *SPE·ED*. We then discuss two ways of applying SPE analysis to component-based systems, both in general and following concrete examples. An important point in this context is how to extract the input parameters of the analysis from the non-functional specifications of the components and the application as a whole. Sect. 7.3 proposes a formal technique based on our specification approach supporting the extraction of the correct information from non-functional specifications.

7.1 Software Performance Engineering and Performance Analysis Using *SPE·ED*

In their book [133], Smith and Williams describe a process for estimating the performance of software at different stages during the development of an application. Figure 7.1 shows an overview of the steps they propose to follow. For any project, one should first make an assessment of the criticality of performance. Depending on the outcome of this assessment, performance should be taken into account earlier or later in the software development cycle. When performance is considered sufficiently important, performance estimation is always done with respect to critical use cases. These are the use cases for which performance matters most, and which, therefore, must be considered first. From there, the process proceeds in two parallel sub-processes. We are mainly concerned with the process on the right, and will only mention that the verification and validation process on the left serves to ensure that our estimates have some relation to reality. For example, in this process we answer questions like "Are the resource requirements we have defined/estimated accurate?" Smith and Williams mention that this may require prototyping and measurement. We add that it may also require decisions regarding container strategies to be used and other context-of-use constraints. In the next step on the right side, we narrow the set of performance-critical situations down to individual scenarios in the critical use cases. These scenarios form the basis for the construction of performance models, which in SPE come in the form of a special type of control-flow graph called software execution model. Before evaluating these models, however, we need to determine the performance objectives and work loads in order to have something against which to evaluate the analysis results later on. The following two steps add resource demand information, which, for reasons of separation of concerns, is done in two steps in SPE. Evaluation of the models is performed using the *SPE·ED* tool; we will discuss the evaluation of each type of model when discussing the models themselves. Depending on the outcome of the analysis, we can either determine that we have met our performance objectives, that we need to modify our design, or that the performance objectives are completely unreasonable and need to be adjusted to a more realistic range.

In SPE, performance models are constructed at two levels of detail:

1. A *Software Execution Model* describes the control flow of an application, together with specifications of resource demands for each step, using so-called *execution graphs* [129]. Steps can be coarse grained—we only care about the points where resource demand changes and about loops and choices. The most important types of nodes in execution graphs can be seen in Fig. 7.2.

   With each basic node in an execution graph, we need to associate elementary performance information. In SPE, this is done in two steps (*cf.* also Fig. 7.1):

   (a) *Add software resource requirements,* and

   (b) *Add computer resource requirements*

   Software resource requirements specify the basic services each node requires—for example, how many database access calls it performs, or how many individual screens it needs to display. Computer resource requirements specify how much of the physical resources are consumed for each unit of each software resource—for example, how much CPU is required and how many network packets are sent for each database access call. They are specified by performance experts through the so-called overhead matrix.

   Evaluation of an execution graph happens by iterative reduction of the graph to one so-called computed node (in effect a basic node, whose resource demand has been computed from the original graph). For each basic node type there is a rule how to transform it into a computed node if all connected nodes are computed or basic nodes. These rules are applied successively until the complete graph has been transformed into a single computed node giving the result of the evaluation. Because for case nodes only execution probabilities for each path are known, the resulting resource demands are only valid for the average case. Software execution models consider only one piece of software independently of other software running on the same system or other parallel invocations of the same piece of software running at the same time. They do not consider resource contention and, therefore, provide optimistic results for the average performance.

2. A *System Execution Model* takes into account the actually available resources and the interaction between different pieces of software having to share them. It is, thus, an extension of the software execution model that can additionally analyse resource-contention effects on average performance. The underlying formalism is Queuing

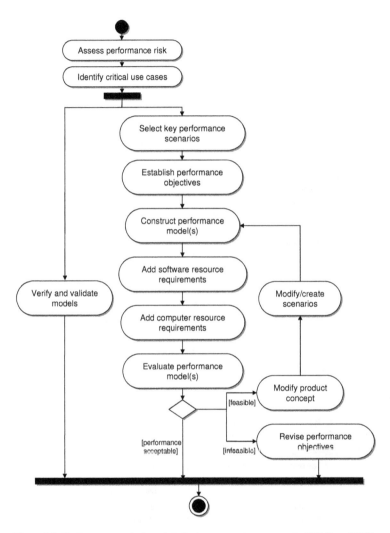

Figure 7.1: Performance analysis and design as an ongoing process in SPE (from [133]). Information exchange between the two main branches ('verification and validation of models' and 'construction and evaluation of performance models') has not been shown

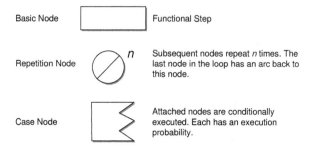

Figure 7.2: Basic node types of execution graphs. From [133]

Networks [79]. Because this formalism is much more complex, Smith and Williams advise that a system execution model be constructed and evaluated only after the software execution model indicates that there are no problems.

Each resource of the system is modelled as a server in the system execution model's underlying queueing network. For each piece of software to run in the system, a new job class is created. The service times for each job class at each server are taken from the solutions to the software execution model of the corresponding piece of software. Solving the queueing network for residence time, throughput and similar metrics then produces average performance results under consideration of resource contention.

Smith and Williams have produced an SPE tool named *SPE·ED* [131], which focuses on software execution models, but can create system execution models from software execution models and can evaluate both types of models. Users of *SPE·ED* do not require deep knowledge of queuing networks, because the tool hides this complexity from them.

7.2   SPE Analysis of Component-Based Specifications

When applying SPE to component-based systems, we represent the number of operation calls performed in each step as a software resource requirement and the resource demand of each operation as the corresponding computer resource requirement. Depending on what we select to be our performance scenario, we can perform two types of analysis:

1. *Use-case–based analysis:* We derive performance scenarios from the system's use cases. The operations under consideration are only those offered directly to the user as part of the system's services. This corresponds to the traditional SPE process, where end-to-end performance metrics are calculated on a per-use-case basis.

    For each use case, we create a software execution model corresponding to the most performance-critical scenario for the use case and determine the performance of this scenario. Such a scenario describes a sequence of calls to operations provided by various encapsulated components in the system. We can, therefore, use an execution graph to model user behaviour (that is, each operation that is invoked is represented by one step in the execution graph) and use the response time of the different service operations (as defined in the example in Sect. 3.5.1) to indicate the time required for each step. When we solve this software execution model, we can determine end-to-end performance of the scenario. In many cases, this will determine worst-case performance values for the scenario. If the scenarios include case nodes, we obtain average case values (because the probability of each choice at the case node is taken into account). We can determine best-case values by using the execution time specification of the components instead of the response time of the service. However, in this case, if we use extended container strategies (*cf.* Sect. 4.3.2) to specify the effect of components used, we also need to take into account all the components used by a called component.

2. *Analysis of one service operation:* Here, we are interested in the average performance of one service operation. We derive performance scenarios from the control flow of this operation. Software and computer resource requirements are based on the (hierarchy of) operations called from this service operation.

   To this end, we model the operation itself as an execution graph, providing one step that uses the complete execution time of the operation, and one step per invocation of an operation of another component—associated with the average performance of that operation. We can perform such an analysis very early in the design phase, even when we have not yet decided what resources will be available or what strategies will be implemented in the container. In this case, the analysis helps determine whether the chosen architecture and component implementations have a chance of providing satisfactory performance at all. Of course such an analysis is comparatively rough and needs to be supported by more precise analysis at later stages in the development when more detailed information is available. Still, it helps designers to quickly assess many design alternatives at the architectural level. The performance values thus determined can also be reused for analysing complete scenarios as discussed in the previous step.

The main difference between these two approaches is, that in the first case we look at the system as a black box, using other techniques—for example, feasibility proofs as in Sect. 3.4—for analysing the properties of individual operations, and use SPE-based analysis to determine the end-to-end performance of complete user scenarios; while in the second case we take the functional structure of our system into account when constructing a software performance model, which we then evaluate to determine the performance of individual operations. In the following, we will discuss two concrete examples, one for each type of performance analysis.

7.2.1 An SPE Model for Use-Case–Based Analysis

In this section, we walk through an analysis of a use-case scenario for the Counter application we discussed in Sect. 3.5.1. Figure 7.3 shows the scenario we have selected for our analysis. It can be seen that we have slightly extended the Counter application: We have added an init () operation that needs to be invoked before any incrementing or reading of the counter value can occur. After that, users can repeatedly invoke the inc () and getValue () operations. We used a UML 2.0 sequence diagram, which provides convenient notation to express loops and branching behaviour.

[133] explains how to derive execution graphs from sequence diagrams. We essentially follow this approach; that is, we transform every message sent by the user into a basic node in the execution graph, every loop into a loop node, and every alternative into a case node. The resulting execution graph can be found in Fig. 7.4 a).

We needed to add some information that we could not determine from the sequence diagram, namely

- The number of times the loop is executed. This number has not been specified in the sequence diagram, which is not concerned with non-functional properties. We can refer to the system requirements, or to an analysis of previously existing systems, to estimate an appropriate average value. For our example, we have chosen a value of 3.

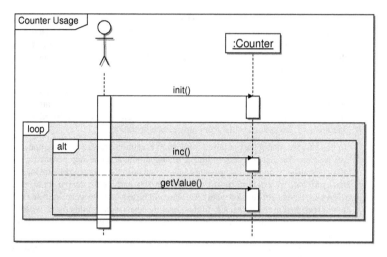

Figure 7.3: Sequence Diagram of a use case scenario for the Counter component: Users first initialize the counter and then repeatedly invoke either inc() or getValue()

- The probability with which inc() or getValue() are chosen at each iteration. Again, this is typically not specified in the sequence diagram, but we can use knowledge of previous systems or information from the system's requirements to come up with a reasonable estimate here. We have specified that in 70% of the cases inc() and in 30% of all cases getValue() is invoked.

As a next step, we need to annotate the execution graph with software resource requirements. We define each operation offered by our system to be one software resource and associate it with the number of times it is invoked in each step. This way we can combine basic nodes which form a sequence of calls to operations of the service into a single basic node with a slightly more complex software resource requirement. In our example, we annotate the first node[1] with 1 call to init(), node number 2 with 1 call to inc(), and node number 3 with 1 call to getValue(). The resulting execution graph with software resource annotations can be found in Fig. 7.4 b).

Next, we need to specify the computer resource requirements; that is, we need to determine the overhead caused by each software resource. The performance expert doing this can make use of the non-functional specification of the system: he is most interested in the time that each operation call takes, and this is exactly the response time of the service represented by that operation. So, if we have components specifying their execution time, a container strategy specification transforming execution time into response time, and a specification of the available resources on our target machine, we can combine these specifications to determine the response time for each service operation, provided the system is feasible. For our example, we can use the specifications from Sect. 3.5.1. Figure 7.5 shows a screen shot from the *SPE·ED* tool. The performance expert has just defined a so-called overhead matrix specifying the respective computer resource demand for each software resource requirement. Each column in an overhead matrix denotes one computer resource. In our case we have defined only one, namely CPU. In the second and third row we define that CPU demand will be specified in millisecond units in the following. Each of the following rows (except the very last row of the matrix, which specifies that one millisecond

---
[1]See the numbers in Fig. 7.4 a).

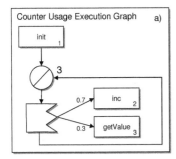
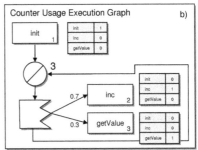

Figure 7.4: Execution Graph representation of the same scenario as in Fig. 7.3. Part a) shows the execution graph derived directly from the functionality as shown in Fig. 7.3, while in Part b) software resource requirements have been added to each step

of CPU time takes one millisecond) defines the CPU demand for one software resource. We have defined one software resource per operation, namely init(), inc(), and getValue(). The times we entered have been taken from the respective specifications. For example, the 50 milliseconds for the getValue() operation have been taken from specification CounterAppResponseTime (cf. Page 172).

Finally, we need to evaluate the model. The *SPE·ED* tool can do so completely automatically, all we need to do is press the 'Solve' button. Figure 7.6 shows the results obtained for our example as a *SPE·ED* screen shot. We find that the complete scenario takes, on average, 434 milliseconds. Note that we had to split out the case node into a separate diagram, because *SPE·ED* accepts only basic nodes in a loop. The double bars surrounding the node inside the loop indicate that the node is extended in a separate diagram, namely the one on the right. The meaning of these two diagrams is exactly the same as the meaning of the one diagram in Fig. 7.4 a). In addition to computing the time spent in the complete scenario, *SPE·ED* has also annotated each node with the average time spend in this node.

7.2.2   An SPE Model for the Analysis of a Single Operation

In this section we perform an early analysis of the Calculator component network from Sect. 4.4. By early analysis we mean that this is an analysis that can be performed very early in the development process, at a time where we have determined the architecture of our system and are selecting component implementations to use, but haven't fixed the precise platform configuration yet. At this point it is important to obtain information about whether the architecture and the selected component implementations have any chance of providing acceptable performance.

Because we are at such an early stage in our design, we cannot use container or resource specifications in our analysis. The only information we have available comes from the functional specification and the component specifications. Because we have separated non-functional component specifications from container and resource specification in our approach, we can easily perform analysis even without knowing about the concrete resources and containers to be used in the final system.

In our example, we are interested in the total execution time of the getResult operation of the calc component (remember from Fig. 4.2 that this is the central component performing the actual calculation). We say 'total execution time of the operation' to distinguish this from response time, which would include effects caused by the container or

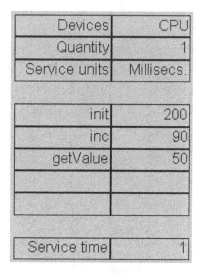

Figure 7.5: Overhead specification for the use-case based analysis

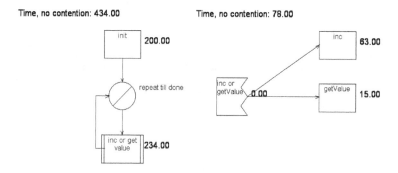

Figure 7.6: Results of *SPE·ED* analysis

by the availability of certain resources. For this analysis, we are only interested in effects due to component implementation and application architecture (i.e., the topology of the component network forming the application).

To perform this analysis, there are two steps which we need to perform:

1. We need to construct a software execution model for getResult(). We do this by using one basic node that we associate with the complete execution time specified for the operation, followed by one extended node for each invocation of an operation in another component. The node's extension is then a similar execution graph for that operation. The order and number of operation invocations we obtain from the functional specification of the Calculator application. The execution times to be associated with the basic nodes can be determined from the non-functional specification by the performance expert.

2. Using the *SPE·ED* tool, we must evaluate the software execution model thus constructed. Depending on our requirements we can evaluate the model for minimum, average, or maximum total execution time. If evaluation of the software execution model indicates satisfactory performance, we can then proceed to constructing and evaluating a system execution model. Analysing the system execution model will provide us with more precise insights about the operation's performance properties by including effects caused by resource contention into the analysis. The system execution model does not include effects due to the container strategies we choose, but by analysing different scenarios (for example, allowing multiple instances of the component to run in parallel) we may get an idea about which container strategies may be appropriate for our application. [133] explains how to derive a system execution model from a software execution model, and how to use the *SPE·ED* tool for this derivation and for the evaluation of the models.

Figure 7.7 shows the software execution model for getResult(). The information in these three diagrams has been taken from the functional specification of the Calculator example. For each invocation of an operation from inside the getResult() operation we have added an extended node which is refined by an execution graph for the called operation (getData() in our case). If an operation is invoked more than once, we simply reuse its execution-graph model and just insert an additional extended node into the model of the calling operation. The execution-graph model differs from a control-flow representation of the functional specification mainly in one place: We always begin the execution graph of an operation with a basic node that we use to represent the accumulated execution time for this operation. For our example, the execution graphs are very simple, but of course we could have loop nodes, case nodes, or any other more complex construction in the graphs for real-world examples.

All that remains to do is to assign resource demands to the basic nodes and to evaluate the model. The only basic nodes in our model are the nodes we introduced to represent the component's execution time, so it is clear that we need to associate the respective execution time as the CPU time demand for these nodes. If a getData() request takes 5 milliseconds, and a getResult() execution takes 13 milliseconds, evaluating the model gives us a total time of 28 milliseconds as the total execution time of the getResult() operation. Because we do not use case nodes in our example, we can influence this result by using minimum, average, or maximum execution times for the individual operations.

In [132], Smith and Williams argue that for analysing the performance of component-based systems it is important to model the semantics of operation calls more precisely. They distinguish three types of operation call (inspired by the terminology from Common Object Request Broker (ORB) Architecture (CORBA)):

1. *synchronous,* where the calling component starts an operation call and is blocked until the result is returned,

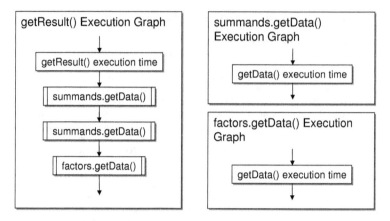

Figure 7.7: Software execution model for the `getResult()` operation from the `Calculator` example from Sect. 4.4

2. *deferred synchronous,* where the calling component starts an operation call, continues working on other tasks, and eventually uses a synchronous call to collect the result, and

3. *asynchronous,* where the calling component starts an operation call, but is not interested in any result value and continues to work.

Smith and Williams provide execution graph notation for each of these three cases. To refine our analysis above, it is of course possible to use this notation, provided that the functional model of our system contains sufficient information.

7.3 Formal Support for Analysis Experts

In the previous section, we discussed two kinds of performance analysis that could be performed on component-based non-functional specifications. In both cases, we required performance experts to extract performance information from the specification and make it available to the analysis tool. This information included such properties as response time of service operations (both maximum and average), or execution time of component operations. So far, we have not discussed how a performance expert—or an *analysis expert* in general—can extract this information from the component specification. In particular, the analysis expert must be able to judge whether a specific property value is indeed the required one; for example, whether it is appropriate to use average execution time for an analysis or if maximum response time would be required instead.

Wherever analysis methods are presented in the literature, their pre-conditions and result values are characterised in natural language only. This leaves room for interpretation. Recently, in the context of MDA, a new concept has been proposed to provide for a more formal representation of model transformation and analysis know-how: MDA components (MDACs) [21]. An MDAC is a collection of related models and meta-models representing knowledge about a specific model transformation. MDACs can be executed in so-called MDA containers integrated into CASE tools. Thus, modelling knowledge can be packaged in interoperable units that can be reused and traded across business boundaries.

A formal description of the analysis technique—in particular its interface—is obviously a key pre-requisite for reusing it as an MDAC.

In our view, an analysis method is nothing but an operation which takes a non-functional specification obeying some additional rules (such as which non-functional constraints are contained in the specification, or what type of application it describes), and produces a constraint over some measurement regarding that specification. We can, therefore, formalise its interface using pre- and post-conditions as for any other operation. The most important difference to normal operation specification is that the parameters of the operations themselves represent specifications again. Providing such a formal specification of the prerequisites for an analysis method would even allow formal proofs of the applicability of the analysis method; but more importantly, it provides an unambiguous description of what input is needed to perform the analysis.

Example 7.1 (Use-Case–Based Analysis) Figures 7.8 and 7.9 show a formal representation of the pre- and post-conditions for use-case–based analysis as we discussed it in Sect. 7.2.1. This specification assumes that use-case–based analysis can be represented as an operation of the general signature

```
spe_analysis (in Nat NumOps, in Scenario Services,
              in Real[] ResponseTimes,
              out Real GlobalTimeConstr)
```

that is, it takes a scenario of NumOps Services being invoked, for each of which the maximum response time (ResponseTimes) is given, and produces a real value for the global time constraint.

The specifications now impose constraints on these parameters (in the following, line numbers refer to the lines in Figs. 7.8 and 7.9):

- Services describes a sequence of service operations which are invoked one after the other (*cf.* Lines 29–60).

- ResponseTimes is an array containing the maximum response time for each service operation in the order in which they are described in Services (*cf.* Line 34).

- GlobalTimeConstr represents an upper bound for the time between the invocation of the first operation in Services and the return of the last such operation (*cf.* Lines 64–80).

The most interesting aspect of this specification is how operation invocations are specified. We have lifted the service operation context model from Sect. 3.5.1 to a sequence of operations by collecting the corresponding state variables in a function Services from the operation number to a tuple containing all the state variables. This function is then used to define an operator $Operation(n)$ (Lines 29*ff.*) that represents an individual operation by its context model. An operation call is then described by including the state machine from that context model (*cf.* Lines 45 and 51). This way, we can reuse the concept of a model mapping (see Sect. 3.2.3) to define the application of the analysis method to a specific application model and a specific sequence of operation calls. The performance expert needs to present such a mapping to validate that he has chosen the right parameter values for the performance analysis.

The specification we saw in the example appears comparatively complex in relation to what it actually expresses. This is so, because it has been written at the semantic level. In a practical application, the same information would be expressed using a more high-level language—for example, a mixture of OCL and CQML$^+$. The following snippet of pseudo-CQML$^+$ and pseudo-OCL defines use-case–based analysis:

```
 1 ┌───────────────────── MODULE SPEAnalysis ─────────────────────┐

 3 EXTENDS RealTime
```

Parameters:

Services	An array containing the state variables for the response time model. This essentially describes the sequence of calls.
ResponseTimes	An array containing the response time constraints for each operation in Services.
NumOps	The number of operations in the sequence of calls.
GlobalTimeConstr	The analysis result value.

```
18 CONSTANT NumOps
19 VARIABLE Services
20 ASSUME Services ∈ [{1 .. NumOps} → [LastResponseTime : Real,
21                                      Start : Real,
22                                      inState : { "Idle", "HandlingRequest" },
23                                      unhandledRequest : BOOLEAN ]]
24 CONSTANT ResponseTimes
25 ASSUME ResponseTimes ∈ [{1 .. NumOps} → Real]
26 CONSTANT GlobalTimeConstr
27 ASSUME (GlobalTimeConstr ∈ Real) ∧ (GlobalTimeConstr ≥ 0)

29 Operation(n) ≜ INSTANCE ResponseTimeConstrainedService
30                  WITH LastResponseTime ← Services[n].LastResponseTime,
31                       Start ← Services[n].Start,
32                       inState ← Services[n].inState,
33                       unhandledRequest ← Services[n].unhandledRequest,
34                       ResponseTime ← ResponseTimes[n]

36 ├────────────────────────────────────────────────────────────┤

38 VARIABLES CurOp, InOp

40 Init ≜ ∧ CurOp = 1
41        ∧ InOp = FALSE

43 DoOp(n) ≜ ∧ CurOp = n
44            ∧ InOp = FALSE
45            ∧ Operation(n)!Serv!StartRequest
46            ∧ InOp' = TRUE
47            ∧ ∀ m ∈ {1 .. NumOps} : m ≠ n ⇒ UNCHANGED Services[m]

49 FinishOp(n) ≜ ∧ CurOp = n
50                ∧ InOp = TRUE
51                ∧ Operation(n)!Serv!FinishRequest
52                ∧ InOp' = FALSE
53                ∧ CurOp' = n + 1
54                ∧ ∀ m ∈ {1 .. NumOps} : m ≠ n ⇒ UNCHANGED Services[m]

56 Next ≜ ∃ n ∈ {1 .. NumOps} : ∨ DoOp(n)
57                               ∨ FinishOp(n)

59 Precond ≜ ∧ Init
60            ∧ □[Next]_{(CurOp, InOp)}
```

Figure 7.8: Formal specification of Use-Case–based analysis. Note that for simplicity we assume that no measurement specification hides any state variable

```
62 ├─────────────────────────────────────────────────────────────────────┤

64  VARIABLES Start, GlobalTime

66  InitGM  ≜  ∧ Start = 0
67              ∧ GlobalTime = 0

69  DoStart ≜  DoOp(1) ⇒ ∧ Start' = now
70                        ∧ UNCHANGED GlobalTime

72  DoEnd  ≜  FinishOp(NumOps) ⇒ ∧ GlobalTime' = now
73                                ∧ UNCHANGED Start

75  NextGM ≜  DoStart ∧ DoEnd

77  PostCond ≜  ∧ Precond
78               ∧ ∧ InitGM
79                 ∧ □[NextGM]₍CurOp, InOp, Start, GlobalTime₎
80                 ∧ □(GlobalTime ≤ GlobalTimeConstr)

82 └─────────────────────────────────────────────────────────────────────┘
```

Figure 7.9: Formal specification of Use-Case–based analysis (end)

```
1   quality_characteristic scenario_time (scenario: Scenario) {
      domain: numeric milliseconds;

      — a Scenario is really just a sequence of OperationCalls
      values: scenario->last().endTime −
6             scenario->first().startTime;
    }

    context spe_analysis (NumOps: Nat, Services: Scenario,
                          ResponseTimes: Sequence(Real)): Real
11  pre: ResponseTimes->size() = NumOps and
         Services->size() = NumOps
    pre: Sequence{1..NumOps}->forAll(i |
             response_time (Services->at(i)) = ResponseTimes->at(i))
    post: result = scenario_time (Services)
```

It uses the `response_time` from Chapt. 6. Additionally, it defines the CQML$^+$ measurement `scenario_time` that represents the total time of a single scenario (a sequence of operation calls). It then uses OCL to specify the interface of `spe_analysis` using the quality characteristics just defined. It is worth noting how the high-level specification language makes individual measurements and context-model elements named entities, so that we can refer to them directly by their names instead of having to quote the structure specification again and again.   ◇

7.4 Summary

In this chapter we have discussed how non-functional specifications following the approach proposed in this thesis can be analysed to gain further insights into the non-functional properties of systems. First of all, we have found that it is not possible to provide one analysis approach that is suitable for all non-functional properties because non-functional properties are much too diverse. For this reason, in this chapter, we have concentrated on performance properties and their analysis following the SPE approach, and using the *SPE·ED* tool.

We have shown two types of performance analysis useful for component-based systems: (i) use-case–based analysis, and (ii) analysis of one operation. The former variant analyses performance-critical scenarios from system use cases and determines end-to-end performance properties for those. The latter variant is more interested in the performance of a single operation as offered by the system. It analyses how the chosen architecture and component implementations affect the performance of individual service operations. Because it uses execution-time data only and ignores resource sharing and container effects, it is useful mainly as a first analysis at very early stages of the development process.

This study opens the way for applying the *SPE·ED* tool to doing performance analysis of component-based systems. Our examples of such analyses have been simple, but the *SPE·ED* tool is capable of performing much more complex analyses, including complete evaluation of queuing networks. All of these possibilities are now available for component-based systems.

Finally, we have shown how our formal specification approach helps to describe precisely the prerequisites and potential results of any non-functional analysis method. As an example, we have shown the formal description of the use-case–based performance analysis. Hence, our generic approach to specifying non-functional properties of component-based software is not only compatible with existing analysis techniques, but it, additionally, allows a more precise and unambiguous description of those analysis methods themselves. An interesting question for future research is how we can use these descriptions of analysis methods to automatically extract analysis input from a system specification.

Chapter 8

Connection to a Development Process

The vision behind CBSE is to increase efficiency by packaging readily-built pieces of software into components and reusing them in different applications, sometimes even trading them on a component market. This requires a special software development process. We have claimed that our specification approach fits well with the different roles in component-based software development. To support this claim, in this chapter, we look at a component-oriented development process and discuss how our specification techniques fit into this process.

8.1 A Development Process for Component-Based Software with Special Consideration of Non-functional Properties

In [118, 119, ?] a software development process for component-based applications has been proposed. This process attaches particular importance to the non-functional properties of the application to be developed. Figure 8.1 shows an overview of the process focusing on the roles involved.

The process distinguishes three roles:

1. *Measurement Designers* define the terminology used by the other players for the specification of non-functional properties. They make their specifications available through a so-called measurement repository accessible to all participants of the process.

2. *Component Developers* build reusable pieces of software, which they package as software components and provide through a component library. Before a component can be made available in the component library, its properties—both functional and non-functional—need to be described. To determine the non-functional properties, component developers use a test container [94] in which the component's properties can be measured. These properties are then documented in a formal component specification using the measurements from the measurement repository, which is placed into the component library together with the actual component.

3. *Application Designers* use components to build applications. In a first step, they decompose the system to be built into subsystems and components. They use the terminology provided by measurement designers to specify the non-functional properties these subsystems and components must have. Next, they select components

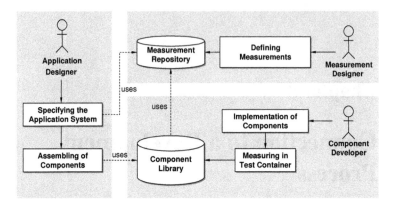

Figure 8.1: A component-based software development process with support for non-functional properties (Adapted from [?])

from the component library and use them to implement their target application. In the selection process, the component properties as specified by the component developer are matched against the requirements as specified by the application designer in the first step of application development.

In the next section, we are going to discuss how our specification approach fits into this development process.

8.2   Specification of Non-functional Properties in the Context of the Development Process

The development process shown in the previous section does not consider deployment of the application on a platform and container. As we have seen in previous chapters, these are, however, critical to the non-functional properties of the system as a whole. We, therefore, extend the development process by two additional roles:

1. *Platform Designers* provide the hardware and basic control software on which the application is running. Platform designers can be the actual developers of the hardware, but they can also buy (and possibly recombine) existing hardware. In any case the platform designers know what resources are provided by the hardware.

2. *Container Designers* develop component containers. In particular, they develop container strategies—whether as individual container components or integrated into monolithic container implementations—and provide them for the deployment of a component-based application.

The five roles thus established can use our specification approach for exchanging information about the non-functional properties of the application to be developed:

- *Measurement Designers* agree on a computational model for the application domain and derive context models from this computational model. Based on these models, they define measurement specifications to be used by the other roles in the development process. In effect, they provide the terminology for the other designers.

- *Component Developers* use the measurement specifications provided by the measurement designers to describe the non-functional properties of the components they develop. In particular, component developers specify intrinsic properties of their components. Because they cannot foretell future usage contexts of the components, they cannot make statements about any extrinsic properties.

- *Platform Designers* provide resource specifications of the resources provided by the platform they have designed. For example, they may provide a specification like that, discussed on Page 46, of a CPU scheduled using RMS. Additionally, they also agree on and provide *abstract* resource specifications (like the abstract specification of a CPU in the above example), which are independent of a concrete platform.

- *Container Designers* use measurement and abstract resource specifications to describe the container strategies they have implemented. These container-strategy specifications become part of the container's documentation and can be used by application designers to reason about the behaviour of the complete application system.

- *Application Designers* use the measurement specifications provided by the measurement designers to describe the non-functional properties of the services realised by their applications. In particular, they describe extrinsic properties of these services and compare them to the requirements as specified by the application's clients.

  Furthermore, application designers use the container and platform specifications provided by container and platform designers, resp., as well as the component specifications provided by the component developers. They select the appropriate specifications from this set and combine them into a complete specification of the system they are building. Based on this specification they can then derive proofs of feasibility of the application architecture they have designed. In this process, feasibility proofs can be useful even if not all components have been selected yet. In such a situation, missing components are replaced by a specification of the properties they *should* have.

8.3   Example

Figure 8.2 shows the architecture of a simple stock syndication application. It shows an active `StockSyndication` component, that periodically queries various providers of stock index information (National Association of Securities Dealers Automated Quotations (NASDAQ) and Deutscher Aktienindex (DAX) in the example, but of course this could be more and could include individual stocks, too). The stock syndicator then filters this information according to rules provided by a client and sends the filtered data on to the client. A non-functional property that is very relevant in this context is the delay between data retrieval from the information providers and delivery of filtered data to the client. We can call this property the up-to-dateness of information delivery.

There are various parties involved in building such a stock syndication application: NASDAQ Inc. provide the NASDAQ component, Deutsche Börse AG provide the DAX component,[1] and some software company provides the actual syndication component and probably also the client component (including, for example, a viewer). The same software company probably also develops the complete application. The components need some runtime environment, provided by a component-container company (e.g., JBoss Inc.), which runs on a hardware platform developed by yet another party.

To enable these different parties to communicate precisely also about the non-functional properties of their components, applications, and systems, *measurement designers* define

---

[1] Both components are, of course, imaginary. No endorsement by any of the companies should be implied.

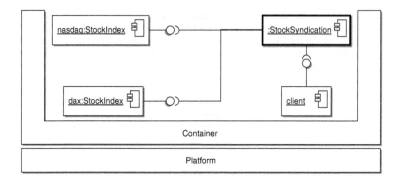

Figure 8.2: Rough architecture of a stock syndication application

a computational model and various measurements to be used. These measurement designers will need to communicate with all parties involved. Therefore, they need to have a
certain international standing. It is probably helpful, if their definitions can be fixed as
an internationally accepted standard—at least for the domain of stock quoting. Using the
pseudo-language from Sect. 2.8, we can define the measurements we are interested in. This
language can be seen as a first sketch of a new specification language taking into account
the results of our studies on semantics for CQML$^+$ from Chapt. 6. Such a language would
of course need a definition of semantics based on our semantic framework, which can follow the same principles that were applied to define the semantics of CQML$^+$ in Chapt. 6.
The following defines the measurements of interest:

```
declare real processing_time   (ComponentEvent eStart,
                                ComponentEvent eEnd) {
  spec = [Time between eStart and eEnd for an execution
          on an empty system with infinite resources.]
}

declare real delay (ServiceEvent eStart,
                    ServiceEvent eEnd) {
  spec = [Time between eStart and eEnd at the service
          level.]
}
```

Here, processing_time defines an intrinsic measurement using two 'events' as its parameters. An example for such an event may be the invocation of an operation. delay
is an extrinsic measurement. Of course, all of these specifications would include a precise
formal definition in TLA$^+$ according to the approach presented in this thesis.

Based on these definitions, the *component developer* of the StockSyndication
component could state

```
declare component StockSyndication {
  uses public Quote[] getStockData();
  uses public void sendFilteredData();

  always processing_time (getStockData,
                          sendFilteredData) <= 10ms;
```

```
}
```

expressing that he implemented the component such that it will take at most 10ms to filter a set of information from the information providers and hand it over to the client.

It may be a user requirement that all information should be at most 50ms old. This can be expressed by the *application designer* as follows:

```
declare service StockSyndication {
  uses public Quote[] getStockData();
  uses public void sendFilteredData();

  always delay (getStockData, sendFilteredData) <= 50ms;
}
```

The StockSyndication component will be executed in a component container. This container provides a container strategy that can manage components with a certain processing_time and provide a service with a certain maximum delay. A *container designer* provides the container and its specification:

```
declare container Cont (procTime, delayTime) {
  requires
    component C {
      uses operation op1;
      uses operation op2;
      always processing_time (op1, op2) <= procTime },
    resource CPU {canSchedule (TaskSet {procTime,
                                        delayTime});

  provides
    service CS implemented by C {
      always delay (op1, op2) <= delayTime;
    }
}
```

This specification reuses the abstract CPU specification from Sect. 2.8. This CPU specification has been provided by the *platform designer* of the platform on which the stock syndication application runs.

We now have a set of specifications provided independently by the different players developing parts of the system. The *application designer* can use these specifications to create a specification of the complete stock syndication system (we only show the parts related to the stock syndication component here):

```
system StockSyndication {
  instance StockSyndication s;
  instance RMS_CPU cpu;
  instance Cont container;

  container uses s, cpu;
  container provides StockSyndication service;
}
```

Finally, the application designer can use this specification to prove that the system is feasible; that is, that it provides the non-functional properties required by its users.

8.4   Summary

In this chapter we have demonstrated how the specification approach relates to a component-based software development process. We have, in particular, seen that the clear separation of the concerns of intrinsic, extrinsic, resource, and container-strategy specification fits very well into the separation of roles often found in CBSE: Component developers provide intrinsic specifications of their components, platform designers provide resource specifications of the resources available on their platforms, and container designers use container strategy specifications to describe the capabilities of their containers. Because all of these specifications are independent of each other, everybody can work in parallel. This is important in the context of a component market where different players provide components, containers, and platforms. Because our specification approach is structured in a composable manner, the application designer can combine the different specifications to derive a description of the complete system. He can use this description to prove feasibility of an application architecture. The measurement designer provides common terminology to all participants in the development process by defining a computational model and measurement specifications.

Part V

Summary

Chapter 9

Related Work

This thesis merges two movements in research: Component-Based Software Engineering (CBSE) and specification of non-functional properties. Consequently, we will review the literature from these two directions and show how the work done in this thesis fits into the picture.

9.1   Application Structuring Techniques

The topic of 'programming in the large' has received considerable interest over roughly the last thirty years. In the second half of the 1970s, software engineers introduced the notion of a *module*—a self-contained piece of software with a well-defined interface which can be combined with other modules to form larger systems—to improve control over increasingly large and complex software systems. In order to manage modules and describe their interconnections, various Module Interconnection Languages (MILs) [107, 142] were defined. We will not review these individual languages as they are of very limited relevance to this work other than forming a historic background to other, more relevant, work. It is, however, interesting to note that already in [142] the interface of a module was defined explicitly to include both the provided *and* the required resources of the module. This consideration of what a module or a component requires has been lost for some time and is still missing in many industrial component systems.

Later, MILs developed into Architecture Description Languages (ADLs) [90, 91, 92]. ADLs model systems as collections of *components,* which are generalisations of modules that can have more than one interface (typically called *ports* and modelled to varying degrees of formality), connected by *connectors* to form a component *configuration.* Connectors are modelled at varying degrees of formality in different ADLs, and can represent any kind of relationship between components: the more common call-relationship, where one component sends messages to another component, but also relations as complex as the sharing of a processor in a real-time system [126].

In the research community, the question 'What is a component?' has led to much discussion and controversy [27, 32, 38, 43, 62, 71, 140]. Nowadays, the definition given by Szyperski in [140] has become more or less accepted:

> "A software component is a unit of composition with contractually specified interfaces and explicit context dependencies only. A software component can be deployed independently and is subject to composition by third parties."
> [140]

Thus, software components are elements of software which need to be composed with other components to form an application. The different components in an application may be developed by different component developers. They can interact because there exists a

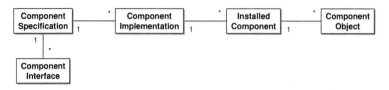

Figure 9.1: Component forms identified in [32]

standardised component runtime environment offering a space to live in to the components. This definition was first formulated at the 1996 European Conference on Object-Oriented Programming (ECOOP) as an outcome of the Workshop on Component-Oriented Programming, and has since become the definition of a component most accepted in the community. If we compare this definition to the component concept in ADLs, two differences become obvious:

1. "A software component is a unit of composition [and] can be deployed independently [...]" This implies that software components are physical components which are deployed into, and can be identified in, the running system. In contrast, ADL components are typically logical components, which do not necessarily map directly into actual runtime entities.

2. "A software component is [...] subject to composition by third parties." In contrast to Szyperski's software components, ADL components are only meant to structure a system, not to be an object of trade. Szyperski and others even envision a market of commercial off-the-shelf (COTS) components where companies no longer produce complete applications, but highly reusable software components which are sold to third parties. Deployment by third parties requires standardised *component runtime infrastructures* (often called *application servers* or *component containers*) with well-defined management interfaces. Examples for such standards include Enterprise JavaBeans (EJB) [95], the Common Object Request Broker (ORB) Architecture (CORBA) Component Model (CCM) [99], or Microsoft's Component Object Model (COM) [114].

It is interesting to see that the idea of a component market is also the motivation behind one of the earliest works on components: McIlroy's address at the NATO conference on Software Engineering 1968 in Garmisch [89]. He was the first to propose the notion of software built by assembling independently implemented software components, which would be available through a commercial component marketplace.

This part of the definition of a software component is, however, controversial. There are those who, like Szyperski, hold that the main benefit in CBSE lies in the ability to reuse pieces of code produced by third parties. On the other hand there are those— for example, Cheesman and Daniels [32]—who claim that the main benefit lies in a gain of flexibility through a strong modularisation and clean separation of concerns in the application structure. The concepts presented in this thesis provide benefits to both sides in this discussion. On the side of Cheesman and Daniels, this thesis shows concepts which allow a modular consideration of non-functional properties in addition to the functional properties. On the other side, as we have shown in Chapt. 8, the concepts allow non-functional specifications of component implementations to be written without knowledge of the contexts in which the component will be deployed. This is an important precondition for a component market.

Cheesman and Daniels [32] also introduce another important notion into the world of CBSE, namely the idea of *component forms*. They argue that the concept of a component varies depending on where in the project life cycle one is. Cheesman and Daniels distinguish the following four major component forms (*cf.* Fig. 9.1):

Component Specification The specification of the behaviour of a unit of software without reference to implementation decisions. Cheesman and Daniels use component interfaces and interface models to define component behaviour.

Component Implementation An actual implementation of a component specification. There can be various implementations for the same component specification as long as they exhibit the same externally observable behaviour.

Installed Component Component implementations are installed into a runtime environment where they will be executed. Although Cheesman and Daniels do not mention it, at this level it would be possible to further distinguish different configurations of the same component implementation, even installed into the same runtime environment.

Component Object Installed components are instantiated to create component objects—sometimes also called *component instances*—which are the entities actually handling any requests. The important thing here is that component objects can have a runtime state, so that two component objects of the same installed component can be distinguished by their respective runtime state.

Non-functional properties will typically be associated with component implementations. In particular, the concept of *intrinsic properties* introduced in this thesis applies to component implementations, capturing all those properties determined by the specific algorithms chosen to implement a component specification as opposed to the properties determined by how the component is used. However, it should be noted that there are some non-functional properties (in addition to the extrinsic properties) that can only be determined at the level of installed component, or even component object. In the response time example in Sect. 3.5.1 we assumed that we could determine the execution time for our component. However, execution time of a component heavily depends on the underlying hardware and runtime environment [33]—for example, the time it takes the specific Central Processing Unit (CPU) to execute certain machine code commands. We call such properties *machine-dependent* properties. The specific CPU to be used can only be determined for an installed component, but still there are some parts of the specification which can already be defined for a component implementation, so that these two aspects should be separated. Mraidha et al. [96] propose a static analysis technique based on symbolic execution to deal with machine dependency for performance properties. Furthermore, execution time very often depends on the specific data to be processed, because the component code may contain branching statements conditional on properties of the data to be processed. We call such properties *data-dependent properties*. Data-dependent properties can only be determined at the level of component objects, once it has been determined what data is to be processed. Sitaraman et al. [127] propose a generalised form of 'Big-O' notation to allow for a more precise expression of data-dependent properties. Their approach is concerned with providing functions as upper bounds for timing and space properties of components. However, they do not explain how such upper-bound functions can be transformed into actual values once the data to be processed is known. Another approach to mitigating the issue of data dependency has been proposed by Bondarev et al. [23]: The authors propose to use explicit application scenarios when describing and analysing non-functional properties. This way, they can provide one scenario for each different execution path, which may give a handle on dealing with data-dependent properties. Neither machine-dependent nor data-dependent properties have been covered in this thesis; both remain for future work. A slightly more detailed discussion of these properties will be given in Chapt. 11.

An important issue in the context of CBSE is *compositionality;* that is the ability to derive properties of a composed system directly from properties of its constituting elements (*viz* the components) without the need to analyse the inner structure of these elements. Werner and Richling [148] have identified five types of compositionality: invariant quality, bound quality, disappearing quality, emerging quality, and transferred quality. The common usage of the term *compositional* seems to imply invariant quality; that is cases where the composed system has the same property as its constituents. In the context of this work we are especially interested in compositionality of properties concerning the behaviour of systems. Writing component specifications in rely–guarantee style—first introduced by Cliff B. Jones [72]—has proven very useful for compositional specifications. Abadi and Lamport have developed a *composition theorem* [2, 5] which allows to compose temporal-logic rely–guarantee specifications expressed in Extended Temporal Logic of Actions (TLA$^+$) [78]. Both TLA$^+$ and the composition principle are an important basis for this thesis. Lund, Braber, and Stølen [85] have shown how these principles can be applied to compositional security risk analysis. Hu and Marcus [67] have studied compositionality from a graph-theoretic viewpoint. Their work is related to [148], but it is more formal than that, presenting 4 different types of compositionality. They distinguish between properties of components, properties of the composition structure (called the *fusion* in their terminology) and properties of the composed system. The relations between these properties determine the different types of compositionality. Cau and Collette [31] generalised the composition principle so that it works for state-based formalisms as well as for message-passing–based approaches.

In recent years, a new approach called service-based software engineering has gained increasing importance. This approach is closely related to role-based software engineering introduced by Reenskaug in 1995 [110]. The actual objects (or components) implementing a software system take a back seat while the features (or *services*) themselves and the *interaction patterns* required to realise them come to the fore. *Roles* and *role patterns* are used to model these interaction patterns. Objects or components are then derived by merging some of the roles. This thesis uses the concept of a service to distinguish between the user's view on a system and the internal view of the same system. Over and above this simple concept of a service, we do not use the more advanced concepts of service-based software engineering defining services as interaction patterns [76] or as partial component specifications [121]. We will therefore refrain from further reviewing the literature in this field.

9.2   Non-functional Properties

The research in the field can be classified into two major categories: work concerning nonfunctional a) requirements, and b) properties of actual software artefacts. While this thesis is in the latter area of non-functional properties, we will review some work from the former field, because the insights gained there are also applicable to the theory of non-functional properties. The area of non-functional properties can be further divided into three subareas:

1. *Basic Contract Concepts:* The work in this area is concerned with general observations of what is required to specify non-functional properties in a contractual manner. The authors do not make any choices about concrete specification languages or styles, but rather attempt to explain how the concept of design by contract (and variants thereof) can be extended to non-functional properties. Most of the work already specifically addresses component-based software.

2. *Characteristic-Specific Approaches:* These approaches introduce new, or extend existing, formal description techniques to deal with specific non-functional properties or classes of such properties.

3. *Measurement-Based Approaches:* Work in this area makes non-functional measurements (often called *characteristics*) first-class citizens of specifications, and thus allows any kind of non-functional property to be expressed as long as the underlying measurement can be formalised in the language. This is also the approach chosen in this thesis, because it is the approach with the greatest flexibility. At the same time, the high degree of generality makes it harder to make such specifications usable in property-specific analysis techniques.

The work of Hissam et al. at the Software Engineering Institute at Carnegie Mellon University does not quite fit into this classification. The authors describe Prediction-Enabled Component Technology (PECT) [66], which is a generic concept for combining a component technology with one or more analysis models for non-functional properties. The name PECT stands both for the generic concept and for an individual instantiation of the concept with a concrete component technology (e.g., EJB) and a concrete analysis model (e.g., Software Performance Engineering (SPE) [130, 133]). Their approach shows some similarity to the approach proposed in this thesis, but the authors do not strive for a formal description of the general notions. Instead, they focus on explaining the application of specific analysis techniques to specific component models using their framework. Also, whether their approach is measurement-based or characteristic-specific seems to depend largely on the concrete analysis technique used.

9.2.1 Non-functional Requirements

Chung et al. [36] present a framework for reasoning about design decisions which lead from non-functional requirements to the actual design and eventually the implementation. They use the notion of a *softgoal* to represent non-functional requirements, which may be imprecise, or subjective. Softgoals are related to each other as well as to *operationalisations* (representing possible realisations for a softgoal) to drive the software development process. Rationale for design decisions is explicitly recorded in the form of *claims.* In contrast to this approach, which is mainly concerned with transforming non-functional requirements into a running system, the approach presented in this thesis focuses on formally specifying non-functional properties of components and applications. The two approaches can be seen as complementary to each other in that the approach in this thesis can be used to formally describe the properties of components which can be used when building applications following the process described in [36].

Various authors have given classifications of non-functional requirements (e.g., [69, 87, 134] some more are also reviewed in [36]), which can equally well be applied to non-functional properties. We will not review all the different classifications and their differences, but rather concentrate on some common characteristics, which seem to be recurrent. We base our explanation on the classification given by Sommerville [134, pp. 130 *ff.*], which to us is the most comprehensive one. A graphical representation of this classification can be found in Fig. 9.2. Sommerville identifies three main classes of non-functional requirements:

1. *Product Requirements:* These are requirements directly concerning the software system to be built. They include requirements relevant to the customer—such as usability, efficiency, and reliability requirements—but also portability requirements which are more relevant to the organisation developing the software.

2. *Process Requirements:* Sometimes also called *organisational requirements,* these requirements "[...] are a consequence of organisational policies and procedures." They include requirements concerning programming language, design methodology, and similar requirements defined by the developing organisation.

3. *External Requirements:* These requirements come neither from the customer nor from the organisation developing the software. They include, for example, require-

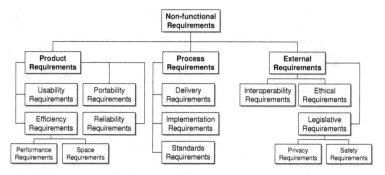

Figure 9.2: Classification of non-functional requirements defined by Sommerville (from [134, p. 131])

ments derived from legislation relevant to the field for which the software is being produced.

This classification is relevant in the context of this thesis because it allows us to express what kinds of non-functional properties our approach supports. It is clear that any classification of non-functional requirements that is not based on how these requirements can be elicited, can also be used as a classification of non-functional properties. Thus, simply replacing "requirements" by "properties" in Fig. 9.2 gives a classification of non-functional properties. We can classify the properties our approach can model as product properties. The examples we have shown in previous chapters typically cover performance properties.

It can also be seen that the classification is not complete. In particular, some product requirements—for example data quality requirements (accuracy of results, etc.)—cannot easily be included in this classification. For this reason, Bandelow [16] extended the classification to support more classes of product properties.

9.2.2 Basic Contract Concepts

Beugnard et al. [20] propose to distinguish 4 levels of contracts, each level depending on all the lower levels:

1. *Syntactic Level:* On this level are contracts describing syntactic interface structures of components. Essentially this covers anything that can be expressed in plain Interface Definition Language (IDL) [70]—that is, interfaces and operation signatures for both used and provided interfaces.

2. *Behavioural Level:* On this level the behaviour of the component is specified. Formal techniques usually employed on this level include pre- and post-conditions, invariants, temporal-logic specifications, and so on.

3. *Synchronisation Level:* On this level one can additionally conclude contracts about synchronisation properties such as reentrancy, mutually exclusive access, call protocols, the order of events emitted by the component, and so on.

4. *Quality of Service (QoS) Level:* This is the level where contracts on non-functional properties of components reside.

A contract can be negotiated the more flexibly the higher its level. It is obvious that syntactic contracts are as good as cast in stone once an interface has been defined. They form the basis for communication between the components so negotiating about them is all but impossible. On the other hand it is not unreasonable to expect components to be able to provide their services in a range of qualities so that clients can select between them and potentially even perform actual negotiations with bids and counter bids being exchanged between component and client. This thesis does not include concepts specifically made for contract negotiation. However, by defining a formal framework, we provide the basis on which negotiation partners can communicate precisely and unambiguously so that negotiations can be performed successfully.

Röttger and Aigner [116], and Selic [124] point out the importance of specifying the required resources in contracts in particular for real-time properties. They both enhance the structure of component contracts—which hitherto essentially described provided and used properties similar to rely–guarantee specifications as described above—by an explicit description of the resources the component requires from its environment. This leads to a layered system where components on one layer are connected through their used and provided properties and the layers are connected by resource associations between components on different layers. In this thesis we show that this approach is not directly feasible, because the resource demand of a component depends largely on how the component is used. We, therefore, separate the resource demand from the component specification and provide the container specification, which is responsible for determining the resource demand based on intrinsic properties of the component and usage decisions made by the runtime environment.

Reussner [111] proposed the concept of parametrised contracts, a more formal representation of dependencies between interfaces provided or required by a component. Parametrised contracts capture the dependencies inside a component as opposed to dependencies between components, which are expressed in more conventional contracts. The concept of parametrised contracts has originally been developed for functional specifications, but Reussner et al. [112, 113] have extended this work to also include non-functional properties. Specifically they have shown how reliability analysis can be supported by the specification of parametrised contracts using Markov-chain models. In accordance with the findings in this thesis parametrised contracts explicitly acknowledge the intra-component dependencies between provided and required properties. In this thesis these dependencies become visible in the expression of intrinsic properties of components, which can be viewed as relations connecting all required and provided properties of a specific component implementation. Moreover, Reussner et al. show for the specific case of reliability that it is important to distinguish between properties inherent to a component implementations and properties which emerge from using the component. This supports the distinction of intrinsic and extrinsic properties proposed in this thesis.

Chimaris and Papadopoulos [34] present a quite different notion of *contracts.* In their view, a contract consists of both a specification of a non-functional property and an aspect (in the sense of Aspect-Oriented Programming (AOP) [51, 73]) that can be used to guarantee that property at runtime. It is thus a combination of our notions of measurement, non-functional property, and container strategy.

9.2.3 Characteristic-Specific Approaches

There are quite a few approaches formalising specific non-functional dimensions. Because this thesis belongs to the strand of measurement-based approaches—to be reviewed in Sect. 9.2.4—we will not review this area in great detail. Instead we review only a few articles selected mostly for their breadth of variance.

Demairy et al. [46] define a kind of ADL which can be used to model multimedia applications. In the context of [46] such applications consist of multimedia components which exchange streams of what the authors call *data frames* via connectors. Components and connectors handle such streams following certain *protocols* (e.g., PCM, MPEG-2, TCP/IP). Apart from defining a data format (which can be considered a functional property), protocols also define timing behaviour—for example, how long it takes to handle a data frame using this protocol. The paper is concerned with two properties:

1. *Protocol Consistency:* This is essentially a functional correctness property which holds if components and connectors are connected in such a way that each component understands the protocol delivered by the adjoining connector and vice versa. Protocols are modelled by an enumeration of protocol identifiers, sets of which are associated with components and connectors. The authors define an ordering relationship over these protocol identifiers which represents compatibility relationships between protocols. This allows them to check any model for protocol consistency.

2. *Timeliness Consistency:* The paper covers probabilistic constraints over three characteristics: a) the time between two successive inputs of a data frame, b) synchronisation between streams received or sent on different ports, and c) the end-to-end delay between two ports. The authors define a set of rules which allow them to derive properties of composed systems from properties of their components, if the composition is constructed from so-called "serial" and "parallel" composition only.

The representation of protocols is very simple: A protocol is represented by a unique name, and knowledge of the meaning of timeliness properties is very much implicit. The approach is, therefore, good for its very narrow purposes, but it seems difficult to extend it to even slightly different properties.

Leue [81] proposes two extensions of temporal logic providing additional operators. He defines Metric Temporal Logic (MTL), which adds the new operators $\diamondsuit_I \Phi$, expressing that Φ holds in the current state or a future state within time interval I, and $\square_I \Phi$, stating that Φ holds in all states within time interval I. On this basis he defines Probabilistic MTL (PMTL) a probabilistic extension, adding the operator $\diamondsuit^p \Phi$, which asserts that with probability p Φ will eventually hold. From these basic operators he derives specification patterns for describing certain non-functional properties, such as response time, jitter, or stochastic reliability. Because the non-functional aspects have been tightly integrated with the operators of the language, evaluation of expressions in MTL or PMTL requires special algorithms. Standard evaluation techniques for temporal-logic expressions cannot be reused directly.

Timed Automata [13] are an extension of the classic theory of finite automata. They add a notion of dense time that can be sampled through so-called clocks. Clocks can be reset at any transition and store the amount of time that has passed since the last reset. Transitions can be guarded by constraints on clocks, the intuitive meaning being that the transition can only be taken when the associated clock constraints hold. Timed automata are good for modelling, and reasoning about, real-time systems where certain deadlines must be respected. However, the approach cannot be extended to other measurements, as the notion of time has been integrated directly into the semantic domain of the approach.

In the context of ongoing research on combining CBSE and SPE, Grassi and Mirandola [61] present a specification language tuned explicitly towards performance analysis of component-based systems. They use Unified Modelling Language (UML) [105] models which they annotate with stereotypes and tagged values according to the UML profile for schedulability, performance and time (SPT) specification [101] to express timing properties of individual operations. An interesting property of the language is that it unifies the concepts of components and resources into one, so that components and resources can all be connected through appropriate connectors. Resource usage is explicitly modelled as calls to services offered by the resource (e.g., statements of the form "CPU: execute five operations"). Then, the authors use activity diagrams to model relevant system states and the control flow (simply called "Flow" in the paper). From this "Flow" the authors can then extract information for performance analysis. Based on this language, Bertolino and Mirandola develop Component-Based SPE (CB-SPE) [18, 19], a component-based extension to SPE. CB-SPE is a process that supports performance analysis of component-based systems. It is structured into two layers: At the *component layer, component developers* implement components and annotate their interfaces with performance indices according to [101]. At the *application layer, system assemblers* use these components to construct systems, derive queuing-network models, and analyse the system performance based on these models. We classify this approach as a characteristic-specific approach, because it is specifically tuned for performance evaluation. However, the approach has some features of a measurement-based approach. In particular, the performance indices are measurements themselves, which are modelled in the semantic framework provided by [101]. Instead of [101], the authors could also use the semantic framework proposed in this thesis. This would come with the added benefit of a clear separation of intrinsic from extrinsic properties; that is, properties that component developers can provide from properties which only system assemblers can derive. At the moment, the authors use very vaguely defined *environment parameters* env-param to represent the usage context of the components. Even though [17, Sect. 5] presents a more detailed discussion of these parameters, their precise structure remains unclear.

Finally, we discuss research that can be seen as situated on the border between characteristic-specific and measurement-based approaches. Because *error functions* are a prominent element of this research we will refer to it as the *error-function–based approach*. Staehli presented, in his dissertation [135] (key results of which have also been reported on in [137]), a technique for specifying the QoS properties of multimedia systems. Staehli distinguishes three view points: content, view, and quality specifications. A *content* specification is a constraint on the possible data values at each point in a three-dimensional space. The three dimensions are: x and y, the planar dimensions of images (not used when specifying audio data), and t the time. Staehli defines various operators such as scale or clip which allow specifiers to construct content specifications by applying transformations to an original data source. A *view* specification describes how the logical space of content specifications is mapped to the space of physical devices. While this mapping considers scaling because of logical application requirements (e.g., viewing only a selected area of the frames, or rendering a video faster or slower than its original timing), it does explicitly not consider issues of discretisation or limited resource capacity. Therefore, the view specification defines an *ideal presentation* which could only be achieved on an non-discrete device with unlimited resources. In order to render multimedia content on an actual device, the system computes a *presentation plan*. This results in an *actual presentation*. The quality of a presentation is then given by the "distance" between actual and ideal presentation. To calculate this distance, Staehli first observes that it is impossible to uniquely derive the ideal presentation behind an actual presentation without additional information. The information missing is given through an *error model,* defining the possible ways in which the actual presentation can deviate from the ideal. Staehli defines *error functions* which can determine measurements such as jitter or shift in an actual presentation. An *error model* is a set of such error functions which are used together to model the quality of a multimedia presentation. Based on this work, Staehli, together with Eliassen, Aagedal, and Blair, proposed a QoS semantics for component-based systems [136]. This article follows a very similar line, modelling an *ideal execution* of a system on a machine with unlimited resources and an *actual execution* on an actual system. Again, an error model is used to describe the perceived quality of the actual execution. The properties supported by this semantics are timeliness and data-quality properties; that is, properties such as response time or accuracy of results. Although the paper has component-based systems in its title, it remains unclear what is specific to component-based systems about the approach. While both applications of Staehli's approach have been very characteristic-specific, the principle seems to be sufficiently general to work for other characteristics, too. The error functions are, in essence, a model of individual measurements, so a generalisation should not be too difficult. Therefore, it would be possible to argue that this approach is in fact measurement-based. We still classify it as characteristic-specific, because so far the authors have not attempted to generalise it into a purely measurement-based approach.

However, we strongly consider this a border-line case.

9.2.4 Measurement-Based Approaches

The approaches combined under this heading all make characteristics first-class citizens of a specification; that is, they allow characteristics to be defined as part of a specification. We call them measurement-based, because characteristics as defined by these approaches are essentially measurements in the sense of measurement theory (see, e.g., [55] for a quick overview). The basic terms employed in this strand of research have been standardised by the International Standardisation Organisation (ISO) and the International Telecommunication Union (ITU) [69]. The most important terms are:

QoS Characteristic "A quantifiable aspect of QoS, which is defined independently of the means by which it is represented or controlled." For the reasons stated above, we also use the term *measurement* to mean characteristic.

QoS Category "A group of user requirements that leads to the selection of a set of QoS requirements." Although it is tempting to view QoS categories as a representation of the classes discussed in Sect. 9.2.1, the definition is actually intended to classify applications into groups with commensurable types of non-functional requirements.

QoS Management "Any set of activities performed by a system or communications service to support QoS monitoring, control and admission."

QoS Mechanism "A specific mechanism that may use protocol elements, QoS parameters or QoS context, possibly in conjunction with other QoS mechanisms, in order to support establishment, monitoring, maintenance, control, or enquiry of QoS."

QoS Policy "A set of rules that determine the QoS characteristics and QoS management functions to be used."

The approach presented in this thesis fits well into the framework provided by these definitions. We, essentially, give formal semantics to QoS characteristics (namely as intrinsic and extrinsic measurements), and to QoS Management, QoS Mechanism, and QoS Policy (namely the container specification). In addition to presenting a formal representation of these concepts, we also give a more detailed analysis and identify more fine-grained distinctions within these definitions. The source for these distinctions is our requirement to provide a semantics specifically targeted to component-based software systems. QoS categories are little more than a convenience grouping mechanism, which has no semantic significance, so we do not support this in our approach.

Measurement-based approaches can be categorised into two groups:

1. *Predicate-Based Approaches:* These approaches use measurements to formulate constraints on the system behaviour. A system either fulfils these constraints or it does not fulfil them, so the underlying semantics is very similar to that of functional specifications: For each system we can decide whether it is a correct implementation of the specification, but over and above that we cannot compare different implementations.

2. *Optimisation-Based Approaches:* These approaches deviate from predicate-based approaches in viewing the achievement of non-functional properties (typically called *quality* in this context) as an optimisation problem. For each system we can still analyse whether it is a correct implementation of a specification, but in addition, we can compare two systems A and B, and, for example, state that A *is a better implementation than* B. Such statements are of course only valid in relation to some *objective function*. Objective functions are typically given as *utility functions* (or *value functions*, *cf.* [52] for an overview) representing users' or clients' preferences on different quality combinations.

The work presented in this thesis falls into the first category, although we believe it is general enough to be extended to support optimisation-based approaches, too. This will be discussed in some more detail in the outlook in Chapt. 11.

Another interesting distinction is based on the degree of formality with which the measurements can be defined in the various approaches. We can distinguish two major cases: A first group of approaches defines measurements as functions of some domain without providing a semantic framework relative to which the meaning of each measurement could be formally defined. We say that these approaches have a *weak semantics,* because measurements are barely more than names for values. The second group of approaches provides a semantic framework—albeit the degree of formality may vary between approaches—and, thus, allows specifiers to define the meaning of measurements formally and precisely. We say that these approaches have a *strong semantics.* It is one of the aims of the approach presented in this thesis to provide a framework for the formal definition of measurements, thus, it is an approach with strong semantics.

We will now review some predicate- and some optimisation-based approaches. For each approach we will also indicate whether it has a strong or weak semantics.

Predicate-Based Approaches

One of the earliest works that proposes a measurement-based specification language for non-functional properties of component-based systems has been written by Xavier Franch [56]. It proposes a language called *NoFun.* The main concept of this language is the *non-functional attribute.* Franch distinguishes basic attributes and derived attributes. While derived attributes are formally specified in terms of other (basic or derived) attributes, basic attributes are not formally specified. They remain names for values, their semantics can only be expressed outside NoFun. Franch's approach therefore is an approach with weak semantics. Nonetheless it already contains many of the concepts found in modern predicate-based approaches.

Abadi and Lamport [4] present an approach which integrates time as a flexible variable into temporal logic specifications. Although this approach is limited to the expression of timeliness properties, we classify it as a measurement-based approach, because—for example in contrast to [81] discussed above—the individual measurements are explicitly modelled as part of the specification (using normal flexible variables of the specification language), and are thus first-class citizens. Also, the approach can be extended to arbitrary measurements, which is what we have done in this thesis. Abadi and Lamport use standard temporal logic as their formal framework in which they also define their measurements. We can, therefore, classify them as an approach with a strong semantics.

In his thesis, Aagedal defines Component Quality Modelling Language (CQML) [1], a specification language for non-functional properties of component-based systems. The definition remains largely at the syntactic level, semantic concepts are mainly explained in plain English without formal foundations. The language is based on the definitions given in [69]. Arbitrary measurements can be defined as quality_characteristics, which have a domain and a semantics given in a values clause. The approach has a strong semantics by our definition of the term, even though the degree of formality of the semantic framework is comparatively low. We have proposed a more explicit representation of the semantic framework in previous work [117, 118] which eventually led to the concept of context models presented in this thesis.

The UML has developed into a well-accepted language for specifying software systems. Consequently, several researchers have investigated using UML to model measurements and non-functional properties of software. Most important among these approaches is probably the UML SPT profile [101], which is based on ideas previously presented by Selic [124]. This standard profile defines a meta-model for the specification of performance- and scheduling-related parameters in UML models. Although it is comparatively flexible, and not specific to one characteristic, it does not consider issues related to CBSE, such as independent development of components and applications, or runtime management of resource allocation and component usage by component runtime environments. Another interesting approach has been chosen by Skene et al. [128]. They present SLAng a language for precisely specifying Service Level Agreements (SLAs). Their work is based on the precise UML (pUML) definition of the semantics of UML [39]. There, UML-like (meta-)models are used to specify both the syntax and the semantics of a modelling language. SLAng leverages the flexibility inherent to such a meta-modelling approach to allow specifiers to define measurements of their own, complete with a tailor-made semantic domain and semantic mapping. Because it uses UML as its semantic framework, it has a strong semantics. Because the semantics of UML itself is not formally defined, the degree of formality of SLAng definitions remains very low.

Optimisation-Based Approaches

Liu et al. [84] present a task-based model to describe QoS properties of applications. The tasks are considered to be so-called *flexible tasks* that "[...] can trade the amounts of time and resources [they] require to produce [their] results for the quality of the results [they] produce." Each task is described by a *reward profile,* which relates the quality of incoming data, the quality of data produced, and the amount of resources used while processing. Resource demand is considered only where it can be adjusted during execution. The model is completely oriented towards adaptation, admission control is not considered. In contrast, we defined the notion of a *feasible system* (*cf.* Sect. 3.4) which captures admission control. If tasks are composed to form applications, they interact in a producer–consumer pattern. Consumers formulate their expectations on quality of incoming data using *value functions*—that is, objective functions over relevant quality measurements. A QoS management system then strives to allocate resources to tasks such that the value functions of corresponding consumers are maximised. [84] uses a weak semantics of measurements.

Sabata et al. [120] also present a task-based model. System specifications are composed from *metrics* and *policies,* and are written from three perspectives:

1. *Application Perspective:* In this perspective one specifies the properties of one application without considering other applications, which might contend for the same resources. The specification uses *metrics,* which are essentially measurement definitions, and *benefit functions*—objective functions used to formulate constraints over *metrics.*

2. *Resource Perspective:* This perspective serves to determine the total resource demand for each individual resource.

3. *System Perspective:* In this perspective one specifies how resource conflicts between different applications can be resolved.

Again, the approach uses a weak semantics. However, the authors provide a classification of different types of *metrics,* so that some additional information about the semantics of a measurement can be derived from its placement in this classification.

In his dissertation [80], Lee presents another approach to modelling non-functional properties of applications and systems as an optimisation problem. In contrast to the two approaches described before, this approach does not consider the internal structure of applications, but is only concerned with balancing the resource allocation to applications contending for shared resources. The approach also features a weak semantics, defining measurements (called *quality dimensions*) as name–value pairs. For each measurement, the author defines an ordering relationship over the value domain. Resource demand and resource allocations are also simplified to name–value pairs. For each application Lee defines a *resource profile* as a relationship between allocated resources and delivered quality. The quality specification of an application is given by a *task profile,* the main part of which is a *utility function* representing the desired quality to be produced by this application. These utility functions are then combined in a weighted sum to form the *system utility*. The system utility is the global objective function to be maximised by allocating resources to applications. Lee has developed several algorithms to solve such optimisation problems efficiently and with sufficient accuracy. The notions of task and system utility are very close to our notion of extrinsic specifications, which makes Lee's approach an interesting candidate for integration with our approach. This would allow our approach to be extended to support optimisation-based techniques, as well as providing a strong semantics to Lee's approach.

9.3 Related Projects

In this section, we review selected research projects working in related areas.

Quite a few projects consider the realisation of component infrastructure supporting non-functional properties. The Quality of Service-Aware Component Architecture (QuA) [14] project at SIMULA in Oslo aims to build a component runtime environment supporting *platform-managed QoS*. In their view, components have a functional specification (called the *QuA type*), an implementation, and a non-functional specification using the error functions introduced in [136]. Clients request a service by specifying a QuA type and some non-functional requirements. Based on this information the runtime environment selects components and QoS-management algorithms to instantiate an application providing the requested service. Our approach is more focused on specification and could be useful as a complimentary technique to the platform realisation in QuA.

In the context of the ADAPTIVE Communication Environment (ACE) project, the distributed object computing group at Washington University, St. Louis (Missouri, USA) have built The ACE ORB (TAO) [123], an efficient ORB with support for real-time guarantees implementing Real-Time CORBA (RT-CORBA) [100, 122]. In another project based on this work—Component Integrated ACE ORB (CIAO) [37]—an implementation of CCM providing support for guaranteeing QoS and real-time properties has been built.

The Components with Quantitative properties and Adaptation (COMQUAD) [8, ?] project aimed at developing specification techniques, runtime support, and development technology for component-based applications with special focus on non-functional properties. The project developed a container architecture, Extended Component Quality Modelling Language (CQML$^+$) [117] an extension of Jan Aagedal's CQML [1] specification language, an integration of this language into UML, and a first component-oriented development process. This thesis has its origins in the COMQUAD project.

The Metropolis project [15, and references therein] defines an integrated development approach for computer systems based on formal methods. The project uses a meta-model based on the concepts *process, port,* and *medium.* So-called *quantities* and *quantity managers* are used to represent non-functional properties of a system. System descriptions can be structured into layers—called platforms in Metropolis. Each layer consists of a network of interacting processes and media, and can make use of services provided by the underlying platform. Many of the concepts are related to work done in this thesis. However, Metropolis does not directly support CBSE. Also, there is only one meta-model which must be used by all specifications following the Metropolis approach. This means that only those properties which can be represented using this meta-model (mainly performance properties) can be used. In contrast, in this thesis we allow designers to freely define context models.

9.4   Summary

In this chapter we have reviewed literature from two main research areas: CBSE and the theory of non-functional properties of software systems. We demonstrated that while research in the area of CBSE has advanced quite far to this day, the theory of non-functional properties still leaves many open questions. In particular, in the area of measurement-based approaches to the specification of non-functional properties of software systems (Sect. 9.2.4), a commonly accepted approach to the semantics of such specifications is missing. In this thesis we aim to close this gap by providing a semantic framework for the specification of non-functional properties of component-based software.

Chapter 10

Conclusions

In this chapter we summarise the work done in this thesis and show how we have solved the problems we identified in Chapt. 1 and how we have provided the contributions we claimed there.

10.1 General Conclusions

In this thesis, we have studied the specification of non-functional properties in a component-based setting. The major driving force for our work was the fact that there are different parties involved, who have only limited knowledge, but need to communicate effectively to produce a complete system. We started from the realisation that component-based systems—and in particular component markets—require precise and formal specifications of all relevant properties of components, and, consequently, also for their non-functional properties. However, existing specification languages for non-functional properties were lacking in at least two ways: 1) they did not have a formal semantics, and 2) their conceptualisations were often not useful in the context of component-based systems.

In our studies we first found that we need to provide a formal basis for a common terminology to be used by the different parties involved in a component market. To this end, we have introduced *measurements*—formal definitions of non-functional dimensions. To anchor measurements in a common formal system for all parties involved, we have introduced *computational models* as a representation of the relevant structures of components and application systems. Computational models are agreed on by domain experts for one domain. Non-functional properties can then be expressed as constraints over measurements applied to a specific component or system.

We have, further, found that it is important to distinguish at least two types of non-functional properties: *intrinsic* and *extrinsic properties*. The former depend only on the implementation of a component, the latter depend on how it is being used. Thus, intrinsic properties can be specified by component developers without regard for possible usage scenarios. Extrinsic properties can be specified by application designers once the usage scenario for each component is known. The transformation from the intrinsic properties of individual components to the extrinsic properties of complete systems is done by *component containers* using *container strategies*. These can be specified in container specifications by container designers. Container strategies may have to use resources of the underlying system to provide certain extrinsic properties.

To evaluate our framework we have used it to define a semantic mapping for a sublanguage of CQML+—a current specification language for component-based systems. Through this, we have identified some deficiencies in CQML+, which can now be fixed based on the insights gained when defining the semantic mapping. Further, we have used our formal specifications to derive analysis parameters for a (exemplary) performance analysis using the *SPE·ED* tool. The approach can also be used to formally describe the inputs and outputs of analysis techniques for non-functional properties in component-based settings. Last but not least, we have shown how our approach integrates into a software development process for component-based systems.

In [125], Mary Shaw presents, among other things, a classification of software engineering research. She distinguishes the following aspects:

Research Setting This covers the essential questions the research strives to answer. Shaw distinguishes studies of feasibility, characterisation, methods and means, generalisation, and selection; giving corresponding generic research questions for each. This thesis fits best into the research setting of "Characterisation". Some corresponding research questions are: What are the important characteristics of X? What, exactly, do we mean by X? In our case, we can set 'non-functional specification of component-based systems' for X.

Research Approach, Method, and Product This covers the variety of approaches taken in software engineering research. Shaw distinguishes them by their tangible results, as follows: qualitative or descriptive model, technique, system, empirical predictive model, analytic model. Our results are "Analytic Models" where they have been developed to full formality, but some of our research has also resulted in "Descriptive Models", because full-fledged formalisation was not currently feasible.

Validation Technique With this aspect, Shaw refers to the techniques used by researchers to convince their audience of the validity of their results. She identifies the following strategies that have been used successfully in the past: persuasion, implementation, evaluation, analysis, experience. In this thesis we have used a mixture of validation techniques. In particular:

- "Analysis" has been used in the formal proofs we provide.
- We have used a form of "Implementation" when presenting the semantics of μCQML in Chapt. 6.
- We have used "Persuasion" when we argued in Chapt. 8 that the specification approach was a good fit with software development processes. Also, all of the examples we provided throughout the thesis are a form of validation by persuasion.
- All in all, we have used "Evaluation" by ticking off our check-list of requirements on our approach in Chapts. 6–8.

There is a certain emphasis on persuasion in our validation strategy. This is only natural as this work stands at the very beginning of a lot of work still to be done in the research area. As the field evolves, we will see work that can be evaluated more formally or based on experience from actual practical use. Our intent was an initial formal characterisation of the field. Persuasion, implementation, analysis, and evaluation appear a good set of validation techniques for this goal.

10.2   Contributions of the Thesis and Problems Solved

In Chapt. 1, we have listed the contributions we claim for this thesis and the problems we claim the thesis solves. In the following, we list these claims again and show how and where they are accounted for in the thesis:

- *Problems Identified (cf. Sect. 1.2):*

– *Existing approaches specialise on one type of property*
One of the problems identified was that most existing approaches focus on one property or on a small set of closely related properties. Our approach is open to any kind of non-functional property, as long as it can be represented in a behavioural specification of the components and the system using temporal logic. We have shown through examples some of the properties which can be handled. These included, in particular, time-related and accuracy-related properties. In general, the approach should be usable for any measurable property relating to a product requirement (as defined by Sommerville [134, pp. 130 *ff*.] (also *cf.* Page 130)). In particular, all properties typically classified as QoS should be treatable by our approach. Work by Lund et al. [85] allows for great optimism that the approach should also be useful for security properties.

– *Existing approaches lack formal semantics*
Another problem identified was that many existing approaches lack a formal basis. In particular, we discussed that the semantics of CQML$^+$ was not entirely clear. Our approach uses formal means throughout to define the concepts identified and to use them for specifying systems. In addition, in Chapt. 6 we have shown how our approach can be used to provide formal semantics for an existing non-functional specification language.

– *Existing approaches often use inadequate concepts, in particular in the areas of resource specification and separation of knowledge*
Finally, we identified some inadequate concepts in existing languages, in particular in the area of specification of resource demand. Our approach introduces separate resource specifications (*cf.* Sect. 3.3.2), which are bound into system specifications through specifications of container strategies that use certain resources to provide certain extrinsic properties. This approach enables a precise and independent specification of resources. Further, it respects the limited knowledge of the various parties involved in a component market, separating their differing concerns into different specifications.

• *Major Contributions (cf. Sect. 1.4.1):*

1. *The thesis provides an approach for the formal specification of non-functional properties of component-based systems*
Chapter 3 presents the basic concepts of our approach. We use TLA$^+$ throughout to formalise our concepts. The approach distinguishes four different parties and, consequently, four different types of specifications: component developers provide specifications of intrinsic properties, container designers provide specifications of container strategies, platform designers provide specifications of available resources, and application designers provide systems specifications, pulling everything together and describing a system with services with certain extrinsic properties.
We have shown through various examples how this approach can be used for the formal specification of non-functional properties of component-based systems. The individual specifications provided by the various parties involved can be composed allowing reasoning about properties of the system as a whole. The composition principle of Abadi and Lamport [2, 5] forms the basis for this. In Sect. C.3.3 we have shown a formal proof of feasibility (a formal property of a system introduced in Sect. 3.4) for an example specification.
As can be seen from our discussions in Chapt. 9, to the best of our knowledge, this is the first such approach available.

2. *The thesis shows that and how non-functional properties can be understood formally as constraints over history-determined variables based on an abstract context-model state machine*

Sect. 3.2.2 presents our definition of a measurement. Non-functional properties are later defined as constraints over measurements. The definition of a
measurement we use in this thesis is essentially an adjusted version of the definition of a history-determined variable from [4]. Thus, measurements are really
history-determined variables as defined by Abadi and Lamport.

In the sections following that definition, we discuss how model mappings can
be employed to relate generic, abstractly defined measurements to concrete application models and their parts. The mapping is defined such that the measurement definition 'observes' the application model and performs corresponding
transitions whenever the application model performs a transition. In analogy
to the definition of a history-determined variable, however, associating a measurement with an application model does not constrain the set of behaviours
allowed by that application model. Such a constraint is only implied by a constraint over the measurement—that is, by specifying a non-functional property.

We give formal rules for the definition of such a model mapping, but also show
that the set of meaningful model mappings cannot be completely characterised
formally. An important result is that we cannot define a completely generic
specification language for non-functional properties, but instead have to at least
agree on a domain, for which we need to define (and agree on) a formal computational model characterising the domain. This is in contrast to some thoughts
in current work on non-functional specification languages (in particular [1]),
stating that the languages proposed are indeed completely generic.

3. *The thesis improves understanding of the concepts underlying non-functional
specifications in particular in the context of CBSE*

Of course, whether the thesis indeed improves the understanding of its readers
must be left for them to judge. However, the thesis introduces concepts that
have not been discussed in the community before and that enable precise description of non-functional properties in a component-based setting—in particular, the notion of separating intrinsic and extrinsic properties, the concept of a
container as a collection of container strategies, each of which is responsible for
a specific set of non-functional properties, and the definition of non-functional
properties as constraints over formally defined measurements. It can, thus, be
said to improve our current understanding of the domain. Also, feedback from
the community regarding the work presented here shows the relevance of the
ideas therein to an international research community.

- *Secondary Contributions (cf. Sect. 1.4.2):*

  1. *The thesis defines the semantics of a sub-language of CQML$^+$*

     Chapter 6 defines μCQML, by reducing CQML$^+$ to its core concepts and using
     sets and functions for the abstract syntax. Based on this definition, we provide
     a mapping function relating μCQML expressions and TLA$^+$ specifications fol-
     lowing our specification approach. In this way, our specification approach is
     used for defining the semantics of μCQML.

  2. *The thesis provides for formal description of analysis methods*

     Chapter 7 discusses the general approach for formally specifying the inter-
     face of an analysis method. The chapter also shows an example of such a
     specification, namely Example 7.1 for use-case–based performance analysis of
     component-based applications.

  3. *The thesis shows how non-functional specifications can be embedded into a
     component-oriented software development process*

     Chapter 8 discusses a component-oriented software development process and
     how the non-functional specifications proposed in this thesis can be used in this

process. In particular, we present a number of specialised roles, each of which is responsible for one type of specification as proposed in this thesis.

4. *The thesis gives a comprehensive overview and classification of related literature*

   Chapter 9 "Related Work" provides an overview of the literature in the component community as well as on research in the field of non-functional specification. In the latter field it provides a classification of research into work on "non-functional requirements", "basic contract concepts", "characteristic-specific approaches", and "measurement-specific approaches". The latter are further categorised into "predicate-based" and "optimisation-based" approaches.

5. *The thesis introduces the notion of a modular component runtime environment consisting of container strategies*

   Section 3.1 introduces a system model where components are executed by a runtime environment called a *container*. This concept is not new *per se*. However, we propose such a container use a set of so-called *container strategies* to manage the components and in particular to support various non-functional properties. Thus, we propose a modularisation of containers, where each container strategy is responsible for transforming a specific set of intrinsic properties into a specific set of extrinsic properties, using a certain amount of resources. Container strategies are specified through so-called *container specifications*.

6. *The thesis shows that and why formal specifications techniques for non-functional properties can never be completely generic*

   Section 3.2.3 shows that in every domain in which non-functional specifications are needed, first of all a common basis for communication must be agreed on. Such a common basis can be given by a formal computational model. Providing such a computational model restricts the set of non-functional properties that can be expressed, because every formal definition of a measurement must take recourse on this computational model. Thus, if a basic concept has not been defined in the computational model, it cannot be introduced later in a measurement definition. Measurement definitions can only introduce concepts that result from a combination of other basic concepts defined in the computational model.

Chapter 11

Outlook

In this thesis, we have proposed an approach for formal specifications of non-functional properties of component-based systems. Of course, there are still areas not covered by our approach. These areas imply a need for further research and subsequent refinement of the specification techniques here proposed. The following is a list of questions that remain for future study. We do not claim that the list is complete, but have attempted some degree of classification of the issues:

1. *Extensions and refinements of the formalism:* This area covers issues not yet covered by our approach or issues covered insufficiently:

   - The major driving force for our specification approach was the fact that the different parties in a component market possess only partial knowledge of the final application. We have designed our specifications such that each party can provide independent specifications using only the knowledge available. This is one form of separation of concerns [47]. In particular, our approach helps to separate the concerns of the component developer and the application designer.

     There are, however, other concerns which also need to be separated. Experience tells us about at least two more concern dimensions that have not been covered in this thesis (we identify them by the roles involved):

     (a) *Component Developer and Platform Designer:* The machinery on which a piece of software is executed, of course, has an influence on its non-functional properties. Some of these influences have been covered by our separation of intrinsic and extrinsic properties through the introduction of resource specifications and incorporation of these through container strategies.

         However, this only covers the available resources, but not their *physical properties.* The most prominent example is probably the speed of a CPU: The performance of an application depends on intrinsic performance properties of the components implementing the application, on the available resources and the scheduling decisions made, but also on the time it takes the CPU to execute each machine-code instruction. In our approach, the latter information must be factored directly into the component specification. It would be much more desirable to separate these concerns into specifications that are *machine independent* (in the same way that intrinsic specifications are context-of-use independent) and specifications that provide *machine-dependent* information.

         As has been discussed in Chapt. 9, some work in this field has been done in the community. For the most part, however, this is still an open research area.

(b) *Component Developer, Application Designer, and Data Provider:* In some
applications, the specific data to be processed can have an enormous im-
pact on non-functional properties of the application. For example, [115]
shows, among other things, that for the same video decoder, decoding time
per frame can vary from about 4–11 ms for one video to about 30–130 ms
for another video. This means, execution times for decoding videos can
vary by as much as an order of magnitude depending on the specific data
to be processed.

Such behaviour cannot be modelled with our approach. Again, we need a
separation of specifications that are *data independent* from such that provide *data-dependent* information. Chapter 9 lists a few initial examples of
work in this direction, but mostly, this is again an open research area.

- The specification approach we have presented in this thesis is a predicate-based
approach (*cf.* Sect. 9.2.4). In Chapt. 1 we said that one important characteristic
of non-functional properties is the fact that they are typically non-BOOLEAN.
The approach presented in this thesis essentially reduces the problem of specifying such complex constraints to one of specifying BOOLEAN constraints.
When assembling applications from components, this kind of constraint is very
useful because it allows us to check whether two components can be composed
to produce a system that maintains some non-functional property.

  However, if our interest lies in using a minimum of available resources while
providing a maximum in terms of extrinsic non-functional properties and user
satisfaction, we need to follow a different approach. Here, optimisation-based
approaches (*cf.* Sect. 9.2.4) can be useful. Some work exists on optimisation-
based approaches, but the formalisations defined do not respect the separation
of concerns between the different parties involved in developing component-
based applications.

  Because of its component-oriented nature, the approach of Lee [80] is an interesting candidate for merging with our approach. Such a merged approach
would result in a formally defined specification technique for optimisation-
based specifications.

- In this thesis, we have used TLA$^+$ as our formal basis. As we have discussed
in Sect. 1.6, this limits our expressive possibilities because TLA$^+$ is not very
good at expressing stochastic behaviours. For some non-functional properties
stochastic definitions may be required.[1] Work presented in [85] allows optimism that some stochastic non-functional properties can still be expressed with
TLA$^+$. We also believe that the concepts identified in this thesis can be expressed in other formalisms, too, maybe even in such formalisms that allow for
expressing stochastic properties. Whether this is indeed true, however, needs
to be studied in future work.

- Using more than one container strategy for one component can become problematic when different parts of the same component have different intrinsic
properties or need to provide for different extrinsic properties. A problem arises
when each property on its own could be treated by a container strategy, the different strategies, however, make conflicting decisions about resource allocation
for the component. This has been partially discussed in Chapt. 5, but a lot
of work still remains to be done. For example, consider our `Counter` component from Sect. 3.5.1. Assume that we have specified execution time for
`increment()` in addition to `getValue()`. We are interested in a specific
response time for `increment()`. This requires that we select a container

---

[1] Note that this does not apply for things like 'average response time'. These *statistic* derivations can be
modelled using temporal logic.

strategy that can manage this operation. We have, thus, two container strategies managing the `Counter` component—one for `getValue()` and another one for `increment()`. If our clients want to invoke both operations of one instance of the component, these two strategies manage the same instance. Resource allocation for the component can only happen once, however. Thus, conflicts can arise. This can be viewed as a form of inconsistency in the component specification. It is, however, not clear whether such specifications can be avoided and whether they can be identified and fixed already by component developers or whether they require collaboration of the other parties. Also, it is unclear, what should be done with components with a specification of this type. All these questions remain for future research. However, the approach proposed in this thesis at least provides the terminology that can be used when studying them.

- As we saw in Sect. 3.5.2 ("A Data Quality Example"), some measurements are more difficult to define than others. The problem with the accuracy measurement was that the *definition* of the measurement depended on the data to be processed. This made this measurement more complicated to specify than, for example, response time. While the latter could be specified completely independently from any concrete application, the definition of accuracy needed to take into account the type and semantics of data to be processed by the concrete application. The definition of accuracy mixes meta-modelling layers, the definition of response time does not. How to deal with such measurements and whether there are other cases that complicate specification are questions for further research.

- In Sect. 3.3.3 we have mentioned in passing that it would be interesting to represent container strategies as rewrite rules over non-functional specifications. We have not followed this research path further in this thesis. However, we still consider it to be a worthwhile area for future work. In particular, it would be interesting to understand what types of container strategies can be expressed in this manner, whether both styles of expressing them can be mixed, and how reasoning capabilities are affected by such a hybrid approach.

2. *Extensions and refinement of other systems:* This refers to changes required to other systems, such as runtime environments or specification languages:

- We have postulated component runtime environments consisting of a set of container strategies, each of which is responsible for a set of non-functional properties. Such runtime environments do not yet exist. Although examples for container strategies can be found in the literature, the actual development of prototypical strategy-based containers remains as future work.

- In Chapt. 6 we have defined a semantic mapping for μCQML. In defining this mapping, we have identified a number of deficiencies of μCQML—and by extension of CQML$^+$. It would be interesting and necessary to use this knowledge to define an extended version of CQML$^+$ that would overcome the problems identified. The concepts have been formally defined in this thesis. What would be needed is to provide appropriate notation in CQML$^+$ for these concepts and to formally define the semantics of such notation using the approach shown in Chapt. 6. The pseudo-language we have used in Chapts. 1 and 8 can be used as a basis for such a notation.

A lot of work remains to be done. The most important contribution of this thesis is the precise and formal definition of basic concepts. This provides the tools for discussing and understanding these further issues.

Part VI

Appendices

Appendix A

Acronyms

This appendix defines all acronyms used in this thesis:

ACE   ADAPTIVE Communication Environment, an object-oriented framework for developing components for client–server applications

ADL   Architecture Description Language [90, 91, 92]

AOP   Aspect-Oriented Programming [51, 73]

ASM   Abstract State Machine [25]

CASE   Computer-Aided Software Engineering. This refers to tool-support, typically including modelling and code-generation capabilities.

CBSE   Component-Based Software Engineering

CB-SPE   Component-Based $^\uparrow$SPE [18, 19]

CCM $^\uparrow$CORBA Component Model [99]

CIAO   Component Integrated $^\uparrow$ACE $^\uparrow$ORB [37]

COM   Microsoft's Component Object Model [114]

COMQUAD Components with Quantitative properties and Adaptation [8, ?], a project at Technische Universität Dresden, Germany

CORBA   Common Object Request Broker (ORB) Architecture

COTS   commercial off-the-shelf, this refers to the concept of a component market, where pre-fabricated, standard components can be bought and used in third-party applications. Components are no longer custom-made for a specific application, rather, specific applications are built from the standard components available.

CPU   Central Processing Unit

CQML   Component Quality Modelling Language [1]

CQML$^+$ Extended Component Quality Modelling Language [117]

DAX   Deutscher Aktienindex, a German stock index.

DROpS   Dresden Real-Time Operating System [65]

ECOOP   European Conference on Object-Oriented Programming

EJB   Enterprise JavaBeans [95]

IDL   Interface Definition Language [70]

IPC   Interprocess Communication, a technique to allow communication between processes running in different address spaces, typically on the same machine. Remote Procedure Call (RPC) is a special case of IPC, where the processes reside on different machines.

ISO   the International Standardisation Organisation

ITU   the International Telecommunication Union, another standardisation organisation.

MDA   Model-Driven Architecture [75, 104], a standard defined by the Object Management Group (OMG) describing a model-based development technique, where platform-independent models are transformed into platform-dependent ones and finally into source code.

MDAC   Model-Driven Architecture (MDA) [75, 104] component [21] (also [†]MDA Tool Component (MDATC)[106]), a technology for packaging model-transformation know-how in a computer-executable form.

MIL   Module Interconnection Language [107, 142]

MOF   Meta-Object Facility [102]

MTL   Metric Temporal Logic an extension to temporal logic defined in [81] adding operators for writing timed specifications.

NASDAQ   National Association of Securities Dealers Automated Quotations, an American electronic stock exchange.

OCL   the Object Constraint Language [103], a textual sublanguage of the [†]UML allowing for the specification of first-order constraints.

OMG   Object Management Group, an industrial standardisation body in computer science. The OMG is the creator of the [†]UML standard.

ORB   Object Request Broker

OWL-S   Semantic Web Specification Language for Web Services [30]

PECT   Prediction-Enabled Component Technology [66]

PMTL   Probabilistic [†]MTL an extension to temporal logic defined in [81] adding operators for writing probabilistic specifications.

pUML   precise [†]UML a group of researchers working to provide a precise and formal basis for the [†]UML

QML   Quality Modelling Language [57], a specification language for [†]QoS. QML is the predecessor language for [†]CQML.

QoS   Quality of Service

QuA   Quality of Service-Aware Component Architecture [14], a project at SIMULA in Oslo building a component runtime environment with platform-managed [†]QoS.

RMS   Rate-Monotonic Scheduling [83]

RPC   Remote Procedure Call

RT-CORBA Real-Time †CORBA [100, 122], an extension of the †CORBA standard supporting real-time applications.

SLA   Service Level Agreement

SPE   Software Performance Engineering [130, 133]

TAO   The †ACE †ORB [123]

TLA   Temporal Logic of Actions [77]

TLA$^+$ Extended Temporal Logic of Actions [78]

UML   Unified Modelling Language [105]

WCET   worst-case execution time

XML   Extended Markup Language [26]

Appendix B

Complete Example Specifications

In this appendix we have collected the full TLA$^+$ specifications of the examples for which there was not sufficient space in the main body of this thesis. All of the specifications have been checked using tlasany [79, p. 207 *ff.*], TLA$^+$'s automatic syntactic and semantic analyser, which found them to be correct.

B.1 A Simple Performance Example Based on Request–Response Communication

Here are the specifications for the example discussed in Sect. 3.5.1. The first module defines the functionality of the Counter component. It uses the specification of the CounterInterface from Fig. 3.9, which it implements.

```
1 ┌──────────────────── MODULE CounterApp ────────────────────┐

3  EXTENDS CounterInterface, Naturals

5    Internal variables:
6  VARIABLE internalCounter
7  VARIABLE doHandle

9  Init ≜  ∧ internalCounter = 0
10         ∧ doHandle = 0
11         ∧ counterState ∈ InitialCounterStates


14 IncrementReq ≜ ∧ DoInc(counterState, counterState')
15               ∧ doHandle = 0
16               ∧ internalCounter' = internalCounter + 1
17               ∧ UNCHANGED doHandle

19 ReceiveGetData ≜ ∧ GetData(counterState, counterState')
20                 ∧ doHandle = 0
21                 ∧ doHandle' = 1
22                 ∧ UNCHANGED internalCounter

24 HandleGetData ≜ ∧ doHandle = 1
25                ∧ doHandle' = 2
26                ∧ UNCHANGED ⟨internalCounter, counterState⟩

28 ReplyStep ≜ ∧ doHandle = 2
29            ∧ doHandle' = 0
```

155

30            $\land\ SendData(internalCounter,\ counterState,\ counterState')$

31            $\land\ \text{UNCHANGED}\ internalCounter$

33   $Next\ \triangleq\ \lor\ IncrementReq$

34            $\lor\ ReceiveGetData \lor HandleGetData \lor ReplyStep$

36   $vars\ \triangleq\ \langle counterState,\ internalCounter,\ doHandle\rangle$

38   $Spec\ \triangleq\ \land\ Init$

39            $\land\ [Next]_{vars}$

41

The next module defines the notion of *time*. It has been taken and slightly modified from [79]. The main modification is that we have separated safety and liveness parts of the specification so that we can use the safety part of the definition independently. Time is captured by the new variable *now*.

1 —————————————————— MODULE *RealTime* ——————————————————

This is based on the original *RealTime* specification from the TLA toolkit, but I removed the lifeness part— that is, $NZ(v)$—— from *RTnow*.

6   EXTENDS *Reals*

Variables:

now - the current system time.

13   VARIABLE *now*

15   A helper definition

16   LOCAL $NowNext(v)\ \triangleq\ \land\ now' \in \{r \in Real : r > now\}$

17                    $\land\ \text{UNCHANGED}\ v$

$RTnow(v)$ asserts two things: a) time never runs backward, b) steps changing now do not change any other variable in v, and vice versa

$RTnow(v)$ is a safety property, that is, it allows systems in which time stops altogether. This is useful for certain proofs. If one needs to explicitly exclude this possibility, one conjoins $NZ(v)$, which adds the required fairness constraints.

29   $RTnow(v)\ \triangleq\ \land\ now \in Real$

30                $\land\ \Box[NowNext(v)]_{now}$

The so called *NonZeno* condition, which asserts that time will eventually exceed every bound. This liveness constraint is only required under certain circumstances.

37   $NZ(v)\ \triangleq\ \forall\, r \in Real : \text{WF}_{now}(NowNext(v) \land (now' > r))$

38

The following module describes the behaviour of a system environment. In particular, it constrains the frequency with which the environment sends request for an operation to a given service. This is done by specifying the minimum amount of time between two requests. The specification is parametrised: The desired minimum time between requests should be passed to the constant *RequestPeriod*. The actual specification is encapsulated in module *Inner* on Lines 63–65. It makes use of the specification of a service from Fig. 3.11.

```
1 ─────────────────── MODULE MaxRequPeriodEnv ───────────────────
```
Specification of a system environment which sends service request with a certain minimum time between individual requests.

Note that this is not a specification of what we expect from an environment but actually a description of a behaviour of one specific system environment. It only becomes a specification of an expectation the way it is used in the system specification.

11 EXTENDS *RealTime*

Parameters:

RequestPeriod – the lower limit for the time between individual requests that should be observed by the environment.

19 CONSTANT *RequestPeriod*
20 ASSUME $(RequestPeriod \in Real) \land (RequestPeriod > 0)$

Variables:

LastDeltaTime – The amount of time between the last two requests.
inState – Current state of the service invoked.
unhandledRequest – TRUE signals that a new request has been put into the system.

30 VARIABLES *LastDeltaTime*
31 VARIABLES *inState*, *unhandledRequest*

```
33 ├────────────────────────────────────────────────────────────┤
34 ├────────────────────── MODULE Inner ───────────────────────┤
```
The actual specification.

38 EXTENDS *Sequences*

Variables:

StartDelta – Start time of the last request.

45 VARIABLE *StartDelta*

47 $TheService \triangleq$ INSTANCE *Service*

```
49 ├────────────────────────────────────────────────────────────┤
```

51 $vars \triangleq TheService!vars \circ \langle LastDeltaTime, StartDelta \rangle$

53 $Init \triangleq \land LastDeltaTime = RequestPeriod$
54 $\land StartDelta = now$

56 $NewRequest \triangleq TheService!RequestArrival$
57 $\Rightarrow \land LastDeltaTime' = now - StartDelta$
58 $\land StartDelta' = now$

60 $ReqPeriod \triangleq \land Init$
61 $\land \Box[NewRequest]_{vars}$

63 $Service \triangleq \land TheService!Service$
64 $\land ReqPeriod$
65 $\land \Box(LastDeltaTime \geq RequestPeriod)$

```
67 └────────────────────────────────────────────────────────────┘
```

69 ┣━━━┫

70 $\_Environment(StartDelta) \triangleq \text{INSTANCE } Inner$

71 $Environment \triangleq \exists\, sd : \_Environment(sd)!Service$

73 ┗━━━┛

The following module defines the context model of a component. It is very similar to the service context model from Fig. 3.11, but it has an additional state 'Blocked', which represents all situations where the system has suspended computation of the component.

```
1 ┌──────────────────── MODULE Component ────────────────────┐
  │ Context Model of a component implementation.                │
  │                                                             │
6 ├─────────────────────────────────────────────────────────────┤
```

Variables:

$unhandledRequest$ – set to TRUE by the environment to indicate that a new request has arrived and should be handled.
$inState$ – the state in which the component is.

15 VARIABLE $inState$
16 VARIABLE $unhandledRequest$

18 $vars \triangleq \langle inState, unhandledRequest \rangle$

```
20 ├─────────────────────────────────────────────────────────────┤
```

The environment specification.

The environment in particular influences the $unhandledRequest$ variable by entering new requests into the system.

29 Initially there are no requests in the system
30 $InitEnv \triangleq unhandledRequest = $ FALSE

32 The environment sets the $unhandledRequest$ flag at some arbitrary moment to indicate a
33 new request.
34 $RequestArrival \triangleq \land unhandledRequest = $ FALSE
35 $\qquad\qquad\qquad\quad \land unhandledRequest' = $ TRUE
36 $\qquad\qquad\qquad\quad \land$ UNCHANGED $inState$

38 Somebody, but not the environment, will collect the request
39 Also, $inState$ changes independently of the environment
40 $CompAgent \triangleq \lor unhandledRequest = $ TRUE $\land unhandledRequest' = $ FALSE
41 $\qquad\qquad\qquad \lor \neg$UNCHANGED $inState$

43 $SpecEnv \triangleq \land InitEnv$
44 $\qquad\qquad\quad \land \Box[RequestArrival \lor CompAgent]_{vars}$

```
46 ├─────────────────────────────────────────────────────────────┤
```

The actual component.

It mainly specifies changes to the $inState$ variable, however it communicates with the environment via the $unhandledRequest$ variable.

55 Initially we start out in the idle state
56 $InitComponent \triangleq inState = $ "Idle"

58 The transition from idle to handling request is triggered by an incoming request
59 $StartRequest \triangleq \land inState = $ "Idle"
60 $\qquad\qquad\qquad \land unhandledRequest = $ TRUE
61 $\qquad\qquad\qquad \land inState' = $ "HandlingRequest" $\lor inState' = $ "Blocked"
62 $\qquad\qquad\qquad \land unhandledRequest' = $ FALSE

64 Request handling can finish any time
65 $FinishRequest \triangleq \land inState = $ "HandlingRequest"
66 $\qquad\qquad\qquad \land inState' = $ "Idle"

67                          $\wedge$ UNCHANGED $unhandledRequest$

69   Also, the runtime environment may at any time take away the CPU from us and assign it
70   to someone else.
71   $SwitchToOther \triangleq \wedge inState =$ "HandlingRequest"
72                          $\wedge inState' =$ "Blocked"
73                          $\wedge$ UNCHANGED $unhandledRequest$

75   But, it may also at any time give back the CPU to us
76   $SwitchBack \triangleq \wedge inState =$ "Blocked"
77                          $\wedge inState' =$ "HandlingRequest"
78                          $\wedge$ UNCHANGED $unhandledRequest$

80   $NextComponent \triangleq \vee StartRequest \vee FinishRequest$
81                          $\vee SwitchToOther \vee SwitchBack$

83   The environment occasionally provides new requests
84   $EnvAgent \triangleq unhandledRequest =$ FALSE $\wedge unhandledRequest' =$ TRUE

86   $SpecComponent \triangleq \wedge InitComponent$
87                          $\wedge \Box[NextComponent \vee EnvAgent]_{vars}$

89 ├───┤

The complete specification

95   $Component \triangleq SpecEnv \xrightarrow{+} SpecComponent$

97 └───┘

Based on the `Component` context model, we can now define the execution time measurement. This specification uses the $Component$ module (Line 49) and attaches actions measuring the time the component spends actually computing (Lines 57–79). The
execution time of the last completed invocation of the operation is stored in variable
$LastExecutionTime$.

1 ┌───────────── MODULE $ExecTimeConstrainedComponent$ ─────────────┐
Specification of a component which offers one operation the execution time of which can be constrained.

6   EXTENDS $RealTime$

Parameters:

$ExecutionTime$ – an upper bound for the execution time of the component's operation.

14   CONSTANT $ExecutionTime$
15   ASSUME $(ExecutionTime \in Real) \wedge (ExecutionTime > 0)$

Variables:

$inState$ – the state in which the component currently is.
$unhandledRequest$ – TRUE if the environment put another request into the system.
$LastExecutionTime$ – the execution time of the last service execution.

25   VARIABLE $inState$

27   VARIABLE $unhandledRequest$
28   VARIABLE $LastExecutionTime$

30 ├───┤

32 ┌───────────────────────── MODULE $Inner$ ─────────────────────────┐

Internal module containing the actual specification.

Variables:

$AccExec$ – The accumulated execution time of the current service execution.
$SegStart$ – The start time of the current service execution.

44 VARIABLE $AccExec$
45 VARIABLE $SegStart$

47 ├──┤

49 $BasicComponent \triangleq$ INSTANCE $Component$ Based on the component context model

51 ├──┤

53 $Init \triangleq \ \wedge AccExec = 0$
54 $\wedge SegStart = 0$
55 $\wedge LastExecutionTime = 0$

57 $StartNext$ reacts to a $StartRequest$ step
58 $StartNext \triangleq BasicComponent!StartRequest \Rightarrow$
59 $\wedge SegStart' = now$
60 $\wedge AccExec' = 0$
61 $\wedge$ UNCHANGED $LastExecutionTime$

63 $RespNext$ reacts to a $FinishRequest$ step
64 $RespNext \triangleq BasicComponent!FinishRequest \Rightarrow$
65 $\wedge LastExecutionTime' =$
66 $AccExec + now - SegStart$
67 $\wedge$ UNCHANGED $\langle SegStart, AccExec \rangle$

69 $STONext$ reacts to a $SwitchToOther$ step
70 $STONext \triangleq BasicComponent!SwitchToOther \Rightarrow$
71 $\wedge AccExec' =$
72 $AccExec + now - SegStart$
73 $\wedge$ UNCHANGED $\langle LastExecutionTime,$
74 $SegStart \rangle$

76 $SBNext$ reacts to a $SwitchBack$ step
77 $SBNext \triangleq BasicComponent!SwitchBack \Rightarrow \wedge SegStart' = now$
78 $\wedge$ UNCHANGED
79 $\langle LastExecutionTime, AccExec \rangle$

81 $Next \triangleq \ \wedge StartNext$
82 $\wedge RespNext$
83 $\wedge STONext$
84 $\wedge SBNext$

86 $vars \triangleq \langle AccExec, SegStart, LastExecutionTime, inState, unhandledRequest \rangle$

88 $Spec \triangleq \ \wedge Init$
89 $\wedge \Box[Next]_{vars}$

91 Compose the various partial specifications
92 $Component \triangleq \ \wedge BasicComponent!Component$
93 $\wedge RTnow(vars)$
94 $\wedge Spec$
95 $\wedge \Box(LastExecutionTime \leq ExecutionTime)$

97

99

101 $\_Component(AccExec, SegStart) \triangleq \text{INSTANCE } Inner$
102 $Component \triangleq \exists ae, ss : \_Component(ae, ss)!Component$

104

The following three specifications deal with the resource CPU. The first module defines what a CPU is: It is a resource that is allocated to requesters one at a time in some fashion. Constant $TaskCount$ is used to identify the number of tasks to be scheduled, variable $AssignedTo$ indicates the requester which has currently been assigned the resource.

1 ┌─────────────── MODULE $CPUScheduler$ ───────────────┐

A CPU Scheduler allocates the resource CPU to various tasks. We model this through a variable $AssignedTo$ holding in each state the number of the task which has currently been allocated the resource.

7 EXTENDS $Naturals$

Parameters:

$TaskCount$ – the number of tasks which need to share the resource.

14 CONSTANT $TaskCount$
15 ASSUME $(TaskCount \in Nat) \wedge (TaskCount > 0)$

Variables:

$AssignedTo$ – holds the number of the task currently assigned the resource

22 VARIABLE $AssignedTo$

24 $AssignedToType \triangleq \{1 .. TaskCount\}$

26 ├───┤

28 $Init \qquad \triangleq AssignedTo \in AssignedToType$

30 The $Switch$ action reassigns the resource from from to to.
31 $Switch(from, to) \triangleq \wedge AssignedTo = from$
32 $\qquad\qquad\qquad\qquad \wedge AssignedTo' = to$

34 The CPU can be switched from any task to any other task.
35 $Next \qquad\qquad \triangleq \exists i \in AssignedToType :$
36 $\qquad\qquad\qquad\qquad \exists j \in AssignedToType : Switch(i, j)$

38 $CPUScheduler \qquad \triangleq \wedge Init$
39 $\qquad\qquad\qquad\qquad \wedge \Box[Next]_{AssignedTo}$

41 └───┘

The next specification adds some history-determined variables (quite similar to measurements) that allow to determine for what amount of time each requester has been allocated the resource. It introduces the parameter $Periods$ storing the request period length per requester, so that times can be determined per period. On Lines 150–151 the specification also introduces a formalisation for a situation where all requesters get a sufficiently large share of the resource. To this end, an additional parameter $Wcets$ is introduced. This parameter captures the requested amount of time per period for each requester.

1 ┌─────────────── MODULE $TimedCPUScheduler$ ───────────────┐

A CPU scheduler for which the time each task is assigned can be measured.

The corresponding formulae are derived by conjoining history variables to the CPU scheduler specification.

8 EXTENDS $RealTime$

Parameters:

$TaskCount$ – the number of tasks which need to share the resource.
$Periods$ – the periods of each task
$Wcets$ – the worst case execution times of the tasks to be scheduled. This is an array with one entry per task.

18 CONSTANT $TaskCount$

19 ASSUME $(TaskCount \in Nat) \wedge (TaskCount > 0)$

21 CONSTANT $Periods$
22 ASSUME $Periods \in [\{1 .. TaskCount\} \rightarrow Real]$

24 CONSTANT $Wcets$
25 ASSUME $Wcets \in [\{1 .. TaskCount\} \rightarrow Real]$

Variables:

$MinExecTime$ – records for each task the minimum amount of execution time it has been allocated over all periods so far.
$AssignedTo$ – holds the number of the task currently assigned the resource

34 VARIABLE $MinExecTime$
35 VARIABLE $AssignedTo$

37 $CPUSched \triangleq$ INSTANCE $CPUScheduler$
38 ├───┤

40 ┌───────────────────────── MODULE $Inner$ ─────────────────────────┐
Inner module with the actual specification. This is done so that we can hide some of the variables which are really only there so that defining the measurement becomes easy.

Variables:

$ExecTimeStart$ – Records for each task the time when it last started executing
$LastExecTime$ – Records the last accumulated execution time for each task.
$LastPeriodStart$ – Records for each task when it last started a period.

58 VARIABLES $ExecTimeStart, LastExecTime, LastPeriodStart$

60 ├───┤

62   A little helper function
63 $Min(a, b) \triangleq$ CASE $a < = b \rightarrow a$
64                    $\Box a > b \rightarrow b$
65 ├───┤
66 $Init \triangleq \wedge ExecTimeStart = [k \in CPUSched!AssignedToType \mapsto 0]$
67              $\wedge LastExecTime = [k \in CPUSched!AssignedToType \mapsto 0]$
68              $\wedge$ IF $(TaskCount > 1)$ THEN
69   We start out with infinity, so that any real execution time
70   will definitely be smaller
71                      $MinExecTime = [k \in CPUSched!AssignedToType \mapsto Infinity]$
72   ELSE
73   We need to handle this case specially for technical reasons
74                      $MinExecTime = [k \in CPUSched!AssignedToType \mapsto Periods[k]]$
75              $\wedge LastPeriodStart = [k \in CPUSched!AssignedToType \mapsto 0]$

77   Next we define what happens when a $CPUSched!Switch$ occurs
78 $OnSwitch(from, to) \triangleq \wedge LastExecTime' = [LastExecTime$ EXCEPT
79 $![from] = @ + now -$
80 $ExecTimeStart[from]$
81 $]$
82                      $\wedge ExecTimeStart' = [ExecTimeStart$ EXCEPT
83 $![to] = now$
84 $]$
85                      $\wedge$ UNCHANGED $\langle MinExecTime, LastPeriodStart \rangle$

87   The *OSNext* action binds *OnSwitch* to corresponding *Switch* actions

88    $OSNext \triangleq \forall i \in CPUSched!AssignedToType :$

89    $\qquad \forall j \in CPUSched!AssignedToType :$

90    $\qquad\qquad CPUSched!Switch(i, j) \Rightarrow OnSwitch(i, j)$

92   The *ExecTime* action determines the accumulated execution time for task i

93   in the next state, but at most to the end of its current period

94    $ExecTime(i) \triangleq LastExecTime[i] +$

95    $\qquad\qquad\qquad$ IF $(AssignedTo = i)$ THEN

96    $\qquad\qquad\qquad\quad Min(now', LastPeriodStart[i] + Periods[i]) -$

97    $\qquad\qquad\qquad\quad ExecTimeStart[i]$

98    $\qquad\qquad\qquad$ ELSE 0

100   The *PeriodEnd* action reacts to the end of a period for task i

101   $PeriodEnd(i) \triangleq \wedge (now' - LastPeriodStart[i]) \geq Periods[i]$ A period

102   $\qquad\qquad\qquad\qquad\qquad\qquad\qquad\qquad\qquad\qquad\qquad$ is going to

103   $\qquad\qquad\qquad\qquad\qquad\qquad\qquad\qquad\qquad\qquad\qquad$ end

105   $\qquad\qquad\qquad\qquad$ The following is the measurement we are really

106   $\qquad\qquad\qquad\qquad$ interested in

107   $\qquad\qquad\qquad\qquad \wedge MinExecTime' = [MinExecTime$ EXCEPT

108   $\qquad\qquad\qquad\qquad\qquad\qquad ![i] = Min(@, ExecTime(i))]$

110   $\qquad\qquad\qquad\qquad$ But we also need to perform some cleanup to prepare for

111   $\qquad\qquad\qquad\qquad$ the next period

112   $\qquad\qquad\qquad\qquad \wedge LastPeriodStart' = [LastPeriodStart$ EXCEPT

113   $\qquad\qquad\qquad\qquad\qquad\qquad ![i] = @ + Periods[i]]$

114   $\qquad\qquad\qquad\qquad \wedge ExecTimeStart' = [ExecTimeStart$ EXCEPT

115   $\qquad\qquad\qquad\qquad\qquad\qquad ![i] = LastPeriodStart'[i]]$

116   $\qquad\qquad\qquad\qquad \wedge LastExecTime' = [LastExecTime$ EXCEPT $![i] = 0]$

118   *CheckPeriods* catches all period ends of all tasks

119   $CheckPeriods \triangleq$ IF $(TaskCount > 1)$ THEN

120   $\qquad\qquad\qquad\qquad \forall k \in CPUSched!AssignedToType : PeriodEnd(k)$

121   $\qquad\qquad\qquad\qquad$ ELSE

122   $\qquad\qquad\qquad\qquad$ If there's only one process it will be allowed to run for

123   $\qquad\qquad\qquad\qquad$ the whole period

124   $\qquad\qquad\qquad\qquad MinExecTime'[1] = Periods[1]$

126   $Next \triangleq OSNext$

128   $vars \triangleq \langle AssignedTo, ExecTimeStart, LastExecTime \rangle$

130   $timeVars \triangleq \langle LastPeriodStart, MinExecTime, now \rangle$

132   $TimingSpecification \triangleq \wedge RTnow(vars)$

133   $\qquad\qquad\qquad\qquad\qquad \wedge Init$

134   $\qquad\qquad\qquad\qquad\qquad \wedge \Box[Next]_{vars}$

135   $\qquad\qquad\qquad\qquad\qquad \wedge \Box[CheckPeriods]_{timeVars}$

137   $TimedCPUScheduler \triangleq \wedge CPUSched!CPUScheduler$

138   $\qquad\qquad\qquad\qquad\qquad \wedge TimingSpecification$

140

142

144   $\_TimedCPUScheduler(ExecTimeStart, LastExecTime, LastPeriodStart)$

145    $\triangleq$ INSTANCE *Inner*
146 *TimedCPUScheduler*
147    $\triangleq \exists\, ets,\, let,\, lps :$
148        $\_TimedCPUScheduler(ets,\, let,\, lps)!TimedCPUScheduler$

150 *ExecutionTimesOk* $\triangleq \forall\, k \in CPUSched!AssignedToType :$
151                        $(MinExecTime[k] \geq Wcets[k])$

153

Finally, *RMSScheduler* below defines an actual CPU which is scheduled using RMS. The main contribution of this specification is the schedulability criterion defined on Lines 56–58. This is the standard RMS schedulability criterion.

1 ──────────────── MODULE *RMSScheduler* ────────────────

A *CPU* Scheduler using *RMS*.

5 EXTENDS *Reals*

Parameters:

TaskCount – the number of tasks to be scheduled on the *CPU*.
Periods – the periods to be scheduled for these tasks. This is an array with one entry per task.
Wcets – the worst case execution times of the tasks to be scheduled. This is an array with one entry per task.

16 CONSTANT *TaskCount*
17 ASSUME $(TaskCount \in Nat) \wedge (TaskCount > 0)$

19 CONSTANT *Periods*
20 ASSUME $Periods \in [\{1 .. TaskCount\} \rightarrow Real]$

22 CONSTANT *Wcets*
23 ASSUME $Wcets \in [\{1 .. TaskCount\} \rightarrow Real]$

Variables:

MinExecTime – records for each task the minimum amount of execution time it has been allocated over all
                periods so far.
AssignedTo – holds the number of the task currently assigned the resource
now   – the current time.

33 VARIABLE *MinExecTime*
34 VARIABLE *AssignedTo*
35 VARIABLE *now*

37 *TimedCPUSched* $\triangleq$ INSTANCE *TimedCPUScheduler*

39├──┤

40 A few helpers

42 bth root of a
43 $sqrt(b,\, a) \triangleq a^{(1/b)}$

45 Sum of all the elements in an array (function)
46 Copied from *Bags.tla*
47 $Sum(f) \triangleq$
48   LET $DSum[S \in$ SUBSET DOMAIN $f] \triangleq$ LET $elt \triangleq$ CHOOSE $e \in S :$ TRUE
49   IN   IF $S = \{\}$
50   THEN 0
51   ELSE $f[elt] + DSum[S \setminus \{elt\}]$
52   IN $DSum[$DOMAIN $f]$

54

55   Schedulable is true if the given task load can be scheduled using RMS.

56   $Schedulable \;\triangleq\; $ LET $usage \;\triangleq\; [k \in \{1 \;..\; TaskCount\} \mapsto (\;Wcets[k]/Periods[k])]$

57   IN

58                         $Sum(usage) \leq (\;TaskCount * (sqrt(\;TaskCount,\;2) - 1))$

60   The actual specification: A $TimedCPUScheduler$ which will meet all deadlines

61   provided the RMS schedulability is met by the tasks to be scheduled.

62   $RMSScheduler \;\triangleq\; \land \; TimedCPUSched!TimedCPUScheduler$

63                         $\land \; \Box Schedulable \overset{+}{\Rightarrow} \Box\, TimedCPUSched!ExecutionTimesOk$

65

Resource allocations, intrinsic component properties, and extrinsic service properties must be related by a container strategy. The following module defines such a container strategy. The specification has been discussed exhaustively in Sect. 3.5.1, so we will not give too many explanations here.

1 ———————————— MODULE *SimpleContainer* ————————————

A container specification for a very simple container. This container manages just one component instance and tries to achieve a certain response time with it.

7   EXTENDS *RealTime*

Parameters:

ResponseTime – the response time the container should achieve.
ExecutionTime – the execution time of the component available.

15   CONSTANT *ResponseTime*
16   ASSUME $(ResponseTime \in Real) \wedge (ResponseTime > 0)$

18   CONSTANT *ExecutionTime*
19   ASSUME $(ExecutionTime \in Real) \wedge (ExecutionTime > 0)$

Variables:

TaskCount   – the number of tasks the container would want to execute on the *CPU*.
Periods   – the periods the container associates with these tasks.
Wcets   – the worst case execution times the container associates with these tasks.

30   VARIABLES *TaskCount*, *Periods*, *Wcets*

32 ├───┤

Specification of required *CPU* scheduling behaviour. Note that this does not make any statement about the actual scheduling regime, but only states what tasks need to be scheduled.

Variables:

CPUMinExecTime – records for each task the minimum amount of execution time it has been allocated over all periods so far.
CPUAssignedTo – holds the number of the task currently assigned the resource.

48   VARIABLES *CPUMinExecTime*, *CPUAssignedTo*

50   _*SomeCPUScheduler*(*TaskCountConstraint*, *PeriodsConstraint*, *WcetsConstraint*)
51     $\triangleq$ INSTANCE *TimedCPUScheduler*
52   WITH *MinExecTime* $\leftarrow$ *CPUMinExecTime*,
53   *AssignedTo* $\leftarrow$ *CPUAssignedTo*,
54   *TaskCount* $\leftarrow$ *TaskCountConstraint*,
55   *Periods* $\leftarrow$ *PeriodsConstraint*,
56   *Wcets* $\leftarrow$ *WcetsConstraint*
57   *CPUCanSchedule*(*TaskCountConstraint*, *PeriodsConstraint*, *WcetsConstraint*)
58     $\triangleq$ $\wedge$ _*SomeCPUScheduler*(*TaskCount*, *Periods*, *Wcets*)!*TimedCPUScheduler*
59        $\wedge$ $\Box$_*SomeCPUScheduler*(*TaskCount*, *Periods*, *Wcets*)!*ExecutionTimesOk*

61 ├───┤

Specification of required component behaviour.

Variables:

CmpInState   – the state in which the component currently is.
CmpUnhandledRequest – TRUE if the environment put another request into the system.
CmpLastExecutionTime – the execution time of the last service execution.

74   VARIABLES *CmpInState*, *CmpUnhandledRequest*, *CmpLastExecutionTime*

76   _*Component*(*ExecutionTimeConstraint*)

77     $\triangleq$ INSTANCE $ExecTimeConstrainedComponent$
78   WITH $ExecutionTime \leftarrow ExecutionTimeConstraint,$
79               $inState \leftarrow CmpInState,$
80               $unhandledRequest \leftarrow CmpUnhandledRequest,$
81               $LastExecutionTime \leftarrow CmpLastExecutionTime$
82 $ComponentMaxExecTime(ExecutionTimeConstraint)$
83     $\triangleq \_Component(ExecutionTimeConstraint)!Component$

This predicate represents the functionality of the component.

88 CONSTANT $CompFun$
89 ASSUME $CompFun \in$ BOOLEAN

This predicate represents the mapping between functionality and context model of the component.

95 CONSTANT $CompModelMapping$
96 ASSUME $CompModelMapping \in$ BOOLEAN

98 ├───┤

Specification of required request interarrival time.

Variables:

$EnvLastDeltaTime$ – The amount of time between the last two requests.
$EnvInState$ – Current state of the service invoked.
$EnvUnhandledRequest$ – TRUE signals that a new request has been put into the system.

111 VARIABLES $EnvLastDeltaTime, EnvInState, EnvUnhandledRequest$

113 $\_MinInterrequestTime(RequestPeriodConstraint)$
114     $\triangleq$ INSTANCE $MaxRequPeriodEnv$
115   WITH $RequestPeriod \leftarrow RequestPeriodConstraint,$
116               $LastDeltaTime \leftarrow EnvLastDeltaTime,$
117               $inState \leftarrow EnvInState,$
118               $unhandledRequest \leftarrow EnvUnhandledRequest$
119 $MinInterrequestTime(RequestPeriodConstraint)$
120     $\triangleq \_MinInterrequestTime(RequestPeriodConstraint)!Environment$

122 ├───┤

Specification of guaranteed service behaviour.

Variables:

$ServLastResponseTime$ – the response time of the last request serviced.
$ServInState$ – the current state of the service machinery.
$ServUnhandledRequest$ – TRUE indicates the arrival of a new request.

134 VARIABLES $ServLastResponseTime, ServInState, ServUnhandledRequest$

136 $\_ServiceResponseTime(ResponseTimeConstraint)$
137     $\triangleq$ INSTANCE $ResponseTimeConstrainedService$
138   WITH $ResponseTime \leftarrow ResponseTimeConstraint,$
139               $LastResponseTime \leftarrow ServLastResponseTime,$
140               $inState \leftarrow ServInState,$
141               $unhandledRequest \leftarrow ServUnhandledRequest$
142 $ServiceResponseTime(ResponseTimeConstraint)$
143     $\triangleq \_ServiceResponseTime(ResponseTimeConstraint)!Service$

This predicate represents the functionality of the service.

148 CONSTANT $ServFun$
149 ASSUME $ServFun \in$ BOOLEAN

This predicate represents the mapping between functionality and context model of the service.

155 CONSTANT $ServModelMapping$
156 ASSUME $ServModelMapping \in$ BOOLEAN

158
159 $ContainerPreCond \triangleq \land ExecutionTime \leq ResponseTime$
160 $\land$ The CPU must be able to schedule exactly one task with a period
161 equal to the requested response time and a wcet equal to the
162 specified execution time of the available component.
163 $\land CPUCanSchedule(1,$
164 $[n \in \{1\} \mapsto ResponseTime],$
165 $[n \in \{1\} \mapsto ExecutionTime])$
166 $\land$ A component with the required execution time is available.
167 $\land ComponentMaxExecTime(ExecutionTime)$
168 $\land CompFun$
169 $\land CompModelMapping$
170 $\land$ The component functionality implements the service
171 functionality.
172 $CompFun \Rightarrow ServFun$
173 $\land$ Requests arrive with a constant period, the length of which is
174 somehow related to the period length requested from the CPU.
175 $\land MinInterrequestTime(ResponseTime)$

178 $ContainerPostCond \triangleq \land$ The promised response time can be guaranteed
179 $\land ServiceResponseTime(ResponseTime)$
180 $\land ServFun$
181 $\land ServModelMapping$
182 $\land$ The container will allocate exactly one task for the component.
183 $\Box \land TaskCount = 1$
184 $\land Periods = [n \in \{1\} \mapsto ResponseTime]$
185 $\land Wcets = [n \in \{1\} \mapsto ExecutionTime]$
186 $\land$ State that the container will hand requests directly to the
187 component, without buffering them in any way. If the container
188 provides buffering, this would need to go here
189 $\Box(CmpUnhandledRequest = EnvUnhandledRequest)$

191 $Container \triangleq ContainerPreCond \overset{+}{\Rightarrow} ContainerPostCond$
192

So far, we have been discussing the non-functional properties in the abstract. The following two specifications define the model mappings for execution time of the Counter component and for response time of the Counter service, resp. Both specifications work in a similar manner: They extend the *CounterApp* specification from Page 155, so that all specifications and variables from that specification are directly available. Then, they import the measurement specification. Eventually, they define the *ModelMapping* formula, which represents the actual model mapping by relating states of the Counter application to states of the context model.

1 ────────────── MODULE *CounterAppExecTime* ──────────────

A module defining execution time of the *GetData*() operation.

5 EXTENDS *CounterApp, Realtime*

Variables:

inState   – the state in which the component currently is.
unhandledRequest – TRUE if the environment put another request into the system.
LastExecutionTime – the execution time of the last service execution.

15 VARIABLE *inState*

17 VARIABLE *unhandledRequest*
18 VARIABLE *ExecutionTime*

20 *ExecTimeSpec(ExecutionTimeConstr)*
21   ≜ INSTANCE *ExecTimeConstrainedComponent*
22   WITH *LastExecutionTime ← ExecutionTime,*
23   *ExecutionTime ← ExecutionTimeConstr*

25 *CompSpec* ≜ *ExecTimeSpec*(20)!*Component*

27 ├──┤

Definition of the context-model–application-model mapping

Note how this maps the *GetData/SendData* operation, but not *DoInc*.

34 *ModelMapping* ≜ ∧ *doHandle* = 0 ⇒ ∧ *inState* = "Idle"
35   ∧ *unhandledRequest* = FALSE
36   ∧ *doHandle* = 1 ⇒ ∧ *inState* = "Idle"
37   ∧ *unhandledRequest* = TRUE
38   ∧ *doHandle* = 2 ⇒ ∧ *inState* ∈ {"HandlingRequest",
39   "Blocked"}
40   ∧ *unhandledRequest* = FALSE
41   Dummy mapping for completeness' sake
42   ∧ (*doHandle* ∉ {0, 1, 2}) ⇒ ∧ *inState* = "Idle"
43   ∧ *unhandledRequest* = FALSE

45 ├──┤

Final model of the counter component.

50 *CounterComponent* ≜ ∧ *Spec*
51   ∧ *CompSpec*
52   ∧ □*ModelMapping*

54 └──┘

```
 1 ┌────────────────── MODULE CounterAppResponseTime ──────────────────┐
    A module defining response time of the GetData() operation.

 5  EXTENDS CounterApp, Realtime

    Variables:

    ResponseTime     – the response time of the last request serviced.
    inState          – the current state of the service machinery.
    unhandledRequest – TRUE indicates the arrival of a new request.

14  VARIABLES ResponseTime, inState, unhandledRequest

16  ResponseTimeSpec(ResponseTimeConstr)
17      ≜ INSTANCE ResponseTimeConstrainedService
18          WITH LastResponseTime ← ResponseTime,
19                  ResponseTime ← ResponseTimeConstr

21  ServSpec ≜ ResponseTimeSpec(50)!Service

23 ├──────────────────────────────────────────────────────────────────┤

    Definition of the context-model–application-model mapping

    Note how this maps the GetData/SendData operation, but not DoInc.
30  ModelMapping ≜ ∧ doHandle = 0 ⇒ ∧ inState = "Idle"
31                                   ∧ unhandledRequest = FALSE
32                   ∧ doHandle = 1 ⇒ ∧ inState = "Idle"
33                                   ∧ unhandledRequest = TRUE
34                   ∧ doHandle = 2 ⇒ ∧ inState = "HandlingRequest"
35                                   ∧ unhandledRequest = FALSE
36                   ∧ (doHandle ∉ {0, 1, 2}) ⇒ ∧ inState = "Idle"
37                                              ∧ unhandledRequest = FALSE

39 ├──────────────────────────────────────────────────────────────────┤

    Final model of the counter service .

44  CounterService ≜ ∧ Spec
45                   ∧ ServSpec
46                   ∧ □ModelMapping

48 └──────────────────────────────────────────────────────────────────┘
```

Now, finally, we are ready to pull everything together. This we do in the system specification. The important bit is on Lines 219–235, where the system specification is composed from the individual elementary specifications. Everything before that is mainly of technical relevance, importing the previous specifications.

1 ┌───────────────── MODULE *SystemSpecification* ─────────────────┐

A sample system specification.

The system contains one counter with an execution time of 20 milliseconds, a *RMS* scheduled *CPU*, and a simple container.

8 EXTENDS *Reals*, *CounterInterface*

Parameters:

RequestPeriod – Part of an environment assertion: The environment promises to send requests with a minimum distance of *RequestPeriod* milliseconds.

17 CONSTANT *RequestPeriod*
18 ASSUME $(RequestPeriod \in Real) \wedge (RequestPeriod > 0)$

Variables:

now – the current time.

25 VARIABLE *now*

27 ├──┤

The counter component. The only intrinsic property offered by this component is its execution time, which is always less than $20ms$.

Variables:

MyCompExec   – The last execution time of a service request handled by *MyComponent*.
MyCompInState   – The current state of component *MyComponent*
MyCompUnhandledRequest – Set to TRUE to send a request to *MyComponent*.

41 VARIABLES *MyCompExec*, *MyCompInState*, *MyCompUnhandledRequest*
42 VARIABLES *MyInternalCounter*, *MyDoHandle*

44 $\_MyComponent \triangleq$ INSTANCE *CounterAppExecTime* WITH
45           $ExecutionTime \leftarrow MyCompExec,$
46           $inState \leftarrow MyCompInState,$
47           $unhandledRequest \leftarrow MyCompUnhandledRequest,$
48           $internalCounter \leftarrow MyInternalCounter,$
49           $doHandle \leftarrow MyDoHandle$

51   The actual component specification.
52 $MyComponent \triangleq \_MyComponent!CounterComponent$
53 $CompMap \triangleq \square\_MyComponent!ModelMapping$

55 $\_MyCompFunc \triangleq$ INSTANCE *CounterApp* WITH
56           $internalCounter \leftarrow MyInternalCounter,$
57           $doHandle \leftarrow MyDoHandle$
58 $MyCompFunc \triangleq \_MyCompFunc!Spec$

60 ├──┤

A *CPU*. The parameters of the specification can be used to indicate the number of tasks to be scheduled, their respective periods as well as their respective worst case execution times.

Variables:

$MYCPU\_MinExecTime$ – records for each task the minimum amount of execution time it has been allocated over all periods so far.
$MYCPU\_AssignedTo$ – holds the number of the task currently assigned the resource

76 VARIABLES $MYCPU\_MinExecTime$, $MYCPU\_AssignedTo$

78 $\_MyCPU(TaskCount, Periods, Wcets)$
79      $\triangleq$ INSTANCE $RMSScheduler$
80   WITH $MinExecTime \leftarrow MYCPU\_MinExecTime$,
81                  $AssignedTo \leftarrow MYCPU\_AssignedTo$
82 $MyCPU(TaskCount, Periods, Wcets)$
83      $\triangleq \_MyCPU(TaskCount, Periods, Wcets)!RMSScheduler$

85├───┤

Environment specification.

Variables:

$EnvLastDeltaTime$ – The amount of time between the last two requests.
$EnvInState$ – Current state of the service invoked.
$EnvUnhandledRequest$ – TRUE signals that a new request has been put into the system.

99 VARIABLES $EnvLastDeltaTime$, $EnvInState$, $EnvUnhandledRequest$

101 $\_Environment(RequestPeriodConstraint)$
102     $\triangleq$ INSTANCE $MaxRequPeriodEnv$
103   WITH $RequestPeriod \leftarrow RequestPeriodConstraint$,
104             $LastDeltaTime \leftarrow EnvLastDeltaTime$,
105             $inState \leftarrow EnvInState$,
106             $unhandledRequest \leftarrow EnvUnhandledRequest$
107 $Environment(RequestPeriodConstraint)$
108     $\triangleq \_Environment(RequestPeriodConstraint)!Environment$

110├───┤

The service the system is to perform.

Variables:

$ServResponseTime$ – the response time of the last request serviced.
$ServInState$ – the current state of the service machinery.
$ServUnhandledRequest$ – TRUE indicates the arrival of a new request.

123 VARIABLES $ServResponseTime$, $ServInState$, $ServUnhandledRequest$
124 VARIABLES $ServInternalCounter$, $ServDoHandle$

126 $\_Service$
127     $\triangleq$ INSTANCE $CounterAppResponseTime$
128   WITH $ResponseTime \leftarrow ServResponseTime$,
129             $inState \leftarrow ServInState$,
130             $unhandledRequest \leftarrow ServUnhandledRequest$,
131             $internalCounter \leftarrow ServInternalCounter$,
132             $doHandle \leftarrow ServDoHandle$
133 $Service \triangleq \_Service!CounterService$
134 $ServMap \triangleq \square\_Service!ModelMapping$

136 $\_MyServFunc \triangleq$ INSTANCE $CounterApp$ WITH
137             $internalCounter \leftarrow ServInternalCounter$,
138             $doHandle \leftarrow ServDoHandle$
139 $MyServFunc \triangleq \_MyServFunc!Spec$

141├───┤

Container specification.

Variables:

$SCCPUMinExecTime$ – records for each task the minimum amount of execution time it has been allocated over all periods so far.
$SCCPUAssignedTo$ – holds the number of the task currently assigned the resource.

$SCCmpInState$ – the state in which the component currently is.
$SCCmpUnhandledRequest$ – TRUE if the environment put another request into the system.
$SCCmpLastExecutionTime$ – the execution time of the last service execution.

$SCEnvLastDeltaTime$ – The amount of time between the last two requests.
$SCEnvInState$ – Current state of the service invoked.
$SCEnvUnhandledRequest$ – TRUE signals that a new request has been put into the system.

$SCServLastResponseTime$ – the response time of the last request serviced.
$SCServInState$ – the current state of the service machinery.
$SCServUnhandledRequest$ – TRUE indicates the arrival of a new request.

169 VARIABLES $SCCPUMinExecTime,\ SCCPUAssignedTo$
170 VARIABLES $SCCmpInState,\ SCCmpUnhandledRequest,\ SCCmpLastExecutionTime$
171 VARIABLES $SCEnvLastDeltaTime,\ SCEnvInState,\ SCEnvUnhandledRequest$
172 VARIABLES $SCServLastResponseTime,\ SCServInState,\ SCServUnhandledRequest$

174 $\_MyContainer(ExecutionTimeConstr,\ ResponseTimeConstr,$
175         $TaskCount,\ Periods,\ Wcets)$
176     $\triangleq$ INSTANCE $SimpleContainer$
177   WITH $ExecutionTime \leftarrow ExecutionTimeConstr,$
178           $ResponseTime \leftarrow ResponseTimeConstr,$
179           $CPUMinExecTime \leftarrow SCCPUMinExecTime,$
180           $CPUAssignedTo \leftarrow SCCPUAssignedTo,$
181           $CmpInState \leftarrow SCCmpInState,$
182           $CmpUnhandledRequest \leftarrow SCCmpUnhandledRequest,$
183           $CmpLastExecutionTime \leftarrow SCCmpLastExecutionTime,$
184           $EnvLastDeltaTime \leftarrow SCEnvLastDeltaTime,$
185           $EnvInState \leftarrow SCEnvInState,$
186           $EnvUnhandledRequest \leftarrow SCEnvUnhandledRequest,$
187           $ServLastResponseTime \leftarrow SCServLastResponseTime,$
188           $ServInState \leftarrow SCServInState,$
189           $ServUnhandledRequest \leftarrow SCServUnhandledRequest,$
190           $CompFun \leftarrow MyCompFunc,$
191           $CompModelMapping \leftarrow CompMap,$
192           $ServFun \leftarrow MyServFunc,$
193           $ServModelMapping \leftarrow ServMap$

195 $MyContainer(ExecutionTimeConstr,\ ResponseTimeConstr,$
196            $TaskCount,\ Periods,\ Wcets)$
197     $\triangleq$ $\_MyContainer(ExecutionTimeConstr,\ ResponseTimeConstr,$
198                $TaskCount,\ Periods,\ Wcets)!Container$

200

The complete system.

Variables:

$TaskCount$ – the number of tasks to be scheduled on the CPU as determined by the container.
Periods – the periods to be scheduled for those tasks as determined by container.
$Wcets$ – the worst case execution times to be considered when scheduling. As determined by the container.

216 VARIABLES $CPUTaskCount,\ CPUPeriods,\ CPUWcets$
217 VARIABLES $SCTaskCount,\ SCPeriods,\ SCWcets$

219 $System\ \triangleq\ \wedge\ MyComponent$

220         $\wedge\ MyCPU(CPUTaskCount,\ CPUPeriods,\ CPUWcets)$

221         $\wedge\ MyContainer(20,\ 50,\ SCTaskCount,\ SCPeriods,\ SCWcets)$

222         $\wedge\ \Box\ \wedge\ ServResponseTime = SCServLastResponseTime$

223            $\wedge\ ServInState = SCServInState$

224            $\wedge\ ServUnhandledRequest = SCServUnhandledRequest$

225         $\wedge\ \Box\ \wedge\ MYCPU\_MinExecTime = SCCPUMinExecTime$

226            $\wedge\ MYCPU\_AssignedTo = SCCPUAssignedTo$

227            $\wedge\ CPUTaskCount = SCTaskCount$

228            $\wedge\ CPUPeriods = SCPeriods$

229            $\wedge\ CPUWcets = SCWcets$

230         $\wedge\ \Box\ \wedge\ SCCmpLastExecutionTime = MyCompExec$

231            $\wedge\ SCCmpInState = MyCompInState$

232            $\wedge\ SCCmpUnhandledRequest = MyCompUnhandledRequest$

233         $\wedge\ \Box\ \wedge\ SCEnvLastDeltaTime = EnvLastDeltaTime$

234            $\wedge\ SCEnvInState = EnvInState$

235            $\wedge\ SCEnvUnhandledRequest = EnvUnhandledRequest$

The external behaviour we require of the system.

240   $ExternalService\ \triangleq\ Environment(RequestPeriod) \overset{+}{\rightarrow} Service$

242 ├──┤

This is the property we need to prove to ensure that we have a feasible system.

248   $IsFeasible\ \triangleq\ System \Rightarrow ExternalService$

250 └──┘

B.2 A Data Quality Example

In the following we show the full TLA$^+$specifications of the data-quality example. These specifications reuse the `Counter` example specifications from Sect. B.1.

The first module defines a context model that can be used for the definition of data-quality measurements. Because, here, we are not interested in the mechanics of an operation invocation, we use the two abstract actions *IncomingRequest* and *SendRequestResult* to describe invocation and return of the operation. We are interested in the state of the component in these two situations and in the result data delivered by the operation call. Consequently, these have been made parameters of the abstract actions. Note, however, that these are not restricted further by the context model specification. In particular, the result value is existentially quantified on Line 52.

An interesting variable is *idealResult*, which is also kept abstract. It will be used when defining measurements, but it will be *defined* only by the model mapping.

1 ─────────────── MODULE *DataQualityCtx* ───────────────

A context model that allows for the definition of data quality properties.

envState is the state of the world around a component. This is the state of the part of the world sending requests.

10 VARIABLE *envState*
11 CONSTANT *InitialEnvironmentStates*

IncomingRequest (*envState*, *envState′*) is TRUE when a request arrives.

16 CONSTANT *IncomingRequest*(_, _)
17 ASSUME ∀ *eSOld*, *eSNew* : *IncomingRequest*(*eSOld*, *eSNew*) ∈ BOOLEAN

SendRequestResult (*envState*, *envState′*, result) is TRUE when the result of a request is being sent to (and received by) the environment.

23 CONSTANT *SendRequestResult*(_, _, _)
24 ASSUME ∀ *eSOld*, *eSNew*, *dta* :
25   *SendRequestResult*(*eSOld*, *eSNew*, *dta*) ∈ BOOLEAN

The states of a component/service:

30 VARIABLE *inState*

At the time of sending the result, *idealResult* contains the ideal result for the current request. This variable is somewhat special, because it will only be set in the model mapping, as the ideal result depends on the functionality and thus can only be determined at the application model level.

39 VARIABLE *idealResult*

41 ├──┤

43 *Init* ≜ ∧ *inState* = "Idle"
44   ∧ *envState* ∈ *InitialEnvironmentStates*

46 *RequestArrival* ≜ ∧ *inState* = "Idle" ∧ *inState′* = "HandlingRequest"
47   ∧ *IncomingRequest*(*envState*, *envState′*)

49 *SendResult*(*dta*) ≜ ∧ *inState* = "HandlingRequest" ∧ *inState′* = "Idle"
50   ∧ *SendRequestResult*(*envState*, *envState′*, *dta*)

52 *Next* ≜ *RequestArrival* ∨ ∃ *dta* : *SendResult*(*dta*)

54 *Spec* ≜ ∧ *Init*
55   ∧ □[*Next*]$_{inState}$

57 └──┘

In the following module, we define the measurement of accuracy. The most important definition is $CheckRequestResult(dta)$ on Lines 55–57. This defines accuracy as the absolute difference between ideal and actual result.

1 ———————————— MODULE *Accuracy* ————————————

A model of accuracy. This model is based on the *DataQualityCtx* context model, but it adds some additional constraints so that result values can only be real values. This allows us to define the accuracy measurement.

7 EXTENDS *Reals*

Parameter specifying the maximum deviation from the correct result that should be allowed.

13 CONSTANT *AccuracyBound*
14 ASSUME $AccuracyBound \in Real \wedge AccuracyBound \geq 0$

envState is the state of the world around a component. This is the state of the part of the world sending requests.

20 VARIABLE *envState*
21 CONSTANT *InitialEnvironmentStates*

IncomingRequest (envState, envState') is TRUE when a request arrives.

26 CONSTANT $IncomingRequest(\_, \_)$
27 ASSUME $\forall eSOld, eSNew : IncomingRequest(eSOld, eSNew) \in$ BOOLEAN

SendRequestResult (envState, envState', result) is TRUE when the result of a request is being sent to (and received by) the environment.

33 CONSTANT $SendRequestResult(\_, \_, \_)$
34 ASSUME $\forall eSOld, eSNew, dta :$
35 $\wedge SendRequestResult(eSOld, eSNew, dta) \in$ BOOLEAN
36 $\wedge dta \notin Real \Rightarrow \neg SendRequestResult(eSOld, eSNew, dta)$

38 VARIABLE *inState*
39 VARIABLE *idealResult*

41 $DataQualityContext \triangleq$ INSTANCE $DataQualityCtx$

LastAccuracy captures the accuracy of the last operation result. This is the measurement we are interested in.

47 VARIABLE *LastAccuracy*

49 |————————————————————————————————|

51 $Init \triangleq LastAccuracy = 0$

53 $Abs(a) \triangleq$ IF $a < 0$ THEN $-a$ ELSE a

55 $CheckRequestResult(dta) \triangleq$
56 $\quad DataQualityContext!SendResult(dta)$
57 $\quad\quad \Rightarrow LastAccuracy' = Abs(idealResult - dta)$

59 $Next \triangleq \forall dta \in Real : CheckRequestResult(dta)$

61 $Spec \triangleq \wedge Init$
62 $\quad\quad\quad \wedge \Box[Next]_{LastAccuracy}$

64 $AccuracySpec \triangleq \wedge DataQualityContext!Spec$
65 $\quad\quad\quad\quad\quad \wedge Spec$
66 $\quad\quad\quad\quad\quad \wedge \Box(LastAccuracy \leq AccuracyBound)$

68 |————————————————————————————————|

For our example, of course, we need a sample component. This is the inaccurate counter presented in the following module. Typically, accuracy would be influenced by other non-functional properties in a trade-off between the properties. Because, in our example, we only have one non-functional property, we cannot do this. This is why we actually have to provide a component with a different implementation. The following specification differs from the one on Page 155 on Line 34, where it states that sometimes, non-deterministically, the counter will not increment its internal data.

```
1 ┌──────────────── MODULE InAccurateCounter ────────────────┐

3  EXTENDS CounterInterface, Naturals

5    Internal variables:
6  VARIABLE doHandle
7  VARIABLE internalCounter

9 ├──────────────────────────────────────────────────────────┤
     An ideal counter which always works correctly. This is only used to define what accuracy means for counters.
14 VARIABLE accurateIC
15 VARIABLE accurateDH
16 VARIABLE accurateCS
17 AccurateCounter ≜ INSTANCE CounterApp
18      WITH internalCounter ← accurateIC,
19           doHandle ← accurateDH,
20           counterState ← accurateCS

22 ├──────────────────────────────────────────────────────────┤

24 Init ≜  ∧ internalCounter = 0
25         ∧ doHandle = 0
26         ∧ counterState ∈ InitialCounterStates
27         ∧ AccurateCounter!Init

30 IncrementReq ≜  ∧ DoInc(counterState, counterState')
31                 ∧ doHandle = 0
32                 ∧ ∨ internalCounter' = internalCounter + 1
33                       But sometimes the counter doesn't work . . .
34                   ∨ UNCHANGED internalCounter
35                 ∧ AccurateCounter!IncrementReq
36                 ∧ UNCHANGED doHandle

38 ReceiveGetData ≜  ∧ GetData(counterState, counterState')
39                   ∧ doHandle = 0
40                   ∧ doHandle' = 1
41                   ∧ UNCHANGED internalCounter

43 HandleGetData ≜  ∧ doHandle = 1
44                  ∧ doHandle' = 2
45                  ∧ UNCHANGED ⟨internalCounter, counterState⟩

47 ReplyStep ≜  ∧ doHandle = 2
48              ∧ doHandle' = 0
49              ∧ SendData(internalCounter, counterState, counterState')
50              ∧ UNCHANGED internalCounter

52 Next ≜  ∨ IncrementReq
53         ∨ ReceiveGetData ∨ HandleGetData ∨ ReplyStep
```

55 $vars \triangleq \langle counterState, internalCounter, doHandle \rangle$

57 $Spec \triangleq \wedge Init$
58 $\qquad \wedge [Next]_{vars}$

60

Finally, we apply the accuracy measurement to the inaccurate counter just defined. In this specification, much of the model mapping happens in the renamings on Lines 9–12. Only the ideal result is defined in *ModelMapping* on Line 17. The specification defines that the inaccurate counter has a maximum accuracy of 7. Note that this implies a constraint on how often the counter may fail to increase the internal variable.

1 —————————————— MODULE *AccuracyLimitedCounter* ——————————————

3 EXTENDS *InAccurateCounter*

5 VARIABLES *inState, idealResult, LastAccuracy*

7 $\_SendResult(eS1, eS2, val) \triangleq SendData(val, eS1, eS2)$
8 $AccuracySpec(AccuracyBound) \triangleq$ INSTANCE *Accuracy*
9 $\qquad$ WITH *InitialEnvironmentStates* $\leftarrow$ *InitialCounterStates*,
10 $\qquad\qquad envState \leftarrow counterState,$
11 $\qquad\qquad IncomingRequest \leftarrow GetData,$
12 $\qquad\qquad SendRequestResult \leftarrow \_SendResult$

14

16 Map *doHandle, internalCounter* auf *envState, currentParams, inState, idealResult*
17 $ModelMapping \triangleq idealResult = accurateIC$

19

21 $CompleteSpec \triangleq \wedge Spec$
22 $\qquad\qquad\qquad \wedge AccuracySpec(7)!Spec$
23 $\qquad\qquad\qquad \wedge \Box ModelMapping$

25

B.3   A Performance Example Based on Stream-Based Communication and an Active Component

This section contains the complete specifications for the example from Sect. 3.5.3. First, we define the context model of an active component; that is, a component that consists of one operation that is being executed continuously. The most interesting bit is the way the starting of the process and the sending of an event are modelled: Both are represented as abstract actions *StartSignal* and *SendData*, resp. This is the right level of abstraction because in the following we will only be interested in *when* these events occur, but not in any more detailed properties.

```
1 ┌──────────────── MODULE ActiveComponent ────────────────┐
    An active component is a component that has a thread of control of its own and, once started, produces some data
    on a periodic basis.


  Variables:

    inState - the execution state of the component.
    envState - the state of the environment of the component.
13  VARIABLE inState
14  VARIABLE envState

16  CONSTANT InitialEnvStates

18  CONSTANT StartSignal(_, _)
19  ASSUME ∀ esOld, esNew : StartSignal(esOld, esNew) ∈ BOOLEAN

21  CONSTANT SendData(_, _)
22  ASSUME ∀ esOld, esNew : SendData(esOld, esNew) ∈ BOOLEAN

24 ├─────────────────────────────────────────────────────────┤

26  Init  ≜  ∧ inState = "Idle"
27            ∧ envState ∈ InitialEnvStates

29  StartWorking  ≜  ∧ inState = "Idle"
30                    ∧ StartSignal(envState, envState′)
31                    ∧ inState′ = "Working"

33  GetBlocked  ≜  ∧ inState = "Working"
34                  ∧ inState′ = "Blocked"

36  GetUnBlocked  ≜  ∧ inState = "Blocked"
37                    ∧ inState′ = "Working"

39  DoSendData  ≜  ∧ inState = "Working"
40                  ∧ SendData(envState, envState′)
41                  ∧ inState′ = "Working"

43  Next  ≜  ∨ StartWorking
44            ∨ GetBlocked
45            ∨ GetUnBlocked
46            ∨ DoSendData

48  Component  ≜  ∧ Init
49                ∧ □[Next]_inState
50 └─────────────────────────────────────────────────────────┘
```

Next, we can define the measurement data rate based on the context model of an active component. The structure of this definition is very similar to that of the definition of execution time.

1 ——————————————— MODULE *DataRate* ———————————————

Measurement definition of data rate of an active component.

5 EXTENDS *RealTime*

This parameter defines the minimum rate to be guaranteed by the component.

10 CONSTANT *RateBound*
11 ASSUME $(RateBound \in Real) \land (RateBound > 0)$

Variables and constants required by the specification.

16 VARIABLE *inState*
17 VARIABLE *envState*

19 CONSTANT *InitialEnvStates*

21 CONSTANT $StartSignal(\_, \_)$
22 ASSUME $\forall esOld, esNew : StartSignal(esOld, esNew) \in$ BOOLEAN

24 CONSTANT $SendData(\_, \_)$
25 ASSUME $\forall esOld, esNew : SendData(csOld, esNew) \in$ BOOLEAN

27   Based on the active component context model.
28 $ActiveComp \triangleq$ INSTANCE *ActiveComponent*

30 |———|

These variables represent the actual measurement itself.

35 VARIABLES *Start, AccInterval, LastInterval*

37 |———|

39 $Init \triangleq \land Start = 0$
40         $\land AccInterval = 0$
41         $\land LastInterval = 0$

43 $OnStartWorking \triangleq ActiveComp!StartWorking \Rightarrow \land Start' = now$
44 $\land AccInterval' = 0$
45 $\land$ UNCHANGED *LastInterval*

47 $OnGetBlocked \triangleq ActiveComp!GetBlocked \Rightarrow \land AccInterval' = AccInterval +$
48 $now - Start$
49 $\land$ UNCHANGED $\langle Start, LastInterval \rangle$

51 $OnGetUnBlocked \triangleq ActiveComp!GetUnBlocked \Rightarrow \land Start' = now$
52 $\land$ UNCHANGED $\langle AccInterval,$
53 $LastInterval \rangle$

55 $OnDoSendData \triangleq ActiveComp!DoSendData \Rightarrow \land LastInterval' = AccInterval +$
56 $now - Start$
57 $\land Start' = now$
58 $\land AccInterval' = 0$

60 $Next \triangleq \land OnStartWorking$
61         $\land OnGetBlocked$
62         $\land OnGetUnBlocked$
63         $\land OnDoSendData$

65 $vars \triangleq \langle inState, Start, AccInterval, LastInterval \rangle$

67 $IntervalSpec \triangleq \wedge Init$
68 $\wedge \Box [Next]_{vars}$

70 $Component \triangleq \wedge ActiveComp!Component$
71 $\wedge RTnow(vars)$
72 $\wedge IntervalSpec$
73 $\wedge \Box ((LastInterval > 0) \Rightarrow (1/LastInterval \leq RateBound))$

75

The next specification defines the context model for an active service—a service implemented by an active component.

1 ———————————— MODULE $ActiveService$ ————————————

An active service is a service that has a thread of control of its own and, once started, produces some data on a
periodic basis.

Variables:

$inState$ - the execution state of the service.
$envState$ - the state of the environment of the service.

13 VARIABLE $inState$
14 VARIABLE $envState$

16 CONSTANT $InitialEnvStates$

18 CONSTANT $StartSignal(\_, \_)$
19 ASSUME $\forall esOld, esNew : StartSignal(esOld, esNew) \in$ BOOLEAN

21 CONSTANT $SendData(\_, \_)$
22 ASSUME $\forall esOld, esNew : SendData(esOld, esNew) \in$ BOOLEAN

24

26 $Init \triangleq \wedge inState =$ "Idle"
27 $\wedge envState \in InitialEnvStates$

29 $StartWorking \triangleq \wedge inState =$ "Idle"
30 $\wedge StartSignal(envState, envState')$
31 $\wedge inState' =$ "Working"

33 $DoSendData \triangleq \wedge inState =$ "Working"
34 $\wedge SendData(envState, envState')$
35 $\wedge inState' =$ "Working"

37 $Next \triangleq \vee StartWorking$
38 $\vee DoSendData$

40 $Service \triangleq \wedge Init$
41 $\wedge \Box [Next]_{inState}$
42

Based on this context model, we define data rate for an active service. Note that for data rate intrinsic and extrinsic measurement have the same informal name. They are still different measurements, because they are based on different context models.

1 ┌──────────────────────── MODULE $DataRateService$ ────────────────────────┐

Measurement definition of data rate of an active service.

5 EXTENDS $RealTime$

This parameter defines the minimum rate to be guaranteed by the service.

10 CONSTANT $RateBound$
11 ASSUME $(RateBound \in Real) \wedge (RateBound > 0)$

Variables and constants required by the specification.

16 VARIABLES $inState,\ envState$
17 CONSTANT $InitialEnvStates$

19 CONSTANT $StartSignal(\_,\ \_)$
20 ASSUME $\forall\ esOld,\ esNew : StartSignal(esOld,\ esNew) \in$ BOOLEAN

22 CONSTANT $SendData(\_,\ \_)$
23 ASSUME $\forall\ esOld,\ esNew : SendData(esOld,\ esNew) \in$ BOOLEAN

25   Based on the active service context model.
26 $ActiveServ \triangleq$ INSTANCE $ActiveService$

These variables represent the actual measurement itself.

31 VARIABLES $Start,\ LastInterval$

33 ├───┤

35 $Init \triangleq \wedge Start = 0$
36 $\qquad\qquad \wedge LastInterval = 0$

38 $OnStartWorking \triangleq ActiveServ!StartWorking \Rightarrow \wedge Start' = now$
39 $\qquad\qquad\qquad\qquad\qquad\qquad\qquad\qquad \wedge$ UNCHANGED $LastInterval$

41 $OnDoSendData \triangleq ActiveServ!DoSendData \Rightarrow \wedge LastInterval' = now - Start$
42 $\qquad\qquad\qquad\qquad\qquad\qquad\qquad\qquad \wedge Start' = now$

44 $Next \triangleq \wedge OnStartWorking$
45 $\qquad\qquad \wedge OnDoSendData$

47 $vars \triangleq \langle inState,\ Start,\ LastInterval \rangle$

49 $IntervalSpec \triangleq \wedge Init$
50 $\qquad\qquad\qquad \wedge \Box[Next]_{vars}$

52 $Service \triangleq \wedge ActiveServ!Service$
53 $\qquad\qquad\quad \wedge RTnow(vars)$
54 $\qquad\qquad\quad \wedge IntervalSpec$
55 $\qquad\qquad\quad \wedge \Box((LastInterval > 0) \Rightarrow (1/LastInterval \leq RateBound))$

57 └───┘

Eventually, we use these two measurements to specify a container strategy that uses components with a given data rate to provide a service with a certain data rate.

1 ┌─────────────── MODULE $SimpleContainer$ ───────────────┐

A container specification for a very simple container. This container manages just one component instance and tries to achieve a certain service data rate with it.

7 EXTENDS $RealTime$

Parameters:

$ServiceDataRate$ – the service data rate the container should achieve.
$ComponentDataRate$ – the data rate of the component available.

15 CONSTANT $ServiceDataRate$
16 ASSUME $(ServiceDataRate \in Real) \wedge (ServiceDataRate > 0)$

18 CONSTANT $ComponentDataRate$
19 ASSUME $(ComponentDataRate \in Real) \wedge (ComponentDataRate > 0)$

Variables:

$TaskCount$ – the number of tasks the container would want to execute on the CPU.
$Periods$ – the periods the container associates with these tasks.
$Wcets$ – the worst case execution times the container associates with these tasks.

30 VARIABLES $TaskCount, Periods, Wcets$

32 ├──┤

Specification of required CPU scheduling behaviour. Note that this does not make any statement about the actual scheduling regime, but only states what tasks need to be scheduled.

39 VARIABLES $CPUMinExecTime, CPUAssignedTo$

41 $\_SomeCPUScheduler(TaskCountConstraint, PeriodsConstraint, WcetsConstraint)$
42    $\triangleq$ INSTANCE $TimedCPUScheduler$
43   WITH $MinExecTime \leftarrow CPUMinExecTime,$
44          $AssignedTo \leftarrow CPUAssignedTo,$
45          $TaskCount \leftarrow TaskCountConstraint,$
46          $Periods \leftarrow PeriodsConstraint,$
47          $Wcets \leftarrow WcetsConstraint$
48 $CPUCanSchedule(TaskCountConstraint, PeriodsConstraint, WcetsConstraint)$
49    $\triangleq \wedge \_SomeCPUScheduler(TaskCount, Periods, Wcets)!TimedCPUScheduler$
50       $\wedge \Box\_SomeCPUScheduler(TaskCount, Periods, Wcets)!ExecutionTimesOk$

52 ├──┤

Specification of required component behaviour.

56 VARIABLES $CmpInState, CmpLastInterval, CmpStart, CmpAccInterval$
57 VARIABLE $CmpEnvState$
58 CONSTANTS $CmpStartSignal(\_, \_), CmpSendData(\_, \_), CmpInitEnvStates$

60 $\_Component(DataRateConstraint)$
61    $\triangleq$ INSTANCE $DataRate$
62   WITH $RateBound \leftarrow DataRateConstraint,$
63          $inState \leftarrow CmpInState,$
64          $LastInterval \leftarrow CmpLastInterval,$
65          $Start \leftarrow CmpStart,$
66          $AccInterval \leftarrow CmpAccInterval,$
67          $StartSignal \leftarrow CmpStartSignal,$
68          $SendData \leftarrow CmpSendData,$
69          $InitialEnvStates \leftarrow CmpInitEnvStates,$
70          $envState \leftarrow CmpEnvState$

71 $ComponentMinRate(DataRateConstraint)$
72      $\triangleq$ $\_Component(DataRateConstraint)!Component$

This predicate represents the functionality of the component.

77 CONSTANT $CompFun$
78 ASSUME $CompFun \in$ BOOLEAN

This predicate represents the mapping between functionality and context model of the component.

84 CONSTANT $CompModelMapping$
85 ASSUME $CompModelMapping \in$ BOOLEAN

87├───┤

Specification of guaranteed service behaviour.

91 VARIABLES $ServInState, ServLastInterval, ServStart, ServEnvState$
92 CONSTANTS $ServStartSignal(\_, \_), ServSendData(\_, \_), ServInitEnvStates$

94 $\_Service(DataRateConstraint)$
95      $\triangleq$ INSTANCE $DataRateService$
96   WITH $RateBound \leftarrow DataRateConstraint,$
97              $inState \leftarrow ServInState,$
98              $LastInterval \leftarrow ServLastInterval,$
99              $Start \leftarrow ServStart,$
100             $StartSignal \leftarrow ServStartSignal,$
101             $SendData \leftarrow ServSendData,$
102             $InitialEnvStates \leftarrow ServInitEnvStates,$
103             $envState \leftarrow ServEnvState$
104 $ServiceMinRate(DataRateConstraint)$
105     $\triangleq$ $\_Service(DataRateConstraint)!Service$

This predicate represents the functionality of the service.

110 CONSTANT $ServFun$
111 ASSUME $ServFun \in$ BOOLEAN

This predicate represents the mapping between functionality and context model of the service.

117 CONSTANT $ServModelMapping$
118 ASSUME $ServModelMapping \in$ BOOLEAN

120├───┤
121 $ContainerPreCond \triangleq$ $\wedge$ Generic sensibility rules
122                              $\wedge$ $ComponentDataRate \geq ServiceDataRate$
123                              $\wedge$ The CPU must be able to schedule exactly one task with a period
124   inferred from the service data rate and a wcet inferred from the
125   data rate of the available component.
126                              $\wedge$ $CPUCanSchedule($
127                                      $1,$
128                                      $[n \in \{1\} \mapsto 1/ServiceDataRate],$
129                                      $[n \in \{1\} \mapsto 1/ComponentDataRate])$
130                              $\wedge$ A component with the required minimum data rate is available.
131                              $\wedge$ $ComponentMinRate(ComponentDataRate)$
132                              $\wedge$ $CompFun$
133                              $\wedge$ $CompModelMapping$
134                              $\wedge$ The component functionality implements the service
135   functionality.
136                                  $CompFun \Rightarrow ServFun$

139   $ContainerPostCond \triangleq \land$ The promised response time can be guaranteed

140                                   $\land ServiceMinRate(ServiceDataRate)$

141                                   $\land ServFun$

142                                   $\land ServModelMapping$

143                          $\land$ The container will allocate exactly one task for the component.

144                             $\Box \land TaskCount = 1$

145                                   $\land Periods = [n \in \{1\} \mapsto 1/ServiceDataRate]$

146                                   $\land Wcets = [n \in \{1\} \mapsto 1/ComponentDataRate]$

148 ├───┤

150   $Container \triangleq ContainerPreCond \overset{+}{\twoheadrightarrow} ContainerPostCond$

151 └───┘

B.4   An Example for Component Network Specification

The first module defines the interface of a `DataDeliverer`: Data deliverers provide one operation `getData`, represented by abstract actions *CallGetData* and *ReturnGetData* in the specification.

```
1 ┌─────────────────── MODULE DataDelivererIntf ───────────────────┐

    Offered interface of the DataDeliverer component. This component offers exactly one operation: getData,
    modelled by two actions CallGetData and ReturnGetData. getData obtains data from some data store and
    returns it.

8   EXTENDS Naturals

10  VARIABLE dataDelivererState     Abstract representation of the DataDeliverer's state
11  CONSTANT initialDataDevState    Set of initial DataDeliverer states


14    CallGetData (dataDelivererState, dataDelivererState') represents invocation of the
15    getData operation.
16  CONSTANT CallGetData(_, _)

18    ReturnGetData (dataDelivererState, dataDelivererState', result) represents the return
19    from invocation for operation getData. result' contains the result as a natural number.
20  CONSTANT ReturnGetData(_, _, _)

22  ASSUME ∀ ddsOld, ddsNew : ∀ result ∈ Nat :
23      ∧ CallGetData(ddsOld, ddsNew) ∈ BOOLEAN
24      ∧ ReturnGetData(ddsOld, ddsNew, result) ∈ BOOLEAN

26 └────────────────────────────────────────────────────────────────┘
```

The following module provides an implementation for this interface. We do not care about the precise data delivered, so we leave this part of the specification open, using an existential quantification on Line 30.

```
1 ┌─────────────────── MODULE DataDeliverer ───────────────────┐

    An implementation for the DataDelivererIntf interface. Simply delivers one data item after the other.

6   EXTENDS DataDelivererIntf

8     Internal process counter
9   VARIABLE step

11 ├────────────────────────────────────────────────────────────┤

13  Init ≜  ∧ dataDelivererState ∈ initialDataDevState
14          ∧ step = 0

16    A new request for a data item has arrived.
17  GetRequest ≜  ∧ step = 0
18                ∧ CallGetData(dataDelivererState, dataDelivererState')
19                ∧ step' = 1

21    A value is being returned in response to a previous request.
22  ReturnData(value) ≜  ∧ step = 1
23                       ∧ ReturnGetData(dataDelivererState,
24                                        dataDelivererState',
25                                        value)
26                       ∧ step' = 0
```

28 $Next \triangleq \ \lor \ GetRequest$
29 $\lor$ We don't really care about the exact algorithm
30 $\exists \, value \in Nat : ReturnData(value)$

32 $DataDeliverer \triangleq \ \land \ Init$
33 $\land \ \Box[Next]_{\langle step, \, dataDelivererState \rangle}$

35

The following two specifications contain the model mappings defining execution time and response time of the getData operation.

1 ———————— MODULE $DataDelivererExecTime$ ————————

A module defining execution time of the $DataDeliverer$'s $getData()$ operation.

6 EXTENDS $DataDeliverer, RealTime$

8 CONSTANT $ExecutionTimeConstr$ Execution time constraint to be applied

Variables:

$inState$ – the state in which the component currently is.
$unhandledRequest$ – TRUE if the environment put another request into the system.
$LastExecutionTime$ – the execution time of the last service execution.

18 VARIABLE $inState$

20 VARIABLE $unhandledRequest$
21 VARIABLE $ExecutionTime$

23 $ExecTimeSpec \triangleq$ INSTANCE $ExecTimeConstrainedComponent$
24 WITH $LastExecutionTime \leftarrow ExecutionTime,$
25 $ExecutionTime \leftarrow ExecutionTimeConstr$

27 $CompSpec \triangleq ExecTimeSpec!Component$

29

Definition of the context-model–application-model mapping

34 $ModelMapping \triangleq \ \land \ step = 0 \Rightarrow \ \land \ inState = \text{"Idle"}$
35 $\land \ unhandledRequest \in \text{BOOLEAN}$
36 $\land \ step = 1 \Rightarrow \ \land \ inState \in \{\text{"HandlingRequest"}, \text{"Blocked"}\}$
37 $\land \ unhandledRequest = \text{FALSE}$
38 Dummy mapping for completeness' sake
39 $\land \ (step \notin \{0, 1\}) \Rightarrow \ \land \ inState = \text{"Idle"}$
40 $\land \ unhandledRequest = \text{FALSE}$

42

Final model of the $DataDeliverer$ component.

47 $DataDelivererComponent \triangleq \ \land \ DataDeliverer$
48 $\land \ CompSpec$
49 $\land \ \Box ModelMapping$

51

1 ┌─────────────── MODULE $DataDelivererResponseTime$ ─────────────┐

A module defining response time of the $DataDeliverer$'s $getData()$ operation.

6 EXTENDS $DataDeliverer$, $RealTime$

8 CONSTANT $ResponseTimeConstr$ Response time constraint to be applied

Variables:

$inState$ – the state in which the component currently is.
$unhandledRequest$ – TRUE if the environment put another request into the system.
$ResponseTime$ – the response time of the last service execution.

18 VARIABLE $inState$

20 VARIABLE $unhandledRequest$
21 VARIABLE $ResponseTime$

23 $ResponseTimeSpec \triangleq$ INSTANCE $ResponseTimeConstrainedService$
24   WITH $LastResponseTime \leftarrow ResponseTime$,
25                         $ResponseTime \leftarrow ResponseTimeConstr$

27 $ServSpec \triangleq ResponseTimeSpec!Service$

29 ├──┤

Definition of the context-model–application-model mapping

34 $ModelMapping \triangleq \land step = 0 \Rightarrow \land inState =$ "Idle"
35                                    $\land unhandledRequest \in$ BOOLEAN
36                   $\land step = 1 \Rightarrow \land inState =$ "HandlingRequest"
37                                    $\land unhandledRequest =$ FALSE
38   Dummy mapping for completeness' sake
39                   $\land (step \notin \{0, 1\}) \Rightarrow \land inState =$ "Idle"
40                                    $\land unhandledRequest =$ FALSE

42 ├──┤

Final model of the $DataDeliverer$ $Service$.

47 $DataDelivererService \triangleq \land DataDeliverer$
48                         $\land ServSpec$
49                         $\land \Box ModelMapping$

51 └──┘

Eventually, we need a container strategy to transform execution time into response time. We reuse the specification from Page 168. However, there is one difference (*cf.* Lines 193– 195): We have to model CPU as a shared resource.

1 ——————————————— MODULE *SimpleContainer* ———————————————

A container specification for a very simple container. This container manages just one component instance and tries to achieve a certain response time with it.

7 EXTENDS *RealTime*

Parameters:

ResponseTime – the response time the container should achieve.
ExecutionTime – the execution time of the component available.

15 CONSTANT *ResponseTime*
16 ASSUME $(ResponseTime \in Real) \land (ResponseTime > 0)$

18 CONSTANT *ExecutionTime*
19 ASSUME $(ExecutionTime \in Real) \land (ExecutionTime > 0)$

Output-Variables:

TaskCount – the number of tasks the container would want to execute on the *CPU*.
Periods – the periods the container associates with these tasks.
Wcets – the worst case execution times the container associates with these tasks.

30 VARIABLES $TaskCount, Periods, Wcets$

32 ├──┤

Specification of required *CPU* scheduling behaviour. Note that this does not make any statement about the actual scheduling regime, but only states what tasks need to be scheduled.

Variables:

CPUMinExecTime – records for each task the minimum amount of execution time it has been allocated over all periods so far.
CPUAssignedTo – holds the number of the task currently assigned the resource.

48 VARIABLES $CPUMinExecTime, CPUAssignedTo$
49   The parameters of the *CPU* provided - Input variables
50 VARIABLES $AllTaskCount, AllPeriods, AllWcets$
51 $\_CPU \triangleq$
52   INSTANCE $TimedCPUScheduler$
53   WITH $MinExecTime \leftarrow CPUMinExecTime,$
54       $AssignedTo \leftarrow CPUAssignedTo,$
55       $TaskCount \leftarrow AllTaskCount,$
56       $Periods \leftarrow AllPeriods,$
57       $Wcets \leftarrow AllWcets$
58 $CPUCanSchedule(TaskCountConstr, PeriodsConstr, WcetsConstr)$
59    $\triangleq \land \_CPU!TimedCPUScheduler$
60       $\land \Box \_CPU!ExecutionTimesOk$
61       $\land$ Our tasks are included in the task set scheduled by the *CPU*
62       $\Box \land AllTaskCount \geq TaskCountConstr$
63       $\land \forall i \in \{1 .. TaskCountConstr\} : \exists j \in \{1 .. AllTaskCount\} :$
64          $\land PeriodsConstr[i] = AllPeriods[j]$
65          $\land WcetsConstr[i] = AllWcets[j]$

67 ├──┤

Specification of required component behaviour.

Variables:

CmpInState   – the state in which the component currently is.

$CmpUnhandledRequest$ – TRUE if the environment put another request into the system.
$CmpLastExecutionTime$ – the execution time of the last service execution.

80 VARIABLES $CmpInState, CmpUnhandledRequest, CmpLastExecutionTime$

82 $\_Component(ExecutionTimeConstraint)$
83 $\triangleq$ INSTANCE $ExecTimeConstrainedComponent$
84 WITH $ExecutionTime \leftarrow ExecutionTimeConstraint,$
85 $inState \leftarrow CmpInState,$
86 $unhandledRequest \leftarrow CmpUnhandledRequest,$
87 $LastExecutionTime \leftarrow CmpLastExecutionTime$
88 $ComponentMaxExecTime(ExecutionTimeConstraint)$
89 $\triangleq \_Component(ExecutionTimeConstraint)!Component$

This predicate represents the functionality of the component.

94 CONSTANT $CompFun$
95 ASSUME $CompFun \in$ BOOLEAN

This predicate represents the mapping between functionality and context model of the component.

101 CONSTANT $CompModelMapping$
102 ASSUME $CompModelMapping \in$ BOOLEAN

104 ├───┤

Specification of required request interarrival time.

Variables:

$EnvLastDeltaTime$ – The amount of time between the last two requests.
$EnvInState$ – Current state of the service invoked.
$EnvUnhandledRequest$ – TRUE signals that a new request has been put into the system.

117 VARIABLES $EnvLastDeltaTime, EnvInState, EnvUnhandledRequest$

119 $\_MinInterrequestTime(RequestPeriodConstraint)$
120 $\triangleq$ INSTANCE $MaxRequPeriodEnv$
121 WITH $RequestPeriod \leftarrow RequestPeriodConstraint,$
122 $LastDeltaTime \leftarrow EnvLastDeltaTime,$
123 $inState \leftarrow EnvInState,$
124 $unhandledRequest \leftarrow EnvUnhandledRequest$
125 $MinInterrequestTime(RequestPeriodConstraint)$
126 $\triangleq \_MinInterrequestTime(RequestPeriodConstraint)!Environment$

128 ├───┤

Specification of guaranteed service behaviour.

Variables:

$ServLastResponseTime$ – the response time of the last request serviced.
$ServInState$ – the current state of the service machinery.
$ServUnhandledRequest$ – TRUE indicates the arrival of a new request.

140 VARIABLES $ServLastResponseTime, ServInState, ServUnhandledRequest$

142 $\_ServiceResponseTime(ResponseTimeConstraint)$
143 $\triangleq$ INSTANCE $ResponseTimeConstrainedService$
144 WITH $ResponseTime \leftarrow ResponseTimeConstraint,$
145 $LastResponseTime \leftarrow ServLastResponseTime,$
146 $inState \leftarrow ServInState,$
147 $unhandledRequest \leftarrow ServUnhandledRequest$
148 $ServiceResponseTime(ResponseTimeConstraint)$
149 $\triangleq \_ServiceResponseTime(ResponseTimeConstraint)!Service$

This predicate represents the functionality of the service.

154 CONSTANT $ServFun$
155 ASSUME $ServFun \in$ BOOLEAN

This predicate represents the mapping between functionality and context model of the service.

161 CONSTANT $ServModelMapping$
162 ASSUME $ServModelMapping \in$ BOOLEAN

---

165 $ContainerPreCond \stackrel{\Delta}{=} \wedge$ Generic sensibility rules
166 $\wedge ExecutionTime \leq ResponseTime$
167 $\wedge$ The CPU must be able to schedule exactly one task with a period
168 equal to the requested response time and a wcet equal to the
169 specified execution time of the available component.
170 $\wedge CPUCanSchedule(1,$
171 $[n \in \{1\} \mapsto ResponseTime],$
172 $[n \in \{1\} \mapsto ExecutionTime])$
173 $\wedge$ A component with the required execution time is available.
174 $\wedge ComponentMaxExecTime(ExecutionTime)$
175 $\wedge CompFun$
176 $\wedge CompModelMapping$
177 $\wedge$ The component functionality implements the service
178 functionality.
179 $CompFun \Rightarrow ServFun$
180 $\wedge$ Requests arrive with a constant period, the length of which is
181 somehow related to the period length requested from the CPU.
182 $\wedge MinInterrequestTime(ResponseTime)$

185 $ContainerPostCond \stackrel{\Delta}{=} \wedge$ The promised response time can be guaranteed
186 $\wedge ServiceResponseTime(ResponseTime)$
187 $\wedge ServFun$
188 $\wedge ServModelMapping$
189 $\wedge \Box(CmpUnhandledRequest = EnvUnhandledRequest)$

---

193 $Container \stackrel{\Delta}{=} \wedge \Box \wedge TaskCount = 1$
194 $\wedge Periods = [n \in \{1\} \mapsto ResponseTime]$
195 $\wedge Wcets = [n \in \{1\} \mapsto ExecutionTime]$
196 $\wedge ContainerPreCond \stackrel{+}{\Rightarrow} ContainerPostCond$

Using this strategy with the data deliverer component creates an encapsulated data deliverer component, specified by the following module. Note that the resource requirements have been made an environment condition of the data deliverer (*cf.* Lines 133–141).

```
1 ┌──────────────────── MODULE DataDelivererService ────────────────────┐
```

This describes the service provided by a *DataDeliverer* component managed by a simple container. It expects the environment to provide for *CPU* which can schedule the task set determined by the container. In addition, the spec. provides parameters to set the response time the service should exhibit.

8 EXTENDS *RealTime*

10 The response time the service should exhibit.
11 CONSTANT *ResponseTimeConstraint*
12 ASSUME $(ResponseTimeConstraint \in Real) \wedge (ResponseTimeConstraint > 0)$

14 The request perdiod for calls to this service.
15 CONSTANT *RequestPeriod*
16 ASSUME $(RequestPeriod \in Real) \wedge (RequestPeriod > 0)$

```
18 ├─────────────────────────────────────────────────────────────────────┤
```

The component implementation.

22 VARIABLES *CmpInState*, *CmpUnhandledRequest*, *CmpLastExecutionTime*

24 VARIABLES *CmpStep*, *CmpDataDelivererState*
25 CONSTANT *CmpInitialDataDevState*
26 CONSTANT $CmpCallGetData(\_,\_)$
27 CONSTANT $CmpReturnGetData(\_,\_,\_)$

29 $\_Component \triangleq$
30   INSTANCE *DataDelivererExecTime*
31   WITH $ExecutionTimeConstr \leftarrow 7,$ As determined by measuring the component
32   implementation
33          $inState \leftarrow CmpInState,$
34          $unhandledRequest \leftarrow CmpUnhandledRequest,$
35          $ExecutionTime \leftarrow CmpLastExecutionTime,$
36          $step \leftarrow CmpStep,$
37          $dataDelivererState \leftarrow CmpDataDelivererState,$
38          $initialDataDevState \leftarrow CmpInitialDataDevState,$
39          $CallGetData \leftarrow CmpCallGetData,$
40          $ReturnGetData \leftarrow CmpReturnGetData$

42 $Component \triangleq \_Component!DataDelivererComponent$

44 $CompFun \triangleq \_Component!DataDeliverer$
45 $CompModelMapping \triangleq \_Component!ModelMapping$

```
47 ├─────────────────────────────────────────────────────────────────────┤
```

The service to be provided.

51 VARIABLES *ServInState*, *ServUnhandledRequest*, *ServLastResponseTime*
52 VARIABLES *ServStep*, *ServDataDelivererState*
53 CONSTANT *ServInitialDataDevState*
54 CONSTANT $ServCallGetData(\_,\_)$
55 CONSTANT $ServReturnGetData(\_,\_,\_)$

57 $\_Service \triangleq$
58   INSTANCE *DataDelivererResponseTime*
59   WITH $ResponseTimeConstr \leftarrow ResponseTimeConstraint,$
60          $inState \leftarrow ServInState,$
61          $unhandledRequest \leftarrow ServUnhandledRequest,$

62   $ResponseTime \leftarrow ServLastResponseTime,$

63   $step \leftarrow ServStep,$

64   $dataDelivererState \leftarrow ServDataDelivererState,$

65   $initialDataDevState \leftarrow ServInitialDataDevState,$

66   $CallGetData \leftarrow ServCallGetData,$

67   $ReturnGetData \leftarrow ServReturnGetData$

69   $Service \;\triangleq\; \_Service!DataDelivererService$

71   $ServFun \;\triangleq\; \_Service!DataDeliverer$

72   $ServModelMapping \;\triangleq\; \_Service!ModelMapping$

74

The CPU to be provided by the environment.

78   VARIABLES $CPUMinExecTime, CPUAssignedTo$

79   Input parameters: What the CPU really does

80   VARIABLES $AllTaskCount, AllPeriods, AllWcets$

81   Output parameters: What we want to be doing with the CPU

82   VARIABLES $TaskCount, Periods, Wcets$

83   $\_CPU \;\triangleq\;$

84   INSTANCE $TimedCPUScheduler$

85   WITH $MinExecTime \leftarrow CPUMinExecTime,$

86     $AssignedTo \leftarrow CPUAssignedTo,$

87     $TaskCount \leftarrow AllTaskCount,$

88     $Periods \leftarrow AllPeriods,$

89     $Wcets \leftarrow AllWcets$

90   $CPUCanSchedule(TaskCountConstr, PeriodsConstr, WcetsConstr)$

91    $\triangleq \;\; \wedge \_CPU!TimedCPUScheduler$

92     $\wedge \;\Box\, \_CPU!ExecutionTimesOk$

93     $\wedge$ Our tasks are included in the task set scheduled by the CPU

94      $\Box \wedge AllTaskCount \geq TaskCountConstr$

95       $\wedge \, \forall\, i \in \{1\,..\,TaskCountConstr\} : \exists\, j \in \{1\,..\,AllTaskCount\} :$

96        $\wedge \, PeriodsConstr[i] = AllPeriods[j]$

97        $\wedge \, WcetsConstr[i] = AllWcets[j]$

99

The call frequency specification.

103   VARIABLE $LastDeltaTime$

104   $\_CallsFromEnv \;\triangleq\;$

105   INSTANCE $MaxRequPeriodEnv$

106   WITH $inState \leftarrow ServInState,$

107     $unhandledRequest \leftarrow ServUnhandledRequest$

108   $EnvCalls \;\triangleq\; \_CallsFromEnv!Environment$

110

The container managing the component.

114   $\_Container \;\triangleq\;$

115   INSTANCE $SimpleContainer$

116   WITH $ResponseTime \leftarrow ResponseTimeConstraint,$

117     $ExecutionTime \leftarrow 7,$

118     $EnvLastDeltaTime \leftarrow LastDeltaTime,$

119     $EnvInState \leftarrow ServInState,$

120     $EnvUnhandledRequest \leftarrow ServUnhandledRequest$

121   $Container \;\triangleq\; \_Container!Container$

123 ├──┤

The actual specification.

128   Internal view
129    $SubSystem \triangleq \land Component$
130                       $\land Container$

132   External view
133    $ExternalService \triangleq \land \Box \land TaskCount = 1$
134                       $\land Periods = [n \in \{1\} \mapsto ResponseTimeConstraint]$
135                       $\land Wcets = [n \in \{1\} \mapsto 7]$
136              $\land \land CPUCanSchedule($
137                       $1,$
138                       $[n \in \{1\} \mapsto ResponseTimeConstraint],$
139                       $[n \in \{1\} \mapsto 7])$
140              $\land EnvCalls$
141              $\overset{+}{\twoheadrightarrow} Service$

143 ├──┤

145   THEOREM $SubSystem \Rightarrow ExternalService$

147 └──┘

Next, we show the specification of the complete system consisting of a calculator and two data deliverers. We use a different specification for DataDeliverer, in which we have removed any information about the internals of this encapsulated component, and only show its external view.

1 ─────────────── MODULE *DataDelivererService* ───────────────

This describes the service provided by a *DataDeliverer* component managed by a simple container. It expects the environment to provide for *CPU* which can schedule the task set determined by the container. In addition, the spec. provides parameters to set the response time the service should exhibit.

8 EXTENDS *RealTime*

10 The response time the service should exhibit.
11 CONSTANT *ResponseTimeConstraint*
12 ASSUME $(ResponseTimeConstraint \in Real) \wedge (ResponseTimeConstraint > 0)$

14 The request perdiod for calls to this service.
15 CONSTANT *RequestPeriod*
16 ASSUME $(RequestPeriod \in Real) \wedge (RequestPeriod > 0)$

18 ├───┤

The service to be provided.

22 VARIABLES *ServInState, ServUnhandledRequest, ServLastResponseTime*

24 VARIABLES *ServStep, ServDataDelivererState*
25 CONSTANT *ServInitialDataDevState*
26 CONSTANT *ServCallGetData(_, _)*
27 CONSTANT *ServReturnGetData(_, _, _)*

29 _Service $\triangleq$
30   INSTANCE *DataDelivererResponseTime*
31   WITH *ResponseTimeConstr ← ResponseTimeConstraint,*
32   *inState ← ServInState,*
33   *unhandledRequest ← ServUnhandledRequest,*
34   *ResponseTime ← ServLastResponseTime,*
35   *step ← ServStep,*
36   *dataDelivererState ← ServDataDelivererState,*
37   *initialDataDevState ← ServInitialDataDevState,*
38   *CallGetData ← ServCallGetData,*
39   *ReturnGetData ← ServReturnGetData*

41 *Service* $\triangleq$ *_Service!DataDelivererService*

43 ├───┤

The *CPU* to be provided by the environment.

47 VARIABLES *CPUMinExecTime, CPUAssignedTo*
48 VARIABLES *AllTaskCount, AllPeriods, AllWcets* The parameters of the *CPU* provided -
49   Input variables
50 _CPU $\triangleq$
51   INSTANCE *TimedCPUScheduler*
52   WITH *MinExecTime ← CPUMinExecTime,*
53   *AssignedTo ← CPUAssignedTo,*
54   *TaskCount ← AllTaskCount,*
55   *Periods ← AllPeriods,*
56   *Wcets ← AllWcets*
57 *CPUCanSchedule(TaskCountConstr, PeriodsConstr, WcetsConstr)*
58     $\triangleq$ $\wedge$ *_CPU!TimedCPUScheduler*
59          $\wedge$ $\Box$*_CPU!ExecutionTimesOk*

```
60          ∧  Our tasks are included in the task set scheduled by the CPU
61             □ ∧ AllTaskCount ≥ TaskCountConstr
62                ∧ ∀ i ∈ {1 .. TaskCountConstr} : ∃ j ∈ {1 .. AllTaskCount} :
63                   ∧ PeriodsConstr[i] = AllPeriods[j]
64                   ∧ WcetsConstr[i] = AllWcets[j]
```

The call frequency specification.

```
70  VARIABLE LastDeltaTime
71  _CallsFromEnv  ≜
72     INSTANCE MaxRequPeriodEnv
73      WITH inState ← ServInState,
74            unhandledRequest ← ServUnhandledRequest
75  EnvCalls  ≜  _CallsFromEnv!Environment
```

```
79  VARIABLES TaskCount, Periods, Wcets   What we want to schedule - Output variables
```

External view
```
82  DataDelivererService  ≜  ∧ □ ∧ TaskCount = 1
83                             ∧ Periods = [n ∈ {1}
84                                          ↦ ResponseTimeConstraint]
85                             ∧ Wcets = [n ∈ {1} ↦ 7]
86                          ∧ ∧ CPUCanSchedule(1,
87                                             [n ∈ {1} ↦
88                                             ResponseTimeConstraint],
89                                             [n ∈ {1} ↦ 7])
90                             ∧ EnvCalls
91                             ⊹▷ Service
```

The following two specifications define the `Calculator` component. The first module represents the interface.

1 ┌─────────────────── MODULE *CalculatorIntf* ───────────────────┐

Offered interface of the Calculator component. This component offers exactly one operation: *getResult*, modelled by two actions *CallGetResult* and *ReturnGetResult*. *getResult* computes some value and returns it.

7 EXTENDS *Naturals*

9 VARIABLE *calculatorState*   Abstract representation of the Calculator's state
10 CONSTANT *initialCalcState*   Set of initial Calculator states

12 *CallGetResult*(*calculatorState*, *calculatorState'*) represents invocation of the *getResult*
13 operation.
14 CONSTANT *CallGetResult*(_, _)

16 *ReturnGetResult* (*calculatorState*, *calculatorState'*, result) represents the return from
17 invocation for operation *getResult*. result' contains the result as a natural number.
18 CONSTANT *ReturnGetResult*(_, _, _)

20 ASSUME ∀ *csOld*, *csNew* : ∀ *result* ∈ *Nat* :
21 ∧ *CallGetResult*(*csOld*, *csNew*) ∈ BOOLEAN
22 ∧ *ReturnGetResult*(*csOld*, *csNew*, *result*) ∈ BOOLEAN

24 └───┘

The following specification is the implementation of the calculator. Note how it refers to the two data deliverers using *DataDelivererIntf* on Lines 14–27 and 29–42.

1 ┌─────────────────── MODULE *Calculator* ───────────────────┐

Our *Calculator* component. It uses two *DataDeliverers*, referred to as summands and factors, adds two values obtained from summands and multiplies the result by a value obtained from factors.

7 EXTENDS *CalculatorIntf*

9 ├───┤

The used interfaces of this component.

14   Interface to a *DataDeliverer* from which we get our summands.
15 VARIABLE *summandsState*
16 CONSTANT *CallSummandGet*(_, _)
17 CONSTANT *ReturnSummand*(_, _, _)
18 CONSTANT *initialSummandState*
19 *summands* ≜ INSTANCE *DataDelivererIntf*
20   WITH *dataDelivererState* ← *summandsState*,
21   *CallGetData* ← *CallSummandGet*,
22   *ReturnGetData* ← *ReturnSummand*,
23   *initialDataDevState* ← *initialSummandState*
24   Some shortcuts to be used with the summands interface
25 *CallGetSummand* ≜ *CallSummandGet*(*summandsState*, *summandsState'*)
26 *GetSummandResult*(*result*)
27   ≜ *ReturnSummand*(*summandsState*, *summandsState'*, *result*)

29   Interface to a *DataDeliverer* from which we get our factors.
30 VARIABLE *factorsState*
31 CONSTANT *CallFactorGet*(_, _)
32 CONSTANT *ReturnFactor*(_, _, _)
33 CONSTANT *initialFactorState*

34 $factors \triangleq$ INSTANCE $DataDelivererIntf$
35   WITH $dataDelivererState \leftarrow factorsState,$
36                  $CallGetData \leftarrow CallFactorGet,$
37                  $ReturnGetData \leftarrow ReturnFactor,$
38                  $initialDataDevState \leftarrow initialFactorState$
39 Some shortcuts to be used with the factors interface
40 $CallGetFactor \triangleq CallFactorGet(factorsState, factorsState')$
41 $GetFactorResult(result) \triangleq ReturnFactor(factorsState, factorsState',$
42 $result)$

44

Internal variables of the calculator: step is a program counter, and acc is an accumulator containing the current result.
49 VARIABLES $step, acc$

51 $Init \triangleq \wedge calculatorState \in initialCalcState$
52          $\wedge step = 0$
53          $\wedge acc \in Nat$

55 Arrival of a new call
56 $GetResultCall \triangleq \wedge step = 0$ Only accept calls if not currently processing one
57                      $\wedge CallGetResult(calculatorState, calculatorState')$
58                      $\wedge step' = 1$ Start work
59                      $\wedge acc' = 0$
60   Requiring $summandsState$ and $factorsState$ to be unchanged enforces
61   synchronisation. If we were not to do so, we could have 'phantom
62   calls', where the interface processes a call that has never been
63   initiated by the calling component.
64                      $\wedge$ UNCHANGED $\langle summandsState, factorsState \rangle$

66 Asking summands for the first summand
67 $RequestFirstSummand \triangleq \wedge step = 1$
68                              $\wedge CallGetSummand$
69                              $\wedge step' = 2$
70                              $\wedge$ UNCHANGED $\langle acc, calculatorState, factorsState \rangle$

72 Summands answers
73 $ObtainFirstSummand \triangleq \wedge step = 2$
74                          $\wedge GetSummandResult(acc')$
75                          $\wedge step' = 3$
76                          $\wedge$ UNCHANGED $\langle calculatorState, factorsState \rangle$

78 Ask summands for the second summand
79 $RequestSecondSummand \triangleq \wedge step = 3$
80                              $\wedge CallGetSummand$
81                              $\wedge step' = 4$
82                              $\wedge$ UNCHANGED $\langle acc, calculatorState, factorsState \rangle$

84 summands answers again
85 $ObtainSecondSummand \triangleq \wedge step = 4$
86                              $\wedge \exists result \in Nat : \wedge GetSummandResult(result)$
87 $\wedge acc' = acc + result$
88                              $\wedge step' = 5$
89                              $\wedge$ UNCHANGED $\langle calculatorState, factorsState \rangle$

91 Ask factors for a factor

92   $RequestFactor \triangleq \land step = 5$
93                     $\land CallGetFactor$
94                     $\land step' = 6$
95                     $\land \text{UNCHANGED} \langle acc,\ calculatorState,\ summandsState \rangle$

97   factors answers
98   $ObtainFactor \triangleq \land step = 6$
99                  $\land \exists\, result \in Nat : \land GetFactorResult(result)$
100                                    $\land acc' = acc * result$
101                  $\land step' = 7$
102                  $\land \text{UNCHANGED} \langle calculatorState,\ summandsState \rangle$

104   Return the final result of the computation
105   $ReturnResult \triangleq \land step = 7$
106                  $\land ReturnGetResult(calculatorState,\ calculatorState',\ acc)$
107                  $\land step' = 0$ Ready to start again
108                  $\land \text{UNCHANGED} \langle acc,\ summandsState,\ factorsState \rangle$

110   $Next \triangleq \lor GetResultCall$
111             $\lor RequestFirstSummand$
112             $\lor ObtainFirstSummand$
113             $\lor RequestSecondSummand$
114             $\lor ObtainSecondSummand$
115             $\lor RequestFactor$
116             $\lor ObtainFactor$
117             $\lor ReturnResult$

119   $vars \triangleq \langle step,\ acc,\ calculatorState,\ summandsState,\ factorsState \rangle$

121   $Calculator \triangleq \land Init$
122               $\land \Box[Next]_{vars}$

124

We use an extended context model of a component. This context model allows for an additional state 'OperationCall', which represents times where the component waits for a call to a used component to return.

1 ┌─────────────────────── MODULE *Component* ───────────────────────┐

Models the functional side of a component impl.

6 ├──┤

Variables:

unhandledRequest – set to TRUE by the environment to indicate that a new request has arrived and should be
handled.
inState   – the state in which the component is.

15 VARIABLE *inState*
16 VARIABLE *unhandledRequest*

18 *vars* $\triangleq$ $\langle inState,\ unhandledRequest \rangle$

20 ├──┤

22   The agent set μ which *SpecEnv* does not constrain and *SpecComponent* constrains
23   at most.
24 LOCAL *SystemAgent* $\triangleq$ $inState' \neq inState$

26 ├──┤

The environment specification.

The environment in particular influences the *unhandledRequest* variable by entering new requests into the
system.

35   The environment sets the *unhandledRequest* flag at some arbitrary moment to indicate a
36   new request.
37 *RequestArrival* $\triangleq$ $\land$ *unhandledRequest* = FALSE
38                          $\land$ *unhandledRequest'* = TRUE
39                          $\land$ UNCHANGED *inState*

41 *NextEnv* $\triangleq$ *RequestArrival*

43 *SpecEnv* $\triangleq$ $\Box[NextEnv \lor SystemAgent]_{vars}$

45 ├──┤

The actual component.

It mainly specifies changes to the *inState* variable, however it communicates with the environment via the
unhandledRequest variable.

54   Initially we start out in the idle state
55 *InitComponent* $\triangleq$ *inState* = "Idle"

57   Initially there are no requests in the system
58   Note that we need to put this in the initialisation of the component, in order to
59   separate the agents correctly
60 *InitEnv* $\triangleq$ *unhandledRequest* = FALSE

62   The transition from idle to handling request is triggered by an incoming request
63 *StartRequest* $\triangleq$ $\land$ *inState* = "Idle"
64                          $\land$ *unhandledRequest* = TRUE
65                          $\land$ *inState'* = "HandlingRequest" $\lor$ *inState'* = "Blocked"
66                          $\land$ *unhandledRequest'* = FALSE

68   Request handling can finish any time

69   $FinishRequest \triangleq \land inState =$ "HandlingRequest"

70                 $\land inState' =$ "Idle"

71                 $\land$ UNCHANGED $unhandledRequest$

73   Also, the runtime environment may at any time take away the CPU from us and assign it

74   to someone else.

75   $SwitchToOther \triangleq \land inState =$ "HandlingRequest"

76                 $\land inState' =$ "Blocked"

77                 $\land$ UNCHANGED $unhandledRequest$

79   But, it may also at any time give back the CPU to us

80   $SwitchBack \triangleq \land inState =$ "Blocked"

81                 $\land inState' =$ "HandlingRequest"

82                 $\land$ UNCHANGED $unhandledRequest$

84   $CallOperation \triangleq \land inState =$ "HandlingRequest"

85                 $\land inState' =$ "OperationCall"

86                 $\land$ UNCHANGED $unhandledRequest$

88   $OperationReturn \triangleq \land inState =$ "OperationCall"

89                 $\land inState' =$ "HandlingRequest"

90                 $\land$ UNCHANGED $unhandledRequest$

92   $NextComponent \triangleq \lor StartRequest$

93                 $\lor FinishRequest$

94                 $\lor SwitchToOther$

95                 $\lor SwitchBack$

96                 $\lor CallOperation$

97                 $\lor OperationReturn$

99   $SpecComponent \triangleq \land InitComponent$

100                 $\land InitEnv$

101                 $\land \Box[NextComponent \lor \neg SystemAgent]_{vars}$

103 ———

    The complete specification

108   $Component \triangleq SpecEnv \overset{+}{\Rightarrow} SpecComponent$

110 ———

112   $TypeInvariant \triangleq \land inState \in \{$"Idle", "HandlingRequest",

113   "Blocked", "OperationCall"$\}$

114                 $\land unhandledRequest \in$ BOOLEAN

115 ———

Based on this context model we can define the call time measurement.

1 ┌─────────── MODULE *CallTimeConstrainedComponent* ───────────┐

Specification of a component which offers one operation. This operation may call other operations, and the
component offers a way to determine the amount of time spent in those calls.

7 EXTENDS *RealTime*

Parameters:

CallTime – an upper bound for the time spent in invocations of other components' operations.

15 CONSTANT *CallTime*
16 ASSUME $(CallTime \in Real) \wedge (CallTime > 0)$

Variables:

inState   – the state in which the component currently is.
unhandledRequest – TRUE if the environment put another request into the system.
LastCallTime   – The invocation time of the last call to other operations.

27 VARIABLE *inState*
28 VARIABLE *unhandledRequest*
29 VARIABLE *LastCallTime*

31 ├──┤

33 ┌──────────────────── MODULE *Inner* ────────────────────┐

Internal module containing the actual specification.

Variables:

SegStart   – The start time of the current call to another operation.

44 VARIABLE *SegStart*

46 ├──┤

We base our specification on the specification of the functional mechanics of a component executing a service.

This is essentially the context model.

54 *BasicComponent* ≜ INSTANCE *Component*

56 ├──┤

58    $Init \triangleq LastCallTime = 0 \wedge SegStart = 0$

60   *StartNext* reacts to a *StartRequest* step
61    $StartNext \triangleq BasicComponent!StartRequest \Rightarrow \wedge LastCallTime = 0$
62 $\wedge$ UNCHANGED *SegStart*

64   *RespNext* reacts to a *FinishRequest* step
65    $RespNext \triangleq BasicComponent!FinishRequest \Rightarrow$ UNCHANGED $\langle SegStart,$
66 $LastCallTime \rangle$

68   *STONext* reacts to a *SwitchToOther* step
69    $STONext \triangleq BasicComponent!SwitchToOther \Rightarrow$ UNCHANGED $\langle LastCallTime,$
70 $SegStart \rangle$

72   *SBNext* reacts to a *SwitchBack* step
73    $SBNext \triangleq BasicComponent!SwitchBack \Rightarrow$ UNCHANGED $\langle LastCallTime,$
74 $SegStart \rangle$

76   *CONext* reacts to a *CallOperation* step
77    $CONext \triangleq BasicComponent!CallOperation \Rightarrow \wedge SegStart' = now$
78 $\wedge$ UNCHANGED $\langle LastCallTime \rangle$

80   *ORNext* reacts to an *OperationReturn* step

81    $ORNext \triangleq BasicComponent!OperationReturn$

82          $\Rightarrow \land LastCallTime' = LastCallTime + now - SegStart$

83          $\land \text{UNCHANGED } \langle SegStart \rangle$

85    $Next \triangleq \land StartNext \land RespNext$

86          $\land STONext \land SBNext$

87          $\land CONext \land ORNext$

inState, *unhandledRequest* are implicit, because whenever they have changed, one of the *Component* actions must have fired.

91    $vars \triangleq \langle SegStart, LastCallTime \rangle$

93    $Spec \triangleq \land Init$

94          $\land \Box[Next]_{vars}$

96   Compose the various partial specifications

97    $Component \triangleq \land BasicComponent!Component$

98          $\land RTnow(vars)$

99          $\land Spec$

100   And don't forget the constraint on call time.

101          $\land \Box(LastCallTime \leq CallTime)$

103 ├───┤

Type invariant

108    $TypeInvariant \triangleq \land (SegStart \in Real) \land (SegStart \geq 0)$

109          $\land (LastCallTime \in Real) \land (LastCallTime \geq 0)$

111 └───┘

113 ├───┤

115    $\_Component(SegStart) \triangleq \text{INSTANCE } Inner$

117    $Component \triangleq \exists ss : \_Component(ss)!Component$

119 └───┘

CalculatorResponseTime maps the response_time measurement for the getResult operation of the calculator service. *CalculatorExecTime* maps execution_time for getResult of the calculator component.

```
1 ┌────────────────── MODULE CalculatorResponseTime ──────────────────┐
  A module defining response time of the Calculator's getResult() operation.

5 EXTENDS Calculator, RealTime

7 CONSTANT ResponseTimeConstr

  Variables:

  ResponseTime    – the response time of the last request serviced.
  inState         – the current state of the service machinery.
  unhandledRequest – TRUE indicates the arrival of a new request.

16 VARIABLES ResponseTime, inState, unhandledRequest


19 ResponseTimeSpec ≜ INSTANCE ResponseTimeConstrainedService
20                      WITH LastResponseTime ← ResponseTime,
21                           ResponseTime ← ResponseTimeConstr

23 ServSpec        ≜ ResponseTimeSpec!Service

25├──────────────────────────────────────────────────────────────────┤

  Definition of the context-model–application-model mapping
30 ModelMapping ≜ ∧ step = 0 ⇒ ∧ inState = "Idle"
31                              ∧ unhandledRequest = FALSE
32                ∧ step = 1 ⇒ ∧ inState = "Idle"
33                              ∧ unhandledRequest = TRUE
34                ∧ step ∈ {2, 3, 4, 5, 6, 7} ⇒ ∧ inState = "HandlingRequest"
35                                              ∧ unhandledRequest = FALSE
36                Dummy mapping for completeness' sake
37                ∧ (step ∉ {0, 1, 2, 3, 4, 5, 6, 7}) ⇒
38                                              ∧ inState = "Idle"
39                                              ∧ unhandledRequest = FALSE

41├──────────────────────────────────────────────────────────────────┤

  Final model of the Calculator service .
46 CalculatorService ≜ ∧ Calculator
47                      ∧ ServSpec
48                      ∧ □ModelMapping

50└──────────────────────────────────────────────────────────────────┘



1 ┌────────────────── MODULE CalculatorExecTime ──────────────────┐
  A module defining execution time of the Calculator's getResult() operation.

5 EXTENDS Calculator, RealTime

7 CONSTANT ExecutionTimeConstr

  Variables:

  inState         – the state in which the component currently is.
  unhandledRequest – TRUE if the environment put another request into the system.
  LastExecutionTime – the execution time of the last service execution.
```

17 VARIABLE *inState*

19 VARIABLE *unhandledRequest*
20 VARIABLE *ExecutionTime*

22 *ExecTimeSpec* $\triangleq$ INSTANCE *ExecTimeConstrainedComponent*
23   WITH *LastExecutionTime* $\leftarrow$ *ExecutionTime*,
24   *ExecutionTime* $\leftarrow$ *ExecutionTimeConstr*

26 *CompSpec* $\triangleq$ *ExecTimeSpec!Component*

28 ├──┤

Definition of the context-model–application-model mapping

33 *ModelMapping* $\triangleq$ $\wedge$ *step* = 0 $\Rightarrow$ $\wedge$ *inState* = "Idle"
34                                      $\wedge$ *unhandledRequest* = FALSE
35                          $\wedge$ *step* = 1 $\Rightarrow$ $\wedge$ *inState* = "Idle"
36                                      $\wedge$ *unhandledRequest* = TRUE
37                          $\wedge$ *step* $\in$ {2, 4, 6} $\Rightarrow$ $\wedge$ *inState* = "OperationCall"
38                                      $\wedge$ *unhandledRequest* = FALSE
39                          $\wedge$ *step* $\in$ {3, 5, 7} $\Rightarrow$ $\wedge$ *inState* $\in$ {"HandlingRequest",
40   "Blocked"}
41                                      $\wedge$ *unhandledRequest* = FALSE
42   Dummy mapping for completeness' sake
43                          $\wedge$ (*step* $\notin$ {0, 1, 2, 3, 4, 5, 6, 7}) $\Rightarrow$
44 $\wedge$ *inState* = "Idle"
45 $\wedge$ *unhandledRequest* = FALSE

47 ├──┤

Final model of the *Calculator* component.

52 *CalculatorComponent* $\triangleq$ $\wedge$ *Calculator*
53                          $\wedge$ *CompSpec*
54                          $\wedge$ $\Box$ *ModelMapping*

56 └──┘

The following module specifies a container strategy that transforms information on execution time and call time into response time of a service.

```
1 ┌──────────────── MODULE ContainerRespectingCalledOperations ────────────────┐
```

A container specification for a simple container that uses the response times of called operations to determine the response time of an operation call. This container manages just one component instance and tries to achieve a certain response time with it.

8 EXTENDS *RealTime*

Parameters:

ResponseTime – the response time the container should achieve.
ExecutionTime – the execution time of the component available.

16 CONSTANT *ResponseTime*
17 ASSUME $(ResponseTime \in Real) \land (ResponseTime > 0)$

19 CONSTANT *ExecutionTime*
20 ASSUME $(ExecutionTime \in Real) \land (ExecutionTime > 0)$

Variables - Outputs of this module:

TaskCount – the number of tasks the container would want to execute on the *CPU*.
Periods   – the periods the container associates with these tasks.
Wcets   – the worst case execution times the container associates with these tasks.

31 VARIABLES *TaskCount*, *Periods*, *Wcets*

Variables - Inputs of this module:

AllTaskCount – the number of tasks the *CPU* actually executes.
AllPeriods – the periods associated with these tasks.
AllWcets – the worst case execution times the associated with these tasks.

41 VARIABLES *AllTaskCount*, *AllPeriods*, *AllWcets*

43 ├──┤

Specification of required *CPU* scheduling behaviour. Note that this does not make any statement about the actual scheduling regime, but only states what tasks need to be scheduled.

Variables:

CPUMinExecTime – records for each task the minimum amount of execution time it has been allocated over all periods so far.
CPUAssignedTo – holds the number of the task currently assigned the resource.

59 VARIABLES *CPUMinExecTime*, *CPUAssignedTo*

61 *_SomeCPUScheduler*
62    $\triangleq$ INSTANCE *TimedCPUScheduler*
63   WITH *MinExecTime* $\leftarrow$ *CPUMinExecTime*,
64   *AssignedTo* $\leftarrow$ *CPUAssignedTo*,
65   *TaskCount* $\leftarrow$ *AllTaskCount*,
66   *Periods* $\leftarrow$ *AllPeriods*,
67   *Wcets* $\leftarrow$ *AllWcets*
68 *CPUCanSchedule*(*TaskCountConstr*, *PeriodsConstr*, *WcetsConstr*)
69    $\triangleq$ $\land$ *_SomeCPUScheduler*!*TimedCPUScheduler*
70      $\land$ $\Box$_*SomeCPUScheduler*!*ExecutionTimesOk*
71      $\land$ Our tasks are included in the task set scheduled by the *CPU*
72        $\Box$ $\land$ *AllTaskCount* $\geq$ *TaskCountConstr*
73          $\land$ $\forall i \in \{1 .. TaskCountConstr\} : \exists j \in \{1 .. AllTaskCount\} :$
74            $\land$ *PeriodsConstr*[i] $=$ *AllPeriods*[j]
75            $\land$ *WcetsConstr*[i] $=$ *AllWcets*[j]

77 ├──┤

Specification of required component behaviour.

Variables:

$CmpInState$ – the state in which the component currently is.
$CmpUnhandledRequest$ – TRUE if the environment put another request into the system.
$CmpLastExecutionTime$ – the execution time of the last service execution.

90 VARIABLES $CmpInState$, $CmpUnhandledRequest$, $CmpLastExecutionTime$
91 VARIABLE $CmpLastCallTime$

93   The execution time constraint
94 $\_Component(ExecutionTimeConstraint)$
95    $\triangleq$ INSTANCE $ExecTimeConstrainedComponent$
96   WITH $ExecutionTime \leftarrow ExecutionTimeConstraint,$
97        $inState \leftarrow CmpInState,$
98        $unhandledRequest \leftarrow CmpUnhandledRequest,$
99        $LastExecutionTime \leftarrow CmpLastExecutionTime$
100 $ComponentMaxExecTime(ExecutionTimeConstraint)$
101   $\triangleq \_Component(ExecutionTimeConstraint)!Component$

103   The call time constraint
104 $\_CompCallTime(CallTimeConstraint)$
105   $\triangleq$ INSTANCE $CallTimeConstrainedComponent$
106   WITH $CallTime \leftarrow CallTimeConstraint,$
107        $inState \leftarrow CmpInState,$
108        $unhandledRequest \leftarrow CmpUnhandledRequest,$
109        $LastCallTime \leftarrow CmpLastCallTime$
110 $ComponentMaxCallTime(CallTimeConstraint)$
111   $\triangleq \_CompCallTime(CallTimeConstraint)!Component$

113   This predicate represents the functionality of the component
114 CONSTANT $CompFun$
115 ASSUME $CompFun \in$ BOOLEAN

117   This predicate represents the mapping between functionality and context model of the
118   component.
119 CONSTANT $CompModelMapping$
120 ASSUME $CompModelMapping \in$ BOOLEAN

122 ├───┤

Specification of required request interarrival time.

Variables:

$EnvLastDeltaTime$ – The amount of time between the last two requests.
$EnvInState$ – Current state of the service invoked.
$EnvUnhandledRequest$ – TRUE signals that a new request has been put into the system.

135 VARIABLES $EnvLastDeltaTime$, $EnvInState$, $EnvUnhandledRequest$

137 $\_MinInterrequestTime(RequestPeriodConstraint)$
138   $\triangleq$ INSTANCE $MaxRequPeriodEnv$
139   WITH $RequestPeriod \leftarrow RequestPeriodConstraint,$
140        $LastDeltaTime \leftarrow EnvLastDeltaTime,$
141        $inState \leftarrow EnvInState,$
142        $unhandledRequest \leftarrow EnvUnhandledRequest$
143 $MinInterrequestTime(RequestPeriodConstraint)$
144   $\triangleq \_MinInterrequestTime(RequestPeriodConstraint)!Environment$

146├───┤

Specification of guaranteed service behaviour.

Variables:

$ServLastResponseTime$ – the response time of the last request serviced.
$ServInState$ – the current state of the service machinery.
$ServUnhandledRequest$ – TRUE indicates the arrival of a new request.

158 VARIABLES $ServLastResponseTime$, $ServInState$, $ServUnhandledRequest$

160 $\_ServiceResponseTime(ResponseTimeConstraint)$
161   $\triangleq$ INSTANCE $ResponseTimeConstrainedService$
162   WITH $ResponseTime \leftarrow ResponseTimeConstraint$,
163            $LastResponseTime \leftarrow ServLastResponseTime$,
164            $inState \leftarrow ServInState$,
165            $unhandledRequest \leftarrow ServUnhandledRequest$
166 $ServiceResponseTime(ResponseTimeConstraint)$
167   $\triangleq \_ServiceResponseTime(ResponseTimeConstraint)!Service$

169 This predicate represents the functionality of the service.
170 CONSTANT $ServFun$
171 ASSUME $ServFun \in$ BOOLEAN

173 This predicate represents the mapping between functionality and context model of the
174 service.
175 CONSTANT $ServModelMapping$
176 ASSUME $ServModelMapping \in$ BOOLEAN

178├───┤
179 $ContainerPreCond(MaxCallTime) \triangleq$
180                          $\wedge$ Generic sensibility rules
181                          $\wedge ExecutionTime + MaxCallTime \leq ResponseTime$
182                          $\wedge$ The CPU must be able to schedule exactly one task with a
183   period equal to the requested response time (minus the
184   component call time) and a wcet equal to the specified
185   execution time of the available component.
186                          $\wedge CPUCanSchedule($
187                               $1,$
188                               $[n \in \{1\} \mapsto (ResponseTime - MaxCallTime)],$
189                               $[n \in \{1\} \mapsto ExecutionTime])$
190                          $\wedge$ A component with the required execution time is available.
191                          $\wedge ComponentMaxExecTime(ExecutionTime)$
192                          $\wedge CompFun$
193                          $\wedge CompModelMapping$
194                          $\wedge$ And the available component has a known call time
195                          $\wedge ComponentMaxCallTime(MaxCallTime)$
196                          $\wedge$ The component functionality implements the service
197   functionality.
198                               $CompFun \Rightarrow ServFun$
199                          $\wedge$ Requests arrive with a constant period, the length of which is
200   somehow related to the period length requested from the CPU.
201                          $\wedge MinInterrequestTime(ResponseTime)$

204 $ContainerPostCond \triangleq \wedge$ The promised response time can be guaranteed
205                          $\wedge ServiceResponseTime(ResponseTime)$
206                          $\wedge ServFun$

207            $\land\ ServModelMapping$

208         $\land$ State that the container will hand requests directly to the

209   component, without buffering them in any way. If the container

210   provides buffering, this would need to go here

211             $\Box(\,CmpUnhandledRequest = EnvUnhandledRequest)$

213   $Container\ \overset{\Delta}{=}\ \exists\, MaxCallTime:$

214      $\land$ The container will allocate exactly one task for the component.

215       $\Box\ \land\ TaskCount = 1$

216         $\land\ Periods = [n \in \{1\} \mapsto ResponseTime - MaxCallTime]$

217         $\land\ Wcets = [n \in \{1\} \mapsto ExecutionTime]$

218     $\land\ ContainerPreCond(MaxCallTime) \xrightarrow{+} ContainerPostCond$

To describe the complete system, we need to specify how components are connected. For this purpose, we define a simple connector that transports messages in no time.

1 ─────────────────── MODULE *SimpleConnector* ───────────────────

A very simple connector that transports requests for data in one direction and the corresponding response in the other direction. This connector is strictly sequencing requests; that is, only one request is processed at a time. This specification also defines the timing behaviour of the connector. This is a little shortcut, we would normally have to use measurements for this, too. But to simplify things we have simply set the specification to say that the connector performs immediate transferral.

12 EXTENDS *Naturals*, *RealTime*

14 CONSTANT *Data*

16 VARIABLE *connector*

Type of connectors. Note that there are two independent state components for the client and the server side. This is so, because for synchronisation reasons both client and server need to be able to assert that their interface state remains UNCHANGED , unless they explicitly issue an event. At the same time, the server needs to be able to change the connector state while the client is waiting for something to be returned.
Here is how this is meant to work:

```
                                      c   s   d
                                    [0,  0,  ?]
   --- PutRequest ---------->
                                    [3,  0,  ?]
                                              --- GetRequest ----->
                                    [3,  1,  ?]
                                              <-- SendResult(x) ---
                                    [3,  2,  x]
   <-- RetrieveResult (x) ---
                                    [2,  2,  x]
                                      . . .
```

You can see, that each action changes either *clientState* or *serverState*, but never both. Still, the difference between the two values always clearly indicates what may happen next.

43 *ConnectorType* $\triangleq$ [*clientState* : *Nat*, *serverState* : *Nat*, *data* : *Data*,
44   *lastEventTime* : *Nat*]
45 *TypeInvariant* $\triangleq$ *connector* $\in$ *ConnectorType*

47 ├──┤

49 *Init* $\triangleq$ $\wedge$ *TypeInvariant*
50          $\wedge$ *connector.clientState* $= 0$
51          $\wedge$ *connector.serverState* $= 0$

53 A *PutRequest* action models sending of a request by the client.
54 *PutRequest* $\triangleq$ $\wedge$ *connector.clientState* = *connector.serverState*
55             $\wedge$ *connector'* = [*connector* EXCEPT !.*clientState* = @ + 3,
56   !.*lastEventTime* = *now*]

58 A *GetRequest* action models the moment when a new request arrives at the server.
59 *GetRequest* $\triangleq$ $\wedge$ *connector.serverState* + 3 = *connector.clientState*
60             $\wedge$ *connector.lastEventTime* = *now*
61             $\wedge$ *connector'* = [*connector* EXCEPT !.*serverState* = @ + 1]

63 A *SendResult* action models the moment when the server sends a result.
64 *SendResult*(*value*) $\triangleq$ $\wedge$ *connector.serverState* + 2 = *connector.clientState*
65                       $\wedge$ *connector'* = [*connector* EXCEPT !.*serverState* = @ + 1,
66   !.*data* = *value*,
67   !.*lastEventTime* = *now*]

69 A *RetrieveResult* action models the moment when the client receives the data.

70   $RetrieveResult(value) \triangleq \wedge connector.serverState + 1 = connector.clientState$
71                         $\wedge connector.data = value$
72                         $\wedge connector.lastEventTime = now$
73                         $\wedge connector' = [connector \text{ EXCEPT}$
74                                     $!.clientState = @ - 1]$

76   $Next \triangleq \vee PutRequest$
77           $\vee GetRequest$
78           $\vee \exists\, val \in Data : \vee SendResult(val)$
79                                     $\vee RetrieveResult(val)$

81   $Spec \triangleq \wedge RTnow(connector)$
82          $\wedge Init$
83          $\wedge \square[Next]_{connector}$

85 ├──┤

87   THEOREM $Spec \Rightarrow \square TypeInvariant$

89 └──┘

Finally, the system specification puts everything together. Note how components and connectors are related through adaptational definitions. For example, on Lines 60–86 an adapter is defined that relates the *serverState* end of connector *calcSumConnector* to the interface of a *DataDeliverer* instance.

```
1 ┌──────────────────────── MODULE System ────────────────────────┐
  A system composed of one calculator and two independent data deliverers.

5 EXTENDS Naturals, RealTime

7 CONSTANT RequestPeriod   The request period we want to use

9 ├──────────────────────────────────────────────────────────────────┤

  A CPU. The parameters of the specification can be used to indicate the number of tasks to be scheduled, their
  respective periods as well as their respective worst case execution times.

  Variables:

  MYCPU_MinExecTime – records for each task the minimum amount of execution time it has been allocated
                      over all periods so far.
  MYCPU_AssignedTo – holds the number of the task currently assigned the resource

25 VARIABLES MYCPU_MinExecTime, MYCPU_AssignedTo
26 VARIABLES CPUTaskCount, CPUPeriods, CPUWcets

28 _MyCPU ≜ INSTANCE RMSScheduler
29              WITH MinExecTime ← MYCPU_MinExecTime,
30                   AssignedTo ← MYCPU_AssignedTo,
31                   TaskCount ← CPUTaskCount,
32                   Periods ← CPUPeriods,
33                   Wcets ← CPUWcets
34 MyCPU ≜ _MyCPU!RMSScheduler

36 ├──────────────────────────────────────────────────────────────────┤
37   Connectors
38 VARIABLE calcSumConnector
39 CalcSumConnector ≜ INSTANCE SimpleConnector
40                       WITH connector ← calcSumConnector,
41                            Data ← Nat

43 VARIABLE calcFactConnector
44 CalcFactConnector ≜ INSTANCE SimpleConnector
45                       WITH connector ← calcFactConnector,
46                            Data ← Nat

48 ├──────────────────────────────────────────────────────────────────┤

  The service the summands component provides.

  Variables:

  ServResponseTime     – the response time of the last request serviced.
  ServInState          – the current state of the service machinery.
  ServUnhandledRequest – TRUE indicates the arrival of a new request.

60 VARIABLES SumServResponseTime, SumServInState, SumServUnhandledRequest
61 VARIABLES SumServStep, SumServLastDeltaTime
62 LOCAL _sumReturnData(a, b, value) ≜ ∧ a = calcSumConnector.serverState
63                                      ∧ b = calcSumConnector'.serverState
64                                      ∧ CalcSumConnector!SendResult(value)
65 LOCAL _sumRequestData(a, b) ≜ ∧ a = calcSumConnector.serverState
66                                ∧ b = calcSumConnector'.serverState
```

67                                    $\wedge\ CalcSumConnector!GetRequest$
68   $\_Summands(TaskCount,\ Periods,\ Wcets)\ \triangleq$
69   INSTANCE $DataDelivererService$
70   WITH $ResponseTimeConstraint \leftarrow 10,$
71              $RequestPeriod \leftarrow 10,$
72              $ServInState \leftarrow SumServInState,$
73              $ServUnhandledRequest \leftarrow SumServUnhandledRequest,$
74              $ServLastResponseTime \leftarrow SumServResponseTime,$
75              $ServStep \leftarrow SumServStep,$
76              $ServDataDelivererState \leftarrow calcSumConnector.serverState,$
77              $ServInitialDataDevState \leftarrow Nat,$
78              $ServCallGetData \leftarrow \_sumRequestData,$
79              $ServReturnGetData \leftarrow \_sumReturnData,$
80              $CPUMinExecTime \leftarrow MYCPU\_MinExecTime,$
81              $CPUAssignedTo \leftarrow MYCPU\_AssignedTo,$
82              $AllTaskCount \leftarrow CPUTaskCount,$
83              $AllPeriods \leftarrow CPUPeriods,$
84              $AllWcets \leftarrow CPUWcets,$
85              $LastDeltaTime \leftarrow SumServLastDeltaTime$
86   $Summands(T,\ P,\ W)\ \triangleq\ \_Summands(T,\ P,\ W)!DataDelivererService$

88 ├───┤

The service the factors component provides.

Variables:

$ServResponseTime$ – the response time of the last request serviced.
$ServInState$ – the current state of the service machinery.
$ServUnhandledRequest$ – TRUE indicates the arrival of a new request.
100 VARIABLES $FactServResponseTime,\ FactServInState,\ FactServUnhandledRequest$
101 VARIABLES $FactServStep,\ FactServLastDeltaTime$
102 LOCAL $\_facReturnData(a,\ b,\ value)\ \triangleq\ \wedge\ a = calcFactConnector.serverState$
103 $\wedge\ b = calcFactConnector'.serverState$
104 $\wedge\ CalcFactConnector!SendResult(value)$
105 LOCAL $\_facRequestData(a,\ b)\ \triangleq\ \wedge\ a = calcFactConnector.serverState$
106 $\wedge\ b = calcFactConnector'.serverState$
107 $\wedge\ CalcFactConnector!GetRequest$
108 $\_Factors(TaskCount,\ Periods,\ Wcets)\ \triangleq$
109   INSTANCE $DataDelivererService$
110   WITH $ResponseTimeConstraint \leftarrow 10,$
111              $RequestPeriod \leftarrow 10,$
112              $ServInState \leftarrow FactServInState,$
113              $ServUnhandledRequest \leftarrow FactServUnhandledRequest,$
114              $ServLastResponseTime \leftarrow FactServResponseTime,$
115              $ServStep \leftarrow FactServStep,$
116              $ServDataDelivererState \leftarrow calcFactConnector.serverState,$
117              $ServInitialDataDevState \leftarrow Nat,$
118              $ServCallGetData \leftarrow \_facRequestData,$
119              $ServReturnGetData \leftarrow \_facReturnData,$
120              $CPUMinExecTime \leftarrow MYCPU\_MinExecTime,$
121              $CPUAssignedTo \leftarrow MYCPU\_AssignedTo,$
122              $AllTaskCount \leftarrow CPUTaskCount,$
123              $AllPeriods \leftarrow CPUPeriods,$
124              $AllWcets \leftarrow CPUWcets,$
125              $LastDeltaTime \leftarrow FactServLastDeltaTime$

126   $Factors(T, P, W) \triangleq \_Factors(T, P, W)!DataDelivererService$

128├───┤

The actual *Calculator* component.

This view on the *Calculator* component is mainly based on execution time, but because we have defined the model mapping intelligently, it also defines when the component is in an external operation call, so that the container can determine the call time of the component.

140   VARIABLES $calcStep$, $calcAcc$, $calcCompUnhandledRequest$, $calcCompInState$
141   CONSTANT $calcCmpInitial$
142   VARIABLE $calcCompExecTime$, $calcIntfState$
143   LOCAL $\_calcFactGet(a, b) \triangleq \ \wedge a = calcFactConnector.clientState$
144                                 $\wedge b = calcFactConnector'.clientState$
145                                 $\wedge CalcFactConnector!PutRequest$
146   LOCAL $\_calcFactReturn(a, b, value)$
147      $\triangleq \ \wedge a = calcFactConnector.clientState$
148         $\wedge b = calcFactConnector'.clientState$
149         $\wedge CalcFactConnector!RetrieveResult(value)$
150   LOCAL $\_calcSumReturn(a, b, value)$
151      $\triangleq \ \wedge a = calcSumConnector.clientState$
152         $\wedge b = calcSumConnector'.clientState$
153         $\wedge CalcSumConnector!RetrieveResult(value)$
154   LOCAL $\_calcSumGet(a, b) \triangleq \ \wedge a = calcSumConnector.clientState$
155                                 $\wedge b = calcSumConnector'.clientState$
156                                 $\wedge CalcSumConnector!PutRequest$
157   CONSTANT $\_calcReturnGetResult(\_, \_, \_)$
158   CONSTANT $\_calcCallGetResult(\_, \_)$
159   $calc \triangleq$ INSTANCE $CalculatorExecTime$
160   WITH $step \leftarrow calcStep$,
161              $acc \leftarrow calcAcc$,
162              $summandsState \leftarrow calcSumConnector.clientState$,
163              $factorsState \leftarrow calcFactConnector.clientState$,
164              $calculatorState \leftarrow calcIntfState$,
165              $initialSummandState \leftarrow Nat$,
166              $initialFactorState \leftarrow Nat$,
167              $initialCalcState \leftarrow calcCmpInitial$,
168              $CallFactorGet \leftarrow \_calcFactGet$,
169              $ReturnFactor \leftarrow \_calcFactReturn$,
170              $CallSummandGet \leftarrow \_calcSumGet$,
171              $ReturnSummand \leftarrow \_calcSumReturn$,
172              $unhandledRequest \leftarrow calcCompUnhandledRequest$,
173              $inState \leftarrow calcCompInState$,
174              $ExecutionTime \leftarrow calcCompExecTime$,
175              $ExecutionTimeConstr \leftarrow 15$,
176              $ReturnGetResult \leftarrow \_calcReturnGetResult$,
177              $CallGetResult \leftarrow \_calcCallGetResult$

179   $CalcCompMap \triangleq \Box calc!ModelMapping$
180   $CalcCompFunc \triangleq calc!Calculator$

182├───┤

Environment specification.

Variables:

EnvLastDeltaTime – The amount of time between the last two requests.
EnvInState – Current state of the service invoked.
EnvUnhandledRequest – TRUE signals that a new request has been put into the system.

196 VARIABLES $EnvLastDeltaTime$, $EnvInState$, $EnvUnhandledRequest$

198 $\_Environment(RequestPeriodConstraint)$
199 $\triangleq$ INSTANCE $MaxRequPeriodEnv$
200 WITH $RequestPeriod \leftarrow RequestPeriodConstraint$,
201 $LastDeltaTime \leftarrow EnvLastDeltaTime$,
202 $inState \leftarrow EnvInState$,
203 $unhandledRequest \leftarrow EnvUnhandledRequest$
204 $Environment(RequestPeriodConstraint)$
205 $\triangleq \_Environment(RequestPeriodConstraint)!Environment$

207 ├───┤

The service the system is to perform.

Variables:

ServResponseTime – the response time of the last request serviced.
ServInState – the current state of the service machinery.
ServUnhandledRequest – TRUE indicates the arrival of a new request.

220 VARIABLES $ServResponseTime$, $ServInState$, $ServUnhandledRequest$
221 CONSTANT $ServInitialIntfState$
222 VARIABLE $ServIntfState$
223 CONSTANT $ServReturnGetResult(\_, \_, \_)$
224 CONSTANT $ServCallGetResult(\_, \_)$

226 $\_CalcService$
227 $\triangleq$ INSTANCE $CalculatorResponseTime$
228 WITH $ResponseTime \leftarrow ServResponseTime$,
229 $inState \leftarrow ServInState$,
230 $unhandledRequest \leftarrow ServUnhandledRequest$,
231 $step \leftarrow calcStep$,
232 $acc \leftarrow calcAcc$,
233 $summandsState \leftarrow calcSumConnector.clientState$,
234 $factorsState \leftarrow calcFactConnector.clientState$,
235 $initialSummandState \leftarrow Nat$,
236 $initialFactorState \leftarrow Nat$,
237 $CallFactorGet \leftarrow \_calcFactGet$,
238 $ReturnFactor \leftarrow \_calcFactReturn$,
239 $CallSummandGet \leftarrow \_calcSumGet$,
240 $ReturnSummand \leftarrow \_calcSumReturn$,
241 $initialCalcState \leftarrow ServInitialIntfState$,
242 $calculatorState \leftarrow ServIntfState$,
243 $ReturnGetResult \leftarrow ServReturnGetResult$,
244 $CallGetResult \leftarrow ServCallGetResult$,
245 $ResponseTimeConstr \leftarrow 50$
246 $CalcService \triangleq \_CalcService!CalculatorService$
247 $CalcServMap \triangleq \Box\_CalcService!ModelMapping$
248 $CalcServFunc \triangleq calc!Calculator$

250 ├───┤

Calculator container.

Variables:

SCCPUMinExecTime – records for each task the minimum amount of execution time it has been allocated over all periods so far.
SCCPUAssignedTo – holds the number of the task currently assigned the resource.

SCCmpInState – the state in which the component currently is.
SCCmpUnhandledRequest – TRUE if the environment put another request into the system.
SCCmpLastExecutionTime – the execution time of the last service execution.

SCEnvLastDeltaTime – The amount of time between the last two requests.
SCEnvInState – Current state of the service invoked.
SCEnvUnhandledRequest – TRUE signals that a new request has been put into the system.

SCServLastResponseTime – the response time of the last request serviced.
SCServInState – the current state of the service machinery.
SCServUnhandledRequest – TRUE indicates the arrival of a new request.

```
278  VARIABLES SCCalcCPUMinExecTime, SCCalcCPUAssignedTo
279  VARIABLES SCCalcCmpInState, SCCalcCmpUnhandledRequest
280  VARIABLES SCCalcCmpLastExecutionTime, SCCalcEnvLastDeltaTime
281  VARIABLES SCCalcEnvInState, SCCalcEnvUnhandledRequest
282  VARIABLES SCCalcServLastResponseTime, SCCalcServInState
283  VARIABLES SCCalcServUnhandledRequest, SCCalcServLastCallTime

285  _CalcContainer(ExecutionTimeConstr, ResponseTimeConstr,
286                  TaskCount, Periods, Wcets)
287     ≜ INSTANCE ContainerRespectingCalledOperations
288        WITH ExecutionTime ← ExecutionTimeConstr,
289             ResponseTime ← ResponseTimeConstr,
290             CPUMinExecTime ← SCCalcCPUMinExecTime,
291             CPUAssignedTo ← SCCalcCPUAssignedTo,
292             AllTaskCount ← CPUTaskCount,
293             AllPeriods ← CPUPeriods,
294             AllWcets ← CPUWcets,
295             CmpInState ← SCCalcCmpInState,
296             CmpUnhandledRequest ← SCCalcCmpUnhandledRequest,
297             CmpLastExecutionTime ← SCCalcCmpLastExecutionTime,
298             EnvLastDeltaTime ← SCCalcEnvLastDeltaTime,
299             EnvInState ← SCCalcEnvInState,
300             EnvUnhandledRequest ← SCCalcEnvUnhandledRequest,
301             ServLastResponseTime ← SCCalcServLastResponseTime,
302             ServInState ← SCCalcServInState,
303             ServUnhandledRequest ← SCCalcServUnhandledRequest,
304             CmpLastCallTime ← SCCalcServLastCallTime,
305             CompFun ← CalcCompFunc,
306             CompModelMapping ← CalcCompMap,
307             ServFun ← CalcServFunc,
308             ServModelMapping ← CalcServMap

310  CalcContainer(ExecutionTimeConstr, ResponseTimeConstr,
311                  TaskCount, Periods, Wcets)
312     ≜ _CalcContainer(ExecutionTimeConstr, ResponseTimeConstr,
313                  TaskCount, Periods, Wcets)!Container
```

The system.

```
319  VARIABLES SCSumTaskCount, SCSumPeriods, SCSumWcets
320  VARIABLES SCFactTaskCount, SCFactPeriods, SCFactWcets
321  VARIABLES SCCalcTaskCount, SCCalcPeriods, SCCalcWcets
```

323 $System \triangleq \land \land Summands(SCSumTaskCount, SCSumPeriods, SCSumWcets)$
324                $\land Factors(SCFactTaskCount, SCFactPeriods, SCFactWcets)$
325                $\land calc!CalculatorComponent$
326       $\land \land CalcSumConnector!Spec$
327                $\land CalcFactConnector!Spec$
328       $\land MyCPU$
329       $\land CalcContainer(calcCompExecTime, ServResponseTime,$
330                          $SCCalcTaskCount, SCCalcPeriods, SCCalcWcets)$
331       $\land$ Container-CPU-Binding
332       $\Box \land CPUTaskCount = SCSumTaskCount +$
333                          $SCFactTaskCount +$
334                          $SCCalcTaskCount$
335          $\land CPUPeriods =$
336              $[n \in \{1 .. CPUTaskCount\} \mapsto$
337   IF $(n \leq SCSumTaskCount)$ THEN $SCSumPeriods[n]$
338   ELSE IF $(n \leq SCSumTaskCount + SCFactTaskCount)$
339   THEN $SCFactPeriods[n - SCSumTaskCount]$
340   ELSE $SCCalcPeriods[n - SCSumTaskCount$
341 $- SCFactTaskCount]$
342              $]$
343          $\land CPUWcets =$
344              $[n \in \{1 .. CPUTaskCount\} \mapsto$
345   IF $(n \leq SCSumTaskCount)$ THEN $SCSumWcets[n]$
346   ELSE IF $(n \leq SCSumTaskCount + SCFactTaskCount)$
347   THEN $SCFactWcets[n - SCSumTaskCount]$
348   ELSE $SCCalcWcets[n - SCSumTaskCount$
349 $- SCFactTaskCount]$
350              $]$
351       $\land$ Bind *Container* service to functional service
352       $\Box \land ServResponseTime = SCCalcServLastResponseTime$
353          $\land ServInState = SCCalcServInState$
354          $\land ServUnhandledRequest = SCCalcServUnhandledRequest$
355       $\land$ Bind *Container* component to corresponding system components for the
356   container
357       $\Box \land SCCalcCmpLastExecutionTime = calcCompExecTime$
358          $\land SCCalcCmpInState = calcCompInState$
359          $\land SCCalcCmpUnhandledRequest = calcCompUnhandledRequest$
360       $\land$ And also bind the environment description to the environment expectation
361   of the container specification, in effect stating that this is indeed the
362   environment in which we are placing this container.
363       $\Box \land SCCalcEnvLastDeltaTime = EnvLastDeltaTime$
364          $\land SCCalcEnvInState = EnvInState$
365          $\land SCCalcEnvUnhandledRequest = EnvUnhandledRequest$

367 $ExternalService \triangleq Environment(RequestPeriod) \xrightarrow{+} CalcService$

369 ├──┤

371 $IsFeasible \triangleq System \Rightarrow ExternalService$

373 └──┘

B.5 Component Specification with Two Non-functional Properties

This is the complete version of the example from Sect. 5.1.

```
1 ┌─────────────────────── MODULE CompleteCounter ───────────────────────┐
  │ A counter component with constraints on accuracy and execution time.              │
5 EXTENDS Reals, CounterInterface, RealTime

7 ├──────────────────────────────────────────────────────────────────────┤
  │ The counter component. This component offers two intrinsic properties: a maximum execution time and a data
  │ quality.
12 VARIABLES MyCompExec, MyCompInState, MyCompUnhandledRequest
13 VARIABLES MyLastAccuracy, MyIdealResult, MyAccurateIC, MyAccurateCS
14 VARIABLES MyAccurateDH, MyInternalCounter, MyDoHandle

16 Worst-case execution time measurement
17 _ExecTimeSpec ≜ INSTANCE CounterAppExecTime
18               WITH ExecutionTime ← MyCompExec,
19                    inState ← MyCompInState,
20                    unhandledRequest ← MyCompUnhandledRequest,
21                    internalCounter ← MyInternalCounter,
22                    doHandle ← MyDoHandle

24 Accuracy measurement
25 _AccuracySpec ≜ INSTANCE AccuracyLimitedCounter
26               WITH LastAccuracy ← MyLastAccuracy,
27                    idealResult ← MyIdealResult,
28                    accurateIC ← MyAccurateIC,
29                    accurateCS ← MyAccurateCS,
30                    accurateDH ← MyAccurateDH,
31                    inState ← MyCompInState,
32                    internalCounter ← MyInternalCounter,
33                    doHandle ← MyDoHandle

35 The actual (combined) component specification.
36 Counter ≜ ∧ _ExecTimeSpec!CounterComponent
37            ∧ _AccuracySpec!CompleteSpec
38            ∧ □(MyCompExec ≥ 4 + (2 − MyLastAccuracy))

40 └──────────────────────────────────────────────────────────────────────┘
```

B.6   Jitter-Constrained Components

First, we define a new resource, namely memory. Memory is a linear resource where a number of requests are matched by a number of allocations. If for each request an allocation can be found, all requests could be satisfied.

```
1 ┌────────────────────── MODULE Memory ──────────────────────────┐
   Memory resource model.

5  EXTENDS Naturals

   Allocation of memory requests to actual chunks of physical memory. This expresses what the resource does with
   the physical memory managed by it.

11 VARIABLES AllocationCount, Allocations

   Requests for memory allocations are issued by clients of the memory resource.

17 VARIABLES RequestCount, Requests

19 TypeInvariant ≜ ∧ ∧ AllocationCount ∈ Nat
20                    ∧ AllocationCount ≥ 0
21                    ∧ Allocations ∈ [{1 .. AllocationCount}
22                                 → [id : Nat, size : Nat,
23                                     allocStart : Nat]]
24                 ∧ ∧ RequestCount ∈ Nat
25                    ∧ RequestCount ≥ 0
26                    ∧ Requests ∈ [{1 .. RequestCount}
27                                 → [id : Nat, size : Nat]]
28                 ∧ ∀ rIdx1 ∈ {1 .. RequestCount} :
29                    ¬∃ rIdx2 ∈ {1 .. RequestCount} :
30                       ∧ rIdx1 ≠ rIdx2
31                       ∧ Requests[rIdx1].id = Requests[rIdx2].id

33 AllocationsMatchRequests ≜ ∀ aIdx ∈ {1 .. AllocationCount} :
34                              ∃ rIdx ∈ {1 .. RequestCount} :
35                                 ∧ Allocations[aIdx].id = Requests[rIdx].id
36                                 ∧ Allocations[aIdx].size = Requests[rIdx].size

38 MemoryInvariants ≜ ∧ □ TypeInvariant
39                     ∧ □ AllocationsMatchRequests

41 AllRequestsSuccessful ≜ ∀ rIdx ∈ {1 .. RequestCount} :
42                           ∃ aIdx ∈ {1 .. AllocationCount} :
43                              ∧ Allocations[aIdx].id = Requests[rIdx].id
44                              ∧ Allocations[aIdx].size = Requests[rIdx].size

46 └───────────────────────────────────────────────────────────────┘
```

The following module defines a very simple memory management, where requests are allocated consecutively without overlap. Thus, the capacity limit is given by the size of the available memory.

```
1 ┌────────────────── MODULE SimpleMemory ────────────────────────┐
   A very simple memory manager that simply allocates memory to requests in the order of the requests, without
   any overlap or unassigned bits of physical memory between allocations.

7  EXTENDS Memory

   Size of the physical memory block managed by this resource.
```

12 CONSTANT *MemSize*
13 ASSUME $(MemSize \in Nat) \wedge (MemSize > 0)$

15 ├──┤
16   Sum the sizes of all requests
17   Copied and adjusted from *Bags.tla*
18 $RequestSum \triangleq$
19   LET $DSum[S \in$ SUBSET DOMAIN $Requests] \triangleq$ LET $elt \triangleq$ CHOOSE $e \in S :$ TRUE
20   IN   IF $S = \{\}$
21   THEN 0
22   ELSE $Requests[elt].size +$
23 $DSum[S \setminus \{elt\}]$
24   IN $DSum[$DOMAIN $Requests]$

26 $CapacityLimit \triangleq RequestSum < = MemSize$

28 $AllocationInvariant \triangleq \forall aIdx \in \{1 .. AllocationCount\} :$
29                       $Allocations[aIdx].allocStart + Allocations[aIdx].size$
30                       $< = MemSize$

32 $SimpleMemory \triangleq \wedge MemoryInvariants$
33                    $\wedge \Box AllocationInvariant$
34                    $\wedge \Box (CapacityLimit \Rightarrow AllRequestsSuccessful)$
35 └──┘

Based on the definition of response time, we define a service with a lower bound on response time; that is, with a bounded jitter.

1 ┌────────────────── MODULE *JitterConstrainedService* ──────────────────┐

Specification of a service with a constraint on the maximum response time for requests.

6 EXTENDS *RealTime*

Parameter:

ResponseTime – Maximum response time a request should exhibit.

13 CONSTANT *ResponseTime*
14 ASSUME $(ResponseTime \in Real) \wedge (ResponseTime > 0)$

Variables:

LastResponseTime – the response time of the last request serviced.
inState   – the current state of the service machinery.
unhandledRequest – TRUE indicates the arrival of a new request.

23 VARIABLES *LastResponseTime, inState, unhandledRequest*

25 ├──┤

27 *RService* $\triangleq$ INSTANCE *ResponseTimeConstrainedService*

29 ├──┤

31 *Service* $\triangleq$ $\wedge$ *RService!Service*
32                     $\wedge$ $\Box(LastResponseTime \geq ResponseTime)$

34 └──┘

The following module presents a simple strategy for ensuring bounded jitter. The container simply delays results at least until the lower bound for response time.

1 ┌────────────────── MODULE *FixedJitterContainer* ──────────────────┐
2 EXTENDS *RealTime*

4 CONSTANT *ResponseTime*
5 ASSUME $(ResponseTime \in Real) \wedge (ResponseTime > 0)$

7 ├──┤

Specification of required component behaviour.

12 VARIABLES *CmpInState, CmpUnhandledRequest, CmpLastExecutionTime*

14 _*Component(ExecutionTimeConstraint)*
15    $\triangleq$ INSTANCE *ExecTimeConstrainedComponent*
16   WITH *ExecutionTime* ← *ExecutionTimeConstraint*,
17   *inState* ← *CmpInState*,
18   *unhandledRequest* ← *CmpUnhandledRequest*,
19   *LastExecutionTime* ← *CmpLastExecutionTime*
20 *ComponentMaxExecTime(ExecutionTimeConstraint)*
21    $\triangleq$ _*Component(ExecutionTimeConstraint)!Component*

23 CONSTANT *CompFun*
24 ASSUME *CompFun* $\in$ BOOLEAN
25 CONSTANT *CompModelMapping*
26 ASSUME *CompModelMapping* $\in$ BOOLEAN

28 ├──┤

Specification of guaranteed service behaviour.

32 VARIABLES $ServLastResponseTime,\ ServInState,\ ServUnhandledRequest$

34 $\_ServiceJitter(ResponseTimeConstraint)$
35     $\triangleq$ INSTANCE $JitterConstrainedService$
36   WITH $ResponseTime \leftarrow ResponseTimeConstraint,$
37           $LastResponseTime \leftarrow ServLastResponseTime,$
38           $inState \leftarrow ServInState,$
39           $unhandledRequest \leftarrow ServUnhandledRequest$
40 $ServiceJitter(ResponseTimeConstraint)$
41     $\triangleq \_ServiceJitter(ResponseTimeConstraint)!Service$

43 CONSTANT $ServFun$
44 ASSUME $ServFun \in$ BOOLEAN
45 CONSTANT $ServModelMapping$
46 ASSUME $ServModelMapping \in$ BOOLEAN

48 ├───┤

The resources required by this container, namely some memory.

This has been simplified for the sake of the example. Actually, the buffer space requirement depends at least on request frequency and worst-case execution time of the component to be managed.

56 VARIABLES $ContAllocationCount,\ ContAllocations$

58 $\_Buffer(Requests,\ RequestCount) \triangleq$ INSTANCE $Memory$ WITH
59        $AllocationCount \leftarrow ContAllocationCount,$
60        $Allocations \leftarrow ContAllocations$
61 $BufferAvailable \triangleq\ \wedge\ \_Buffer([n \in \{1\} \mapsto [id \mapsto 0,\ size \mapsto 1024]],\ 1)$
62        $!MemoryInvariants$
63        $\wedge\ \Box(\_Buffer([n \in \{1\} \mapsto [id \mapsto 0,\ size \mapsto 1024]],\ 1)$
64        $!AllRequestsSuccessful)$

66 ├───┤
67 $ContainerPreCond \triangleq\ \wedge$ A component with some execution time is available.
68        $\wedge\ \exists\ ExecutionTime :$
69           $ComponentMaxExecTime(ExecutionTime)$
70        $\wedge\ CompFun$
71        $\wedge\ CompModelMapping$
72        $\wedge$ There is sufficient buffer space
73        $\wedge\ BufferAvailable$
74        $\wedge$ The component functionality implements the service functionality.
75        $CompFun \Rightarrow ServFun$

77 VARIABLES $ContRequestCount,\ ContRequests$

79 $ContainerPostCond \triangleq\ \wedge$ The promised jitter can be guaranteed
80        $\wedge\ ServiceJitter(ResponseTime)$
81        $\wedge\ ServFun$
82        $\wedge\ ServModelMapping$
83        $\wedge$ The container will allocate a buffer for the requests
84        $\Box\ \wedge\ ContRequestCount = 1$
85        $\wedge\ ContRequests = [n \in \{1\} \mapsto [id \mapsto 0,$
86                 $size \mapsto 1024]]$

88 $Container \triangleq ContainerPreCond \overset{+}{\Rightarrow} ContainerPostCond$
89 └───┘

The system specification puts everything together.

```
 1 ┌─────────────────────── MODULE System ───────────────────────┐
   A sample system specification.

   The system contains one counter with an execution time of 20 milliseconds, a RMS scheduled CPU, and a
   simple container.

 8 EXTENDS Reals, CounterInterface

   Parameters:

   RequestPeriod – Part of an environment assertion: The environment promises to send requests with a minimum
                   distance of RequestPeriod milliseconds.

17 CONSTANT RequestPeriod
18 ASSUME (RequestPeriod ∈ Real) ∧ (RequestPeriod > 0)

   Variables:

   now – the current time.

25 VARIABLE now

27 ├─────────────────────────────────────────────────────────────┤

   The counter component. The only intrinsic property offered by this component is its execution time, which is
   always less than 20ms.

   Variables:

   MyCompExec            – The last execution time of a service request handled by MyComponent.
   MyCompInState         – The current state of component MyComponent
   MyCompUnhandledRequest – Set to TRUE to send a request to MyComponent.

41 VARIABLES MyCompExec, MyCompInState, MyCompUnhandledRequest
42 VARIABLES MyInternalCounter, MyDoHandle

44 _MyComponent ≜ INSTANCE CounterAppExecTime WITH
45                 ExecutionTime ← MyCompExec,
46                 inState ← MyCompInState,
47                 unhandledRequest ← MyCompUnhandledRequest,
48                 internalCounter ← MyInternalCounter,
49                 doHandle ← MyDoHandle

51   The actual component specification.
52 MyComponent ≜ _MyComponent!CounterComponent
53 CompMap     ≜ □_MyComponent!ModelMapping

55 MyCompFunc ≜ INSTANCE CounterApp WITH
56                 internalCounter ← MyInternalCounter,
57                 doHandle ← MyDoHandle
58 MyCompFunc ≜ _MyCompFunc!Spec

60 ├─────────────────────────────────────────────────────────────┤

   A CPU. The parameters of the specification can be used to indicate the number of tasks to be scheduled, their
   respective periods as well as their respective worst case execution times.

   Variables:

   MYCPU_MinExecTime – records for each task the minimum amount of execution time it has been allocated
                       over all periods so far.
   MYCPU_AssignedTo – holds the number of the task currently assigned the resource

76 VARIABLES MYCPU_MinExecTime, MYCPU_AssignedTo

78 _MyCPU(TaskCount, Periods, Wcets)
```

79      $\triangleq$ INSTANCE *RMSScheduler*
80   WITH *MinExecTime* ← *MYCPU_MinExecTime*,
81   *AssignedTo* ← *MYCPU_AssignedTo*
82 *MyCPU(TaskCount, Periods, Wcets)*
83      $\triangleq$ *_MyCPU(TaskCount, Periods, Wcets)!RMSScheduler*

85 ├───┤

The actual memory resource. This is a very simple memory.

Variables:

MYMEM_ACount – holds the number of allocations managed by the memory.
MYMEM_Allocs – holds the actual allocations managed by the memory.

97 VARIABLES *MYMEM_ACount, MYMEM_Allocs*

99 *_MyMemory(RequestCount, Requests)* $\triangleq$ INSTANCE *SimpleMemory* WITH
100   *MemSize* ← 65536,
101   *AllocationCount* ← *MYMEM_ACount*,
102   *Allocations* ← *MYMEM_Allocs*
103 *MyMemory(RequestCount, Requests)*
104      $\triangleq$ *_MyMemory(RequestCount, Requests)!SimpleMemory*

106 ├───┤

Environment specification.

Variables:

EnvLastDeltaTime – The amount of time between the last two requests.
EnvInState   – Current state of the service invoked.
EnvUnhandledRequest – TRUE signals that a new request has been put into the system.

120 VARIABLES *EnvLastDeltaTime, EnvInState, EnvUnhandledRequest*

122 *_Environment(RequestPeriodConstraint)*
123      $\triangleq$ INSTANCE *MaxRequPeriodEnv*
124   WITH *RequestPeriod* ← *RequestPeriodConstraint*,
125   *LastDeltaTime* ← *EnvLastDeltaTime*,
126   *inState* ← *EnvInState*,
127   *unhandledRequest* ← *EnvUnhandledRequest*
128 *Environment(RequestPeriodConstraint)*
129      $\triangleq$ *_Environment(RequestPeriodConstraint)!Environment*

131 ├───┤

The service the system is to perform.

Variables:

ServResponseTime   – the response time of the last request serviced.
ServInState   – the current state of the service machinery.
ServUnhandledRequest – TRUE indicates the arrival of a new request.

144 VARIABLES *ServResponseTime, ServInState, ServUnhandledRequest*
145 VARIABLES *ServInternalCounter, ServDoHandle*

147 *_Service*
148      $\triangleq$ INSTANCE *CounterAppResponseTime*
149   WITH *ResponseTime* ← *ServResponseTime*,
150   *inState* ← *ServInState*,
151   *unhandledRequest* ← *ServUnhandledRequest*,

152           $internalCounter \leftarrow ServInternalCounter,$
153           $doHandle \leftarrow ServDoHandle$
154 $Service \triangleq \_Service!CounterService$
155 $ServMap \triangleq \square\_Service!ModelMapping$

157 $\_MyServFunc \triangleq$ INSTANCE $CounterApp$ WITH
158           $internalCounter \leftarrow ServInternalCounter,$
159           $doHandle \leftarrow ServDoHandle$
160 $MyServFunc \triangleq \_MyServFunc!Spec$

162 ├───┤

Container specification 1: The Response-time guaranteeing container.

Variables:

$SCCPUMinExecTime$ – records for each task the minimum amount of execution time it has been allocated over all periods so far.
$SCCPUAssignedTo$ – holds the number of the task currently assigned the resource.

$SCCmpInState$ – the state in which the component currently is.
$SCCmpUnhandledRequest$ – TRUE if the environment put another request into the system.
$SCCmpLastExecutionTime$ – the execution time of the last service execution.

$SCEnvLastDeltaTime$ – The amount of time between the last two requests.
$SCEnvInState$ – Current state of the service invoked.
$SCEnvUnhandledRequest$ – TRUE signals that a new request has been put into the system.

$SCServLastResponseTime$ – the response time of the last request serviced.
$SCServInState$ – the current state of the service machinery.
$SCServUnhandledRequest$ – TRUE indicates the arrival of a new request.

190 VARIABLES $SCCPUMinExecTime, SCCPUAssignedTo$
191 VARIABLES $SCCmpInState, SCCmpUnhandledRequest, SCCmpLastExecutionTime$
192 VARIABLES $SCEnvLastDeltaTime, SCEnvInState, SCEnvUnhandledRequest$
193 VARIABLES $SCServLastResponseTime, SCServInState, SCServUnhandledRequest$

195 $\_SchedulingContainer(ExecutionTimeConstr, ResponseTimeConstr,$
196                     $TaskCount, Periods, Wcets)$
197     $\triangleq$ INSTANCE $SimpleContainer$
198   WITH $ExecutionTime \leftarrow ExecutionTimeConstr,$
199             $ResponseTime \leftarrow ResponseTimeConstr,$
200             $CPUMinExecTime \leftarrow SCCPUMinExecTime,$
201             $CPUAssignedTo \leftarrow SCCPUAssignedTo,$
202             $CmpInState \leftarrow SCCmpInState,$
203             $CmpUnhandledRequest \leftarrow SCCmpUnhandledRequest,$
204             $CmpLastExecutionTime \leftarrow SCCmpLastExecutionTime,$
205             $EnvLastDeltaTime \leftarrow SCEnvLastDeltaTime,$
206             $EnvInState \leftarrow SCEnvInState,$
207             $EnvUnhandledRequest \leftarrow SCEnvUnhandledRequest,$
208             $ServLastResponseTime \leftarrow SCServLastResponseTime,$
209             $ServInState \leftarrow SCServInState,$
210             $ServUnhandledRequest \leftarrow SCServUnhandledRequest,$
211             $CompFun \leftarrow MyCompFunc,$
212             $CompModelMapping \leftarrow CompMap,$
213             $ServFun \leftarrow MyServFunc,$
214             $ServModelMapping \leftarrow ServMap$

216 $SchedulingContainer(ExecutionTimeConstr, ResponseTimeConstr,$
217                 $TaskCount, Periods, Wcets)$
218     $\triangleq \_SchedulingContainer(ExecutionTimeConstr, ResponseTimeConstr,$

219                          $TaskCount,\ Periods,\ Wcets)!Container$

221 |——————————————————————————————————|

Container specification 2: The Jitter-constraing guaranteeing container.

227 $\_JitterContainer(ResponseTimeConstr,\ MemReqCount,\ MemRequests)$
228     $\triangleq$ INSTANCE $FixedJitterContainer$
229   WITH $ResponseTime \leftarrow ResponseTimeConstr,$
230             $CompFun \leftarrow MyCompFunc,$
231             $CompModelMapping \leftarrow CompMap,$
232             $CmpInState \leftarrow SCCmpInState,$
233             $CmpUnhandledRequest \leftarrow SCCmpUnhandledRequest,$
234             $CmpLastExecutionTime \leftarrow SCCmpLastExecutionTime,$
235             $ContRequestCount \leftarrow MemReqCount,$
236             $ContRequests \leftarrow MemRequests,$
237             $ContAllocationCount \leftarrow MYMEM\_ACount,$
238             $ContAllocations \leftarrow MYMEM\_Allocs,$
239             $ServLastResponseTime \leftarrow SCServLastResponseTime,$
240             $ServInState \leftarrow SCServInState,$
241             $ServUnhandledRequest \leftarrow SCServUnhandledRequest,$
242             $ServFun \leftarrow MyServFunc,$
243             $ServModelMapping \leftarrow ServMap$

245 $JitterContainer(ResponseTime,\ MemReqCount,\ MemRequests)$
246     $\triangleq \_JitterContainer(ResponseTime,$
247                     $MemReqCount,\ MemRequests)!Container$

249 |——————————————————————————————————|

The complete system.

Variables:

$TaskCount$ – the number of tasks to be scheduled on the CPU as determined by the container.
Periods – the periods to be scheduled for those tasks as determined by container.
$Wcets$ – the worst case execution times to be considered when scheduling. As determined by the container.

265 VARIABLES $CPUTaskCount,\ CPUPeriods,\ CPUWcets$
266 VARIABLES $MEMRequestCount,\ MEMRequests$
267 VARIABLES $SCTaskCount,\ SCPeriods,\ SCWcets$

269 $System \triangleq \wedge MyComponent$
270             $\wedge MyCPU(CPUTaskCount,\ CPUPeriods,\ CPUWcets)$
271             $\wedge MyMemory(MEMRequestCount,\ MEMRequests)$
272             $\wedge SchedulingContainer(MyCompExec,\ ServResponseTime,$
273                             $SCTaskCount,\ SCPeriods,\ SCWcets)$
274             $\wedge JitterContainer(ServResponseTime,$
275                             $MEMRequestCount,\ MEMRequests)$
276             $\wedge$ This connects the service promised by the container to the service
277   expected from the system
278                 $\Box \wedge ServResponseTime = SCServLastResponseTime$
279                 $\wedge ServInState = SCServInState$
280                 $\wedge ServUnhandledRequest = SCServUnhandledRequest$
281             $\wedge$ This connects $MyCPU$ and the CPU requested by the container essentially
282   stating that $MyCPU$ is indeed the one the container can use.
283                 $\Box \wedge MYCPU\_MinExecTime = SCCPUMinExecTime$
284                 $\wedge MYCPU\_AssignedTo = SCCPUAssignedTo$

285 $\quad\quad\quad\quad \wedge\ CPUTaskCount = SCTaskCount$

286 $\quad\quad\quad\quad \wedge\ CPUPeriods = SCPeriods$

287 $\quad\quad\quad\quad \wedge\ CPUWcets = SCWcets$

288 $\quad\quad\quad \wedge$ Tell the container which component to use

289 $\quad\quad\quad\quad \square \wedge\ SCCmpLastExecutionTime = MyCompExec$

290 $\quad\quad\quad\quad\quad \wedge\ SCCmpInState = MyCompInState$

291 $\quad\quad\quad\quad\quad \wedge\ SCCmpUnhandledRequest = MyCompUnhandledRequest$

292 $\quad\quad\quad \wedge$ And also bind the environment description to the environment expectation

293 $\quad\quad\quad\quad$ of the container specification, in effect stating that this is indeed the

294 $\quad\quad\quad\quad$ environment in which we are placing this container.

295 $\quad\quad\quad\quad \square \wedge\ SCEnvLastDeltaTime = EnvLastDeltaTime$

296 $\quad\quad\quad\quad\quad \wedge\ SCEnvInState = EnvInState$

297 $\quad\quad\quad\quad\quad \wedge\ SCEnvUnhandledRequest = EnvUnhandledRequest$

299 $\quad$ The external behaviour we require of the system.

300 $\ ExternalService \ \overset{\Delta}{=}\ Environment(RequestPeriod) \overset{+}{\rhd} Service$

302 ├───┤

304 $\quad$ This is the property we need to prove to ensure that we have a feasible system.

305 $\ IsFeasible \ \overset{\Delta}{=}\ System \Rightarrow ExternalService$

307 └───┘

B.7   Reliable Components

In order to define reliability, we need a context model of a component that enables us to determine whether a component operation has been executed successfully. This is defined in the following module. The specification defines an additional state `Exception` which represents situations where the operation call returned the wrong result.

1 ┌─────────────────────── MODULE *Component* ───────────────────────┐

Models the functional side of a component impl.

A component impl is what makes a service "live". This is an extension of the standard component model with an added state for exceptional return.

A component specification is an open specification, because there is an environment sending in requests.

12 ├──┤

Variables:

unhandledRequest – set to TRUE by the environment to indicate that a new request has arrived and should be handled.
inState   – the state in which the component is.

21 VARIABLE *inState*
22 VARIABLE *unhandledRequest*

24 $vars \triangleq \langle inState, unhandledRequest \rangle$

26 ├──┤

28   The agent set μ which *SpecEnv* does not constrain and *SpecComponent* constrains
29   at most.
30 LOCAL $SystemAgent \triangleq inState' \neq inState$

32 ├──┤

The environment specification.

38   The environment sets the *unhandledRequest* flag at some arbitrary moment to indicate a
39   new request.
40 $RequestArrival \triangleq$ $\land unhandledRequest =$ FALSE
41                             $\land unhandledRequest' =$ TRUE
42                             $\land$ UNCHANGED $inState$

44 $NextEnv \triangleq RequestArrival$

46 $SpecEnv \triangleq \Box[NextEnv \lor SystemAgent]_{vars}$

48 ├──┤

The actual component.

54   Initially we start out in the idle state
55 $InitComponent \triangleq inState =$ "Idle"

57   Initially there are no requests in the system
58 $InitEnv \triangleq unhandledRequest =$ FALSE

60   The transition from idle to handling request is triggered by an incoming request
61 $StartRequest \triangleq \land inState =$ "Idle"
62                          $\land unhandledRequest =$ TRUE
63                          $\land inState' =$ "HandlingRequest" $\lor inState' =$ "Blocked"
64                          $\land unhandledRequest' =$ FALSE

66   Request handling can finish any time
67   $FinishRequest \triangleq \land inState =$ "HandlingRequest"
68                                   $\land inState' =$ "Idle"
69                                   $\land$ UNCHANGED $unhandledRequest$

71   An exception occured while handling the request
72   $Exception \triangleq \land inState =$ "HandlingRequest"
73                              $\land inState' =$ "Exception"
74                              $\land$ UNCHANGED $unhandledRequest$

76   The exception has been handled, the component is ready for the next request
77   $ExceptionHandled \triangleq \land inState =$ "Exception"
78 $\land inState' =$ "Idle"
79 $\land$ UNCHANGED $unhandledRequest$

81   Also, the runtime environment may at any time take away the CPU from us and assign it
82   to someone else.
83   $SwitchToOther \triangleq \land inState =$ "HandlingRequest"
84                                   $\land inState' =$ "Blocked"
85                                   $\land$ UNCHANGED $unhandledRequest$

87   But, it may also at any time give back the CPU to us
88   $SwitchBack \triangleq \land inState =$ "Blocked"
89                              $\land inState' =$ "HandlingRequest"
90                              $\land$ UNCHANGED $unhandledRequest$

92   $NextComponent \triangleq \lor StartRequest$
93                                     $\lor FinishRequest$
94                                     $\lor Exception$
95                                     $\lor ExceptionHandled$
96                                     $\lor SwitchToOther$
97                                     $\lor SwitchBack$

99   $SpecComponent \triangleq \land InitComponent$
100                                     $\land InitEnv$
101                                     $\land \Box[NextComponent \lor \neg SystemAgent]_{vars}$

103 ├──┤

The complete specification

109   $Component \triangleq SpecEnv \xrightarrow{+} SpecComponent$

111 ├──┤

113   $TypeInvariant \triangleq \land inState \in \{$"Idle",
114   "HandlingRequest",
115   "Blocked",
116   "Exception"$\}$
117                                     $\land unhandledRequest \in$ BOOLEAN
118 └──┘

Based on the context model, the measurement of reliability is defined.

1 ┌──────────── MODULE $ReliabilityConstrainedComponent$ ────────────┐

A reliability-constrained component is a component with a constraint placed on the reliability of an operation call.

6 EXTENDS $Reals$

8 VARIABLES $inState$, $unhandledRequest$

10 $\_Component \triangleq$ INSTANCE $Component$

12 ├───┤

14 VARIABLES $AllRequests$, $SuccessfulRequests$

16 $Init \triangleq \land AllRequests = 0$
17 $\qquad\quad\ \land SuccessfulRequests = 0$

19 $OnFinishRequest \triangleq \_Component!FinishRequest \Rightarrow$
20 $\qquad\qquad\qquad\qquad\quad \land AllRequests' = AllRequests + 1$
21 $\qquad\qquad\qquad\qquad\quad \land SuccessfulRequests' = SuccessfulRequests + 1$

23 $OnException \triangleq \_Component!Exception \Rightarrow \land AllRequests' = AllRequests + 1$
24 $\qquad\qquad\qquad\qquad\qquad\qquad\qquad \land$ UNCHANGED $SuccessfulRequests$

26 $Component \triangleq \land Init$
27 $\qquad\qquad\quad\ \land \_Component!Component$
28 $\qquad\qquad\quad\ \land \Box[OnFinishRequest \land OnException]_{\langle AllRequests,\ SuccessfulRequests\rangle}$

30 $Reliability(ReliabilityConstr) \triangleq \Box \lor AllRequests = 0$
31 $\qquad\qquad\qquad\qquad\qquad\qquad\quad \lor (SuccessfulRequests/AllRequests)$
32 $\qquad\qquad\qquad\qquad\qquad\qquad\qquad \geq ReliabilityConstr$

34 └───┘

Appendix C

Detailed Proofs

C.1 Proofs on the specification schemes

In this section we will prove two things about the specification schemes defined in Defs. 3.2 and 3.4: First, we will prove that measurements specified in this form are indeed measurements according to Def. 3.3. Then, we will show that the measurement specification scheme essentially appends additional clauses to the actions of the context model. This result will be useful in further proofs.

C.1.1 The Measurement Specification Scheme Produces Measurements

In this section we show that measurements specified following the specification schemes are indeed measurements.

ASSUME: 1. $S_{Ctx} \triangleq \land INIT_{Ctx}$
$\land \Box[NEXT_{Ctx}]_{vars_{Ctx}}$

2. $NEXT_{Ctx} \triangleq \bigvee_i A_i$

3. $\forall i, j : (i \neq j) \Rightarrow (A_i \Rightarrow \neg A_j)$

4. $MeasureSpec_m \triangleq \land m = INIT_m$
$\land \Box[NEXT_m \land vars'_{Ctx} \neq vars_{Ctx}]_{vars}$

5. m does not occur free in $INIT_m$.

6. $vars \triangleq \langle m, vars_{Ctx} \rangle$

7. $NEXT_m \triangleq \land \bigwedge_i (A_i \Rightarrow m' = B_i)$
$\land (\forall i \cdot \neg A_i) \rightarrow \text{UNCHANGED } m$

8. m' does not occur free in any B_i.

PROVE: $\exists f, g, v : MeasureSpec_m \Rightarrow Hist(m, f, g, v)$, m does not occur free in f, v; m' does not occur free in g.

PROOF SKETCH: The proof is constructive, by giving values for f, g, v:

1. $f \triangleq INIT_m$
Proof assumptions 4 and 5. □

2. $v \triangleq vars_{Ctx}$
Proof assumptions 4 and 6. □

3. $g \triangleq$ **if** (A_1)
        then B_1
        else if (A_2)
            then B_2
            else ...
            else m

3.1. $m' = g \equiv \land \bigwedge_i(\bigwedge_{j<i}\neg A_j) \land A_i \Rightarrow m' = B_i$
$\qquad \land (\forall i : \neg A_i) \Rightarrow \text{UNCHANGED } m$

We use rule (16.2) from [78, p. 295] to transform the IF-clauses into implications. $\square$

3.2. $\forall i : ((\forall j < i : \neg A_j) \land A_i) = A_i$

Proof assumption 3.

3.3. Q.E.D.

3.1, 3.2, and proof assumptions 7, 8.

4. Q.E.D.

C.1.2   The Measurement Specification Scheme is a Simple Extension of the Context Model

In this subsection we prove that measurement specifications are a simple extension to the context model.

ASSUME: 1. $S_{Ctx} \stackrel{\Delta}{=} \land INIT_{Ctx}$
$\qquad\qquad \land \Box[NEXT_{Ctx}]_{vars_{Ctx}}$

2. $NEXT_{Ctx} \stackrel{\Delta}{=} \bigvee_i A_i$

3. $\forall i,j : (i \neq j) \Rightarrow (A_i \Rightarrow \neg A_j)$

4. $MeasureSpec_m \stackrel{\Delta}{=} \land m = INIT_m$
$\qquad\qquad\qquad \land \Box[NEXT_m \land vars'_{Ctx} \neq vars_{Ctx}]_{vars}$

5. m does not occur free in $INIT_m$.

6. $vars \stackrel{\Delta}{=} \langle m, vars_{Ctx} \rangle$

7. $NEXT_m \stackrel{\Delta}{=} \land \bigwedge_i(A_i \Rightarrow m' = B_i)$
$\qquad\qquad\quad \land (\forall i : \neg A_i) \Rightarrow \text{UNCHANGED } m$

8. m' does not occur free in any B_i.

9. $\forall i : (A_i \Rightarrow \neg\text{UNCHANGED } vars_{Ctx})$

PROVE: $(S_{Ctx} \land MeasureSpec_m) \equiv \land \land INIT_{Ctx}$
$\qquad\qquad\qquad\qquad\qquad\qquad\qquad \land m = INIT_m$
$\qquad\qquad\qquad\qquad\qquad\qquad\qquad \land \Box[\land \bigvee_i(A_i \land m' = B_i)$
$\qquad\qquad\qquad\qquad\qquad\qquad\qquad\qquad \land (\forall i : \neg A_i) \Rightarrow \text{UNCHANGED } m]_{vars}$

PROOF SKETCH: The proof works by comparison of conjuncts following the structure of the right-hand side of the equivalence. The first conjunct is trivially equivalent, so we use only one substep which focuses on the second conjunct.

1. $\land \Box[NEXT_{Ctx}]_{vars_{Ctx}} \qquad\qquad\qquad \equiv \Box[\land \bigvee_i(A_i \land m' = B_i)$
$\quad \land \Box[NEXT_m \land vars'_{Ctx} \neq vars_{Ctx}]_{vars} \qquad \land (\forall i : \neg A_i)$
$\qquad\qquad\qquad\qquad\qquad\qquad\qquad\qquad\qquad\quad \Rightarrow \text{UNCHANGED } m]_{vars}$

1.1. $\text{UNCHANGED } vars_{Ctx} \land \text{UNCHANGED } vars \equiv \text{UNCHANGED } vars$

Proof assumption 6. $\square$

1.2. $NEXT_{Ctx} \land \text{UNCHANGED } vars \equiv \text{FALSE}$

Proof assumptions 2 and 9. $\square$

1.3. $NEXT_m \land \text{UNCHANGED } vars_{Ctx} \equiv \text{UNCHANGED } vars$

Proof assumptions 6, 7, and 9.

1.4. $NEXT_m \land NEXT_{Ctx} \equiv \land (\bigvee_i A_i \land m' = B_i)$
$\qquad\qquad\qquad\qquad\qquad\qquad \land ((\forall i : \neg A_i) \Rightarrow \text{UNCHANGED } m)$

1.4.1. $(\bigvee_i A_i) \land (\bigwedge_i A_i \Rightarrow m' = B_i) \equiv \bigvee_i(A_i \land m' = B_i)$

By iteration through the conjuncts of the right conjunct, and proof assumption 9. The iteration terminates, because there are only finitely many A_i in a context model.

1.4.2. Q.E.D.

1.1 thru 1.4, and the definition of $[A]_b$.

1.5. Q.E.D.

2. Q.E.D.

C.2   Proving Conditions $\Phi 1$ thru $\Phi 3$ for ϕ_{App}^{Ctx}

In this section we will prove that conditions $\Phi 1$ thru $\Phi 3$ are indeed sufficient to guarantee that ϕ_{App}^{Ctx} will fulfil Equation (3.2). We begin by showing that from any behaviour $\sigma \models \Pi_{App}$ we can construct another behaviour that is stuttering equivalent to σ except for the values it assigns to the flexible variables of a context model, and that satisfies the model mapping and the context-model specification. This is the core of the complete proof, because it is essentially just another way of stating (3.2) as we will show after the first proof. Finally, we extend our proof to also encompass the weakened form of $\Phi 2$.

ASSUME: 1. ϕ_{App}^{Ctx} is a model mapping satisfying conditions $\Phi 1$ thru $\Phi 3$.

$$\Pi_\phi \triangleq \square \left(\langle v_{App}, v_{Ctx} \rangle \in \phi_{App}^{Ctx} \right).$$

2. Π_{App} is the externally visible property of an application model with states Σ_{App}, initial states F_{App}, and next−state relation N_{App}. v_{App} denotes the flexible variables representing the application−model state.

3. Π_{Ctx} is the externally visible property of a context model with states Σ_{Ctx}, initial states F_{Ctx}, and next−state relation N_{Ctx}. v_{Ctx} denotes the flexible variables representing the context−model state.

4. $v_{Ctx} \cap v_{App} = \emptyset$

PROVE: $\forall \sigma \in \Sigma_{App}^\infty : \sigma \models \Pi_{App} \Rightarrow \exists \tau \in (\Sigma_{App} \times \Sigma_{Ctx})^\infty :$
$$\wedge \; \sigma \simeq_{v_{Ctx}} \tau$$
$$\wedge \; \tau \models \Pi_\phi \wedge \Pi_{Ctx}$$

PROOF SKETCH: The proof is by induction over the states in σ.

1. $\forall \sigma_0 \in F_{App} : \exists \tau_0 \in (F_{App} \times F_{Ctx}) : \wedge \pi_{App} (\tau_0) = \sigma_0$
$$\wedge \; \tau_0 \in \phi_{App}^{Ctx}$$

    PROOF: This follows directly from $\Phi 1$. $\square$

2. ASSUME: 1. $\sigma|_n \models \Pi_{App}$

               2. $\tau|_n \models \Pi_\phi \wedge \Pi_{Ctx}$

               3. $\sigma|_n \simeq_{v_{Ctx}} \tau|_n$

      PROVE: $\forall \sigma_{n+1} \in \Sigma_{App} : \sigma|_n \circ \sigma_{n+1} \models \Pi_{App}$
$$\Rightarrow \exists \tau_{n+1} \in (\Sigma_{App} \times \Sigma_{Ctx}) :$$
$$\wedge \; (\sigma|_n \circ \sigma_{n+1}) \simeq_{v_{Ctx}} (\tau|_n \circ \tau_{n+1})$$
$$\wedge \; \tau|_n \circ \tau_{n+1} \models \Pi_\phi \wedge \Pi_{Ctx}$$

PROOF SKETCH: There are two parts to this proof: We first show that the conditions ensure that we can always construct some τ_n from any σ_n and then we show that such a τ_n always satisfies Π_{Ctx}.

2.1. $\forall \sigma_{n+1} \in \Sigma_{App} : \exists \tau_{n+1} \in (\Sigma_{App} \times \Sigma_{Ctx}) :$
$$\wedge \; \pi_{App} (\tau_{n+1}) = \sigma_{n+1}$$
$$\wedge \; \tau_{n+1} \in \phi_{App}^{Ctx}$$

    PROOF: The first conjunct is trivially valid. The second conjunct follows from $\Phi 3$, completeness. $\square$

2.2. CASE: $\sigma_{n+1} = \sigma_n$

    PROOF: Pick $\tau_{n+1} = \tau_n$. Any legal TLA$^+$ property must allow stuttering steps, and $\langle \sigma_n, \pi_{Ctx} (\tau_n) \rangle \in \phi_{App}^{Ctx}$ by the assumptions of the induction step, namely $\sigma|_n \simeq_{v_{Ctx}} \tau|_n$. $\square$[1]

2.3. CASE: $\sigma_{n+1} \neq \sigma_n$

    PROOF: Because of the assumptions of the induction step, $\langle \sigma_n, \sigma_{n+1} \rangle \in N_{App}$, and thus by $\Phi 2$ (strict version),
$$\exists \tau_{n+1} : \langle \sigma_{n+1}, \tau_{n+1} \rangle \in \phi_{App}^{Ctx} \wedge (\langle \tau_n, \tau_{n+1} \rangle \in N_{Ctx} \vee \tau_n = \tau_{n+1})$$
which satisfies Π_{Ctx}. $\square$

2.4. Q.E.D.

---

[1] Note that ϕ_{App}^{Ctx} may also allow other choices for τ_{n+1} that are consistent with Π_{Ctx}, but we only need to find one for our proof.

3. Q.E.D.
PROOF: By induction over the states in σ. $\square$

From the definition of $\exists$ (*cf.*, e.g., the appendix of [4]) it follows that

$$\models \Pi_{App} \equiv \exists\, v_{Ctx} : \Pi_{Ctx}^{App}$$

is equivalent to

$$\forall \sigma \in \Sigma_{App}^{\infty} : \sigma \models \Pi_{App} \Rightarrow \exists \tau \in (\Sigma_{App} \times \Sigma_{Ctx})^{\infty} : \wedge \tau \simeq_{v_{Ctx}} \sigma \\ \wedge \tau \models \Pi_{Ctx}^{App}$$

Using the definition of Π_{Ctx}^{App} (*cf.* (3.1)) and after some simple transformations following the rules for $\models$, this can be written as

$$\forall \sigma \in \Sigma_{App}^{\infty} : \sigma \models \Pi_{App} \Rightarrow \exists \tau \in (\Sigma_{App} \times \Sigma_{Ctx})^{\infty} : \wedge \tau \simeq_{v_{Ctx}} \sigma \\ \wedge \tau \models \Pi_{App} \\ \wedge \tau \models \Pi_{Ctx} \wedge \Pi_{\phi}$$

borrowing the Π_{ϕ} notation from the proof above. Because of

$$\forall \sigma \in \Sigma_{App}^{\infty}, \tau \in (\Sigma_{App} \times \Sigma_{Ctx})^{\infty} : (\sigma \models \Pi_{App} \wedge \tau \simeq_{v_{Ctx}} \sigma \wedge v_{App} \cap v_{Ctx} = \emptyset) \\ \Rightarrow \tau \models \Pi_{App}$$

we can remove the second conjunct from above and obtain

$$\forall \sigma \in \Sigma_{App}^{\infty} : \sigma \models \Pi_{App} \Rightarrow \exists \tau \in (\Sigma_{App} \times \Sigma_{Ctx})^{\infty} : \wedge \tau \simeq_{v_{Ctx}} \sigma \\ \wedge \tau \models \Pi_{Ctx} \wedge \Pi_{\phi}$$

which is precisely what we proved at the beginning of this section. We have, therefore, also proved that conditions $\Phi 1$ through $\Phi 3$ are sufficient to produce a model mapping which satisfies (3.2).

So far, our proof only covers the strict version of $\Phi 2$. We have also provided a weakened form, in which the context model may observe an application-model step using a sequence of context-model states, all of which except the last have been mapped to the first application-model state. To show that this rule is also sufficient to satisfy (3.2), we need to modify the above proof as follows (we only show the parts with relevant changes):

2. ASSUME: 1. $\sigma|_n \models \Pi_{App}$
            2. $\tau|_m \models \Pi_{\phi} \wedge \Pi_{Ctx}$
            3. $\sigma|_n \simeq_{v_{Ctx}} \tau|_m$
            4. $m \geq n$
PROVE: $\forall \sigma_{n+1} \Sigma_{App} : \sigma|_n \circ \sigma_{n+1} \models \Pi_{App}$
               $\Rightarrow \exists \tau_{m+1}, \ldots, \tau_{m+r} \in (\Sigma_{App} \times \Sigma_{Ctx}), r > 0 :$
               $\wedge\, (\sigma|_n \circ \sigma_{n+1}) \simeq_{v_{Ctx}} (\tau|_m \circ \tau_{m+1} \circ \cdots \circ \tau_{m+r})$
               $\wedge\, \tau|_m \circ \tau_{m+1} \circ \cdots \circ \tau_{m+r} \models \Pi_{\phi} \wedge \Pi_{Ctx}$
2.3. CASE: $\sigma_{n+1} \neq \sigma_n$
The argument is essentially as above. $\Phi 2$ in its weakened form allows us to find a corresponding sequence of τ_i so that the context model is satisfied. $\square$

The idea here is to allow τ to grow by a number of states when σ grows by only one state. Because $\simeq$ will add or remove stuttering steps as necessary, the different number of states in σ and τ is not a problem.

C.3   Proofs for the Example Specifications

C.3.1   Proving That Response Time Is a Measurement

In this section we are going to prove that our definition of response time is indeed equivalent to the measurement shown in Equation (3.7). This requires that we show that

$$Hist(m_{RT}, f_{RT}, g_{RT}, v_{RT}) \equiv RespSpec$$

Because both terms are conjunctions of two elements, an easy way to show this equivalence would be to show that the first two and the second two conjuncts are equivalent; that is

$$m_{RT} = \langle 0, 0 \rangle \quad \equiv \quad Init$$
$$\Box[m_{RT}' = g_{RT} \wedge v'_{RT} \neq v_{RT}]_{\langle m_{RT}, v_{RT} \rangle} \quad \equiv \quad \Box[Next \wedge ctxvars' \neq ctxvars]_{vars}$$

The first equivalence holds trivially.

To check the second equivalence, we first note that $vars \equiv \langle m_{RT}, v_{RT} \rangle$ up to order, and that $v_{RT} \equiv ctxvars$. Thus, we only need to show that

$$m_{RT}' = g_{RT} \equiv Next$$

After expanding the IF/THEN/ELSE expressions in g_{RT},[2] we obtain:

$$
\begin{aligned}
m_{RT}' = g_{RT} \equiv\ & \wedge\ Serv!StartRequest \Rightarrow m_{RT}' = \langle now, LastResponseTime \rangle \\
& \wedge\ \neg Serv!StartRequest \\
& \quad \Rightarrow (Serv!FinishRequest \Rightarrow m_{RT}' = \langle Start, now - Start \rangle) \\
& \wedge\ \neg Serv!StartRequest \\
& \quad \Rightarrow (\neg Serv!FinishRequest \\
& \qquad \Rightarrow m_{RT}' = \langle Start, LastResponseTime \rangle)
\end{aligned}
$$

Again, we can compare each individual conjunct with the corresponding conjunct in $Next$. The first and the last are trivially equivalent to their respective counterpart. Also for the second conjunct, the equivalence becomes apparent if we consider that

$$Serv!FinishRequest \Rightarrow \neg Serv!StartRequest$$

that is, that our system cannot perform a $FinishRequest$ and a $StartRequest$ step at the same time (this is mainly due to our explicit usage of UNCHANGED clauses); and that, for any predicates A, B, and C, the following is a tautology:

$$((B \Rightarrow \neg A) \wedge (\neg A \Rightarrow (B \Rightarrow C))) \Rightarrow (B \Rightarrow C)$$

C.3.2   Proving That (3.12) Is a Model Mapping

To do this proof, we need to show that the model mapping specified by the constraints in (3.12) satisfy conditions $\Phi 1$ thru $\Phi 3$. The context model is given by the specification on Pages 159–160. The corresponding application model is given by the specification on Page 155. Figure C.1 shows a visualisation of the model mapping. Note that we have abstracted the two state machines by showing only the states determined by the flexible variables referred to by the model mapping.

We begin with $\Phi 1$, which states that all initial application states are mapped to some initial state in the context model. For every initial application state holds $doHandle = 0$. For such states, (3.12) stipulates that the context model should be in a state with $inState =$ "Idle" $\wedge\ unhandledRequest = $ FALSE. Such states are indeed initial states of the context model.

We now show that $\Phi 2$ holds. There are four state transitions, which we inspect individually:

---

[2]We can pull out the IF-clauses and convert them into implications by using rule (16.2) from [78, p. 295].

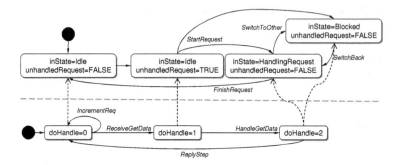

Figure C.1: Visualisation of the model mapping from (3.12)

- IncrementReq: this transition produces a stuttering step in the application and in the context model.

- ReceiveGetData and HandleGetData: These two transition are mirrored by similar transitions in the context model.

- ReplyStep: There are two cases for this transition: First, if the context model is in the state with $inState =$ "HandlingRequest", it can follow the application-model state transition in just one step. Otherwise, if the context model is in a state with $inState =$ "Blocked", then we need to make use of the weak form of $\Phi 2$, which allows the context model to follow the transition in two steps.

Next we prove that the mapping is complete; that is, that each application state is mapped to some context-model state. For this purpose, we first observe that the rules in *ModelMapping* completely cover all possible application states. Moreover, they all map to something that is indeed a (set of) context-model state(s). Thus, the mapping is complete, condition $\Phi 3$ is satisfied.

C.3.3   Proving Feasibility

In this section we will proof the *IsFeasible* property defined in (3.13).

It can be seen that *IsFeasible* has a structure which is very similar to the structure of the conclusion of the proof rule of Theorem 3.2. We are going to show how the hypotheses apply, and how the composition rule can be applied. To help with this objective, [5] defines the following two propositions:

Proposition C.1 (Derived from Proposition 4 from [5]) If E, M, and, for all
$j = 1, \ldots, n$, M_j are safety properties, and
$$\models E \wedge \bigwedge_{j=1}^{n} M_j \Rightarrow M$$
$$\models \bigwedge_{j=1}^{n} M_j \Rightarrow E \bot M$$
then $\models E_{+v} \wedge \bigwedge_{j=1}^{n} M_j \Rightarrow M$ where v a tuple of variables containing all the variables occurring free in M.   □

Proposition C.2 (Derived from Proposition 5 from [5])
If $\models E = Init_E \wedge \Box[N_E]_{\langle x,e \rangle}$
$\models M = Init_M \wedge \Box[N_M]_{\langle y,m \rangle}$
then
$\models (\exists x : Init_E \vee \exists y : Init_M) \wedge Disjoint(e, m) \Rightarrow \exists x : E \bot \exists y : M$ □

We therefore have the following proof plan:

1. Identify the individual components comprising the specification and their corresponding E_i and M_i.

2. Show $\forall i \in \{1..n\} : \models E \wedge \bigwedge_{j=1}^{n} M_j \Rightarrow E_i$.

3. Show $\models E \wedge \bigwedge_{j=1}^{n} M_j \Rightarrow M$.

4. Show $\models E_{+v} \wedge \bigwedge_{j=1}^{n} M_j \Rightarrow M$. We divide this proof further into the following steps:

   (a) Show $\models \bigwedge_{j=1}^{n} M_j \Rightarrow E \bot M$. For this we need to:

   i. Assuming $\quad Init_E \;\triangleq\; \wedge\, EnvLastDeltaTime = RequestPeriod,$
   $$\wedge\, StartDelta = now$$
   $$\wedge\, EnvInState = \text{"Idle"}$$
   $$Init_M \;\triangleq\; ServInState = \text{"Idle"}$$
   show $\models \bigwedge_{j=1}^{n} M_j \Rightarrow \exists\, StartDelta : Init_E \vee Init_M$

   ii. Show that
   $$Disjoint(\langle RequestPeriod,$$
   $$EnvLastDeltaTime,$$
   $$EnvInState,$$
   $$EnvUnhandledRequest \rangle,$$
   $$\langle ServLastResponseTime,$$
   $$ServInState,$$
   $$ServUnhandledRequest,$$
   $$ServInternalCounter,$$
   $$ServDoHandle \rangle)$$
   can be conjoined to the specification without causing inconsistencies.

   iii. Show that $\quad \models E = Init_E \wedge \Box[N_E]_{\langle StartDelta, e \rangle}$
   $$\models M = Init_M \wedge \Box[N_M]_{\langle m \rangle}$$
   for some e, m, N_E, N_M.

   iv. Q.E.D. by Proposition C.2.

   (b) Q.E.D. by Proposition C.1, 3, 4a.

5. Q.E.D. all above, and Theorem 3.2.

Identifying the Components

In order to apply the composition theorem we first must identify the individual components and their respective E_i and M_i. E is easily identified to be $Environment(RequestPeriod)$, M is equal to $ResponseTimeSpec(50)! Service \wedge ServFunc \wedge ServMap$.

$System$ provides the following distinct components:

$\Pi_1 \; ExecTimeSpec(20)! Component \wedge CompFun \wedge CompMap$

$\Pi_2 \; MyCPU(CPUTaskCount, CPUPeriods, CPUWcets)$

$\Pi_3 \; MyContainer(20, 50, SCTaskCount, SCPeriods, SCWcets)$

$\Pi_4 \; \Box \wedge ServLastResponseTime = SCServLastResponseTime$
$\qquad \wedge\, ServInState = SCServInState$
$\qquad \wedge\, ServUnhandledRequest = SCServUnhandledRequest$

$\Pi_5 \quad \Box \wedge\ MYCPU\_MinExecTime = SCCPUMinExecTime$
$\qquad \wedge\ MYCPU\_AssignedTo = SCCPUAssignedTo$
$\qquad \wedge\ CPUTaskCount = SCTaskCount$
$\qquad \wedge\ CPUPeriods = SCPeriods$
$\qquad \wedge\ CPUWcets = SCWcets$

$\Pi_6 \quad \Box \wedge\ SCCmpLastExecutionTime = MyCompLastExec$
$\qquad \wedge\ SCCmpInState = MyCompInState$
$\qquad \wedge\ SCCmpUnhandledRequest = MyCompUnhandledRequest$

$\Pi_7 \quad \Box \wedge\ SCEnvLastDeltaTime = EnvLastDeltaTime$
$\qquad \wedge\ SCEnvInState = EnvInState$
$\qquad \wedge\ SCEnvUnhandledRequest = EnvUnhandledRequest$

Taking a closer look at these components, we can see that some of them can be further split into individual components:

1. $\Pi_1 = \Pi_{11} \wedge \Pi_{12} \wedge \Pi_{13} \wedge \Pi_{14}$ where

   $\Pi_{11} \quad SpecEnv \overset{+}{\Rightarrow} SpecComponent$

   $\Pi_{12} \quad RTnow(\langle AccExec_1, SegStart_1, MyCompLastExec\rangle)^{34}$

   $\Pi_{13} \quad \wedge\ Init_{ExecutionTimeConstrainedComponent}$ [5]
   $\qquad \wedge\ \Box[Next_{ExecutionTimeConstrainedComponent}]_{\langle AccExec_1,}$
   $\qquad\qquad\qquad\qquad\qquad\qquad\qquad\qquad\qquad\qquad\quad {}_{SegStart_1,}$
   $\qquad\qquad\qquad\qquad\qquad\qquad\qquad\qquad\qquad\qquad\quad {}_{MyCompLastExec\rangle}$

   $\Pi_{14} \quad \Box(MyCompLastExec \leq 20)$

   $\Pi_{15} \quad CompFun \wedge CompMap$

2. $\Pi_2 = \Pi_{21} \wedge \Pi_{22}$ where

   $\Pi_{21} \quad TimedCPUSched!\,TimedCPUScheduler$

   $\Pi_{22} \quad \Box Schedulable \overset{+}{\Rightarrow} \Box\, TimedCPUSched!\,ExecutionTimesOk$

Now that we have identified the individual components, we need to identify their respective E_i and M_i. Quite a few of the components do have no environment condition, so that $E_i \overset{\triangle}{=} \text{TRUE} \wedge M_i \overset{\triangle}{=} \Pi_i$. We list only the exceptions in the following:

$\Pi_{11}\ E_{11} \overset{\triangle}{=} SpecEnv \wedge M_{11} \overset{\triangle}{=} SpecComponent$

$\Pi_{22}\ E_{22} \overset{\triangle}{=} \Box Schedulable \wedge M_{22} \overset{\triangle}{=} \Box\, TimedCPUSched!\,ExecutionTimesOk$

$\Pi_3\ E_3 \overset{\triangle}{=} \wedge\ 20 \leq 50$
$\qquad\qquad\quad \wedge\ CPUCanSchedule(1, [1 \mapsto 50], [1 \mapsto 20])$
$\qquad\qquad\quad \wedge\ ComponentMaxExecTime(20)$
$\qquad\qquad\quad \wedge\ MinInterrequestTime(50)$
$\qquad\qquad\quad \wedge\ CompFun \wedge CompMap$
$\qquad\qquad\quad \wedge\ CompFun \Rightarrow ServFun$

---

[3]We use only the variable names from $SystemSpecification$, placing them where they have been put by renaming operators.

[4]$AccExec_1, SegStart_1$ are hidden variables. Proposition 2 from [5] allows us to create a proof with the hidden variables visible and use this to prove statements about the specifications with these variables hidden.

[5]It should be noted that the syntax chosen here is simplifying some aspects: The subscripts are used to signify the module from which the formula has been taken. The component needs to be taken into consideration to perform the correct variable renamings before attempting to prove anything!

$$M_3 \quad \triangleq \quad \wedge\; ServiceResponseTime(50)$$
$$\wedge\; \Box\wedge\; SCTaskCount = 1$$
$$\wedge\; SCPeriods = [1 \mapsto 50]$$
$$\wedge\; SCWcets = [1 \mapsto ExecutionTime]$$
$$\wedge\; \Box(SCCmpUnhandledRequest = SCEnvUnhandledRequest)$$
$$\wedge\; ServFun \wedge ServMap$$

Showing the hypotheses of the proof rule

Let us now prove the hypotheses of Abadi/Lamport's theorem.

Showing that all environment conditions are fulfilled We will first prove that all environment conditions are provided for by one of the other components, or by the system environment itself. Because for most components $E_i = \text{TRUE}$ we only need to consider the three components named above which in fact have an $E_i \neq \text{TRUE}$.

We begin with E_{11}:

$$E_{11} = \wedge\; MyCompUnhandledRequest = \text{FALSE}$$
$$\wedge\; \Box[\vee \wedge MyCompUnhandledRequest = \text{FALSE}$$
$$\wedge\; MyCompUnhandledRequest' = \text{TRUE}$$
$$\wedge\; \text{UNCHANGED}\; MyCompInState$$
$$\vee\; SystemAgent]_{vars}$$

We observe that this is implied by $E \wedge M_3 \wedge M_6 \wedge M_7$, because the container specification, namely M_3 connects the two in the conjunct $\Box(SCCmpUnhandledRequest = SCEnvUnhandledRequest)$. Note that $SCCmpUnhandledRequest$ is connected to $MyCompUnhandledRequest$ in M_6 and $SCEnvUnhandledRequest$ is connected to $EnvUnhandledRequest$ in M_7 in a similar manner.

The next environment condition is E_{22}:

$$E_{22} \quad = \quad \Box Schedulable$$
$$= \quad \Box\textbf{let}\; usage \;\triangleq\; [k \in \{1..SCTaskCount\} \mapsto (SCWcets[k]/SCPeriods[k])]$$
$$\textbf{in}\quad Sum(usage) \leq (SCTaskCount * (sqrt(SCTaskCount, 2) - 1))$$

Looking at $M_3 \wedge M_5$, we find that E_{22} can be derived easily, because $20/50 \leq 1$ holds.

Last but not least, we need to consider E_3. This condition is a bit more complex, and actually consists of six conjuncts, which we are going to check individually:

1. $20 \leq 50$ This is trivially TRUE.

2. $CPUCanSchedule(1, [1 \mapsto 50], [1 \mapsto 20])$ This is implied by $M_{22} \wedge M_{21}$ and the renaming performed in M_5.

3. $ComponentMaxExecTime(20)$ This is the rule that states that the container expects a component with a specified upper bound on its execution time to be available. This can be derived from $M_{11} \wedge M_{12} \wedge M_{13} \wedge M_{14}$ together with a renaming in M_6 already.

4. $MinInterrequestTime(50)$ This is implied by $E \wedge M_7$, and a constraint on the specification parameter $RequestPeriod$. The strongest such constraint is $RequestPeriod = 50$, but the implication can be shown for some weaker conditions, too.

5. $CompFun \wedge CompMap$ This is implied directly by M_{15}.

6. $CompFun \Rightarrow ServFun$ This can be shown directly from the definition of $CompFun$ and $ServFun$ without using any M_i.

We have now shown the second hypothesis of the proof rule, namely

$$\forall\, i \in \{1..n\} : \models E \wedge \bigwedge_{j=1}^{n} M_j \Rightarrow E_i$$

We have identified that we need to place the following conditions on the specification parameter: $RequestPeriod = 50$.

Showing M   In this section we are going to show $\models E \wedge \bigwedge_{j=1}^{n} M_j \Rightarrow M$. It is easy to see that M_3 together with M_4 imply M, because M_4 makes the conjunct

$$ServiceResponseTime(50)$$

from M_3 identical to M. Because

$$\models \forall A, B, C \in \textsc{boolean} : ((A \wedge B) \Rightarrow C) = ((A \Rightarrow C) \vee (B \Rightarrow C)) \qquad \text{(C.1)}$$

we do not need to consider E nor the other M_j.

Showing Disjointness   In this section we are going to perform the 4th step of our proof plan, namely to prove $\models E_{+v} \wedge \bigwedge_{j=1}^{n} M_j \Rightarrow M$. In particular, this requires us to prove $\models \bigwedge_{j=1}^{n} M_j \Rightarrow E \bot M$.

We can see from the specification that $\models M_3 \wedge M_4 \Rightarrow ServInState = \text{"Idle"}$ and therefore $\models M_3 \wedge M_4 \Rightarrow Init_M$, and therefore, again by (C.1):

$$\models \bigwedge_{j=1}^{n} M_j \Rightarrow \exists\, StartDelta : Init_E \vee Init_M \qquad \text{(C.2)}$$

In order to show step 4(a)ii of our proof plan, we need to show that none of the variables in the first tuple are required to change in the same step as any of the variables in the second tuple in any action in our specification. This is not the case, so we can conjoin the $Disjoint$ property without causing an inconsistency.

We are now going to show step 4(a)iii of our proof plan. This requires us to show two things:

1. $\forall\, \sigma \in \Sigma : ((\sigma \models E \Rightarrow \sigma \models Init_E) \wedge (\sigma \models M \Rightarrow \sigma \models Init_M))$.

2. For each state s: $(s \models Init_E) \Rightarrow (\exists\, \sigma : (\sigma[0] = s) \wedge \sigma \models E))$ and $(s \models Init_M) \Rightarrow (\exists\, \sigma : (\sigma[0] = s) \wedge \sigma \models M))$.

Because we only used $Init_M$ in proving Lemma C.3.3, it will be sufficient to perform these proofs for M only. M is defined as follows:

$$
\begin{aligned}
M &\triangleq EnvSpec \overset{+}{\Rightarrow} ServiceSpec \\
EnvSpec &\triangleq \wedge InitEnv \\
&\quad \wedge \Box[NextEnv]_{ServUnhandledRequest} \\
ServiceSpec &\triangleq \wedge InitServ \\
&\quad \wedge \Box[NextServ]_{vars}
\end{aligned}
$$

Because both $NextEnv$ and $NextServ$ are conjunctions of actions, they will be satisfied by any initial behaviour, so

$$
\begin{aligned}
(\forall\, \sigma \in \Sigma : (\sigma \models (InitEnv \overset{+}{\Rightarrow} InitServ) &\Rightarrow \sigma \models Init_M)) \\
\Rightarrow (\forall\, \tau \in \Sigma : (\tau \models M &\Rightarrow \tau \models Init_M))
\end{aligned}
$$

A behaviour σ satisfies $InitEnv \overset{+}{\Rightarrow} InitServ$ by definition of $\overset{+}{\Rightarrow}$, iff[6]

---

[6] The notation used is not completely rigorous, especially in the second condition, cf. [78, page 316] for a more precise definition.

1. $\sigma \models InitEnv \Rightarrow InitServ$, and

2. $\forall\, n \in Nat\; :\; \sigma|_{n-1} \models InitEnv \Rightarrow \sigma|_n \models InitServ$

This implies, in particular,

$$\wedge\, \sigma[0] \models InitEnv \Rightarrow InitServ$$
$$\wedge\, (\exists\, \tau : \tau \models InitEnv) \Rightarrow \sigma[0] \models InitServ$$

The second conjunct is created by letting $n \triangleq 0$. This is a special case, which demands only that $InitEnv$ can be fulfilled at all by any behaviour. See [78, page 316] for further details. Because $InitEnv$ can certainly be fulfilled by some behaviours, the above can be simplified to

$$\sigma[0] \models InitServ$$

which is equivalent to

$$\sigma \models Init_M \tag{C.3}$$

We have thus shown the first proof obligation $\models M \Rightarrow \models Init_M$.

To show the other direction we first observe that we can certainly always find a suitable extension to a behaviour, as long as s fulfils the initial-state conditions given by M. We have derived these already above, to be equal to $InitServ$, or—in fact—$Init_M$. Thus, step 4(a)iii of our proof plan has been discharged.

We have thus discharged all proof obligations and have proved all the hypotheses from Theorem 3.2, and thereby the property $IsFeasible$ for our example system.

List of Figures

2.1 Overview of the semantic framework 12

3.1 System model 21
3.2 An example of a context model defining the relevant steps in an operation call 24
3.3 An example of an application model describing a simple Counter component 25
3.4 An example model mapping 27
3.5 Typical mappings for initial application states 29
3.6 Two examples for mappings constrained by $\Phi2$ 30
3.7 An example mapping that violates rule $\Phi3$ 31
3.8 Relations between the major model types in our approach 35
3.9 Interface specification for the counting application 41
3.10 State-machine representation of the service context model. Note that this is the same as in Fig. 3.2 42
3.11 TLA$^+$ representation of the service context model 43
3.12 TLA$^+$ representation of the response time measurement 44
3.13 TLA$^+$ representation of the response time measurement (end) 45
3.14 State-machine representation of the response time measurement 45
3.15 State-machine representation of the component context model with attached specifications for the execution time measurement 46
3.16 State-machine representation of data rate for an active component 49

4.1 Three approaches to specifying container strategies for component networks 53
4.2 Architecture of the example application 60
4.3 State machine with context model and measurement definition for call time 61

5.1 Sample component specification showing a relation between accuracy and execution time 67
5.2 A container guaranteeing a minimum response time 70
5.3 A container guaranteeing a minimum response time (end) 71
5.4 Using jitter-constrained and response-time container together 72
5.5 Using jitter-constrained and response-time container together (ctd.) 73
5.6 Using jitter-constrained and response-time container together (end) 74
5.7 Container strategy for recovery block software redundancy 75
5.8 Container strategy for recovery block software redundancy (end) 76
5.9 State-machine representation of the reliability measurement 77

6.1 Core concepts of CQML$^+$ 82
6.2 Static structure diagram of the CQML context model for the definition of response time 83
6.3 Context model for use in defining the μCQML semantics 87
6.4 Context model for use in defining the μCQML semantics (end) 88

6.5   Measurement definition template for the semantic mapping of service op-
      erations 89
6.6   Measurement definition template for the semantic mapping of component
      operations 90
6.7   The TLA$^+$ specification for response_time 91
6.8   Constraint template for the semantic mapping of service operations 92
6.9   Constraint template for the semantic mapping of component operations . . 93
6.10 The TLA$^+$ specification for good_response 94
6.11 Profile mapping template 94
6.12 The TLA$^+$ specification for good 95
6.13 System specification mapping template 96

7.1   Performance analysis and design as an ongoing process in SPE (from [133]) 105
7.2   Basic node types of execution graphs. From [133] 106
7.3   Sequence Diagram of a use case scenario for the Counter component 108
7.4   Execution Graph representation of the same scenario as in Fig. 7.3 109
7.5   Overhead specification for the use-case based analysis 110
7.6   Results of *SPE·ED* analysis 110
7.7   Software execution model for the getResult() operation from the
      Calculator example from Sect. 4.4 112
7.8   Formal specification of Use-Case–based analysis 114
7.9   Formal specification of Use-Case–based analysis (end) 115

8.1   A component-based software development process with support for non-
      functional properties (Adapted from [?]) 118
8.2   Rough architecture of a stock syndication application 120

9.1   Component forms identified in [32] 126
9.2   Classification of non-functional requirements defined by Sommerville
      (from [134, p. 131]) 130

C.1   Visualisation of the model mapping from (3.12) 238

List of Examples

1.1 Insufficiencies in CQML$^+$ 4
2.1 Implementation vs Usage 11
3.1 Container Strategy for Responsibility 22
3.2 Response time 23
3.3 Context Model and Application Model 24
3.4 Model Mapping 27
3.5 Bad Model Mapping 31
3.6 A Simple Performance Example Based on Request–Response Communication . 41
3.7 A Data Quality Example 48
3.8 A Performance Example Based on Stream-Based Communication and an Active Component 49
4.1 Global Container Strategies 52
4.2 Shared Resources 55
4.3 Extending intrinsic specifications 58
4.4 An Example for Component Network Specification 59
5.1 Accuracy and Execution Time 66
5.2 Container Strategy Selection 68
5.3 Jitter-Constrained Components 69
5.4 Reliable Components 71
6.1 A simple CQML$^+$ specification 82
6.2 Parameter types and induced names 84
6.3 A simple μCQML specification 85
6.4 Semantics of `response_time` 89
6.5 Semantics of `good_response` 91
6.6 Semantics of `good` profile 92
7.1 Use-Case–Based Analysis 113
8.1 Connection to Development Process – Stock Syndication Application 119

List of Definitions, Propositions, and Theorems

Definition 3.1   Context Model and Application Model 24
Definition 3.2   Specification Scheme for Context Models 25
Definition 3.3   Measurement 26
Definition 3.4   Specification Scheme for Measurements 26
Theorem 3.1   Conditions for Model-Mappings 30
Definition 3.5   Computational Model 32
Definition 3.6   Measurement Mapping 32
Definition 3.7   Component Model 34
Definition 3.8   Interface Model 34
Definition 3.9   Meta-model (derived from [40]) 34
Definition 3.10   Non-functional Property 35
Definition 3.11   Intrinsic vs Extrinsic Specifications 36
Definition 3.12   Resource Specification 38
Definition 3.13   Container Specification 39
Definition 3.14   System Specification 39
Definition 3.15   Feasible System 40
Theorem 3.2   Composition Principle (simplified from Theorem 3 from [5]) 40
Definition 4.1   Encapsulated Component 54
Definition 4.2   Shared Resource 55
Definition 4.3   Composite Encapsulated Component 57
Definition 5.1   Container Specification (Multiple Container Strategies) 68
Definition 6.1 μCQML helper concepts 83
Definition 6.2 μCQML language constructs 84
Proposition C.1   Derived from Proposition 4 from [5] 238
Proposition C.2   Derived from Proposition 5 from [5] 238

Bibliography

[1] Jan Øyvind Aagedal. *Quality of Service Support in Development of Distributed Systems*. PhD thesis, University of Oslo, 2001.

[2] M[artín] Abadi and L[eslie] Lamport. Composing specifications. In J. W. de Bakker, W.-P. de Roever, and G. Rozenberg, editors, *Stepwise Refinement of Distributed Systems – Models, Formalisms, Correctness*, volume 430 of *LNCS*, pages 1–41, Berlin, Germany, 1989. Springer-Verlag.

[3] Martín Abadi and Leslie Lamport. The existence of refinement mappings. *Theoretical Computer Science*, 82(2):253–284, 1991.

[4] Martín Abadi and Leslie Lamport. An old-fashioned recipe for real time. *ACM ToPLaS*, 16(5):1543–1571, September 1994.

[5] M[artín] Abadi and L[eslie] Lamport. Conjoining specifications. *ACM ToPLaS*, 17(3):507–534, May 1995.

[6] Gregory [D.] Abowd, Robert Allen, and David Garlan. Using style to understand descriptions of software architecture. In David Notkin, editor, *SIGSOFT '93: Proc. 1st ACM SIGSOFT Symposium on Foundations of Software Engineering*, pages 9–20, New York, NY, USA, 1993. ACM Press.

[7] Gregory D. Abowd, Robert Allen, and David Garlan. Formalizing style to understand descriptions of software architecture. *ACM Transactions on Software Engineering Methodology*, 4(4):319–364, October 1995.

[8] Ronald Aigner, Elke Franz, Steffen Göbel, Hermann Härtig, Heinrich Hußmann, Klaus Meißner, Klaus Meyer-Wegener, Marcus Meyerhöfer, Andreas Pfitzmann, Christoph Pohl, Martin Pohlack, Simone Röttger, Alexander Schill, Frank Wehner, and Steffen Zschaler. Zwischenbericht der DFG-Forschergruppe 428 "Components with Quantitative Properties and Adaptivity (Comquad)". Technical Report TUD FI03-10-August 2003, Technische Universität Dresden, Fakultät Informatik, 2003.

[9] Ronald Aigner, Christoph Pohl, Martin Pohlack, and Steffen Zschaler. Tailor-made containers: Modeling non-functional middleware service. In Bruel et al. [29]. Technical Report TUD-FI04-12 Sept.2004 at Technische Universität Dresden.

[10] Ronald Aigner, Martin Pohlack, Simone Röttger, and Steffen Zschaler. Towards pervasive treatment of non-functional properties at design and run-time. In *Proc. Int'l Conf. on Software & Systems Engineering and their Applications (ICSSEA)*, Paris, December 2003.

[11] Robert John Allen. *A Formal Approach to Software Architecture*. PhD thesis, Carnegie-Mellon University, 1997.

[12] Lloyd Allison. *A Practical Introduction to Denotational Semantics*. Cambridge Computer Science Texts. Cambridge University Press, February 1987.

251

[13] Rajeev Alur and David L. Dill. A theory of timed automata. *Theoretical Computer Science*, 126(2):183–235, 1994.

[14] Sten Amundsen, Ketil Lund, Frank Eliassen, and Richard Staehli. QuA: platform-managed QoS for component architectures. In *Proc. of the Norwegian Informatics Conf. (NIK), Stavanger, Norway*. Tapir Akademisk Forlag, Trondheim, Norway, November 2004.

[15] Felice Balarin, Yosinori Watanabe, Harry Hsieh, Luciano Lavagno, Claudio Passerone, and Alberto Sangiovanni-Vincentelli. Metropolis: An integrated electronic system design environment. *IEEE Computer*, 36:45–52, April 2003.

[16] Dirk Bandelow. Entwicklung einer CQML$^+$-Basisbibliothek. Diplomarbeit, Technische Universität Dresden, February 2004. In German.

[17] Steffen Becker, Lars Grunske, Raffaela Mirandola, and Sven Overhage. Performance prediction of component-based systems: A survey from an engineering perspective. In *Dagstuhl Seminar 04511: Architecting Systems with Trustworthy Components*, volume 3938 of *LNCS*. Springer, 2006. To Appear.

[18] Antonia Bertolino and Raffaela Mirandola. Towards component based software performance engineering. In *Proc. 6th Workshop on Component-Based Software Engineering: Automated Reasoning and Prediction at ICSE 2003*, pages 1–6. ACM/IEEE, May 2003.

[19] Antonia Bertolino and Raffaela Mirandola. Software performance engineering of component-based systems. In Dujmović et al. [49], pages 238–242.

[20] Antoine Beugnard, Jean-Marc Jézéquel, Noël Plouzeau, and Damien Watkins. Making components contract aware. *IEEE Computer*, 32(7):38–45, July 1999.

[21] Jean Bézivin, Sébastien Gérard, Pierre-Alain Muller, and Laurent Rioux. MDA components: Challenges and opportunities. In Andy Evans, Paul Sammut, and James S. Willans, editors, *Proc. 1st Int'l Workshop Metamodelling for MDA*, pages 23–41, York, UK, 2003.

[22] Milind Bhandarkar and L. V. Kalé. An interface model for parallel components. In H. Dietz, editor, *Proc. Workshop on Languages and Compilers for Parallel Computing (LCPC 2001), Cumberland Falls, KY, August 2001*, volume 2624 of *LNCS*, pages 209–222. Springer, 2003.

[23] Egor Bondarev, Johan Muskens, Peter de With, Michel Chaudron, and Johan Lukkien. Predicting real-time properties of component assemblies: a scenario-simulation approach. In Steinmetz and Mauthe [138], pages 40–47.

[24] Egon Börger. The ASM refinement method. *Formal Aspects of Computing*, 15(2–3):237–257, November 2003.

[25] Egon Börger and Robert Stärk. *Abstract State Machines – A Method for High-Level System Design and Analysis*. Springer, 2003.

[26] Tim Bray, Jean Paoli, C. M. Sperberg-McQueen, and Eve Maler. Extensible markup language (XML) 1.0 (second edition), October 2000. W3C Recommendation.

[27] Manfred Broy, Anton Deimel, Juergen Henn, Kai Koskimies, František Plášil, Gustav Pomberger, Wolfgang Pree, Michael Stal, and Clemens Szyperski. What characterizes a (software) component? *Software – Concepts & Tools*, 19(1):49–56, June 1998.

[28] Jean-Michel Bruel, editor. *Proc. 1st Int'l Workshop on Quality of Service in Component-Based Software Engineering, Toulouse, France.* Cépaduès-Éditions, June 2003.

[29] Jean-Michel Bruel, Geri Georg, Heinrich Hussmann, Ileana Ober, Christoph Pohl, Jon Whittle, and Steffen Zschaler, editors. *Workshop on Models for Non-functional Aspects of Component-Based Software (NfC'04) at UML conference 2004*, September 2004. Technical Report TUD-FI04-12 Sept.2004 at Technische Universität Dresden.

[30] Mark Burstein, Anupriya Ankolenkar, Massimo Paolucci, Naveen Srinivasan, Katia Sycara, Monika Solanki, Ora Lassila, Deborah McGuiness, Grit Denker, David Martin, Bijan Parsia, Evren McIlraith, Jerry Hobbs, Marta Sabou, and Drew McDermott. OWL-S: Semantic markup for web services. OWL Services Coalition White Paper acc. Version 1.0 of the OWL-S Specification, April 2006. URL http://www.daml.org/services/owl-s/1.0/owl-s.pdf.

[31] A. Cau and P. Collette. Parallel composition of assumption–commitment specifications: A unifying approach for shared variable and distributed message passing concurrency. *Acta Informatica*, 33(2):153–176, 1996.

[32] John Cheesman and John Daniels. *UML Components: A Simple Process for Specifying Component-Based Software.* Addison Wesley Longman, Inc., 2001.

[33] Shiping Chen, Ian Gorton, Anna Liu, and Yan Liu. Performance prediction of COTS component-based enterprise applications. In Ivica Crnkovic, Heinz Schmidt, Judith Stafford, and Kurt Wallnau, editors, *Proc. 5th ICSE Workshop on Component-Based Software Engineering (CBSE'2002): Benchmarks for Predictable Assembly*, May 2002.

[34] Avraam Chimaris and George A. Papadopoulos. Implementing QoS aware component-based applications. In Robert Meersman and Zahir Tari, editors, *On the Move to Meaningful Internet Systems 2004: CoopIS, DOA, and ODBASE: OTM Confederated Int'l Confs.*, volume 3291 of *LNCS*, pages 1173–1189, Agia Napa, Cyprus, October 2004. Springer.

[35] J.-Y. Chung, J. W. S. Liu, and K.-J. Lin. Scheduling periodic jobs that allow imprecise results. *IEEE Trans. on Computers*, 39(9), 1990.

[36] Lawrence Chung, Brian A. Nixon, Eric Yu, and John Mylopoulos. *Non-Functional Requirements in Software Engineering.* The Kluwer international series in software engineering. Kluwer Academic Publishers Group, Dordrecht, Netherlands, 1999.

[37] Ciao website. http://www.cs.wustl.edu/ schmidt/CIAO.html.

[38] O. Ciupke and R. Schmidt. Components as context-independent units of software. In *WCOP 96, In Special Issues in Object-Oriented Programming, Workshop Reader of the 10th European Conference on Object-Oriented Programming ECOOP96*, pages 139–143. d.punkt Verlag, Heidelberg, 1996.

[39] Tony Clark, Andy Evans, and Stuart Kent. Engineering modelling languages: A precise meta-modelling approach. In R.-D. Kutsche and H. Weber, editors, *Proc. 5th Int'l Conf. on Fundamental Approaches to Software Engineering (FASE 2002)*, volume 2306 of *LNCS*, pages 159–173, Grenoble, France, April 2002. Springer.

[40] Tony Clark, Andy Evans, Paul Sammut, and James Willans. *Applied Metamodelling – A Foundation for Language Driven Development.* 2004. version 0.1, published on-line August 2004 at http://www.xactium.com/.

[41] Wolfgang Clesle and Andreas Pfitzmann. Rechnerkonzept mit digital sig-
nierten Schnittstellenprotokollen erlaubt individuelle Verantwortungszuweisung.
Datenschutz-Berater, 14(8–9):8–38, 1991. In German.

[42] Stefan Conrad and Klaus Turowski. Temporal OCL: Meeting specification demands
for business components. In K. Siau and T. Halpin, editors, *Unified Modeling Language: Systems Analysis, Design and Development Issues*, pages 151–165. IDEA
Group Publishing, 2001.

[43] William T. Councill and George T. Heinemann. Definition of a software compo-
nent and its elements. In George T. Heinemann and William T. Councill, editors,
Component-Based Software Engineering – Putting the Pieces Together, pages 5–20.
Addison-Wesley, 2001.

[44] Ivica Crnkovic, Magnus Larsson, and Otto Preiss. Concerning predictability in
dependable component-based systems: Classification of quality attributes. In
R. de Lemos et al., editors, *Architecting Dependable Systems III*, volume 3549 of
LNCS, pages 257–278. Springer, 2005.

[45] Ivica Crnkovic, Stig Larsson, and Judith Stafford. Component-based software en-
gineering: Building systems from components. *Software Engineering Notes*, 27(3),
May 2002. Summary of a workshop at 9th IEEE Conference and Workshops on
Engineering of Computer-Based Systems.

[46] Erwan Demairy, Emmanuelle Anceaume, and Valérie Issarny. On the correctness
of multimedia applications. In *Proc. 11th Euromicro Conf. on Real-Time Systems
(ECRTS'99)*, York, UK, June 1999. IEEE.

[47] Edsger Wybe Dijkstra. On the role of scientific thought. published as [48], August
1974. URL http://www.cs.utexas.edu/users/EWD/ewd04xx/EWD447.PDF.

[48] Edsger Wybe Dijkstra. On the role of scientific thought. In *Selected Writings on
Computing: A Personal Perspective*, pages 60–66. Springer-Verlag New York, Inc.,
Secaucus, NJ, USA, 1982.

[49] Jozo Dujmović, Virgilio Almeida, and Doug Lea, editors. *Proc. 4th Int'l Workshop
on Software and Performance WOSP 2004*, California, USA, January 2004. ACM
Press.

[50] Henrik Eichenhardt, Elke Franz, Simone Röttger, and Ute Wappler. Adapting component models to support responsibility. In Tiziana Margaria and Bernhard Steffen,
editors, *Proc. 1st Int'l Symposium on Leveraging Application of Formal Methods*,
2004.

[51] Robert E. Filman, Tzilla Elrad, Siobhan Clarke, and Mehmet Akşit. *Aspect-Oriented
Software Development*. Addison-Wesley Professional, 2004.

[52] Peter Fishburn. Preference structures and their numerical representations. *Theoretical Computer Science*, 217(2):359–383, April 1999.

[53] Stephan Flake and Wolfgang Mueller. Past- and future-oriented time-bounded temporal properties with OCL. In J. R. Cuellar and Z. Liu, editors, *Proc. 2nd Int'l Conf.
on Software Engineering and Formal Methods (SEFM 2004)*, pages 154–163. IEEE
Computer Society Press, 2004.

[54] Gary Ford. *Lecture Notes on Engineering Measurement for Software Engineers*.
Carnegie Mellon University, 1993. CMU/SEI report CMU/SEI-93-EM-9.

[55] Gary Ford. Measurement theory for software engineers. In *Lecture Notes on Engineering Measurement for Software Engineers* [54]. CMU/SEI report CMU/SEI-93-EM-9.

[56] Xavier Franch. Systematic formulation of non-functional characteristics of software. In *Proc. 3rd Int'l Conf. on Requirements Engineering*, pages 174–181. IEEE Computer Society, 1998.

[57] Svend Frølund and Jari Koistinen. Quality of service specification in distributed object systems design. In *Proc. 4th USENIX Conf. on Object-Oriented Technologies and Systems (COOTS)*, Santa Fe, New Mexico, April 1998.

[58] David Garlan, Robert Allen, and John Ockerbloom. Exploiting style in architectural design environments. In *SIGSOFT '94: Proc. 2nd ACM SIGSOFT Symposium on Foundations of Software Engineering*. ACM Press, December 1994.

[59] David Garlan, Robert Allen, and John Ockerbloom. Architectural mismatch or why it's hard to build systems out of existing parts. In *Proc. 17th Int'l Conf. on Software Engineering (ICSE'95)*, pages 179–185, Seattle, Washington, April 1995. IEEE Computer Society.

[60] A[ndrzej] Gościński. *Distributed Operating Systems: The logical design*. Addison-Wesley Publishers Ltd., 1991.

[61] Vincenzo Grassi and Raffaela Mirandola. Towards automatic compositional performance analysis of component-based systems. In Dujmović et al. [49], pages 59–63.

[62] Frank Griffel. *Componentware*. dpunkt.verlag, Heidelberg, 1998.

[63] Claude-Joachim Hamann. On the quantitative specification of jitter constrained periodic streams. In *Proc. 5th Int'l Workshop on Modeling, Analysis, and Simulation of Computer and Telecommunication Systems (MASCOTS'97)*. IEEE Computer Society, 1997.

[64] Claude-Joachim Hamann and Steffen Zschaler. Scheduling real-time components using jitter-constrained streams. In *Proc. Workshop on Advances in Quality of Service Management (AQuSerM'06)*, 2006. To Appear.

[65] Hermann Härtig, Rainer Baumgartl, Martin Borriss, Claude-Joachim Hamann, Martin Hohmuth, F. Mehnert, Lars Reuther, S. Schönberg, and Jean Wolter. DROPS: OS support for distributed multimedia applications. In *Proc. 8th ACM SIGOPS European Workshop: Support for Composing Distributed Applications*, Sintra, Portugal, September 1998.

[66] Scott A. Hissam, Gabriel A. Moreno, Judith A. Stafford, and Kurt C. Wallnau. Packaging predictable assembly. In J. Bishop, editor, *Proc. IFIP/ACM Working Conf. on Component Deployment (CD 2002)*, volume 2370 of *LNCS*, pages 108–126, Berlin, Germany, June 2002. Springer-Verlag.

[67] Tim Hu and Leo Marcus. Semantic foundations of an adaptive security infrastructure: Delegation. Unpublished, 2005.

[68] IASTED. *Proc. IASTED Int'l Conf. on Software Engineering (IASTED SE'04)*, Innsbruck, Austria, February 2004. ACTA Press.

[69] Information technology – quality of service: Framework. ISO/IEC 13236:1998, ITU-T X.641, 1998.

[70] Information technology – open distributed processing – interface definition language. ISO/IEC 14750:1999, January 2005.

[71] Ivar Jacobson, Martin Griss, and Patrik Jonsson. *Software Reuse – Architecture, Process and Organization for Business Success.* ACM Press and Addison Wesley Longman, 1997.

[72] C[liff] B. Jones. Specification and design of (parallel) programs. In R. E. A. Manson, editor, *Proceedings of IFIP '83*, pages 321–332. IFIP, North-Holland, 1983.

[73] Gregor Kiczales, John Lamping, Anurag Mendhekar, Chris Maeda, Cristina V. Lopes, Jean-Marc Loingtier, and John Irwin. Aspect-oriented programming. In Mehmet Akşit and Satoshi Matsuoka, editors, *11th European Conf. on Object-Oriented Programming (ECOOP'97)*, volume 1241 of *LNCS*, pages 220–242. Springer, 1997.

[74] Claude Kirchner and Hélène Kirchner. Rewriting, solving, proving. A preliminary version of a book available at http://www.loria.fr/~ckirchne/rsp.ps.gz, 1999.

[75] Anneke Kleppe, Jos Warmer, and Wim Bast. *MDA Explained: The Model Driven Architecture: Practice and Promise.* Addison Wesley Professional, April 2003.

[76] Ingolf H. Krüger. Service specification with MSCs and roles. In *Proc. IASTED Int'l Conf. on Software Engineering (IASTED SE'04)* [68].

[77] Leslie Lamport. A temporal logic of actions. *ACM ToPLaS*, 16(3):872–923, May 1994.

[78] Leslie Lamport. *Specifying Systems: The TLA+ Language and Tools for Hardware and Software Engineers.* Addison-Wesley, 2002.

[79] Edward D. Lazowska, John Zahorjan, G. Scott Graham, and Kenneth C. Sevcik. *Quantitative System Performance – Computer System Analysis Using Queueing Network Models.* Prentice-Hall, NJ, USA, 1984.

[80] Chen Lee. *On Quality of Service Management.* PhD thesis, Carnegie Mellon University, August 1999.

[81] Stefan Leue. QoS specification based on SDL/MSC and temporal logic. In G. v. Bochmann, J. de Meer, and A. Vogel, editors, *Workshop on Multimedia Applications and Quality of Service Verification*, Montreal, 1994.

[82] J. L. Lions. Report by the inquiry board, "ARIANE 5 flight 501 failure". Technical report, European Space Agency, 1996.

[83] Jane W. S. Liu. *Real-Time Systems.* Prentice Hall, NJ, 2000.

[84] J[ane] W. S. Liu, K[lara] Nahrstedt, D[avid] Hull, S[higang] Chen, and B[aochum] Li. EPIQ QoS characterization. ARPA Report, Quorum Meeting, July 1997.

[85] Mass Soldal Lund, Folker den Braber, and Ketil Stølen. A component-oriented approach to security risk analysis. In Bruel [28], pages 99–110.

[86] Michael R. Lyu, editor. *Handbook of Software Reliability Engineering.* McGraw-Hill, 1996.

[87] Ruth Malan and Dana Bredemeyer. Defining non-functional requirements. Bredemeyer Consulting, White Paper. http://www.bredemeyer.com/papers.htm, 2001.

[88] D. F. McAllister and M. A. Vouk. Fault-tolerant software reliability engineering. In Lyu [86], pages 567–614.

[89] M. Douglas McIlroy. Mass produced software components. In Peter Naur and Brian Randell, editors, *Software Engineering – Report on a conference sponsored by the NATO Science Committee*, pages 138–155, Garmisch, Germany, January 1969.

[90] Nenad Medvidovic and David S. Rosenblum. Domains of concern in software architectures and architecture description languages. In *Proc. 1997 USENIX Conf. on Domain-Specific Languages*, Santa Barbara, California, USA, October 1997.

[91] Nenad Medvidovic and Richard N. Taylor. A framework for classifying and comparing architecture description languages. In *Proc. 6th European Software Engineering Conf. together with 5th ACM SIGSOFT Symposium on the Foundations of Software Engineering (ESEC-FSE97)*, pages 60–76, Zurich, Switzerland, September 1997.

[92] Nenad Medvidovic and Richard N. Taylor. A classification and comparison framework for software architecture description languages. *IEEE Transactions on Software Engineering*, 26(1):70–93, January 2000.

[93] Stephan Merz. Isabelle/TLA. Website on integration of TLA into Isabelle, http://www.loria.fr/~ merz/projects/isabelle-tla/index.html, accessed May 11, 2006.

[94] Marcus Meyerhöfer and Christoph Neumann. TESTEJB – a measurement framework for EJBs. In Ivica Crnkovic, Judith A. Stafford, Heinz W. Schmidt, and Kurt Wallnau, editors, *Proc. 7th Intl. Symposium on Component-Based Software Engineering (CBSE'04)*, volume 3054 of *LNCS*, pages 294–301. Springer, 2004.

[95] Sun Microsystems. Enterprise JavaBeans Specification, version 2.0. Final Release, August 2001.

[96] Chokri Mraidha, Sébastien Gérard, François Terrier, and David Lugato. Worst-case execution time analysis from UML-based RT/E applications. In Susanne Graf, editor, *Proc. Int'l Workshop on Specification and Validation of UML models for Real Time and Embedded Systems (SVERTS'2006)*, 2004. published on-line: http://www-verimag.imag.fr/EVENTS/2004/SVERTS.

[97] Gleb Naumovich and Lori A. Clarke. Classifying properties: An alternative to the safety–liveness classification. In *Proc. of the 8th ACM SIGSOFT Int'l Symposium on Foundations of Software Engineering*, pages 159–168, New York, NY, USA, 2000. ACM Press.

[98] Jörg Nothnagel. Ressourcenverwaltung in DROPS. Diplomarbeit, Technische Universität Dresden, July 2002. In German.

[99] Object Management Group. CORBA 3.0 new component chapters. OMG Document, October 1999. URL http:// www.omg.org/ cgi-bin/ doc?ptc/ 99-10-04.

[100] Object Management Group. Real-time CORBA joint revised submission. OMG Document, March 1999. URL http:// cgi.omg.org/ cgi-bin/ doc?orbos/ 99-02-12 or http:// cgi.omg.org/ cgi-bin/ doc?orbos/ 99-03-29.

[101] Object Management Group. UML profile for schedulability, performance, and time specification. OMG Document, March 2002. URL http:// www.omg.org/ cgi-bin/ doc?ptc/02-03-02.

[102] Object Management Group. Meta object facility (MOF) specification version 1.4. OMG Document, April 2002. URL http://www.omg.org/cgi-bin/doc?formal/2002-04-03.

[103] Object Management Group. UML 2.0 OCL specification. OMG Document, October
       2003. URL http://www.omg.org/cgi-bin/doc?ptc/03-10-14.

[104] Object Management Group. MDA guide version 1.0.1. OMG Document, June 2003.
       URL http://www.omg.org/ cgi-bin/doc?omg/03-06-01.

[105] Object Management Group. Unified modeling language: Superstructure version
       2.0. OMG Document, July 2003. URL http://www.omg.org/cgi-bin/doc?ptc/03-08-
       02.pdf.

[106] Object Management Group. Request for proposals: MDA tool component. OMG
       Document, July 2006. URL http:// www.omg.org/ cgi-bin/ doc?ad/ 2006-06-09.

[107] Ruben Prieto-Diaz and James M Neighbors. Module interconnection languages. *J.
       Syst. Softw.*, 6(4):307–334, 1986.

[108] R. Rajkumar, C. Lee, J. Lehoczky, and D. Siewiorek. A resource allocation model
       for QoS management. In *Proc. IEEE Real-Time Systems Symposium*, December
       1997.

[109] R. Rajkumar, C. Lee, J. Lehoczky, and D. Siewiorek. Practical solutions for QoS-
       based resource allocation problems. In *Proc. IEEE Real-Time Systems Symposium*,
       December 1998.

[110] Trygve Reenskaug. *Working With Objects: The OOram Software Engineering
       Method*. Prentice Hall, 1995.

[111] Ralf H. Reussner. *Parametrisierte Verträge zur Protokolladaption bei Software-
       Komponenten*. Logos Verlag, Berlin, 2001. In German.

[112] Ralf H. Reussner, Iman H. Poernomo, and Heinz W. Schmidt. Contracts and quality
       attributes for software components. In Wolfgang Weck, Jan Bosch, and Clemens
       Szyperski, editors, *Proc. 8th Int'l Workshop on Component-Oriented Programming
       (WCOP'03)*, June 2003.

[113] Ralf H. Reussner, Iman H. Poernomo, and Heinz W. Schmidt. Reasoning about soft-
       ware architectures with contractually specified components. In A. Cechich, M. Pi-
       attini, and A. Vallecillo, editors, *Component-Based Software Quality: Methods and
       Techniques*, volume 2693 of *LNCS*, pages 287–325. Springer, 2003.

[114] Dale Rogerson. *Inside COM: Microsoft's Component Object Model*. Microsoft
       Press, 1997.

[115] Michael Roitzsch. Principles for the prediction of video decoding times applied
       to MPEG-1/2 and MPEG-4 Part 2 video. Großer Beleg, Technische Universität
       Dresden, Germany, June 2005.

[116] Simone Röttger and Ronald Aigner. Modeling of non-functional contracts in
       component-based systems using a layered architecture. In *Component Based Soft-
       ware Engineering and Modeling Non-functional Aspects (SIVOES-MONA), Work-
       shop at UML 2002*, October 2002.

[117] Simone Röttger and Steffen Zschaler. CQML$^+$: Enhancements to CQML. In Bruel
       [28], pages 43–56.

[118] Simone Röttger and Steffen Zschaler. Model-driven development for non-functional
       properties: Refinement through model transformation. In Thomas Baar, Al-
       fred Strohmeier, Ana Moreira, and Stephen J. Mellor, editors, *Proc. 7th Int'l
       <<UML>> Conf. 2004 – The Unified Modeling Language – Modeling Languages
       and Applications*, volume 3273 of *LNCS*, pages 275–289. Springer, October 2004.

[119] Simone Röttger and Steffen Zschaler. A software development process supporting non-functional properties. In *Proc. IASTED Int'l Conf. on Software Engineering (IASTED SE'04)* [68].

[120] Bikash Sabata, Saurav Chatterjee, Michael Davis, Jaroslaw J. Sydir, and Thomas F. Lawrence. Taxonomy for QoS specifications. In *Proc. 3rd Int'l Workshop on Object-oriented Real-Time Dependable Systems (WORDS'97)*, Newport Beach, California, February 1997.

[121] Christian Salzmann and Bernhard Schätz. Service-based software specification. In *Proc. Int'l Workshop on Test and Analysis of Component-Based Systems (TACOS) ETAPS 2003*, Electronic Notes in Theoretical Computer Science, Warsaw, Poland, April 2003. Elsevier.

[122] D.C. Schmidt and F. Kuhns. An overview of the real-time CORBA specification. *IEEE Computer*, pages 56–63, June 2000.

[123] Douglas C. Schmidt, David L. Levine, and Sumedh Mungee. The design of the TAO real-time object request broker. *Computer Communications*, 21(4), April 1998.

[124] Bran Selic. A generic framework for modeling resources with UML. *IEEE Computer*, 33(6):64–69, June 2000.

[125] Mary Shaw. The coming-of-age of software architecture research. In *Proc. 23rd Int'l Conf. on Software Engineering (ICSE'01)*, pages 656–664a. IEEE Computer Society, 2001.

[126] Mary Shaw, Robert DeLine, and Gregory Zelesnik. Abstractions and implementations for architectural connections. In *3rd Int'l Conf. on Configurable Distributed Systems*. IEEE Press, May 1996.

[127] Murali Sitaraman, Greg Kulczycki, Joan Krone, William F. Ogden, and A. L. N. Reddy. Performance specification of software components. In Paul G. Bassett, editor, *Proc. 2001 Symposium on Software Reusability*, pages 3–10. ACM Press, 2001.

[128] James Skene, D. Davide Lamanna, and Wolfgang Emmerich. Precise service level agreements. In *Proc. 26th Int'l Conf. on Software Engineering (ICSE'04)*, pages 179–188, Edinburgh, Scotland, May 2004. IEEE Computer Society.

[129] Connie U. Smith. *Performance Engineering of Software Systems*. SEI Series in Software Engineering. Addison-Wesley, 1990.

[130] Connie U. Smith. Origins of performance engineering: Highlights and outstanding problems. In Reiner Dumke, Claus Rautenstrauch, and Andreas Schmietendorf, editors, *Performance Engineering: State of the Art and Current Trends*, volume 2047 of *LNCS*, pages 96–118. Springer-Verlag, 2001.

[131] Connie U. Smith and Lloyd G. Williams. Performance engineering evaluation of object-oriented systems with SPE·ED. In Raymond A. Marie, Brigitte Plateau, Maria Calzarossa, and Gerardo Rubino, editors, *9th Int'l Conf. Computer Performance Evaluation: Modelling Techniques and Tools*, volume 1245 of *LNCS*, pages 135–154, St. Malo, France, June 1997. Springer.

[132] Connie U. Smith and Lloyd G. Williams. Performance engineering of CORBA-based distributed systems with SPE·ED. In Ramón Puigjaner, Nunzio N. Savino, and Bartomeu Serra, editors, *10th Int'l Conf. Computer Performance Evaluation: Modelling Techniques and Tools, TOOLS'98*, volume 1469 of *LNCS*, pages 321–335, Palma de Mallorca, Spain, September 1998. Springer.

[133] Connie U. Smith and Lloyd G. Williams. *Performance Solutions: A Practical Guide to Creating Responsive, Scalable Software*. Object-Technology Series. Addison-Wesley, 2002.

[134] Ian Sommerville. *Software Engineering*. Addison-Wesley, 1996.

[135] Richard Staehli. *Quality of Service Specification for Resource Management in Multimedia Systems*. DPhil thesis, Oregon Graduate Institute of Science & Technology, 1996.

[136] Richard Staehli, Frank Eliassen, Jan Øyvind Aagedal, and Gordon Blair. Quality of service semantics for component-based systems. In *Middleware 2003 Companion, 2nd Int'l Workshop on Reflective and Adaptive Middleware Systems*, 2003.

[137] Richard Staehli, Jonathan Walpole, and David Maier. Quality of service specification for multimedia presentations. *Multimedia Systems*, 3(5/6), November 1995.

[138] Ralf Steinmetz and Andreas Mauthe, editors. *Proc. EUROMICRO Conf. 2004*, Rennes, France, September 2004. IEEE Computer Society.

[139] Colin Stirling. *Modal and Temporal Properties of Processes*. Texts in Computer Science. Springer, 2001.

[140] Clemens Szyperski. *Component Software: Beyond Object-Oriented Programming*. Component Software Series. Addison-Wesley Publishing Company, second edition, 2002.

[141] Andrew S. Tanenbaum. *Modern Operating Systems*. Prentice Hall, 2nd edition, 2002.

[142] Walter F. Tichy. Software development control based on module interconnection. In *Proc. 4th Int'l Conf. on Software Engineering (ICSE'79)*, pages 29–41, Pittsburgh, PA, USA, September 1979. IEEE Computer Society Press.

[143] Markus Völter. A generative component infrastructure for embedded systems. In Markus Voelter, Michael Kircher, Christa Schwanninger, Uwe Zdun, and Alexander Schmid, editors, *Proc. Workshop on Reuse in Constrained Environments at OOPSLA'03*, October 2003.

[144] Markus Völter. Model-driven development of component infrastructures for embedded systems. In Torsten Klein, Bernhard Rumpe, and Bernhard Schätz, editors, *Proc. Dagstuhl-Workshop Modellbasierte Entwicklung eingebetteter Systeme (MBEES 2005)*, Dagstuhl, Germany, 2005. Internationales Begegnungs- und Forschungszentrum (IBFI), Schloss Dagstuhl, Germany. http://drops.dagstuhl.de/opus/volltexte/2005/31.

[145] Yair Wand and Richard Y. Wang. Anchoring data quality dimensions in ontological foundations. *Communications of the ACM*, 39(11):86–95, 1996.

[146] Ute Wappler. Sicherung der Integrität von Softwarekomponenten. Großer Beleg, Technische Universität Dresden, 2003. In German.

[147] Ute Wappler. Systemseitige Umsetzung ausgewählter Sicherheitsanforderungen in einer Komponentenarchitektur. Diplomarbeit, Technische Universität Dresden, 2004. In German.

[148] Matthias Werner and Jan Richling. Komponierbarkeit nichtfunktionaler Eigenschaften – Versuch einer Definition. In *GI Fachtagung Betriebssysteme 2002*, Gesellschaft für Informatik, Berlin, 2002. In German.

[149] Charles Zhang and Hans-Arno Jacobsen. Resolving feature convolution in middle-ware systems. In John M. Vlissides and Douglas C. Schmidt, editors, *Proc. 19th Annual ACM SIGPLAN Conf. Object-Oriented Programming, Systems, Languages, and Applications (OOPSLA 2004)*, pages 188–205, Vancouver, BC, Canada, October 2004. ACM.

[150] Paul Ziemann and Martin Gogolla. An extension of OCL with temporal logic. In Jan Jurjens, Maria Victoria Cengarle, Eduardo B. Fernanez, Bernhard Rumpe, and Robert Sandner, editors, *Proc. Int'l Workshop on Critical Systems Development with UML (CSDUML'02)*, pages 53–62. TUM, Institut für Informatik, September 2002. Appeared as TUM-I0208.

[151] Steffen Zschaler. Formal specification of non-functional properties of component-based software. In Bruel et al. [29]. Technical Report TUD-FI04-12 Sept.2004 at Technische Universität Dresden.

[152] Steffen Zschaler. Towards a semantic framework for non-functional specifications of component-based systems. In Steinmetz and Mauthe [138].

Index

adaptation, 136, *see* adaptivity
adaptivity, 81–83
analysis, 15, 103, 104, 107, 111, 129
   performance -, 103, 107, 112, 113, 132, 140
   of one service operation, 107, **109–112**
   use-case–based -, 106, **107–109**, 113, 142
   technique, 7, 103
   formal description of -, 6, **112, 113**, 140, 142
application model, 16, **24**, 27–31, 33–35, 66, 84, 86, 91–93, 97, 113, 142, 235–238
architectural style, **54**
architecture, *see* network of components
architecture description language, 51, 54, 57–59, 125, 126, 131, 151
aspect-oriented programming, 67, 131, 151

characteristic, *see* measurement
component, **12**, 13–17, **21**, 22–24, 34, 36–39, 45–49, 51, 52, 54, 55, 57–61, 65, 66, 68, 69, 71, 74, 77, 81, 82, 84, 86, 89, 92, 93, 95, 97, 103, 107–109, 111, 112, 117, 119, 121, 125, 128, 131–133, 139, 141, 143, 145, 146, 155, 159, 160, 168, 171, 177, 179, 185, 194, 199, 202, 206, 212, 214, 230, 241
   active -, **49**, 181–183
   encapsulated -, **54**, 55–58, 60–62, 69, 106, 194, 197
   composite -, **57**
   forms, **127**
   hardware -, 13
   market, **3**, 4–6, 11, 32, 117, 126, 139, 141, 145
   model, **34**, 35
   network, *see* network of components
   software -, 3, 13, **21**, 117, 119, **125**, 126

component-based software engineering, 3, **3**, 6, 11, 36, 51, 117, 122, 125–128, 132, 135, 137, 138, 142, 151
composition principle, *see* composition theorem
composition theorem, 6, 16, **40**, 48, 128, 141, 238, 239, 243
compositionality, **128**
computational model, 7, **32**, 33–35, 41, 77, 83–86, 88–91, 97, 98, 118, 120, 139, 142, 143
configuration, *see* network of components
connector, 51, **57**, 60, 125, 131, 132, 212, 214
container, 7, **13**, 17, **22**, 23, 36, **39**, 46–48, 57, 60, 61, 63, 66–68, 107, 109, 118, 119, 121, 126, 127, 139, 142, 143, 147, 241
   specification, 15, 18, 36, 47, 65, **67, 68**, 134, 139, 143, 241
   strategy, 7, **22**, 23, 36, 38, 39, **39**, 47, 48, 51, 52, 54, 57, 58, 60, 61, 63, 65–69, 74, 77, 93, 95, 97, 104, 107, 108, 111, 118, 119, 121, 131, 139, 141–143, 145–147, 168, 185, 191, 194, 208, 223
     combination of -, 65, 67, 69
     global -, **52**, 56–58
     interactions between -, **68**
     local -, **54**, 55–57, 60
     selection of -, **68**
   specification, **39**, 46, 47, 49, 50, 58, **68**, 69
context model, **13**, 16, 23, **24**, 25–35, 38, 41, 42, 45, 46, 48, 49, 57, 60, 66, 74, 77, 82, 83, 86, 88, 91, 113, 115, 118, 135, 137, 159, 160, 171, 177, 181–184, 202, 204, 230, 232, 233–238
   specification scheme, **25**
context of use, *see* usage context

development process, *see* software develop-

ment process
domain, 32, 41

execution graph, **104**, 106–108, 111, 112
extended component quality modelling language, viii, 4–7, 18, 28, 81–83, 85, 86, 88, 90, 92, 95–99, 113, 115, 120, 137, 139, 141, 142, 147, 151, 245, 247
extended temporal logic of actions, vii, 3, 5–7, **7**, 8, 9, 16, 24–27, 33, 39, 41–46, 57, 61, 74, 83, 85, 86, 88–95, 97, 98, 120, 128, 141, 142, 146, 153, 235, 245, 246
    action, **8**, 9
    behaviour, **7**, 9
    flexible variable, 5, **8**
    history variable, *see* history-determined variable
    history-determined variable, **26**
    initial state, **9**
    liveness property, **40**
    module, **9**
    next-state relation, **9**
    predicate, **8**, 9
    property, **9**
    safety property, **40**
    state, 7, **8**, 9
    state component, *see* flexible variable
    state function, **8**
    state machine, **9**
    state variable, *see* flexible variable
    step, **8**
    stuttering equivalent, **8**
    stuttering step, **8**
    tooling, **9**, 155
    trace, 8, **8**
    transition function, **8**
extrinsic, 95, *see* measurement, *see* property

feasibility proof, 119, *see* feasible system
feasible system, **15**, 18, **40**, 48, 55, 60, 66, 95, 103, 107, 121, 136, 141, 238, 243
feature interaction, *see* property, non-functional -, interaction of -

interface model, **34**, 127
intrinsic, 95, *see* measurement, *see* property

MDA component, 6, 112, 113, 152
MDA tool component, *see* MDA component
measurement, 5, 11, **13**, 16, 23–25, **26**, 27, 28, 31, 32, 35, 38, 41, 42, 45, 47,

49, 57, 58, 60, 61, 66, 74, 77, 82, 88, 91, 96, 113, 115, 117, 119, 120, 129, 131–137, 139, 142, 143, 147, 160, 163, 171, 177, 178, 180, 182, 184, 185, 204, 206, 232, 233, 237
    extrinsic -, **13**, 14, **36**, 37, 39, 120, 134, 184
    intended semantics, 32
    intrinsic -, **14**, **36**, 37, 39, 120, 134, 184
    mapping, **33**, 34, *see* model mapping
    repository, 117
    specification scheme, 26, 42, 233
meta-model, 24, 32, **34**, 35, 82, 112, 135, 137, 147
model mapping, 16, 24, **27–34**, 35, 46, 47, 49, 57, 61, 66, 86, 91, 92, 97, 113, 142, 171, 177, 180, 189, 206, 235–238
model-driven architecture, 6, 112, 152

network of components, 12, 17, **51**, 52, 54, 55, 58, 109, 111, 125
non-functional dimension, *see* measurement

performance model, 104
property, **35**
    functional -, 3, 13, 22, 28, 47, 49, 57, 59, 109, 117, 126, 131, 132, 134
    non-functional -, 3, 6, 12, 13, **14**, 22, 23, 28, **35**, 36, 41, 45, 51, 57, 65–68, 71, 81, 85, 92, 93, 97, 98, 103, 107, 117–119, 125–127, **128–137**, 139–143, 145–147, 171, 179
    classification schemes -, 129
    difference to functional -, **4**
    extrinsic -, 11, 14, **36**, 38, 41, 54, 57, 66, 95, 119, 127, 131, 137, 139, 141, 143, 146
    interaction of -, **65**, 66
    intrinsic -, 11, 14, **36**, 38, 39, 45, 54, 57, 58, 65, 66, 68, 119, 127, 131, 133, 139, 141–143, 145, 146, 168

queuing networks, 106, 133

resource, **12**, 13, 15, 17, 22, 36, 38, 46, 47, 54–56, 60, 61, 68, 69, 81, 93, 95, 97, 104, 106, 107, 109, 111, 118, 119, 132, 133, 136, 137, 139, 141, 143, 145–147, 163, 168, 194, 221
    demand, 5, 14, 38, 39, 51, 54, 55, 57, 60–62, 81, 82, 95, 104, 106, 108, 111, 131, 136, 141

shared -, **55**, 56, 61, 191
specification, 14, 17, 36, **38**, 39, 69

semantic mapping, 139, 147
semantic mapping function, 6, 85, **86**, **88–92**, 95, 97, 142
service, **12**, 13–17, **22**, 23, 36, 41, 42, 46–49, 52, 54, 59, 65, 66, 77, 82–84, 86, 89, 90, 92, 93, 95, 97, 106–108, 113, 119, 121, 141, 157, 171, 185, 206, 208, 223
    active -, **49**, 183, 184
software component, *see* component, software -
software development process, 6, 7, 103, 109, **117–122**, 129, 137, 140, 142
    roles, 117, 118, 143
        analysis expert, 112
        application designer, 11, 16, 33, 36, 57, 86, **117, 118**, 119, 121, 139, 141, 145, 146
        component developer, 11, 16, 23, 34, 36, 37, 45, **117**, 118–120, 125, 133, 139, 141, 145–147
        container designer, 35, 47, 67, **118**, 119, 121, 139, 141
        data provider, 146
        measurement designer, **117**, 118–120
        performance expert, 104, 108, 111–113
        platform designer, **118**, 119, 121, 141, 145
        system assembler, 133
        system user, 36, 41
software execution model, **104**, 106, 111
software performance engineering, viii, 7, 103–107, 109, 115, 129, 132, 151, 153, 246
specification
    data-dependent vs. -independent -, 37, 127, 146
    functional -, *see* property, functional -
    machine-dependent vs. -independent -, 37, 127, 145
    non-functional -, *see* property, non-functional -
specification language, 81, 115, *see* extended component quality modelling language
    μCQML, viii, 81, 83–91, 93, 95, 98, 99, 140, 142, 147, 245, 247, 249
    pseudo-code notation, 16, 98, 120, 147
system execution model, **104, 106**, 111

system model, **21**, 23, 143
system specification, 17, 18, **39**, 48, 55, 56, 68, 69, 88, 93, 97, 119, 141, 173, 197, 214, 225

usage context, 4, 5, 11, 14, 16, 36, **37**, 45, 54, 104, 119, 126, 127, 131, 133, 139, 145

www.ingramcontent.com/pod-product-compliance
Lightning Source LLC
Chambersburg PA
CBHW071412050326
40689CB00010B/1839